Judgments, Decisions, and Public Policy

Behavioral decision theory draws on experimental research in cognitive psychology to provide a descriptively accurate model of human behavior. It shows that people systematically violate the normative assumptions of economic rationality by miscalculating probabilities and making choices based on one economic criterion. Behavioral decision theory's ability to capture the complexity of human judgments and choices makes it a useful foundation for improving public policy analysis, design, and implementation.

This volume showcases the research of leading scholars who are working on applications of behavioral decision theory in diverse policy settings. It is designed to give policy analysts and practitioners who are nonpsychologists a clearer understanding of the complexities of human judgment and choice and an idea of how to integrate behavioral decision theoretic insights into the policy sciences. This interdisciplinary volume should be insightful and useful wherever people's judgments and choices matter for policy formulation, acceptance, and effectiveness.

Rajeev Gowda is Associate Professor of Economics and Social Sciences at the Indian Institute of Management–Bangalore. Dr. Gowda coedited *Integrating Insurance and Risk Management for Hazardous Wastes* (1990), and his articles have been published in the *Journal of Policy Analysis and Management, Policy Sciences, Risk Analysis, Risk: Health, Safety, Environment*, and the *Bulletin of the American Meteorological Society*, among others.

Jeffrey C. Fox is Assistant Professor of Political Science at Catawba College in Salisbury, North Carolina. He has published several articles in *Social Science Quarterly* and the *Bulletin of the American Meteorological Society*.

Cambridge Series on Judgment and Decision Making

Publications Board
Jonathan Baron, Chair
University of Pennsylvania

Michael Birnbaum
California State University

William M. Goldstein
University of Chicago

Past Members
Hal R. Arkes, Chair
Ohio University

John S. Carroll
Massachusetts Institute of Technology

Kenneth R. Hammond
University of Colorado, Boulder

Don N. Kleinmuntz, Chair
University of Illinois at Urbana–Champaign

Lola Lopes
University of Iowa

James Shanteau
Kansas State University

The purpose of the series is to convey the general principles of and findings about judgment and decision making to the many academic and professional fields to which these apply. The contributions are written by authorities in the field and supervised by highly qualified editors and the Publications Board. The series will attract readers from many different disciplines, largely among academics, advanced undergraduates, graduate students, and practicing professionals.

Judgments, Decisions, and Public Policy

Edited by

Rajeev Gowda
Indian Institute of Management–Bangalore

Jeffrey C. Fox
Catawba College

CAMBRIDGE
UNIVERSITY PRESS

CAMBRIDGE UNIVERSITY PRESS
Cambridge, New York, Melbourne, Madrid, Cape Town, Singapore,
São Paulo, Delhi, Dubai, Tokyo, Mexico City

Cambridge University Press
The Edinburgh Building, Cambridge CB2 8RU, UK

Published in the United States of America by Cambridge University Press, New York

www.cambridge.org
Information on this title: www.cambridge.org/9780521660846

© Cambridge University Press 2002

First published 2002

A catalogue record for this publication is available from the British Library

Library of Congress Cataloguing in Publication data
Judgments, decisions, and public policy/edited by Rajeev Gowda,
Jeffrey C. Fox.
p. cm. – (Cambridge series on judgment and decision making)
Includes bibliographical references and index.
ISBN 0 521 66084 X
1. Policy sciences. 2. Decision making. I. Rajeev Gowda, M. V.
(Mothakapalli Venkatappa) II. Fox, Jeffrey, 1966– III. Series.
H97.J853 2001
320´.6 – dc21   00-054658

ISBN 978-0-521-66084-6 Hardback
ISBN 978-0-521-17995-9 Paperback

Contents

Contributors

Jonathan Baron is a Professor in the Department of Psychology at the University of Pennsylvania.

Max H. Bazerman is a Professor in the Department of Organizational Behavior, Kellogg Graduate School of Management, at Northwestern University.

Sharon Dunwoody is the Evjue-Bascom Professor of Journalism and Mass Communication at the University of Wisconsin–Madison.

Rick Farmer is an Assistant Professor of Political Science at the University of Akron.

Jeffrey C. Fox is an Assistant Professor of Political Science at Catawba College in Salisbury, North Carolina.

Lee S. Friedman is a Professor in the Richard and Rhoda Goldman School of Public Policy at the University of California at Berkeley.

Rajeev Gowda is an Associate Professor of Economics and Social Sciences at the Indian Institute of Management, Bangalore, India.

Robert J. Griffin is a Professor in the Department of Journalism and Director of the Center for Mass Media Research at Marquette University.

Jack L. Knetsch is a Professor Emeritus in the Department of Economics at Simon Fraser University.

Howard Kunreuther is a Professor of Decision Sciences and Public Policy and Management at the University of Pennsylvania. He is also the Codirector of the Risk Management and Decision Processes Center at the University of Pennsylvania.

Robert J. MacCoun is a Professor at the Richard and Rhoda Goldman School of Public Policy at the University of California at Berkeley.

Douglas MacLean is a Professor in the Department of Philosophy at the University of Maryland, Baltimore County.

Anthony Patt is an Assistant Professor in the Department of Geography at Boston University.

Eldar Shafir is a Professor in the Department of Psychology at Princeton University.

Paul Slovic is the president of Decision Research in Eugene, Oregon.

Cass R. Sunstein is the Karl N. Llewellyn Professor of Jurisprudence at the University of Chicago Law School.

Chris Swoyer is a Professor in the Department of Philosophy at the University of Oklahoma.

Philip E. Tetlock is a Professor in the Department of Psychology at The Ohio State University.

Richard J. Zeckhauser is the Frank Plumpton Ramsey Professor of Political Economy in the John F. Kennedy School of Government at Harvard University.

Acknowledgments

This book is largely based on conference panels on behavioral decision theory organized for the annual meeting of the Association for Public Policy Analysis and Management in 1997. Many of the contributors to this book attended the conference and agreed to include their work here. We wish to thank the authors for their support and responsiveness in making this book happen. We also want to thank Cambridge University Press, and the Judgment and Decision Making section in particular, for helping to make this work possible. Our former editor, Julia Hough, and our new editor, Philip Laughlin, have provided invaluable assistance. We also wish to thank the reviewers for their valuable insights and comments. We also want to thank great mentors like Jonathan Baron, Howard Kunreuther, and Colin Camerer for their work and encouragement in this area.

Most of all, we want to express our thanks to our spouses and children for enduring our absence while we completed the manuscript. We owe a great debt to Sharmila, Vaibhav, and Rishika in the Gowda home and to Julie, Madison, Mallory, and Maren in the Fox household. We thank them for their love, support, and forbearance during this project.

Introduction

Jeffrey C. Fox and Rajeev Gowda

What are the chances that you will be the victim of a crime on your way home this evening? How likely is it that you will contract cancer from smoking, eating unhealthy foods, or ingesting environmental toxins? Statisticians and scientists have a set of tools to answer these questions – statistics and rationality. What about the rest of us? Most people, when faced with questions like how common, how often, how probable, or how likely, are unable to respond with firm, confident replies. Most people have only an intuitive "feel" when making judgments about probabilities. But they must still make judgments about and choices between alternative risk management strategies or whom to support in public policy debates about health, safety, and the environment.

On what basis do people make such probability judgments? How rational are these judgments? How do such judgments affect how people make choices? Why are people's choices, especially under conditions of risk and uncertainty, seemingly inconsistent? These are the key questions facing scholars who seek to understand judgment and decision making. Researchers working at the intersection of psychology, economics, and the policy sciences have found that people do have a systematic way of arriving at these judgments and choices. But this systematic pattern does not conform to the rational decision process advocated and used by economists and statisticians. Instead, people seem to follow certain *heuristics* or rules of thumb that often do a reasonably good job of helping people make judgments under conditions of uncertainty and low levels of information. At other times, these same heuristics can fail miserably and leave people worse off than they would have been if they had been more systematically rational.

Thus, it is important to understand these systematic deviations from rationality and to examine their implications for policy outcomes. These heuristics may help explain some policy failures, paradoxes, and inefficiencies that policy scientists sometimes attribute to people's irrational behavior (Stone, 1997; Sunstein, 1990). Some examples of these paradoxes include (1) people's failure to purchase flood insurance, even at subsidized rates (Kunreuther, 1978); (2) policies that mandate inefficient, zero-risk solutions such as complete cleanup of Superfund sites allegedly to satisfy people's preferences (Breyer, 1993); (3) policies that allocate relatively more resources to airline safety than to highway safety because people fear airline accidents more, even though more deaths result from highway accidents (Zeckhauser & Viscusi, 1996); (4) people's tendency to use vastly different discount rates for short versus long periods (Knetsch, 1995); and (5) people's tendency to value losses more than commensurate gains, which leads to a disparity between their willingness to pay to avoid environmental harms and their willingness to accept them (Knetsch 1995).

A fundamental reason for these and other paradoxes may lie in the assumptions, approaches, and methods policy analysts bring to their work, particularly their assumptions about human behavior. Most policy analysis builds on the foundational assumption that people are rational actors, that is, expected utility maximizers. Expected utility maximization may be an appropriate normative standard for people's behavior. However, if people's behavior does not conform to expected utility maximization, then policies based on that assumption may lead to policy failures, paradoxes, and inefficiencies. Incorporating descriptively accurate models of decision making in policy analysis may help resolve some of these paradoxes and inefficiencies.

Behavioral decision theory is one alternative approach to understanding human behavior. Behavioral decision theory provides a more descriptively accurate model of human behavior by capturing the complexity of human judgments and choices. It builds on evidence from experimental research in cognitive psychology that shows that people make judgments and decisions in a fundamentally different way from the way they are assumed to act in the economic model (Kahneman, Slovic, & Tversky, 1982).

According to behavioral decision theory, people systematically violate the normative assumptions of economic rationality by (1) miscalculating probabilities and (2) making choices between competing options based on noneconomic criteria (Camerer, 1995; Kahneman et al., 1982). This more complex but more accurate description of how people behave may reveal areas where people's behavior leads to outcomes different from what traditional analysis would predict due to the use of judgmental heuristics. In such cases, behavioral decision theory may pinpoint areas where education and debiasing could prove useful, and may also help in designing policies that anticipate and counter cognitive errors.

In general, behavioral decision theoretic insights should be particularly useful wherever people's judgments and choices matter for policy formulation, acceptance, and implementation. It is possible that public policy could be improved with the integration of more accurate assumptions about people's motivations, how well they understand specific information, how aggressively they will pursue information needed to serve their own interest, and how effectively they can make decisions. Incorporating behavioral decision theory's insights will enhance the realism of existing policies, help in devising ones more likely to achieve their intended goals, and enable us to understand the limits of effective regulation. Further, an increase in the accuracy and realism of analysis that may emerge from integrating this perspective could lead to better utilization of policy analysis in the political sphere.

Unfortunately, behavioral decision theoretic insights have yet to be well integrated into the analysis of public policy issues. "Although taking greater account of this evidence could substantially improve the analysis of a wide range of economic issues and policy options, conventional practice continues much as before. There is seldom any reckoning, or even acknowledgment, of these contrary findings and virtually no serious attempt to exploit this evidence to improve policy design and choice" (Knetsch, 1995, p. 68). This is partly because of the dominance of the economic-rational approach in policy analysis. Another reason may be that public policy scholars and practitioners have yet to encounter an accessible introduction to the essence of the behavioral decision theoretic approach that demonstrates its applicability to public policy issues. Although many scholars profess great interest in the insights of behavioral decision theory, they point out that they are unable to grasp these insights well enough to integrate them into their own work. This is because most behavioral decision theoretic writing is confined to psychology and economics. There are few works written for the wider public policy community.

We hope this book will help remedy this deficiency by showcasing various insights and applications of behavioral decision theory in public policy. The chapters are written by leading scholars working on behavioral decision theory in diverse policy settings. The book is designed to give policy analysts and practitioners who are nonpsychologists a clearer understanding of the complexities of human judgment and choice and an idea of how to integrate behavioral decision theoretic insights into the policy sciences.

The book is divided into five parts. Part I introduces the basics of behavioral decision theory and contrasts it with theories of rational choice. Chris Swoyer's chapter starts the book with a comprehensive overview of the research findings that comprise behavioral decision theory, as well as its boundary conditions and criticisms. Douglas MacLean examines the implications of this *nonrational* judgment and choice process for the policy process and public opinion. Eldar Shafir considers the implications of behavioral insights about human cognition for setting policy guidelines. His chapter demonstrates that presenting people with information either separately or comparatively can significantly alter their evaluations and choices.

Part II considers the relationship between behavioral insights and traditional economic methodologies and assumptions. Jack Knetsch explores the policy implications of the endowment effect, the behavioral foundation of the disparity between willingness to pay and willingness to accept. He also explores valuation over time on the basis of relevant behavioral findings and shows how it differs from standard discounting techniques in economics. Robert MacCoun addresses the question of whether some systematic deviations from rationality (biases) among individuals can be eliminated in group settings. He explores the difference between individual and group judgments using theoretical thought experiments that identify some of the conditions that determine *relative bias*, that is, the difference between group and individual bias. He finds that group interactions do not always attenuate individual-level biases identified by behavioral decision theory. Finally, Lee Friedman explores whether the insights of behavioral decision theoretic research can be operationalized in econometric research. He investigates the topic of energy purchasing by pitting a standard utility-maximizing model against a *bounded rationality* model. He finds that the bounded rationality model best describes natural gas purchasing behavior in an actual market setting.

Public policy is neither made nor executed in a vacuum. Political institutions and processes also affect policy. Part III provides some perspective on how the insights of behavioral decision theory help us better understand and evaluate institutional decision-making procedures and their impact on people's behavior and the policy process. This part includes discussions about the media, the courts, and the impact of political advertising on informed policy choices. Sharon Dunwoody and Robert Griffin argue that any news story is the product of a host of small, individual-level decisions that are determined by fairly standardized decision heuristics that greatly influence the news-making process in a nonrational way. Jeffrey Fox and Rick Farmer then explore how behavioral findings can help us understand and evaluate the effects of political advertising. Cass Sunstein demonstrates how behavioral findings are creating a new field of *behavioral law and economics*. He traces some of the principal findings that emerge from behavioral research, and shows how they bear on positive and prescriptive work in law.

Part IV is devoted to applications of behavioral decision theory to environmental policy, risk perception and management, negotiation, and stigmatization. In the first chapter of Part IV, Rajeev Gowda considers how behavioral decision theoretic research, coupled with risk analysis, can generate useful insights into the potential effectiveness and popularity of innovative policy tools such as information provision laws. Anthony Patt and Richard Zeckhauser present an overview of how behavioral decision theoretic insights fundamentally challenge many of the assumptions involved in environmental policy analysis. Howard Kunreuther and Paul Slovic demonstrate how behavioral features such as imagery, affect, and emotion contribute to stigmatization, demonstrate how stigma arises in a variety of policy contexts, and explore ways to manage it better. Jonathan Baron and Max Bazerman then show how behavioral features affect the resolution of policy disputes. Their focus is on how disputes could be remedied by people sacrificing small losses for large gains. The barrier to such solutions is that people resist such trade-offs because they resist integrating the losses and gains and attending to the net benefit. This takes the form of the *mythical fixed-pie assumption* in negotiation and is also found in the *do-no-harm* heuristic that leads to a bias toward harmful omissions as distinct from harmful acts.

The book concludes in Part V with a commentary by Philip Tetlock. Drawing on his perspective as both a psychologist and a political scientist, Tetlock strikes a cautionary note and points to the enormous challenges that lie ahead as we strive to understand how people really behave when they make judgments and choices.

References

Breyer, S. (1993). *Breaking the vicious circle: Toward effective risk regulation.* Cambridge, MA: Harvard University Press.

Camerer, C. (1995). Individual decision making. In J. H. Kagel and A. E. Roth (Eds.), *The handbook of experimental economics* (pp. 587–673). Princeton, NJ: Princeton University Press.

Kahneman, D., Slovic, P., & Tversky, A. (Eds.). (1982). *Judgment under uncertainty: Heuristics and biases*. Cambridge: Cambridge University Press.

Knetsch, J. L. (1995). Assumptions, behavioral findings, and policy analysis. *Journal of Policy Analysis and Management, 14*, 68–78.

Kunreuther, H. (1978). *Disaster insurance protection: Public policy lessons*. New York: Wiley.

Stone, D. (1997). *Policy paradox*. New York: W. W. Norton.

Sunstein, C. R. (1990). Paradoxes of the regulatory state. *University of Chicago Law Review, 57*, 407–441.

Zeckhauser, R. J., & Viscusi, W. K. (1996). The risk management dilemma. *Annals of the American Academy of Political and Social Science, 545*, 144–155.

Part I

The Fundamentals of Behavioral Decision Theory

1 Judgment and Decision Making: Extrapolations and Applications

Chris Swoyer

People who make or implement public policy must often estimate probabilities, predict outcomes, and make decisions that affect the welfare, values, and lives of many others. Until recently, many of the disciplines that study policy employed a model of individuals and organizations as rational agents whose predictions conform to the prescriptions of probability theory and whose actions maximize their expected gains in conformity with classical decision theory.

Such theories lead a double life. They are sometimes viewed as *normative models* that tell us what we should do in order to be rational (even if we rarely manage to pull it off). Construed this way, they offer advice: We should have logically consistent beliefs, coherent probability assignments, and consistent preferences, and we should maximize expected utilities. But these same theories have also been viewed as *descriptive models*; construed this way, they are meant to provide an approximate characterization of the behavior of real people. It is this interpretation that has played a central role in economics, management science, and parts of political science, sociology, and the law.

Since the early 1970s, this descriptive picture of judgment and decision making has come under increasing attack from scientists working in behavioral decision theory, the field concerned with the ways in which people actually judge, predict, and decide. Much of the criticism

I am grateful to Neera Badhwar, Hugh Benson, Monte Cook, Michael Dougherty, Jim Hawthorne, Eve Ogden, Susanne Z. Riehemann, Rajeev Gowda, Jeff Fox and (much longer ago) Charles Gettys, William Graziano, Paul Meehl, and Thomas Monson for comments on this chapter or discussions on the topics it involves. They are not responsible for shortcomings.

derives from the work of Tversky, Kahneman, and others working in the *heuristics and biases tradition*. Scientists in this tradition argue that people often fail, sometimes quite dramatically, to conform to the strictures of the relevant normative models. Instead, they argue, people frequently employ judgmental heuristics, quick and relatively effortless reasoning strategies that produce accurate results in many circumstances but that are biased in ways that lead to systematic errors under inauspicious conditions.

The heuristics and biases tradition is now just one current in the large stream of behavioral decision theory, and many scientists in the field reject various aspects of this approach. Most agree, however, that people's judgments and decisions often don't fit the guidelines of classical normative models, and there is now no going back to the view that such models are descriptively accurate.

In hindsight, it is difficult to see why our failures to conform to normative models should have seemed a surprise. After all, precise versions of normative theories were formulated only with great effort rather late in human history. Despite millennia of gambling, the basics of probability theory were not hammered out until the middle of the seventeenth century, three more centuries passed before decision theory was formalized, and even today many students find parts of these theories difficult and counterintuitive. Furthermore, there has never been any solid body of evidence showing that we live up to such normative standards, nor does any theory with serious empirical support entail that we do. Indeed, there is much reason to think that we couldn't.

As Herbert Simon (1956) has stressed since the mid-1950s, human rationality is bounded. We have very limited attention, working memory, and computational capacities, and these limitations alone would make it impossible for us to perform the calculations normative theories often require. Moreover, although evolution doubtless equipped us with cognitive mechanisms that were reasonably accurate in the hunter-gatherer environment in which our species evolved, there is no reason to think that it could, much less did, attune us to the subtleties of Bayesian updating or the intricacies of expected utilities. Finally, almost any newscast or history book chronicles miscalculations and follies that are utterly self-defeating, even by the agents' own lights. But although it shouldn't come as news that people's inferences and decisions are sometimes suboptimal, what is surprising is that many of our cognitive and volitional lapses are quite systematic (or biased), and systematic in ways that would have been difficult to predict.

This isn't to say that our judgments and decisions are hopelessly flawed. Indeed, the spotty picture emerging from several decades of research suggests that people have the ability to reason well under some conditions. This ability is fragile and unstable, however, and it can be affected, diverted, and even subverted by a variety of influences. In particular, many subtle features of the contexts in which people judge and decide influence *how* they judge and decide. In fact, one of the most pressing questions in the field, particularly when we are considering applications to politics or policy, is whether reasonably robust generalizations about human judgment and decision making can be found amid all the contextual variability.

My goal here is to sort out some of the issues involved in interpreting, evaluating, and applying work in behavioral decision theory to real-life situations involving policy, politics, and related matters. I will discuss the sorts of considerations that are relevant to settling various disputes about such work and its applications and note several obstacles to applying it to problems in the real world. There is enormous variability in the ways that policies are made and implemented, and it is unlikely that any simple morals will apply to all of them, but the general tenor of the discussion here is cautionary. Behavioral decision theory has produced many important empirical findings and promising models, but at this stage of the game it is difficult to apply many (though not all) of its findings to areas of policy with great confidence. I will end with a brief consideration of the status of normative models and their potential for improving policymaking and implementation.

The Checklist: What? Where? When? Who? Why?

The checklist for the behavioral decision theorist is much like that for the reporter (though the order is a bit different). The first step is to discover *phenomena* or *effects* (like insensitivity to sample size or preference reversals). These rough regularities in human behavior tell us *what* people tend to do. Once a phenomenon has been discovered, questions arise about its boundary conditions: *Where* and *when* does it occur? Which conditions produce, accentuate, attenuate, or eliminate it? Although little work has been done on individual differences in judgment and choice, these differences are often substantial, and researchers are beginning to ask: *Who* reasons in which ways? Finally, a basic goal of most science is to explain *why* the phenomena in its domain obtain; what causal processes or mechanisms mediate a given effect? I will discuss each topic in turn, with an eye to separating issues that are sometimes conflated and to showing how considerations involving each issue affect applications in the world outside the lab.

What? Target Phenomena

Three decades of research in behavioral decision theory have produced a long list of putative phenomena or effects, rough regularities that hold "for the most part." Any exact count of effects would be somewhat arbitrary, but it is now upward of 50. In some cases there is disagreement as to whether an alleged phenomenon really obtains, but for the moment I will treat the phenomena as genuine and I won't worry about qualifications or boundary conditions until the next section.

Table 1.1 lists 13 phenomena or effects, including several classical examples, a few newer ones, and one from the nearby field of social cognition (the fundamental attribution error). The table merely provides a sampling to indicate the *range* of phenomena that are likely to be relevant to policy studies, and many additions would be possible. In the remainder of this section I will describe a few of these phenomena in more detail, point out potential applications to policy, but also note impediments to such applications.

Hindsight Bias

People who know how something (like the implementation of a new program to reduce violent crime) turned out have a tendency to think that they could have predicted the outcome in advance (Fischhoff, 1975). Their confidence is often misplaced, however, because unforeseen and unintended consequences are common in the real world, and it is often very difficult to be sure about the results of new policies and initiatives. How much global warming is occurring, and what can we do to reverse it? Even the best analysts will be wrong about such things some of the time. But after the fact, it is easy to think that they *should* have been able to predict the things that actually happened. This means that people who get things right may get too much credit (and so be relied on too much in the future) and those who get things wrong may get too much blame (and so be ignored when they shouldn't be).

Table 1.1. *Selective Catalog of Phenomena*

Phenomenon/ Effect	Description	Example
Insensitivity to base rates	Not fully using base rates (information about relative frequencies) in judging probabilities and making predictions	Thinking that a person has a high probability of having cancer after testing positive on an accurate but not perfect test, without taking into account the low incidence of cancer in the population
Insufficiently regressive prediction	Prediction that neglects the fact that more extreme outcomes or performances tend to be followed by ones closer to the mean (i.e., closer to average)	Predicting that Sam's score the second time he takes the Graduate Record Examination will be in the top 1% since that's where his score was the first time
Insensitivity to sample size	Willingness to draw an inference about a population from a sample that is too small to support it	Judging that a hospital averaging 100 births a day and one averaging 15 a day will have about the same number of days where over 65% of the births are boys
Conjunction fallacy	Taking a conjunction to be more probable than either of its conjuncts	Example 1: It's more likely that Linda is a bank teller and a feminist rather than a bank teller (a probability version). Example 2: There are more six-letter words ending in -*ing* than having *n* as their fifth letter (a frequency version).
Gambler's fallacy	Treating probabilistically independent events as though they were dependent	Bob and Ann have had seven boys in a row, so they are due for a girl.
Hindsight bias	Tendency to overestimate the likelihood that one would have predicted an outcome after learning it occurred	Monday morning quarterbacking, second guessing ("I knew it all along")
Overconfidence	Tendency to overestimate the probability that one's judgments or predictions are correct	Assigning high probabilities to hypotheses or claims that frequently turn out to be false

(continued)

Table 1.1 *(continued)*

Phenomenon/ Effect	Description	Example
Suboptimal integration of information (actuarial vs. intuitive prediction)	In many cases, an actuarial model (often a simple linear regression equation with just a few predictor variables) provides more accurate predictions than experts do.	Expert diagnoses (e.g., in clinical psychology) or predictions (e.g., of sporting events) are often less accurate than predictions by a formula.
Preference reversals (and framing effects)	Logically equivalent and often seemingly trivial changes in the way options are described lead to reversals of preferences.	Preferring one option to a second when the two are described in terms of rate of employment but preferring the second to the first when they are given equivalent descriptions in terms of unemployment
Preference reversals (and elicitation effects)	Seemingly equivalent methods for eliciting preferences lead to preference reversals.	Selecting one of two options when asked to choose between them and the other option when asked to reject one of them
Fourfold pattern of risk seeking and aversion	Being risk averse with respect to gains and risk seeking with respect to losses when probabilities are moderate to high and the reverse when probabilities are low	Preferring a sure gain of $500 to a 50% chance of winning $1,000 but a 50% chance of losing $1,000 to a sure loss of $500
Subadditive probabilities	Judged probability of a disjunction can be less than the sum of the judged probabilities of its disjuncts.	Judging that the probability of death in an accident is less than the sum of the judged probability of death in an auto accident and the judged probability of death in any other sort of accident
Fundamental attribution error	Tendency to overestimate the role of other people's dispositions and traits, and to underestimate the importance of the context, in explaining their behavior	Thinking that people in a crowd who don't help an injured person are unusually uncaring, when in fact many people in such situations are reluctant to help

Insufficient Attention to Base Rates

Problem solving and policy implementation often require classification, diagnosis, and prediction. Is Jones likely to violate parole or to jump bail? How likely is Smith to be infected by the human immunodeficiency virus (HIV) given his positive test result? In such cases, we need to *integrate* information about the specific case (e.g., that Smith tested positive) with information about base rates in a relevant reference class. Among people like Smith (the reference class), what percentage are infected by the virus? There are difficult problems about selecting an appropriate reference class, but I will set these aside until the seventh section.

The importance of base rates is vividly illustrated by examples like the following. Suppose that we have a test for the HIV virus; the probability that a person who really has the virus will test positive is .90, whereas the probability that a person who does *not* have it will test positive is .20. Finally, suppose that the probability that a person in the general population has the virus (the base rate of the virus) is .01. How likely is Smith, whose test came back positive, to be infected? Because the test is fairly accurate, many people suppose that the chances are quite high, maybe even 90%. But when we plug the numbers into Bayes's theorem, we find that the probability of someone in this situation being infected is 1 chance in 23. It is not difficult to see how policymakers, or the public to which they respond, can make very inaccurate assessments of probabilities, and hence poor decisions about risks and remedies, if they neglect base rates.[1]

Insufficient Attention to Regression Effects

Extreme performances and outcomes tend to be followed by ones that are more average (that regress toward the mean). In the first game you see Ann play, she hits 80% of her three-point shots. It is natural to predict that she will hit about the same percentage the next time around. But in fact, if her average shooting percentage is lower, she is likely to do worse. Her performance is likely to regress toward the mean.

People do not have a good intuitive understanding of this basic statistical phenomenon.[2] When Ann's shooting percentage drops in the next game, it will be tempting to attribute it to her lack of focus or to a better opposing defense, but in fact it may simply result from regression to the mean. Similarly, when the implementation of a new policy (e.g., tougher sentencing laws) is followed by an increase in something desirable (safer streets) or a decrease in something undesirable (a drop in violent crime), it is tempting to conclude that the measure is responsible for the change. But it might well have occurred without the measure, simply as a consequence of regression toward the mean. In such cases, the policy will be given credit it doesn't deserve; more money is likely to be channeled to it and away from alternatives that might be more effective.

Conjunction Fallacy

A person commits the conjunction fallacy if he or she judges that a conjunction is more probable than one of its conjuncts (probability version) or that the frequency of a conjunctive attribute (e.g., being a feminist and a bank teller) in a population is greater than the frequency of one of the attributes taken alone (e.g., being a bank teller).

When people are told that Linda majored in philosophy, has been deeply concerned with issues of discrimination and social justice, and participated in antinuclear demonstrations, many of them conclude that the conjunction (Linda is a feminist and a bank teller) is more probable than the second conjunct (Linda is a bank teller). If we take this result at face value, it is a clear violation of the very basic principle that a conjunction can *never* be more probable than either of its conjuncts. It is unlikely that much policy turns on blatant commissions of this fallacy, but it is noteworthy because it suggests a flaw in our probabilistic reasoning that may result from mechanisms that bias probabilistic judgments in other, more common cases.

Risk Aversion and Risk Seeking: The Fourfold Pattern

Numerous studies show that people evaluate prospects or outcomes differently depending on whether they see them as gains or as losses. We often construe things as gains or losses relative to the status quo, but sometimes we do so relative to an opportunity we let slip by (if I had just invested in Intel . . .) or to a level of aspiration (compared to the raise I deserved . . .). There is a good deal of evidence that we tend to be risk averse with respect to gains and risk seeking with respect to losses when the probabilities of relevant outcomes are judged to be moderate to high, but that pattern is reversed when the probabilities are judged to be low (Tversky & Kahneman, 1992).

Most people, for example, prefer a sure gain of $500 to a 50% chance of winning $1,000, despite the fact that the two options have the same expected value; here in the domain of gains (with moderately high probabilities), people avoid the risky choice. But most people prefer a 50% chance of losing $1,000 to a sure loss of $500; here in the domain of losses (again with moderately high probabilities), people prefer the risk to a certain loss. These findings take on added interest because the way that alternatives are presented or framed seems to affect what people see as the reference point. This determines whether they see something as a gain or as a loss, which in turn affects whether their choices will exhibit risk aversion or risk seeking.

For example, Tversky and Kahneman (1986) asked people to imagine that we were preparing for the outbreak of a virulent Asian disease that would kill 600 people if no countermeasures were taken. They were asked to choose between two alternatives, one of which would save 200 lives and the other of which had a 1/3 probability of saving everyone and a 2/3 probability of saving no one. Here the outcomes are stated in positive terms (lives saved), and most people preferred the first option (thus showing risk aversion). But when exactly the same options were presented in negative terms (deaths), as either 400 people dying or a 1/3 probability that no one would die and a 2/3 probability that 600 would die, most people chose the second, riskier option.

Preference Reversals

This study provides an example of a preference reversal. It was theorized that it occurred because the first description of the two options presents or *frames* things in terms of a *gain* (saving lives) in relationship to the reference point (600 are expected to die), so that people are risk averse. But the second pair of descriptions frames the same options in a way that places the reference point at the status quo; here the options involve a *loss* (people dying), and so respondents are now willing to select the more risky alternative.

Different ways of framing the same options often influence people's preferences. It makes a difference whether alternatives are framed in terms of employment or unemployment; again, people's preferences are affected by whether options are framed in terms of crime rates or law-obedience rates (Quattrone & Tversky, 1988). Framing effects surely play a large role in politics and policy, where choices between uncertain options are ubiquitous and people with competing interests will represent them in quite disparate ways.

Where and When? Boundary Condition

Most phenomena in psychology (and in many other sciences) obtain only within a certain range of circumstances, within *boundary conditions*, and research is often aimed at delineating the range of circumstances in which an effect holds. We can ask about the extent to which a phenomenon holds across cultures or age groups (as in Park, Nisbett, & Hedden, 1999). But it turns out that very small differences in circumstances can lead to very large differences in judgments and preferences, and I will focus on these.

Hindsight Bias

This phenomenon is reasonably robust in the range of contexts in which it has been studied, but some boundary conditions are known. For example, when people are asked to explain how possible outcomes that did not come to pass (e.g., George Bush's being reelected president) could have, the bias is reduced. It is further reduced if people are asked to explain how each of two incompatible outcomes could have happened before they learn which of the two actually occurred. And the phenomenon is small or even reversed in the case of outcomes that would have been very difficult to predict, (here "I knew it all along" gives way to "I would never have guessed that"; see Hawkins & Hastie, 1990, for a general review).

Conjunction Fallacy

The conjunction fallacy is quite robust when it involves vignettes stated in terms of probabilities. When subjects are asked whether it is more probable that Linda is (1) a bank teller or (2) a bank teller and active in the feminist movement, well over half of the respondents often pick the conjunction (option 2). Fewer people commit the fallacy when it is stated in terms of frequencies (out of 100 people who fit Linda's profile, (1') how many are bank tellers and (2') how many are bank tellers and active feminists?), although the effect doesn't disappear. The fallacy persists when pains are taken to make the nature of the task clear and even in gambling situations where subjects stand to win nontrivial amounts of money (Tversky & Kahneman, 1983).

The effect is particularly strong when a sentence that initially seems unlikely ("There will soon be a war with Russia") is conjoined with another sentence that gives a plausible causal story about how the first sentence could be true ("The war will result from a flareup in the Middle East that spirals out of control due to a series of misunderstandings"). And it diminishes or disappears when the two conjuncts are seen as incompatible ("Sam is lazy, and he works 60 hours a week").

Base Rates

There have been a great many studies of people's use of base rate information. Although not all of the findings are consistent, the overall pattern suggests that people typically make *some* use of base rate information (especially when no other information is available), but that they do not give it as much weight as Bayes's theorem would require. Furthermore, a good deal is now known about the boundary conditions that affect people's use of base rates.

People are more likely to use base rate information when it is causal than when it is merely statistical. In a typical vignette, subjects are told that 85% of the cabs in town are green and 15% are blue (statistical base rates). An eyewitness (with, say, the same sensitivity and false alarm rates as the HIV test imagined earlier) thinks that the cab he saw in a late-night hit-and-run accident was blue. When subjects are asked the probability that the witness is right, they tend to neglect the low base rate of blue cabs and give a higher estimate than Bayes's theorem would prescribe. But if we tell them that the green cabs belong to a cut-rate company with reckless drivers and that 85% of the accidents involving cabs are *caused* by this company's cabs, people do take this base rate information into account (cf. Kahneman & Tversky, 1996; Tversky & Kahneman, 1982).

People are also more likely to use base rate information that they find relevant to the problem at hand (Bar-Hillel, 1990), and they do a better job using base rates when the subject matter is familiar (Gigerenzer, Hell, & Blank, 1988). Various studies also suggest that people make greater use of base rate information when the base rates are presented after the specific case information (e.g., a personality description), when base rates are varied across trials, and when people are encouraged to "think as statisticians" (see Kahneman & Tversky, 1996, p. 584 for references). People do take base rate information more fully into account when they are asked to make aggregate frequency judgments than when they are asked to make probability judgments (Gigerenzer et al., 1988), although their judgments still do not coincide with the prescriptions of the Bayesian model (Griffin & Buehler, 1999).

Some of the conclusions drawn from these studies may turn out to be wrong. But the important point here is that this research clearly illustrates the *ways* in which a phenomenon can be affected by contextual features. It also shows how successive studies can sharpen our understanding of the conditions under which a phenomenon will be strong, weak, or even nonexistent. And it emphasizes the point that when we apply work from behavioral decision theory to predict or explain complex things like politics or policy, we must be very sensitive to context.

Effect Size: Is It Big Enough to Matter?

The difficulties that contextual variation pose for applications are exacerbated by the fact that although many of the effects found in the lab are dramatic, others are relatively small. Small effects can be of theoretical interest, and in some cases they are also of practical importance; a treatment that improves the chances of surviving a dangerous surgical procedure by a few percentage points can save many lives over the long haul. But small effects cannot be used with much confidence to underwrite predictions or explanations about what will happen in complex situations outside the lab.

Death by a Thousand Qualifications?

Perhaps the most important question about the boundary conditions of each phenomenon is whether it now seems robust simply because researchers have yet to examine most of the conditions under which it would fail. Will there turn out to be a reasonably short list of conditions that promote or impede a given effect (e.g., the use of base rates)? Or when experimenters investigate a wider range of tasks, types of information, formats for judgments, and the like, will the effect dissolve into a fog of ever higher-order interactions (specific information increases sensitivity to base rates, unless it is difficult to weave it into a causal scenario around it, but even then it increases sensitivity if it is also the case that . . . , unless . . .)?

Some generalizations may end up being relatively unqualified. But it is also possible that further investigation will show that some phenomena must be hedged with so many qualifications that it will be almost impossible to predict with any confidence when they would occur outside the lab or, in the worst case, to determine in retrospect that they had occurred.

The fact that equivalent representations and small differences in methods of elicitation can lead to markedly different responses suggests that many of our preferences and beliefs are not fixed, inert, preexisting things. Instead, they are to some degree constructed on the spot, and the output of the construction process can be influenced by the context. So the issues noted in the previous paragraph might be better posed by asking: How do various contextual features influence this construction, and do they affect it in ways that can be explained without countless qualifications? And the answer is that in many cases we simply do not know. But we do know enough about the importance of context to realize that we must take it into account when applying results or theories from behavioral decision making to complex human affairs.

Who? Individual Differences

Many experimenters have noted that there are substantial individual differences in people's reasoning. For example, people with training in probability and statistics are less prone to certain kinds of errors (Nisbett, 1993; cf. Tversky & Kahneman, 1983). In most empirical work individual differences are treated as error variance, but researchers are beginning to investigate individual differences (e.g., Stanovich & West, 1999). This is important, because it is difficult to form a clear picture about individual reasoning from group data; indeed, in some cases, individual patterns may be in conformity with a norm even when group averages are not. The importance of individual differences sounds yet another cautionary note: People who make or implement policy are very likely to differ substantially in their proclivities to error. Hence, bald generalizations that average out differences can easily ignore factors that matter.

Why? Causal Mechanisms

Once a phenomenon or regularity is discovered (and its boundaries perhaps charted a bit), the next step is to *explain* it. *Why* does it occur? What causal mechanisms or processes produce it? As in many other areas of science the goal is explanatory unification, to explain as many phenomena as possible with the fewest mechanisms. Once a mechanism is discovered, it is possible to ask for a deeper explanation of it, and in fact the line between phenomena and underlying explanations is not always sharp. But at the current stage of research, most of the mechanisms that have been proposed are not very far below the surface phenomena.

The search for underlying mechanisms that causally mediate effects is important for several reasons. First, we want to know why we reason and choose in the ways that we do. Second, a knowledge of mechanisms often allows us to make more robust predictions than we could from knowledge of a regularity alone; the regularity will hold only in those cases where the causal mechanisms that generate it do, and so it may well fail in novel circumstances in ways that can be foreseen only if we know what causes it.

Third, knowledge of mechanisms often allows us to predict new phenomena whose existence could not simply be extrapolated from known phenomena. Fourth, it is often most effective to treat symptoms by intervening with the underlying mechanisms that produce them (e.g., killing microrganisms that cause a disease). Similarly, it may often be easier to improve reasoning by designing interventions that work on the mechanisms that produce suboptimal results rather than by trying to work on the symptoms directly (e.g., by exhorting people to use base rates). Knowing about the mediating processing does not in itself tell us how to intervene, but it suggests a place to begin.

Debunking Explanations: Explaining Results Away

Before turning to substantive explanations, we should note a genre of explanations that attribute various phenomena to errors or oversights on the part of the researcher. For example, Gigerenzer, Hoffrage, and Kleinbolting (1991) argue that the overconfidence effect is largely an artifact stemming from a biased set of test questions (see Brenner, Koehler, Liberman, & Tversky, 1996, for a reply). But the most common debunking accounts are variations on the theme that an apparent phenomenon results from misleading instructions or stimuli that subjects interpret in ways the experimenter didn't foresee. Such criticisms have become a cottage industry in the case of the conjunction fallacy, where it has been argued that subjects interpret words like *and* or *probability* in a way the experimenter didn't intend. Hence, it is urged, subjects' responses stem from their construal of the situation rather than from defective reasoning.

It is surely true that many experiments contain such flaws, but it isn't plausible to think that all of the hundreds of studies in behavioral decision theory are defective in these ways. Still, it always bears repeating that a single study can't show very much and that we need careful manipulation checks, process tracing (where feasible), detailed postexperimental interviews, conceptual replications, and follow-up studies to see whether an apparent effect is really genuine. Tversky and Kahneman's (1983) follow-up work on the conjunction fallacy illustrates some of these strategies. So do several recent studies on the use of base rates. In many early studies base rates were rather artificially defined by the experimenter, but in two recent studies they were actually reported by subjects before they made a probability judgment (Griffin & Buehler, 1999) or the base rates employed were determined by the subject rather than the experimenter (Dawes, Mirels, Gold, & Donahue, 1993).

Such follow-up work may, of course, confirm the suspicion that a phenomenon really *doesn't* exist. But if a pattern of results turns up repeatedly across a range of contexts with different stimulus materials and differently worded instructions, something is going on. And if something is going on, it needs to be explained. Table 1.2 lists a few of the many mechanisms that have been invoked to provide (nondebunking) explanations of the phenomena in Table 1.1, along with a list of the normative prescriptions each phenomenon is often thought to violate. These matters will be our concern in the rest of the chapter.

Explanations in the Heuristics and Biases Tradition

Human judgments and choices are often the result of many interacting partial causes. These include moods, emotions, self-interested motives, and habit, but behavioral decision theorists focus on more purely cognitive mechanisms and I will follow suit here. It is now generally agreed that many phenomena can arise from the operation of different mechanisms (in different circumstances) and that sometimes more than one mechanism is involved. Indeed, the systematically varied patterns of reasoning that people exhibit under different conditions suggest that they have a repertoire of cognitive mechanisms and that they use different mechanisms in different contexts. So the researcher's task is rarely to seek a necessary and sufficient causal condition for a given effect. It is to discover which mechanisms are sufficient for the effect, to determine which mechanism is most likely to be activated in a given range of circumstances, and to learn how mechanisms interact.

Early work in the heuristics and biases paradigm relied heavily on three heuristics: representativeness, availability, and anchoring and adjustment. Over the years a number of additional explanatory concepts

Table 1.2. *Selective Catalogue of Mechanisms and Normative Analyses*

Phenomenon/ Effect	Some Proposed Mechanisms	Normative Status
Insensitivity to base rates	Representativeness	If base rates are equated with prior probabilities, then failure to use them when estimating relevant conditional probabilities violates Bayes's theorem.
Insufficiently regressive prediction	Representativeness	If certain common assumptions are satisfied, an item sampled from a distribution after an extreme one is sampled will usually fall closer to the population mean.
Insensitivity to sample size	Representativeness	Larger samples are more likely to reflect the features of their parent population than smaller samples are.
Conjunction fallacy	Representativeness; availability (for example 2, involving frequencies, in Table 1.1); failure to unpack a relevant explicit disjunction (support theory)	In standard probability theory (and its nonstandard variants) a conjunction can never be more probable than its conjuncts.
Gambler's fallacy	Representativeness	Independent events should be treated as independent.
Hindsight bias	Anchoring on the current belief and not adjusting enough when estimating the likelihood that we would have predicted it	This is a case of inaccurate assessment of probabilities.
Overconfidence	People focus on strength (e.g., extremeness) of evidence and tend to neglect its weight (credibility).	Judges should be well calibrated, i.e., when they judge the probability to be .X they should be right X% of the time.
Suboptimal integration of information (actuarial vs. intuitive prediction)	Many of the effects mentioned here, e.g., failure to attend to base rates, as well as unclarity about the best predictor variables, the weights they should be given, and consistency in applying them	In cases where the predictions can be assessed for accuracy, the model makes a higher proportion of correct predictions than the person.

Phenomenon/ Effect	Some Proposed Mechanisms	Normative Status
Preference reversals (and framing effects)	People edit or code situations (e.g., as gains or losses), and this affects how they subsequently think about them.	Preferences should not depend on differences between logically equivalent ways of describing the same options.
Preference reversals (and elicitation effects)	People's preferences tend to be compatible with the format in which they are elicited.	Preferences should not depend on trivial differences between ways of eliciting them.
Fourfold pattern of risk seeking and aversion	Diminishing sensitivity (impact of a given change diminishes with distance from a reference point) for values and for weighted probabilities	In standard utility theory, risk aversion follows a concave utility function.
Subadditive probabilities	Availability (for implicit disjunctions); anchoring and adjustment and repacking (for explicit) disjunctions	Standard probabilities are additive (the probability of a disjunction of mutually exclusive disjuncts equals the sum of their individual probabilities).
Fundamental attribution error	Increased salience of the actor in the observer's perceptual field; some dual-process models in which we don't discount enough for the power of the situation	It is difficult to assess the accuracy of many of our explanations of behavior, but much evidence shows that situations account for more of the variance in behavior than we typically suppose.

have been added, but the major architects of this tradition still believe that our everyday judgments and predictions are often (at least partially) mediated by the original judgmental heuristics (e.g., Kahneman & Tversky, 1996).

Heuristics

The notion of a heuristic has never been precisely defined, but the basic idea is that we do not typically use formal rules (e.g., those of the probability calculus) in making judgments or decisions. Rather, we routinely make assessments of similarity, frequency, and causal connections of phenomena in the world around us. These processes are usually not carried out at a conscious level, but they often have a substantial influence on our judgments and predictions. The heuristics and biases tradition is not monolithic, but the following sampling of explanations is typical of work in it.

Anchoring and Adjustment

When we make a judgment, particularly one involving numerical values (like probabilities), we often begin by setting a cognitive "anchor" that provides a reference point for our subsequent reasoning. In many cases we realize that the anchor value isn't exactly right, and we make adjustments (up or down) to correct for the error. But often we do not adjust *enough*, and so the original anchor skews our final judgment. Anchoring effects are strong; they can occur even when anchoring values are known to be arbitrary, when they are ridiculously extreme, and when people are given strong incentives to be accurate.

In his seminal work, Fischhoff (1975) explained hindsight bias as the result of anchoring on a current, after-the-fact belief. We know (now) with certainty how things turned out, and we then adjust (insufficiently) to estimate how likely we would have thought it to be *before* we learned that it occurred. It is difficult to think back and accurately reconstruct how we thought about things before we learned what the outcome was, and our present knowledge skews our ability to do this. Additional mechanisms have been proposed to explain hindsight bias (see Dougherty, Gettys, & Ogden, 1999; Hawkins & Hastie, 1990), but Fischhoff's account is a classic example of the use of a heuristic to explain at least some instances of a phenomenon.

Anchoring and (insufficient) adjustment have also been invoked to explain other phenomena, including our tendency to overestimate the probability of conjunctions and to underestimate the probability of disjunctions. We anchor on the probability of one of the pair, then fail to adjust downward enough (for conjunctions) or upward enough (for disjunctions).

Representativeness

The representativeness heuristic has been invoked by one theorist or another to explain a very wide range of phenomena (e.g., insensitivity to regression effects, insensitivity to sample size, the gambler's fallacy, the fundamental attribution error). It is not clear that the more general descriptions of this heuristic pick out a single psychological process, but in some cases it can be characterized, reasonably straightforwardly, in terms of similarity. For example, a person is representative of a category, say an occupation (bank teller) or personality type (bleeding-heart liberal), to the degree that her salient features are similar to those of a stereotypical member of that category.

According to the *representativeness hypothesis*, the probability that x (e.g., Linda) will be judged to be an A (e.g., a feminist bank teller) will depend on the degree to which x resembles (is representative of) the stereotypical A. As we noted earlier in the Linda problem, subjects are given a personality sketch of Linda: She was a philosophy major deeply concerned with issues of discrimination and social justice who participated in demonstrations. Independent studies show that most people find this profile much more representative of (much more similar to) their stereotype or mental picture of a feminist than of their stereotype of a bank teller.

This allows us to pit representativeness against probability theory: Will subjects find it more probable that Linda is a feminist and a bank teller (as the representativeness hypothesis suggests) or that she is simply a bank teller (as probability theory assures us)? And the representativeness hypothesis is supported by the fact that in many studies a large percentage of subjects commit the conjunction fallacy: They judge that Linda is more likely to be a feminist and a bank teller than to be a bank teller.

The use of a heuristic often leads to the relative neglect of other considerations, and representativeness has been used to explain some cases where base rates are underweighted. The personality profile of a hypothetical student, Tom W (bright, compulsive, and a mechanical thinker), is highly representative of many people's stereotype of a computer science major. And in one study more than 90% of the subjects judged that this was in fact Tom's major, even though they had just stated that there were many more students with numerous other majors (or there were in 1973; Kahneman & Tversky, 1973). Here, it is argued, the strong focus on representativeness explains subjects' relative neglect of relevant base rates (the proportions of students in various majors).

Explanations Employing Newer Constructs

Compatibility

Some preference reversals (like that involving the Asian disease) involve framing effects. In other cases the options are framed in the same way, but people's evaluations are *elicited* in different ways. The most popular explanation of this sort of preference reversal in the heuristics and biases tradition is that it results from a *compatibility* between the way responses are elicited and the responses they elicit. For example, if subjects are offered one of two options and asked to *choose* one of the pair, they tend to focus on the positive features of the two things (which is thought to be *compatible* with the instruction to choose). But when they are asked to *reject* one of the two (which leads to exactly the same result, namely, getting one of the two things), they focus more on negative features (which is thought to be more compatible with the instruction to reject). In a range of cases, responses seem tailored to be compatible with the statement of the problem or task, and this can lead to preference reversals (Shafir, 1995).

Cumulative Prospect Theory

The introduction of the compatibility construct is just one of the ways the heuristics and biases tradition has expanded its original arsenal of explanatory mechanisms. Indeed, it now includes several complex explanatory models. For example, support theory aims to explain various aspects of probabilistic judgments, including the fact that they are often subadditive, as well as at least some cases of the conjunction fallacy (Tversky & Koehler, 1994, p. 561). But the most ambitious addition is cumulative prospect theory (Tversky & Kahneman, 1992), which is intended as a more descriptively adequate alternative to classical decision theories. The basic idea here is that value attaches to gains and losses relative to a reference point (rather than to levels of total wealth, as in classical theories). The classical concave utility function is replaced by a value function that is concave for gains, convex for losses, and steeper for losses than for gains, and a weighting function that transforms cumulative (rather than individual) probabilities is employed.

Cumulative prospect theory has been mobilized to explain a large number of phenomena. The shapes of the curves for the value and weighting functions provide pictorial representations of some of them, but they are *explained* by the underlying psychological mechanisms of *loss aversion* and *diminishing sensitivity*. Loss aversion means that losses loom larger than corresponding gains. This is invoked to explain the status quo bias and the endowment effect, our preference to keep things pretty much as they are and the fact that we value items we possess (our endowment) more than we would value them if we didn't have them. The theory explains these phenomena – which are clearly germane to public policies involving regulatory takings – in terms of loss aversion. Once we have something, giving it up is seen as a loss, and so we require more in compensation for it than we would be willing to expend to acquire it (cf. Thaler, 1991, ch. 1).

Diminishing sensitivity means that the psychological impact of change diminishes with its distance from a reference point. This explains the shapes of both the value function (changes here have less impact the further they are from the reflection point) and the probability weighting function (changes here have less impact the further they are from the natural boundaries of certainty and impossibility).

Diminishing sensitivity to changes in payoffs helps explain why most people prefer a sure gain of $500 to a 50% chance of winning $1,000; the two options have the same expected payoff, but because of diminishing sensitivity, $1,000 is not felt to be worth twice as much as $500. Diminishing sensitivity to changes in probabilities explains why most people find changes near the endpoints of the probability scale (e.g., from a probability of .9 to 1.0) more significant than equal changes further from the endpoints (e.g., from a probability of .4 to .5). And the two mechanisms together help explain why we tend to be risk averse with respect to gains and risk seeking with respect to losses when probabilities are judged to be moderate to high and why the situation is reversed when probabilities are judged to be low.

Criticisms of the Heuristics and Biases Approach

The heuristics and biases tradition is not without its critics. Some state that the phenomena announced by its proponents are overblown or even nonexistent. Others agree that these phenomena are genuine but disagree with the explanations workers in this tradition offer for them. I will note the more persistent criticisms, since they involve issues that are important in evaluating work in behavioral decision theory, motivate alternative approaches, and point to difficulties in applying ideas from this field. I will also note possible rejoinders, since such criticisms are sometimes accepted too readily, and some, if credible, would preclude almost any applications of behavioral decision theory to complex human affairs.

The Evidential Base Is Narrow and Artificial

Some of the research in the heuristics and biases paradigm involves unrealistic settings in which subjects have little incentive to think carefully about problems. Sometimes, for example, students in a classroom are given questionnaires that describe vignettes about characters (Linda, Tom W) and situations (taxi cabs, the dreaded Asian diseases) from Heuristics and Biases Central Casting, and they are simply asked to check off answers from a list of alternatives.

It is undeniable that such methods have their limitations and that their results are difficult to extrapolate to complex situations in the real world. But there is nothing about the heuristics and biases approach that precludes other research strategies, including high-impact experiments common in social psychology. Some studies have also provided strong incentives for accuracy (which induces better performance with some types of reasoning, though not with others), and some work has been done in the field (e.g., Lichtenstein & Slovic, 1973, found that varying elicitation methods produced preference reversals in seasoned gamblers in the Four Queens Casino in Las Vegas). But clearly more work of this sort is desirable, and the extent to which it will support the heuristics and biases approach remains to be seen.

Heuristics Are Too Vague

It is often charged that heuristics are too vaguely specified for claims about them to be informative or even testable. Worries about vagueness are not entirely unfounded. The representativeness heuristic may well involve more than one process, availability has meant different things (e.g., the number of instances easily recalled, a general sense that certain things are easier to recall), and compatibility isn't the most precise construct around. But some critics go further, arguing that these constructs are really just redescriptions of the things they are invoked to explain (Gigerenzer, 1998). Whether these more serious charges are fair depends on whether claims involving heuristics are testable and enlightening, which takes us to the next charge.

It's All Post Hoc

It is sometimes charged that although heuristics are too vaguely specified to underwrite testable predictions, some heuristic or other can always be fitted, after the fact, to explain almost any outcome (Gigerenzer, 1998). This isn't a fair characterization of much of the work in the heuristics and biases tradition. For example, in studies of the conjunction fallacy, representativeness is usually assessed independently of judgments of probability, and the fact that so many people doubt that subjects really commit this fallacy shows that the representativeness hypothesis makes a very risky prediction that could easily have turned out wrong.

But although the charge of ad hocery is not a fair criticism of most studies, it is an ever-present danger when such explanatory frameworks are carried outside of the lab to explain specific events, or types of events, involving politics or policy. Here it often *is* difficult to make an independent assessment of representativeness, availability, or compatibility. Again, predictions based on cumulative prospect theory would often require a reasonably detailed knowledge of a person's reference point (perhaps it is some level of aspiration, but which one?), probabilities, and values. And it will often be possible – and sometimes tempting – to tailor assessments of such variables, after the fact, to accommodate the way things turned out.

But the heuristics and biases paradigm is scarcely alone here. To determine whether someone is satisficing (Simon, 1956), we must have some idea what his or her level of aspiration is, and while this is sometimes possible to determine (as when a business has a *bright line* targeted increase in third-quarter profits), it is often quite difficult. Indeed, similar problems arise in applying *any* explanatory apparatus from behavioral decision theory to complex situations. The moral is not that such applications are impossible, but that they require detailed scrutiny of the context in which they are applied and that they are almost always subject to a great deal of uncertainty.

When and Where Revisited

The questions of *where* and *when* arise at the level of mechanisms as well as at the level of phenomena. We want to know what conditions will trigger or suppress the operation of a heuristic, and it is sometimes charged that their proponents have little to say about this. In fact, though, we do know something about this. For example, the specification of boundary conditions for a phenomenon often casts light on the boundary conditions for an underlying mechanism. Thus, if current accounts are right, people are more responsive to base rate information that is vivid and causal, and so in conditions in which such information is salient, the representativeness heuristic should play a less dominant role.

Tversky and Kahneman appear pessimistic about finding formal or detailed accounts specifying which mechanisms will be triggered when; judgment and choice depend on too many subtle contextual features for that (e.g., Tversky & Kahneman, 1992, p. 317). They may be unduly pessimistic, but however this may be, critics of the heuristics and biases tradition also have few answers to questions about which psychological mechanisms will be activated when. Questions about when a given cognitive mechanism will be employed and how it will interact with other processes are important, but here much remains to be learned.

You Can't Assign Probabilities to Single Events

This objection rests on the view that the *only* legitimate interpretation of the probability calculus is that probabilities are *relative frequencies* or *proportions* of an attribute class (e.g., the class of people who suffer a heart attack) in a reference class (e.g., the class of smokers). And since probabilities are frequencies, it doesn't make sense to assign probabilities to single events.

If this is correct, many of the classical results in behavioral decision theory have been badly misinterpreted. For example, subjects who have been thought to commit probabilistic versions of the conjunction fallacy (as in the original Linda problem) or to neglect base rates when judging the probability of a single event (as with the taxi cab problem) are not making errors. They are just doing their best to cope with an incoherently posed problem.

Is this charge fair? There are two well-known interpretations of the probability calculus that make sense of the probabilities of individual outcomes or events. According to the first interpretation, probabilities are dispositional properties known as *propensities*; for example, the propensity of a photon in a particular state to pass through a polarizer set at a 15 degree angle might be 0.4. According to the second (not incompatible) interpretation, probabilities are subjective degrees of belief. Neither interpretation is problem free (though neither are frequency interpretations), but there are certainly no theorems or arguments demonstrating that either of them is wrong.

Our penchant for reasoning with frequencies is sometimes defended on evolutionary grounds, but our hunter-gatherer ancestors often had to bet on the single case (how likely are *these* purple berries to be poisonous?). So do we. Suppose you have a fatal illness and can choose between two drugs (deadly in combination); 99% of those who have taken drug A recovered fully, but only .05% who took drug B did. It seems more than sensible to choose drug A. One theoretical rationale for this might be that frequencies provide relevant evidence about the propensities of the two drugs. But however this may be, if it is illegitimate to engage in probabilistic reasoning about a specific case, you have no clear reason for preferring drug A to drug B.

Theoretical Extensions and Alternatives

There are now numerous alternatives to the heuristics and biases program. I will note three in order to convey a sense of the range of alternatives now available. One very recent approach adapts a mathematical model of recognition memory to explain judgment and decision phenomena. This model, MINERVA-DM (Dougherty et al., 1999), is an extension of Hintzman's (1988) global-matching memory model MINERVA2. Its authors use it to explain a wide range of judgmental phenomena *and* several heuristics (representativeness and availability) that are often thought to underlie them, and so it is more an extension or a deeper account of work in the heuristics and biases tradition than a rejection of it.

The model, in conjunction with testable empirical auxiliary assumptions about memory encoding, memory search, and the structure of stored information, predicts many of the effects discussed in the heuristics and biases literature. There are open questions as to how the memory-retrieval processes employed in the model dovetail with higher-order cognitive mechanisms. But because MINERVA-DM is formulated as a detailed process model implemented in a computer program, it provides the unification (based on the common underlying mechanism of memory retrieval) and precision that are lacking in much of the work on heuristics and biases.

Gigerenzer and his coworkers have proposed a much more radical alternative to the heuristics and biases paradigm. On Gigerenzer's (1998; Gigerenzer & Goldstein, 1996) view, reasoning and choice often involve heuristics. But his heuristics (like "take the best") are step-by-step rules (unlike those in the heuristics and biases tradition), they are not based on consistency or coherence (as many normative rules are), and they do not attempt to integrate numerous pieces of information (as many normative models do).

Because these heuristics are simple and run on relatively little information, they wouldn't produce accurate results in all possible environments. But we don't need accurate results in all possible environments. We only need accuracy in our actual environment and, Gigerenzer argues, his *fast and frugal* heuristics provide this because they involve biological adaptations that are attuned to the structure of information in the ecological setting where our species evolved. They contain built-in, often quite domain-specific information, and when used in the environments to which they are geared, they can be quite accurate.

Normative questions about accuracy are quite different from descriptive questions about when (if ever) people actually use such heuristics, but in both cases there isn't yet enough evidence to be very sure. Among other things, the range of real-life circumstances in which such heuristics yield accurate information is still not well understood. But although evolutionary considerations seem rather distant from the world of policy, mechanisms like Gigerenzer's will probably have a place in future discussions of judgment and choice.

Finally, a number of recent theorists have proposed dual-process accounts of cognition. Different theorists develop this idea in different ways, but the rough idea is that human beings have two quite different cognitive subsystems (or two *types* of subsystems). There is an *explicit* subsystem that is largely conscious, symbolic, verbal, rule governed, serial, flexible, and capable of reflection. But there is also an *implicit* subsystem that is largely nonconscious, associative, impulsive, affective, and that reacts automatically to stimuli (e.g., Sloman, 1996, and many of the papers in Chaiken & Trope, 1999).

Dual-process accounts needn't be incompatible with earlier work on judgment and decision; for example, it might be the case that use of the representativeness heuristic proceeds on automatic pilot, while calculations of probabilities involve a more conscious sort of processing. Dual-process models open new vistas, however, including the intriguing possibility that two subsystems in a single person will sometimes draw conflicting conclusions about the same thing.

Where does this leave us? We know much more than we did 30 years ago about judgment and choice, and a number of theoretical frameworks for dealing with them have emerged. It remains true that none of these frameworks can be applied to any but the simplest real-life cases with great confidence; often the most we can say is that some event or phenomenon is consistent with the operation of this or that psychological mechanism. As accounts of the underlying causal mechanisms become clearer, however, such applications should become easier. But how do we choose among such accounts?

Evaluating the Alternatives: Science as Judgment and Decision Making

Philosophy's graveyard is full of failed universal methodologies for the evaluation of scientific models and theories (the hypothetico-deductive method, Popper's falsificationism, Lakatos's research programs, Bayesian confirmation theory). Each of these accounts pinpoints something important about science, or some parts of some sciences, but they all break down when their more imperialistic partisans try to cram all of science into a single favored pattern.

A more useful and realistic picture depicts the scientist as an information processor with a set of conflicting goals operating in an uncertain environment. She must make judgments (How well has this model performed to date?), predictions (Is it about played out?), and choices (Is it promising enough for me to invest two years working on it?). She does have tools and institutions (training in probability and statistics, a sophisticated theory of experimental design, accountability to peers) that encourage judgments and choices with good normative credentials. But she is still in the same boat (though equipped with a life jacket and good swimming skills) as the agents studied in behavioral decision theory.

Scientists working in behavioral decision theory face conflicting goals because (1) there are various, often incompatible, desiderata for models, and (2) competing descriptive models of probabilistic judgment (e.g., support theory, MINERVA-DM) and choice (e.g., cumulative prospect theory, Loomis and Sugden's 1982 regret theory, Fishburn's 1984 skew symmetric bilinear [SSB] utility theory) possess varying combinations of these features.

Accuracy is typically the most important feature in a model. Models inevitably involve idealizations, approximations, and other simplifications, however, so everyone knows at the outset that accuracy will be a matter of degree. It is also important to have models that apply to a relatively wide range of cases, but there is a familiar trade-off between precise and accurate predictions, on the one hand, and scope or generality or informativeness, on the other. For example, mathematical models of some aspects of memory now deliver quite accurate predictions, but at the price of covering a relatively narrow range of phenomena.

Simplicity is also desirable. Combined with the goal of generality, this means that we want a model with a small number of mechanisms (e.g., a handful of judgmental heuristics) that explains a large number of phenomena (e.g., base rate neglect, insufficiently regressive prediction, overconfidence). There are various sorts of simplicity, some of which can be in tension with others, but one sort that will be increasingly important as models become more formal is the number of free parameters. With more free parameters one can fit a data set more closely (thus increasing accuracy), but as the number increases, it becomes too easy to establish a good fit and too difficult to discern a general underlying pattern.

Another desideratum is explanatory depth. For example, explaining the representativeness heuristic in terms of a memory retrieval process is satisfying because it gives a deeper explanation than merely explaining the conjunction fallacy in terms of the representativeness heuristic. Detail is also good. *Paramorphic models* (Hoffman, 1960) of judgment and reasoning (e.g., linear regression models of experts, some applications of Bayesianism as a descriptive theory) treat the subject as a black box and simply claim that the input–output relations are pretty much what they would be *if* she actually went through the steps prescribed by the models (taking a weighted average of several predictor variables, multiplying prior odds by a likelihood ratio). By contrast, *process models* aim to trace the internal cognitive processes as a person engages in a stretch of reasoning. And when such models are formulated as computer programs, as they increasingly are, they often provide clear and detailed predictions that more loosely formulated models can rarely match.

The downside is that such programs often require details (to make computations run smoothly) that appear to describe psychological processes that lie beyond the reach of any evidence we can obtain. Indeed, at a certain point it becomes difficult (or impossible) to find evidence that can distinguish between competing models. This is a philosophical problem, known as the *underdetermination of theory by data*, but it can be a practical problem in cognitive science, where rival models are often formulated as computer programs and what can be done by one can often be done, with a bit of tinkering, by its competitors.

These trade-offs, approximations, and compromises needn't mean that the mechanisms and processes described in a model are not real (though, of course, in any particular case they may). But they do mean that different theorists may elect different trade-offs, and sometimes one model will provide a more accurate treatment of some aspects of a phenomenon, whereas a different model provides a more accurate treatment of others.

Models Do Not Apply Themselves

One of the most important features of formal (and quasi-formal) models, particularly when we are interested in using them to predict or explain complex behavior outside the lab, is that they do not apply themselves. The theory of rational choice, for example, is typically specified by a handful of axioms that govern the behavior of a few primitive notions like a preference relation over outcomes given our choices. But such axioms cannot tell us how to divide the world up into choices and outcomes or how to ascertain a person's preferences.

There are, to be sure, more or less canonical methods for applying such models and making such measurements, such as gauging preferences by asking the agent to choose between pairs of options or ascertaining her degree of belief by seeing which gambles she will accept. There are two ways to construe these kinds of behavior. They can be viewed as operationalistic or behavioristic definitions of preference and belief. This is how they were often construed when they were introduced (during the heyday of behaviorism), but this now seems less plausible given the known infirmities of operationalism and behaviorism. Alternatively, we might find well-confirmed empirical claims to the effect that specific behaviors (e.g., accepting certain gambles) are highly correlated with genuine underlying psychological states (e.g., having certain degrees of belief about their outcomes).

In the natural sciences, there often are compelling empirical reasons for believing that a measurement procedure really does measure some magnitude (like electrical resistance), but there are no well-confirmed theories in behavioral decision theory to assure us that procedures for assessing preferences or degrees of belief really do so. Hence the fact, trivial in itself, that models do not apply themselves means that it will often be unclear, prior to making various substantive auxiliary assumptions, whether a descriptive model applies to a given situation. It also means that competing models may both work reasonably well *if* we make the right sorts of auxiliary assumptions (e.g., about measurement processes) to support them.[3]

Adding Things Up: The Problem of Unknown Interactions

There is a final feature of psychological models that bears on their applications. Even if you have models for three psychological mechanisms (say representativeness, compatibility, and loss aversion), you can't automatically paste them together to obtain a model that handles all three at once.

In the physical sciences it is sometimes possible to create conditions that shield disturbing influences so that we can ascertain the source, magnitude, and direction of a force whose influence is swamped outside the lab. Once we have learned this, we know that the force will add together with other forces, in conformity with the rules of vector addition, and that an object acted on by this sum of forces will behave (by accelerating in accordance with Newton's second law) in just the way that it would if this resultant force vector were the only force acting on it. Of course, we can't determine all of the forces in the real world, and when it comes to predicting where a leaf blowing in the wind will land, the natural scientist's predictive powers aren't that far ahead of the psychologist's. But we *do* have a simple theoretical picture about how forces interact (by vector addition), and the point here is that we don't have anything like this for the psychological mechanisms involved in judgment and decision making.

When several psychological mechanisms operate at the same time, they may reinforce each other, cancel each other out, exhibit some sort of interference effect, or interact in a way that depends on 37 of the other psychological processes then taking place. So learning about mechanisms in the lab cannot tell us (without checking on a vast number of potential interactions, which would require a vast number of subjects), even in principle, what those mechanisms will do over a range of circumstances in the actual world. This problem is exacerbated by the fact that in the psychology laboratory individual differences (and, to a lesser extent, other sources of variability) mean that the unaccounted-for variance in an experiment will often be greater than the variance accounted for by an experimental manipulation.

Do these difficulties mean that we should abandon studies of processes and mechanisms and simply search for surface-level generalizations with ecological validity (ones that apply to a range of situations in the real world)? Not at all. Most actual behavior results from some unknown combination of causal factors – attention, expectations, reasoning mechanisms, emotions, habits, fatigue. In any particular case, some specific amalgam of these factors will give rise to a piece of behavior, but this exact combination of psychological mechanisms is not likely to arise frequently. This means that there are unlikely to be many surface regularities that are not highly qualified. Hence, an understanding of why these regularities hold, in the situations and to the extent that they do, will require a knowledge of the underlying causal mechanisms that produce them, and fastidious experimentation is the only way to discover this.

Normative Issues

When we focus on the descriptive study of policy, it doesn't matter whether phenomena (like ignoring regression effects) violate normative models. But when we step back and consider the impact of policy on people's lives, suboptimal judgments, predictions, and decisions are clearly bad. To view such things as suboptimal or wrong requires standards for getting things right, and these are provided by normative models. Various people have objected that it is often impossible to identify and apply the right normative model in many actual situations, however, and if this is true, it will be difficult to improve policy by improving reasoning.

Competing Normative Models

Perhaps the most compelling objection is that there are always competing normative models and that they sometimes offer conflicting advice. There are alternative logics (e.g., classical logic, intuitionistic logic), probability theories (e.g., the classical theory, Shafer's, 1976, belief functions), schools of statistics (e.g., Fisher's, Neyman and Pearson's, the ill-motivated blend of the two often taught today), and decision theories (e.g., evidential decision theories like that of Jeffrey, 1992, various causal decision theories, regret theory). And if the experts can't agree about which model is best, how can we expect people who formulate or apply policy to do so?

It is true that there are always competing normative models, but they needn't be viewed as package deals to be accepted in all-or-none fashion. Usually some aspects of a model will be more compelling and defensible than others, and when it comes to this more solid core, many of the competing models agree. For example, classical and intuitionist logic disagree about whether the law of excluded middle is valid, but there is no logical system (with any adherents) in which the inference pattern known as *modus ponens* (If A then B; A, therefore B) is invalid. Similarly, although there are alternative normative models of probability, none of them permits a conjunction to be more probable than either of its conjuncts. Furthermore, even when there is no uniquely correct answer to a problem, it doesn't follow that every possible answer is equally good. This is reflected in the fact that when competing models do not agree on a precise answer, they often agree that the answer falls within a certain range.

In short, the existence of competing normative models does not undermine the idea that such models can play a legitimate role in evaluating people's judgments and choices. But it does mean that empirical studies will provide pertinent evidence about our reasoning abilities only when they involve clear cases in which competing normative models either agree or when they at least determine a range within which correct answers must fall.

Alternative Applications

Even when people agree that a particular normative model applies to a given situation, they may disagree about *how* to apply it. For example, people may agree that a situation calls for Bayesian reasoning and that the relevant prior probabilities are base rates of characteristics (like developing lung cancer) in a population or reference class. But *which* reference class – all people, smokers, heavy smokers, people who smoked but quit? Up to a point smaller reference classes are likely to underwrite better predictions, and we will also be interested in reference classes that seem causally relevant to the characteristic we care about. But if a reference class becomes too small, it won't generate stable frequencies, and it will often be difficult to obtain data on smaller classes neatly tailored to our particular concerns.

There is no one right answer to the question of which reference class is correct, any more than there is one simple scientific methodology. Both cases require judicious, often delicate, sometimes controversial trade-offs. Selection of a reference class often involves weighing the costs of a wrong prediction against the payoffs of extreme accuracy, or the value of more precise information against the costs of acquiring it and the fact that the number of reference classes grows exponentially with each new predictor variable. But although there is no uniquely correct way to use base rates, it doesn't follow that it is always sensible to ignore them. Relevance comes in degrees, and failure to take pertinent base rate information into account will often lead to bad policy.

Alternative Goals

Another objection to the use of normative models is that people have many goals besides consistency and accuracy. Human beings are not merely intuitive scientists or intuitive statisticians: They are also intuitive lobbyists and defense attorneys, conflict negotiators and counselors, gossip columnists and romance novelists, televangelists and inquisitors. The spirit of this criticism is right; it often makes sense to violate the prescriptions of normative models when we have additional goals like drawing quick conclusions; or avoiding decisions that could lead to regret, disappointment, guilt, or embarrassment; or making choices that will minimize conflict or allow deniability. And of course, people who make or implement policy have such goals just as much as the rest of us. Nevertheless, when we entrust people with these responsibilities, we should expect them to make judgments and choices that are well conceived and responsive to the evidence. Hence, normative models are relevant in evaluating what they do on the job and in trying to find ways to help them do better.

The Good News and the Bad News: A Not Entirely Optimistic Conclusion

Behavioral decision theory has opened new and important vistas on human judgment and decision making. In the short term, the clearest lessons for policy studies are probably negative: The old normative models can rarely be used, even as rough approximations, to describe the behavior of real people. On the positive side, some phenomena (e.g., the fact that people treat gains and losses very differently) are robust and can be used to illuminate many actual situations. Many phenomena depend in quite intricate ways on context, however, and it is more risky to base predictions on them or to cite them in explanations of complex behavior. The counsel here is not skepticism, however, but caution and patience. Current work offers insights of a sort that would not have been possible even a few decades ago, and we are learning more every day.

The Good News

Can what we are learning from behavioral decision theory promote better policy? Sometimes. In areas where the same sorts of issues arise repeatedly and records of past performance are available (e.g., with decisions about parole or allocation of scarce medical resources), a crash course on the proper use of base rates and sample size may well improve the implementation of policy. This is especially likely when people are taught to recognize cues that signal the relevance of a formal theory (like the probability calculus) to a given problem (Anderson, Reder, & Simon, 1996; Nisbett, 1993).

In cases where the application of such probabilistic and statistical concepts are fairly routine, however, it often turns out that a formula, frequently a simple linear regression equation with just a few predictor variables, will do a better job at diagnosing and predicting things (e.g., various psychological and medical conditions, parole violation, success on the job, bankruptcy of firms) than experts do (for a recent meta-analysis see Grove, Zald, Lebow, Snitz, & Nelson, 2000). So it is possible that in many of those cases where people can most easily learn to do better, a formula could do better still.

The Bad News: How-to Manuals for Manipulation

The bad news is that it will often be easier to apply lessons from behavioral decision theory to exploit human fallibility than to reduce it. For example, when policymaking is poll driven, shifting the views of 2% or 3% of the electorate may determine what law gets enacted. A 30-second spot warning people about regression effects is unlikely to have much impact on this process, but an attack that manages to frame an issue in a frightening way very well may. The 1993 Harry and Louise commercials framed Clinton's health-care package as a case of big government taking away our choices about health care (and hence as a loss), and some people turned against it.

The art of the spin doctor is in large part skillful framing, but it also re-lies on many of the other biases uncovered in behavioral decision theory. These include exploiting people's susceptibility to anchoring effects by staking out extreme positions, focusing on vivid and memorable sorts of dangers (even if their risk is much less than that of more pallid dangers), and inflating the likelihood of some risk by ignoring base rates. But it is doubtful that successful opinion makers needed to wait for behavioral decision theory to learn about tactics like these.

Notes

1 Bayes's theorem provides a simple and appealing normative model for updating probabilities. It gives the *posterior probability* of a hypothesis H in light of a piece of new evidence e as

$$P(H \mid e) = (P(H)P(e \mid H))/(P(e)) \tag{1}$$

where $P(H)$ is the prior probability of the hypothesis, $P(e \mid H)$ is the likelihood of e given H, and $P(e)$ is the prior probability of obtaining the evidence e. Updating beliefs in light of the new evidence e means setting $NewP(H) = OldP(H \mid e)$, with $OldP(H \mid e)$ determined in accordance with (1). Particularly when we are concerned with mutually exclusive and disjoint hypothesis (e.g., HIV vs. no HIV), the odds version of Bayes's theorem

$$(P(H \mid e))/(P(\sim H \mid e)) = (P(H))/(P(\sim H)) \times (P(e \mid H))/(P(e \mid \sim H)) \tag{2}$$

is often more useful (here $\sim H$ is the negation of H). The expression on the left gives the posterior odds of the two hypotheses, $P(H)/P(\sim H)$ gives their prior odds, and $P(e \mid H)/P(e \mid \sim H)$ is the likelihood (or diagnostic) ratio. Our background knowledge of base rates is reflected in the prior odds, our knowledge about the specific case is represented by the likelihood ratio, and (2) tells us how to integrate the two. For example, if e represents a positive test result for the HIV virus and H represents having the virus, then $P(e \mid H)$ gives the hit rate (sensitivity) of the test and $P(e \mid \sim H)$ gives the rate of false alarms. As the multiplicative relation in (2) indicates, when the prior odds are quite low, even a relatively high likelihood ratio won't raise the posterior odds dramatically. In the example in the text, $P(e \mid H) = .9$, $P(e \mid \sim H) = .2$, $P(H) = .01$, and $P(\sim H) = .99$. Hence $(P(H \mid e))/(P(\sim H \mid e)) = (P(H))/(P\sim H) \times (P(e \mid H))/(P(e \mid \sim H)) = (.9)/(.2) \times (.01)/(.99) = 1/22$ (this gives the odds: 22 to 1 against Smith's being infected). Hence $P(H \mid e) = (1)/(23)$.

2 The unintuitive nature of regression effects is compounded by the fact that, as with base rates, there is a problem about reference class. *Which* average will Ann's shooting percentage regress to: her season average, her recent average, her team's average? We will return to the matter of the reference class in the seventh section.

3 This also raises questions concerning claims about violations of procedural invariance of decision theory (e.g., Tversky, Slovic, & Kahneman, 1990). The fact that different methods for trying to elicit preferences (choosing one of two gambles vs. selecting a lowest selling price for each) seem to produce preference reversals could instead be interpreted as evidence that one of the two methods for eliciting preferences really doesn't measure preference in all cases (perhaps in one of the two cases additional factors, e.g., compatibility effects, influence our response).

References

Anderson, J. R., Reder, L. M., & Simon, H. A. (1996). Situated learning and education. *Educational Researcher, 25*, 5–11.

Bar-Hillel, M. (1990). Back to base rates. In R. M. Hogarth (Ed.), *Insights in decision making: A tribute to Hillel J. Einhorn* (pp. 200–216). Chicago: University of Chicago Press.

Brenner, L. A., Koehler, D. J., Liberman, V., & Tversky, A. (1996). Overconfidence in probability and frequency judgments: A critical examination. *Organizational Behavior and Human Decision Processes, 65,* 212–219.

Chaiken, S., & Trope, Y. (1999). *Dual-process theories in social psychology.* New York: Guilford Press.

Dawes, R. M., Mirels, H. L., Gold, E., & Donahue, E. (1993). Equating inverse probabilities in implicit personality judgments. *Psychological Science: A Journal of the American Psychological Society, 4,* 396–400.

Dougherty, M. R. P., Gettys, C. F., & Ogden, E. E. (1999). MINERVA-DM: A memory processes model for judgments of likelihood. *Psychological Review, 106,* 180–209.

Fischhoff, B. (1975). Hindsight != foresight: The effect of outcome knowledge on judgment under uncertainty. *Journal of Experimental Psychology: Human Perception and Performance, 1,* 288–299.

Fishburn, P. C. (1984). SSB utility theory: An economic perspective. *Mathematical Social Sciences, 8,* 63–94.

Gigerenzer, G. (1998). Surrogates for theories. *Theory and Psychology, 8,* 195–204.

Gigerenzer, G., & Goldstein, D. G. (1996). Reasoning the fast and frugal way: Models of bounded rationality. *Psychological Review, 103,* 650–669.

Gigerenzer, G., Hell, W., & Blank, H. (1988). Presentation and content: The use of base rates as a continuous variable. *Journal of Experimental Psychology: Human Perception & Performance, 14,* 513–525.

Gigerenzer, G., Hoffrage, U., & Kleinbolting, H. (1991). Probabilistic mental models: A Brunswikian theory of confidence. *Psychological Review, 98,* 506–528.

Griffin, D., & Buehler, R. (1999). Frequency, probability, and prediction: Easy solutions to cognitive illusions? *Cognitive Psychology, 38,* 48–74.

Grove, W. M., Zald, D. H., Lebow, B. S., Snitz, B. E., & Nelson, C. (2000). Clinical vs. mechanical prediction: A meta-analysis. *Psychological Assessment, 12,* 19–31.

Hawkins, S. A., & Hastie, R. (1990). Hindsight: Biased judgments of past events after the outcomes are known. *Psychological Bulletin, 107,* 311–321.

Hintzman, D. L. (1988). Judgments of frequency and recognition memory in a multiple-trace memory model. *Psychological Review, 95,* 528–551.

Hoffman, P. J. (1960). The paramorphic representation of clinical judgment. *Psychological Bulletin, 57,* 116–131.

Jeffrey, R. (1992). *The logic of decision.* Cambridge: Cambridge University Press.

Kahneman, D., & Tversky, A. (1973). On the psychology of prediction. *Psychological Review, 80,* 237–251.

Kahneman, D., & Tversky, A. (1996). On the reality of cognitive illusions. *Psychological Review, 103,* 582–591.

Lichtenstein, S., & Slovic, P. (1973). Response-induced reversals of preference in gambling: An extended replication in Las Vegas. *Journal of Experimental Psychology, 101,* 16–20.

Loomis, G., & Sugden, R. (1982). Regret theory: An alternative theory of rational choice under uncertainty. *Economic Journal, 92,* 805–824.

Nisbett, R. E. (1993). *Rules for reasoning.* Hillsdale, NJ: Erlbaum.

Park, D. C., Nisbett, R., & Hedden, T. (1999). Aging, culture, and cognition. *Journals of Gerontology: Series B: Psychological Sciences & Social Sciences, 54B*, 75–84.

Quattrone, G. A., & Tversky, A. (1988). Contrasting rational and psychological analyses of political choice. *American Political Science Review, 82*, 719–736.

Shafer, G. (1976). *A mathematical theory of evidence*. Princeton, NJ: Princeton University Press.

Shafir, E. (1995). Compatibility in cognition and decision. *The Psychology of Learning and Motivation, 32*, 247–274.

Simon, H. A. (1956). Rational choice and the structure of the environment. *Psychological Review, 63*, 129–138.

Sloman, S. A. (1996). The empirical case for two systems of reasoning. *Psychological Bulletin, 119*, 3–22.

Stanovich, K. E., & West, R. F. (1999). Discrepancies between normative and descriptive models of decision making and the understanding/acceptance principle. *Cognitive Psychology, 38*, 349–385.

Thaler, R. H. (1991). *Quasi-rational economics*. New York: Sage.

Tversky, A., & Kahneman, D. (1982). Evidential impact of base rates. In D. Kahneman, P. Slovic, & A. Tversky (Eds.), *Judgment under uncertainty: Heuristics and biases* (pp. 153–161). Cambridge: Cambridge University Press.

Tversky, A., & Kahneman, D. (1983). Extensional versus intuitive reasoning: The conjunction fallacy in probability judgment. *Psychological Review, 90*, 292–315.

Tversky, A., & Kahneman, D. (1986). Rational choice and the framing of decisions. *Journal of Business, 59*, S251–S278.

Tversky, A., Slovic, P., & Kahneman, D. (1990). The causes of preference reversal. *American Economic Review, 80*, 204-217.

Tversky, A., & Kahneman, D. (1992). Advances in prospect theory: Cumulative representation of uncertainty. *Journal of Risk and Uncertainty, 5*, 297–323.

Tversky, A., & Koehler, D. J. (1994). Support theory: A nonextensional representation of subjective probability. *Psychological Review, 101*, 547–567.

2　Some Morals of a Theory of Nonrational Choice

Douglas MacLean

Individuals and organizations often have powerful incentives to shape our preferences, influence our judgments, and get us to make choices that serve their interests, whether or not they serve our own. We depend on our rational instincts, democratic institutions, and other rules and procedures to protect us from being exploited by these forces. To the extent that our preferences are shaped in nonrational ways, however, and to the extent that others can find ways to bypass our rational faculties, we need to worry about our susceptibility to manipulation. If our nonrational tendencies are deep and pervasive, this worry may be justified, even when we have in place procedures and robust institutions aimed at steering us toward rational deliberation, and even when we want and try to act reasonably. This chapter is an examination of the grounds for this worry.

I

One of the central aims of behavioral decision theory is to discover and analyze the causal processes of preference formation. Behavioral decision theory is not a single theory but an amalgamation of findings, hypotheses, and research projects in different areas of the social sciences, which are united by their interest in discovering the empirical bases of judgment and choice. Some of the most interesting research in this

Earlier versions of this chapter were presented to the Twentieth Annual Research Conference of the Association for Public Policy Analysis and Management and to audiences at the University of Maryland, College Park, the University of Colorado, and Philamore. The chapter has improved as a result of those discussions. I am especially grateful to Henry Richardson, Paul Slovic, and Susan Wolf for their suggestions.

area comes from psychologists who show how preferences are often determined in predictable but nonrational ways, with the implication that most of us can easily be led to make choices that we would also admit are not rationally justifiable.

These results have drawn much attention and provoked controversy. Some critics of this research have looked for flaws in the research designs, hoping to dismiss the results. Other critics have accepted the results but attempted to explain away their significance by arguing that the research shows at most that we are not perfectly rational, not that we are systematically irrational. Even the most careful among us err in our judgments and choices, which is hardly surprising. Much of the psychological research shows how we rely on shortcuts or heuristics for processing information that forms the basis for judgments and decisions, but these heuristics are generally reliable ways of coping with the natural limitations of time, information, and our normal computational abilities. Like any shortcut, these heuristics can, of course, lead us astray in some situations and in carefully contrived experiments, but this does not show that we are irrational for relying on them.

Prospect theory, which is one of the most important contributions of psychology to this field, challenges in a particularly interesting way these dismissive or reductionist criticisms of those who would draw strong conclusions from the findings of behavioral decision theory (Kahneman & Tversky, 1979). Prospect theory defends a formal behavioral theory of choice among risky prospects whose central claims are incompatible with utility theory, which is the standard normative theory of rational choice. The axioms of utility theory cannot be constrained, weakened, or amended in any way that would allow utility theory to explain the findings of prospect theory and still express any of our core intuitions about rationality. If we accept utility theory as an account of rational choice, then prospect theory tells us that some of the rules of preference formation are fundamentally nonrational. Prospect theory also explains how we are easily led to make judgments and decisions that are not simply imperfect but plainly irrational. It tells us something disturbing and important about our behavior, and I believe it has interesting implications for moral and political philosophy.

Now utility theory, as its critics often point out, is not an uncontroversial account of rationality, primarily because of what it fails to address. Any conception of rationality adequate for moral theory, for example, would have to include norms that allow us to deliberate among different ends and reject some for being immoral, destructive, or simply crazy.

Utility theory is famously silent about the rationality or irrationality of different ends or objects of preference. A complete theory of rationality would have to explain whether some goods might reasonably be incommensurable with others, but utility theory simply assumes that all alternatives can be seen as commensurable. A complete theory of rationality would help us understand whether some rational choices can only be represented as expressing certain values, not as maximizing anything at all, but utility theory simply assumes that rationality consists in maximizing something.

Utility theory's silence on such matters, however, also helps to account for its robustness in the social sciences. For though it does not address these normative issues, it succeeds brilliantly in defining a simple and useful structure for thinking about preference and choice across a wide range of contexts and behavior. Utility theory certainly characterizes part of the core of our understanding of rationality, even if it does not give sufficient or even necessary conditions for all rational decisions. Any theory of choice that is not dealing in the realm of possibly incommensurable or purely expressive values and is nevertheless incompatible with utility theory, therefore, cannot be describing a rational process, or so it would seem.

Prospect theory is also distinct from some earlier important psychological contributions to behavioral decision theory. In the 1950s, Herbert Simon developed an influential information-processing model of human choice based on a concept of bounded rationality (Simon, 1956). Simon characterized human agents as *satisficers*, rather than utility maximizers, because they follow rules that allow them to make decisions that are good enough, if not maximally good. This research led directly to the discovery and characterization of decision-making heuristics that individuals with bounded rationality tend to employ (Kahneman, Slovic, & Tversky, 1982). But this work is broadly compatible with utility theory, because we can interpret the heuristics we commonly employ as approximations of utility-maximizing strategies by agents acting under certain common natural constraints. Prospect theory, in contrast, presents a deeper challenge to the assumption that we act in basically rational ways. It says that the rules we follow are not approximations of rules of rationality but something altogether different.

My first aim in this chapter is to explain in more detail how prospect theory differs from utility theory and why it should be interpreted as a theory of nonrational choice. Then I will examine some of the most important basic nonrational findings of behavioral decision theory and explore some of their normative implications. These implications do not presuppose that all of the details and predictions of prospect theory are correct. They depend, rather, on accepting only the general conclusion that the causes of preference formation, judgment, and choice are fundamentally nonrational because of the way that they are incompatible with utility theory.

II

The claims of prospect theory may be best appreciated by seeing explicitly how they contrast with utility theory, and thus also with theories of choice in economics, the analysis of games, and elsewhere in the social sciences (Kahneman, 1994). Utility theory consists of a set of axioms that define existence and coherence conditions for preferences. The main theorem of utility theory says that rational preferences maximize expected utility. This means that if an individual's preferences are coherent, in the sense defined by the axioms, then it is possible to assign utilities and probabilities to the alternative possible outcomes so that the most preferred alternative is the one that maximizes expected utility.

Utility theory sees rationality, therefore, in terms of preferences for outcomes or states. Utilities are weights assigned to outcomes in a decision context, which represent the strength of desire or preference for those outcomes. Prospect theory, in contrast, assigns values to changes in one's situation, which are perceived as gains or losses from a reference point. In this sense, prospect theory assigns values to events, not outcomes.

The second central feature of prospect theory is its claim about loss aversion, which says, first, that people tend to weigh perceived losses more heavily than perceived gains and, second, that most people are risk seeking to avoid losses but risk averse with gains. The third main feature of prospect theory is that the reference point from which changes are perceived as gains or losses is susceptible to framing effects. The reference point for a prospect may be determined by the status quo, but it can also be a point other than the status quo, which can be determined by different ways of framing or describing a prospect. Prospect theory includes some more precise claims about such things as decision weights and the shape of the *loss function*, but the three general features just described are sufficient for understanding some of the most significant findings of this research.

Framing effects combine with loss aversion to yield predictions that cannot be explained by utility theory. This point is well illustrated with a simple experiment conducted by Amos Tversky and Daniel Kahneman, which demonstrates what they call the *isolation effect* (Tversky & Kahneman, 1986).

Problem 1

Assume yourself richer by $300 than you are today.
You have to choose between

a sure gain of $100
a 50% chance to gain $200 and a 50% chance to gain nothing

Problem 2

Assume yourself richer by $500 than you are today.
You have to choose between

a sure loss of $100
a 50% chance to lose nothing and a 50% chance to lose $200

It is easy to see that these two problems are equivalent in terms of wealth. Each offers a choice between a sure gain of $400 and a gamble with an equal chance to gain either $300 or $500. If wealth completely defines the outcomes in these problems, then a rational person should choose the same option in both problems. But in fact, most people presented with these problems choose the sure gain in Problem 1 and the gamble in Problem 2. Prospect theory explains this difference in terms of framing effects, which can lead one to see the prospects either as gains or as losses, and loss aversion, which leads to the different preferences in the two problems.

The preference reversal that results from these different ways of framing the prospect would seem to be irrational in the sense defined by utility theory. If utilities are assigned to outcomes, then this pair of choices cannot be represented as coherent. Someone might suggest, however, that the popular pair of choices in the two problems is not irrational and can in fact be represented as coherent by offering an explanation like the following. Suppose we assume that a person actually reaches the stages described in the opening line of the problems and then confronts the prospect from one or the other of those wealth positions. The person facing a choice in Problem 1 has already realized a gain and must now decide whether to accept an additional $100 with certainty or take a risk to gain $200 or nothing. If he takes the risk and wins, he will indeed be happy, but if he gambles and loses, he will regret not having chosen the certain gain, and his feeling of regret at losing might be far stronger than the joy he will feel if he gambles and wins. Thus he chooses to avoid the gamble and the possibility of regret. The person facing the choice in Problem 2, however, seems to be in a different situation. Either he will lose $100 for sure, or he can gamble on losing $200 or losing nothing. Since he may lose in any event, he might reasonably believe that he would feel little additional regret if he gambles and loses more, so he is willing to take a chance at losing nothing. The outcomes in these situations turn out to be different after all, for one has a potential to cause regret that is lacking in the other. The worse outcome in Problem 1 is different from and worse than the worse outcome in Problem 2, although the positions are identical in terms of wealth. If the outcomes are indeed different, then no preference reversal has occurred, and the choices can be represented as rational by utility theory (see, e.g., Bell, 1982; Loomes & Sugden, 1982).

The problem with this kind of explanation is that it fails to understand how framing effects work. Most people can be led to adopt either one of the reference points, even when they are not richer than they are by $300 or $500 and have no good reason to adopt either wealth position as a reference point. Seeing the prospect in terms of gains or losses is merely a framing effect. The regret that attaches to one decision frame may be real, but it is a consequence of adopting the decision frame, not of the options or the context of choice. A theory of rational choice can accommodate differences like these only if we are willing to individuate outcomes in a way that includes their descriptions along with their other properties, but the result of individuating outcomes in such a way would be to make the theory of rational choice vacuous. No set of preferences would ever be incoherent, because some description is always available that could distinguish alternatives in a way that eliminates any inconsistencies among preferences. A theory of choice that is so open-ended that it makes no set of preferences incoherent is not a theory of anything.

When we redescribe a decision problem or frame it differently, it is often true that we bring to light some important aspect of it, which had perhaps been hidden or ignored. We should expect reasonable people to change their preferences as a result of becoming aware of important features of a prospect that had gone unnoticed. It seems correct to say of such cases that framing the problem differently changes the outcomes, for the outcomes over which we form preferences are outcomes as we conceive them, and when we add new information to them, we conceive different outcomes. We may also agree that a person *should* regret certain decisions, and this potential regret should be a salient feature of her deliberations. Someone pondering a risky investment might think, "I started out with nothing, so I can't possibly end up a loser here." If the return on this investment is needed to pay for her children's education, however, or to take care of her retirement needs, then it might be useful to urge her to see the problem differently. "That isn't your situation now. Your choice really amounts to locking in some gains that will meet most of your needs or taking a gamble on losing it all." There may be good reasons for framing a problem one way rather than another and for adopting one reference point rather than a different one. In the experiment illustrating the isolation effect, however, the different decision frames do nothing more than shift the reference point. The different frames are merely different descriptions of the same problem that call attention to no facts of the situation that would justify feeling differently about the prospect or changing one's preferences.

These considerations should lead us to accept what John Broome (1991) has called rational requirements of indifference, which allow us to distinguish mere redescriptions of identical prospects from descriptions of different prospects. Given unlimited latitude on how we can individuate outcomes, it is hard to find any preferences for which utilities and probabilities that satisfy the axioms cannot be assigned. Rational requirements of indifference are needed to keep utility theory from being vacuous. I will not try to formulate such requirements here, but however we formulate these requirements, they would have to be violated in situations where preferences track the frame or description and not any underlying facts about the situation. If there is no reason for adopting one reference point rather than another, then it is irrational to let the choice of a reference point determine one's preferences.

III

The literature on this subject shows that decision theorists disagree about when alternatives should be regarded as genuinely different prospects and when they should be regarded as merely different descriptions of the same prospect. This point is well illustrated in discussions of one of the classic paradoxes of utility theory, which is attributed to Maurice

Allais (1979). We can illustrate the Allais paradox with the following pair of choices given by Tversky and Kahneman (1981). I have chosen this formulation for reasons that will be evident presently.

Problem 3

You have to choose between

A: a sure gain of $30,000
B: an 80% chance to gain $45,000 and a 20% chance to gain nothing.

Problem 4

You have to choose between

C: a 25% chance to gain $30,000 and a 75% chance to gain nothing
D: a 20% chance to gain $45,000 and an 80% chance to gain nothing.

Most people prefer A to B in Problem 3 and D to C in Problem 4, and this pair of choices is also intuitively reasonable. It seems reasonable, that is, to choose the sure gain and avoid a gamble in Problem 3, and it seems reasonable to opt for the chance of the greater gain in Problem 4, where you must gamble and are likely to lose in any case. The paradox is that this pair of preferences seems to violate the utility axioms and thus to be incoherent according to the standard theory of rational choice. To see this, we can assign a utility of 0 to the outcome in which nothing is gained, $U(\$0) = 0$, and a utility of 1 to the outcome in which $45,000 is gained, $U(\$45,000) = 1$. The utility assigned to $30,000 will be somewhere between 0 and 1. Let this utility be X, so that $U(\$30,000) = X$, where $0 < X < 1$. If A is preferred to B in Problem 1, then $U(\$30,000) > .80U(\$45,000) + .20U(0)$; thus, $X > .80$. If D is preferred to C in Problem 2, however, then assuming that the utilities are the same, $.20U(\$45,000) + .80U(\$0) > .25U(\$30,000) + .75U(\$0)$. By substitution, $.20 > .25X$; thus, $X < .80$. The pair of preferences A and D is incoherent.

Some writers have tried to explain away the Allais paradox by arguing that the outcomes in the two problems should be described differently because of the difference in potential regret.[1] A person who gambles and loses in Problem 3 might reasonably experience strong decision regret, because he could have avoided a risk of losing, whereas the same person might not feel regret in Problem 4, because he was likely to lose no matter which gamble he chose to take. The outcomes in the two problems thus appear to be different, because the worst outcome in Problem 3 is the one in which a person wins nothing and regrets his decision, which is worse than the worst outcome in Problem 4, in which he merely wins nothing.

Tversky and Kahneman conducted an experiment that verifies that the popular choices in the Allais paradox are A in Problem 3 and D in Problem 4, but they also present people with a third prospect (Tversky & Kahneman, 1981).

> *Problem 5*
>
> Consider the following two-stage game. In the first stage, there is a 75% chance to end the game without winning anything and a 25% chance to move into the second stage. If you reach the second stage you have a choice between:
>
> E: a sure gain of $30,000;
> F: an 80% chance to gain $45,000 and a 20% chance to gain nothing.

Your choice must be made before the outcome of the first stage is known. Predictably, E is the popular choice in Problem 5. Tversky and Kahneman argued that this result shows that the popular choice in the Allais paradox is an instance of the isolation effect. Any attempt to rationalize A over B in Problem 3 would also rationalize E over F in Problem 5, but Problem 5 is clearly a redescription of the identical Problem 4. If any attempt to rationalize A also rationalizes E, then the preference for A over B in Problem 3 cannot be made compatible with the preference for D over C in Problem 4. Adding Problem 5 to the set of choices forces us to see that the preferences expressed in Problem 3 and Problem 4 demonstrate the isolation effect and thus violate the rational requirement of indifference. The popular preferences turn out to be induced by framing effects and loss aversion and should not be seen as rationally coherent.

IV

Framing effects show how different ways of describing identical prospects can generate preference reversals for those prospects.

Psychologists have also discovered that they can generate preference reversals by varying the procedure or method used to elicit preferences for identical prospects. For example, one can use a method of direct comparison to elicit a preference by presenting people with the alternatives and asking them to choose the one they most prefer. Or one can use a method of independent evaluation by asking people to rate prospects one at a time. The preferences can be inferred from the ratings. This situation is analogous to that of using different methods to determine which is the heavier of two physical objects. You can compare objects directly by placing them on either end of a balance scale, or you can weigh each separately on a bathroom scale and infer which is heavier from the weights. Either method should pick out the same object as the heavier of the two. Similarly, the order of preferences should not vary as a function of the elicitation method, but often it does. This is called the *response mode effect*.

Sarah Lichtenstein and Paul Slovic (1971), the first researchers to study the response mode effect, asked people to express their preferences between two gambles that had similar expected monetary outcomes. One gamble (the H bet) offered a high probability of a modest payoff and the other gamble (the L bet) offered a lower probability of a larger payoff.

> H bet: 29/36 chance to win $2
> L bet: 7/36 chance to win $9

Most people who are asked which of the two gambles they would prefer to play choose the H bet, but when they are asked to evaluate the gambles independently by indicating how much money they would be willing to pay for the right to play each one, most people assign a higher value to the L bet. Moreover, a large majority of those who prefer the H bet in the direct comparison indicate a willingness to pay more to play the L bet, thus reversing their preferences with the different elicitation method.

What explains this response mode effect? Some psychologists have proposed a compatibility hypothesis, which claims that the compatibility of the response mode with one element of a prospect causes that element to be weighed more heavily in the formation of a person's preference (Slovic, Griffin, & Tversky, 1990). Thus, when the method of independent evaluation asks people to rank the gambles on a monetary scale, the monetary outcomes are more salient than the probabilities and the L bet becomes relatively more attractive. In order to test this hypothesis, Tversky and colleagues ran one experiment in which people were asked to rate the H bet and the L bet independently, but instead of using a monetary metric, each bet was rated on a 0–20 scale of attractiveness (Tversky, Slovic, & Kahneman, 1990). When people used this rating method, they expressed a strong preference for the H bet, which suggests that the better chance of winning was seen to be more attractive than the amount won. This result agrees with the outcome obtained by the method of direct comparison, which in turn seems to support the compatibility hypothesis as an explanation of the preference reversal that is caused by using the pricing metric.

One problem with the compatibility hypothesis, however, is that it does not explain why most people prefer the H bet when their preferences are elicited using either a direct comparison method or a nonmonetary rating scale. Why should the higher probability be more attractive than the greater winning amount? Nor can the compatibility hypothesis explain some of the more deeply puzzling effects on preferences that occur when the L bet is modified by adding the risk of a small loss to the gamble. For example, Slovic has measured preferences for the L bet and for what should be a less attractive L′ bet.

> L bet: 7/36 chance to win $9.
> L′ bet: 7/36 chance to win $9; 29/36 chance to lose $.05

It turns out that the L′ bet is preferred by most people to the L bet, and this result occurs regardless of the elicitation method, as long as the bets are not directly compared to each other. In an experiment using the 0–20 attractiveness scale, for example, the mean value for the L bet was 9.4, whereas the mean value for the L′ bet rose to 14.9 (Slovic, Finucane, Peters, & MacGregor, in press). In another experiment in which subjects were asked to express their preferences for these bets by directly comparing each to the alternative of receiving $2, one third of the subjects preferred the L bet to $2, whereas nearly two thirds preferred the L′ bet to $2 (Slovic et al., in press).

Some psychologists have recently suggested different hypotheses to explain these effects. Christopher Hsee (1996), for example, proposes an evaluability hypothesis, which says that some ways of presenting information are easier to evaluate than others. In one experiment, for example, Hsee asked people to imagine that they were music scholars seeking a music dictionary, and he asked them to evaluate two dictionaries that were identical in all respects except the following: Dictionary A had 10,000 entries and no defects, and dictionary B had 20,000 entries but a slightly torn cover. When people were shown both dictionaries and asked to express how much they were willing to pay for each, the mean willingness to pay for B was much greater than that for A, presumably because B contains the greater number of entries. When the dictionaries were shown to different groups, however, and people were asked to express a willingness to pay for the one they saw, the mean willingness to pay for A was much greater than that for B. Hsee hypothesizes that this is because the torn cover is easier to evaluate than the number of entries in a given dictionary. People do not have a clear notion of how good or bad 10,000 (or 20,000) entries is, but they can easily evaluate the condition of the cover.

Numbers presented as proportions or percentages also appear to be easier to evaluate than numbers presented in other forms, such as amounts of money. A gamble with a greater than 50% chance to win is naturally perceived to be good, because the gambler is more likely to win than to lose. A gamble with a less than 50% chance to win is naturally seen as bad, because the gambler is more likely to lose than to win. In contrast, it is hard to evaluate how good it is to win $9 or $2. This seems to be the reason that probabilities dominate the outcomes for most of the elicitation methods used in the gambles that Slovic et al. (in press) have studied.[2] When a slight loss is added to the gamble, however, instead of making the gamble less attractive, as it should, the small loss establishes a contrast with the much greater gain, and this induces a positive feeling associated with the winning amount that is not otherwise there. Adding a $.05 loss to the prospect triggers an attractiveness response to $9.

Slovic et al. (in press) call this phenomenon the *affect heuristic* and suggest that different ways of presenting information (or eliciting preferences) can induce affects associated with the information that make the information easier to evaluate (see also Kunreuther and Slovic, this volume). The result of one further study helps to illustrate the nonrational nature of the affect heuristic: People are willing to pay more for a government program that is estimated to save 95% of 150 lives (or 90% or even 85%) than for a program that is estimated to save 150 lives. The number of lives saved does not seem to trigger a precise positive affective feeling, which makes it relatively difficult to evaluate, while a 90% chance of getting something good triggers a strong positive affective feeling.

The behavior described by the evaluability hypothesis and the affect heuristic, together with the behavior described by prospect theory, seem to support a general conclusion about the nonrational causes of preference and choice. Many of our preferences are not determined

cognitively as a function of understanding relevant facts and information but are shaped instead by affect and feelings that arise in response
to framing, the elicitation method, or the manner of presentation. These
feelings can be prompted by images or descriptions, and they tend to
make the relevant information more or less easy to evaluate. Information
that is less easy to evaluate may be ignored or underemphasized, even
when we agree that it is the most relevant information for determining rational preferences. In these different ways, preferences often track
descriptions rather than facts.

V

One might wonder why decision theorists have appeared so reluctant to
accept the nonrational basis of preference formation. The Allais paradox,
for example, has been known for a long time, and a normal response
to it, as I have indicated, is to attempt to accommodate the popular
preferences within a normative theory of rational choice rather than to
dismiss the popular preferences as irrational. One obvious explanation
of this tendency among decision theorists is that the popular preferences
also seem intuitively to be reasonable, so they should be compatible
with a normative theory of rational choice. But I believe that the desire
to reconcile utility theory with widely held preferences also shows a
certain equivocation in some quarters about the normative status of
utility theory.

Some decision theorists, to be sure, insist that utility theory is strictly
a normative or rational theory of choice that should not be expected
to give a good predictive or empirical account of the subject. Howard
Raiffa (1968), for example, wonders why we should even be interested
in a normative theory of rationality unless it differs significantly from
our actual behavior and could be used prescriptively to correct it.[3] But
those theorists who also regard utility theory as part of the core of formal
work in the behavioral sciences have also tended to be less clear about
its strictly normative status. This common view is nicely illustrated in a
remark made several decades ago by James March (1978):

According to conventional dogma, there are two kinds of theories of human
behavior: descriptive (or behavioral) theories that purport to describe actual
behavior of individuals or social institutions, and prescriptive (or normative)
theories that purport to prescribe optimal behavior. In many ways, the distinction leads to an intelligent and fruitful division of labor in social science,

reflecting differences in techniques, objectives, and professional cultures. For a variety of historical and intellectual reasons, however, such a division has not characterized the development of the theory of choice. Whether one considers ideas about choice in economics, psychology, political science, sociology, or philosophy, behavioral and normative theories have developed as a dialectic rather than as separate domains. Most modern behavioral theories of choice take as their starting point some simple ideas about rational human behavior. As a result, new developments in normative theories of choice have quickly affected behavioral theories. (p. 588)

Behavioral decision theory shows how preferences are nonrational because of the ways they track descriptions rather than facts and thus cannot be represented as maximizing anything. To the extent that these findings are well confirmed and the explanations of them are correct, preferences fail to obey the norms of rationality at the core of utility theory. Behavioral and normative theories of choice must be distinguished, for they tell different stories. Once this point is clearly recognized, the further development of each theory is likely to follow its own course, which will emphasize the independence of each from the other. We should consider carefully the implications of this separation.

Behavioral scientists have responded to prospect theory and preference reversals in different ways, but at least some of them have recognized the implications of the gulf that seems to exist between the findings of behavioral decision theory and even minimal conditions of rationality. Thus, David Grether and Charles Plott (1979) have remarked:

Taken at face value the data are simply inconsistent with preference theory and have broad implications about research priorities within economics. The inconsistency is deeper than the mere lack of transitivity or even stochastic transitivity. It suggests that no optimization principles of any sort lie behind the simplest of human choices and that the uniformities in human choice behavior which lie behind market behavior may result from principles which are of a completely different sort from those generally accepted. (p. 623)

Framing effects, response mode effects, and other related hypotheses predict behavior that violates what Kenneth Arrow (1982) describes as "a fundamental element of rationality, so elementary that we hardly notice it" (1). This fundamental element is the assumption that rational preferences should not vary merely with different descriptions of a problem. Behavioral decision theory shows that our preferences violate this invariance assumption in systematic and predictable ways that are easy to induce. Tversky, Slovic, and Kahneman (1990) thus conclude:

These developments highlight the discrepancy between the normative and the descriptive approaches to decision making. . . . Because invariance . . . is normatively unassailable and descriptively incorrect, it does not seem possible to construct a theory of choice that is both normatively acceptable and descriptively adequate. (p. 215)

VI

How important are the findings of behavioral decision theory for choices that matter? The nonrational causes of choice are not simply manifestations of imperfect rationality, nor do they result solely from our reliance on heuristics or rules of thumb. We do compute roughly, and we are led astray by heuristics, but we can live with our errors, often more easily than we can correct them, and it is usually at least debatable whether we would be better off relying on more accurate but more complicated rules instead. The deeper worry, as I have argued, is that our preferences are formed to a significant degree by processes that are altogether independent of our rational capacities. Our preferences track descriptions rather than facts, and this tendency may persist even though we are aware of it and deplore it. We are at risk of being manipulated, and it is a risk that is difficult to escape.

But how worrisome is this? Marketing experts may or may not have heard of prospect theory, framing effects, or the affect heuristic. But they have powerful incentives to try to figure out how to shape the preferences of their customers, and they have discovered, for instance, that it is better to advertise cash discounts rather than credit card surcharges. The reference point is thus set at the higher price, and customers will perceive a gain by paying cash but not necessarily a cost to using their credit cards (Thaler, 1980). If behavioral decision theory has discovered truths about preference formation, then we can expect firms and advertisers to discover and exploit these same truths, just as we can expect the mice to find the bird food in the tool shed, no matter how well hidden it is (Hanson & Kyasar, 1999).

Nevertheless, with regard to economic preferences, we can probably warn the buyer to beware and live without suffering very much from the fact that we buy things we don't need or pay more than we should for the things we buy.

The more troubling implications of behavioral decision theory lie elsewhere. Slovic has suggested that the truths about preference formation may play a critical role in explaining addictions, which are no minor marketing or economic matter (Slovic, 2000). But I will consider here the implications of behavioral decision theory in the realm of political choice and the formation of public policy, where powerful incentives also exist to shape public opinion and the consequences of irrationality are also serious. Phenomena such as framing effects, response mode effects, and the affect heuristic begin to tell us why "spin control" works so well, and this fact has consequences that should concern us.

I want to draw attention to these implications in two areas. In some situations, we are bound to follow public opinion. For example, we select political officials for the most part through elections. In situations where democratic principles force us to accede directly to citizen preferences, we may have good reasons to be pessimistic about the effects of our susceptibility to having our preferences manipulated. In other political settings, however, including those in which important laws and public policies are made, we are not bound simply to follow public opinion or satisfy majority preferences. In these situations, we can respond to citizen interests in a more deliberate and constructive manner. I will elaborate briefly on these two different decision-making contexts, beginning with the bad news.

Consider the deplorable state of campaigns for high political office in the United States. Money is a prerequisite to getting elected to high political office today, and the amount of money raised and spent by candidates at the national, state, and local levels in the 2000 elections increased almost exponentially over previous elections. Of course, the dependence on money biases access to high office in favor of those who have it or who can raise it, namely, the wealthy and the politically well positioned, especially incumbents. This dependence raises serious questions about justice and the representativeness of the political system, but just as troubling are issues about how the money is spent. Highly paid advisors run well-financed campaigns, and increasingly these advisors are experts not so much in politics as in shaping public opinion. They take polls and run focus groups; they learn which issues should be emphasized and which should be avoided. Most importantly, they know how the messages should be framed in order to manipulate voter preferences most effectively. In 1997, Frank Luntz, a Republican pollster, advised his clients that it was not their policies but the way they were being packaged that was keeping them from winning more elections. He advised them that key phrases were more important to winning votes than the content of their policies. For example: "Women consistently respond to the phrase 'for the children' regardless of the context" (see, e.g., Dowd,

2000). Candidates like George W. Bush used his advice successfully. The clear message here is that images are more powerful than words, and that winning hearts is more effective than winning minds. Worse, the fact that we can easily understand and recognize manipulative strategies at work (and journalists are quick now to point them out to us) does not seem to have much impact in blunting their effectiveness. Other formulae for success in winning votes include: Take cautious positions on key issues; avoid details or specific proposals if possible; and unless you have a comfortable lead in the polls, attack your opponent. "First create doubt" is a slogan of modern political campaigning.

Attacking works better than defending, so candidates are better off saying little for which they can be held accountable. Candidates have to worry about a possible backlash, however, so they must be careful not to be too negative or to be perceived as mudslingers. One strategy for avoiding this risk is the increasingly common though obvious practice of running TV ads that attack one's opponent without showing a picture and scarcely mentioning the name of the candidate whose campaign is sponsoring the ads, hoping thus to distance the candidate from the attack. Another strategy, which was made popular in the 2000 presidential campaign, is to accuse your opponent of being the first candidate to go negative and then attack him for doing so. The goal of the campaign manager is to focus attention on what people will lose by voting for an opponent, not on what they will gain by voting for the candidate the campaign manager is trying to elect. This is one way that framing effects appear to work in politics. You can win more votes by making your opponent look bad than you can by emphasizing your own strengths.

Here too the fact that we understand the strategy of negative campaigning and are quick to criticize it, as polls suggest we are, does not seem to matter much. We may like to think that we ourselves are above these tactics and prepared to make our decisions on rational grounds, but our preferences are all being shaped in ways that play to our nonrational tendencies. Negative campaigning is roundly criticized, but it persists for a simple reason: It works![4]

We could reform the rules governing political campaigns in the United States and make them considerably fairer and more serious than they are today. We could control how money is raised and spent in order to bring an increased measure of justice to politics and ensure political access to a wider and more representative range of perspectives. Independent groups could publicize the records and platforms of candidates, for anyone who cares to see them, and we could bring other kinds of pressure to bear on politicians to limit the extent and kind of negative campaigning that occurs. But all of these reforms together would not address the underlying problem of our susceptibility to manipulation. If preferences really do track descriptions and images rather than facts, then politicians will not be able to refrain from exploiting these forces so long as they need our votes. We cannot easily control the language or images a politician uses to manipulate preferences as long as we value freedom of speech. A politician who is strongly motivated to win, caught in a tight race, and listening to expert advisors about how to improve his standing in the polls can hardly avoid doing what will work.[5] The better they understand tendencies like framing effects, loss aversion, the affect heuristic, and other causes of preference formation, the more we can expect them to rely directly on such techniques.[6]

We could probably be more effective in keeping the forces of irrationality at bay if we exercised a kind of political precommitment, which has a long tradition in politics but appears to be weakening today, especially in the United States. Precommitment is a generally effective strategy for countering irrational tendencies such as weakness of will. Ulysses asked to be bound to the mast of his ship so that he would be unable to succumb to the call of the Sirens. The counterpart in political life would be to cultivate the virtue of strong party loyalties as an antidote to the currently popular tendency to think that it is reasonable and good to be a political independent and uncommitted to either party. Of course, it is hard to be loyal to a political party these days in a country where there are only two major parties, each stumbling over the other to find the political center and appeal directly to the increasing number of uncommitted "swing voters." These uncommitted voters are now the most important voting bloc in most large elections. Moreover, because these uncommitted voters are without strong party loyalties, they are the people most likely to be swayed by appeals to nonrational tendencies. They are the easiest voters to manipulate.

The worries I am describing about our political life apply not only to elections but also to other areas where public opinion drives decisions. This was demonstrated during the process leading to the impeachment of President Bill Clinton. Because of the questionable legal merits of the case brought against the president, both sides involved in this highly political struggle worked hard to shape public opinion. At a critical moment in September 1998, opponents of the president pressed for release of the video recording of the president's testimony to Independent Counsel Kenneth Starr's grand jury. No doubt the president's opponents believed that broadcasting this record of Clinton's responses to detailed questions about his sexual conduct with Monica Lewinsky would turn public opinion strongly against him and in favor of impeachment. Many people were surprised, therefore, when the president's approval ratings went up after the tapes were aired.

Some reporters argued that this surprising support for President Clinton reflected the public's disapproval of Kenneth Starr's tactics, or it showed that people believed the president was doing a good job and that his sexual misconduct should not have been a public concern. No doubt the polls did reflect these and other opinions, but there was also another factor at work, which was not so widely noticed. Leaks about the president's testimony led people to expect that the tapes would show the president looking much worse than he did. According to some reports, even Clinton's advisors, who had not seen the tapes in advance but were well aware of everything they contained, encouraged the rumors that set expectations about what the tapes would show.[7] These expectations set the reference point that guided what viewers saw, and the result was that the president looked better than had been expected, and his approval ratings went up.

Friends and foes of the president may both have hoped that he would have been judged rationally on the basis of relevant facts. But the preferences that influenced the impeachment process were also shaped to a significant degree by nonrational considerations, such as whether his taped performance was better or worse than the public expected it to be, regardless of the relevance of any evidence it may have contained. Clever framing shaped these expectations. In this instance, it appears that the president's advisors understood the effects of spin control and framing better than his enemies did.

VII

When we turn from these problems of direct democracy to examine the role of public opinion in the design and justification of laws and policies, we can be less pessimistic about the implications of behavioral decision theory. This is because in designing laws and policies, we are not bound to follow public opinion, whatever it may be, but can instead probe it in a more controlled manner. We have at least the possibility of avoiding the tyranny of nonrational preferences and relying instead on a more deliberative process.

I will focus on policies. Most analysts would agree that good policies must understand and incorporate public values and preferences. But the

findings of behavioral decision theory should force us to examine this assumption. Why should public opinion or unexamined preferences drive
morally important decisions? Some might defend a principle of citizens'
sovereignty and argue that public policies are justified in a democracy
only if they reflect the will of the majority. According to this view, only
one moral value is relevant to justification: the maximum satisfaction of
citizen preferences. But we can reject this argument. Other moral values,
such as concern for distributive justice or respect for individual rights,
are obviously involved in many policy decisions, and this interpretation
of citizens' sovereignty simply begs the question against the relevance
of these other moral values.

A different and more widely accepted interpretation of citizens'
sovereignty is even less plausible. Someone might think that policymakers have no business, in their public roles, arguing for moral values
and making decisions based on the conclusions of these arguments. The
morally right thing in making policies is simply to do what the majority
believes to be right. Concerns for rights and justice can shape policies,
according to this view, if the majority prefers that they should. We should
find out what people think is best, all things considered, and aggregate
their preferences.

The first thing we should notice in considering this suggestion is that
moral preferences are shaped by framing effects and other elements described by behavioral decision theory, just as other preferences are, so
our moral intuitions have the same nonrational pedigree and exhibit
similar irrationalities (Kahneman, Knetsch, & Thaler, 1986). But the interpretation of citizens' sovereignty we are now considering fails for
a more basic reason. If what is right for public policies simply means
what the majority believes to be right, then how should individuals, who
are concerned to do the right thing, think about which policy alternatives are better than others? If someone asks whether a proposed policy
would be the morally right thing to do, and if she understands what
right means in this context, then she must be asking what the majority
believes to be right. If other people do not understand the meaning of
right and wrong, then she has no reason to pay attention to them. If they
do understand, then she must ask what each of them believes that the
majority believes to be right, and so on. This interpretation of citizens'
sovereignty turns out to be incoherent, because it lands us in a vicious
infinite regress, so it must be rejected.[8]

If the will of the people means anything at all for understanding how
moral values should inform laws and policies, then their will must refer
to the values people hold after reflection and discussion and the reasons

they give to support these values. At this point, however, we confront the problems of the implications of nonrational preference formation. If moral preferences also track descriptions rather than facts, then how do we ask people about their values in a way that will not generate the kinds of incoherence due to framing and response mode effects that we have been examining? How do we write the surveys or conduct the focus groups?

To illustrate this problem, we can consider some recent research of a group of health policy analysts who attempted to measure public values regarding allocation policies for organ transplants. They found in a number of studies that people tended to express a preference for equality over efficiency in allocation rules (Ubel & Loewenstein, 1995). In this context, equality means giving priority to *medical urgency*, or the most critically ill patients, while efficiency would call for giving priority to patients who are likely to benefit most from receiving a new organ. Greater benefit could mean more complete recovery, more years of added life, or other things. To elicit these preferences, people were presented with descriptions of patients and asked to determine which patients should be given priority for receiving an organ transplant.

Apparently bothered by the result of these studies, DeKay, McClelland, Asch, and Ubel (1997) designed a different protocol in which they described different patients by attributes and asked people to assign priority ratings to each patient independently. The preferences were then derived from these ratings. In this study, subjects ranked increased life expectancy, an efficiency-based value, most highly.

Now a student of behavioral decision theory would be quick to point out that these different results show a response mode effect and are exactly what one would expect to find by using different methods for eliciting preferences. The method of direct comparison will lead subjects to give greater weight to attributes like urgency for survival, because such attributes are the easiest to compare. An independent response mode that requires people to rate patients independently as they are presented with a set of attributes will lead people to give greater weight to attributes that may be less easy to evaluate comparatively across subjects, such as increased life expectancy or improved quality of life. Different attributes turn out to be more or less salient in different response modes.

At this point, some people will be tempted to ask which method (or what combination of methods) is correct. What they mean to ask is: Which method gives a more accurate reflection of someone's *true* values? If preferences are inextricably tied to descriptions, however, then perhaps it is more accurate to see them as constructed in the elicitation process than as revealed by it. If this is right, then the proper question to ask is: Which values are being overemphasized or unduly neglected in the way people are thinking about these questions? If we can understand the empirical processes underlying preference formation, then we can sometimes give a defensible answer to this question and figure out a way to counter the framing or response mode effects.

This conclusion suggests that we cannot avoid taking a more explicitly normative approach to eliciting preferences in the manner illustrated in the example we have just considered. One psychologist, Eldar Shafir, proposes in chapter 3 of this book the following policy guideline:

In general, which mode of evaluation, comparative or independent, ought to be preferred will depend on the nature of the problem and on the purposes of the evaluation. When the main concern is an insufficient sensitivity to differences that really ought to count ... a comparative evaluation is likely to help make those differences discernible. On the other hand, if the concern is with a general principle that may overwhelm otherwise valid distinctions ... then an independent evaluation may help trigger the correct sensitivities without the corrupting influence of the overarching principle.

The general idea Shafir proposes seems exactly right. Rather than ask which elicitation method is more neutral or which method better reveals a person's true values, we have to ask which values should guide us in deciding to use one elicitation method or another. The moral principles cannot be read off from the expression of preferences or intuitions but must be articulated, defended, and used to justify the manner of eliciting (and constructing) the preferences that will guide a decision. The organ transplant policy example is simply a vivid illustration of what we should take to be the proper role of moral reasons in justifying important decisions and policies. It helps to illustrate the conceptual independence of moral reasoning and justification from widely held preferences and intuitions.

According to the view I am defending, policymakers cannot assume that if they have elicited public opinions for policy alternatives and responded to the preferences that are expressed, then their laws or policies are justified as expressing the will of the citizens whose views they must try to represent. These preferences are likely to have been shaped by the nonrational tendencies we have been considering. The policy analyst is inevitably complicit in the construction of these preferences. Her role, therefore, must not be restricted to a neutral recording of public opinion but must also include moral reasoning and express moral values.

We need to understand citizen sovereignty in a way that emphasizes the respect due to all citizens. This respect does not mean merely that everyone's preferences should be weighed equally in deciding what is best, which leads to a tyranny of irrational preferences. Rather, laws and policies can be justified by appealing to values and reasons that the majority can accept or that nobody could reasonably reject. This kind of justification shows a deeper concern for citizens than a preference-maximizing view. It treats people not merely as the bearers of labile preferences but also as agents who are ideally rational, or at least as agents who can struggle to become less irrational than they often are.

Notes

1   See, e.g., Jeffrey (1987). Other writers have tried to capture the popular behavior in the Allais paradox in different ways. Some have proposed relaxing one of the axioms of utility theory, either transitivity (e.g., Fishburn, 1982) or the assumption of the independence of irrelevant alternatives or the *sure thing* principle (e.g., Machina, 1982). Still others have proposed different ways of assigning probabilities within utility theory (e.g., Viscusi, 1989). Each of these articles presents an interesting argument for modifying the theory of rational choice and, together with articles previously cited, constitutes an important development in the theory of rational choice, although none of them succeeds in correctly diagnosing the popular responses in the Allais paradox.

2   Presumably, the pricing metric makes the winning amounts easier to evaluate, perhaps by triggering an *anchoring and adjustment* heuristic. The metric caused people to anchor on the $2 win, and the increased value of winning $9 is thus made more salient.

3   The interpretation of axiomatized decision theory as normative and different from an empirical theory of choice, so that it can be used prescriptively, is a general theme in Raiffa's writing. To cite just one example: "These lectures do not present a descriptive theory of actual behavior, nor a positive theory of behavior for a fictitious superintelligent being, but rather present an approach designed to help us erring folk to reason and act a bit more systematically – when we choose to do so!" (Raiffa, 1968, p. 128).

4   Consider, e.g., this report on Sen. Barbara Boxer's 1998 campaign for reelection to the Senate. "Just a few weeks ago, the Democratic incumbent trailed her lesser-known Republican challenger, 48 percent to 44 percent in Mervin Field's California Poll and seemed headed for defeat. But a new survey by the *Los Angeles Times* has her ahead, 49 percent to 44 percent. The turnaround is tied to Boxer's aggressively negative campaign. ...." (Whitcover, 1998, p. A1).

5   Politicians who avoid such tactics do so at their peril. One who tried was Sen. Russell Feingold of Wisconsin, a leading advocate of campaign reform. "I realize it puts me in danger that I don't get up and say all these negative things on TV," Feingold is quoted as saying during his last campaign. "But I have faith in the people of this state." Feingold won, but that is hardly the point, for

had the results been different by a mere 1%, he would have lost. The important consequence of the senator's faith was to turn a campaign in which he had a strong natural advantage into a cliffhanger. "'Feingold, by taking this stand, has issued a challenge to the whole political establishment, to see if anyone can run under these conditions,' said Kenneth Mayer, a political scientist at the University of Wisconsin at Madison and a Feingold sympathizer. 'If he had run as a typical incumbent, he'd be up by 15 points right now, and we wouldn't even be talking'" (Weisman, 1998, p. A1).

6 Some researchers have already shown directly how prospect theory and other findings of behavioral decision theory apply to political advertising. See, e.g., the chapter by Fox and Farmer, in this volume.

7 "Republican pollster Whit Ayres says Clinton 'clearly came across better than people expected, and what it's done is stop the Democrats' free fall. . . . [W]hen CBS News quoted congressional sources as saying Clinton had stormed out of the session, White House staffers made no effort to correct the mistake. Paul Begala, a senior Clinton aide, denies that the White House tried to manipulate expectations. 'We're not as Machiavellian as people make us out to be,' he says" (West, 1998, p. A1).

8 For this point, I am indebted to John Broome.

References

Allais, M. (1979). The foundations of a positive theory of choice involving risk and a criticism of the postulates and axioms of the American school. In M. Allais & O. Hagen (Eds.), *Expected utility hypotheses and the Allais paradox* (pp. 27–145). Dodrecht, the Netherlands: Reidel.

Arrow, K. (1982). Risk perception in psychology and economics. *Economic Inquiry, 20*, 1–9.

Bell, D. (1982). Regret in decision making under uncertainty. *Operations Research, 30*, 961–981.

Broome, J. (1991). *Weighing goods.* Oxford: Basil Blackwell.

DeKay, M. L., McClelland, G. H., Asch, D. A., & Ubel. P. A. (1997, November). *Public values and organ allocation policy.* Paper presented at the meeting of the Association of Public Policy Analysis and Management, Washington, DC.

Dowd, M. (2000, April 5). The Erin factor. *The New York Times*, p. A23.

Fishburn, P. (1982). Intransitive measurable utility. *Journal of Experimental Psychology: Learning, Memory, and Cognition, 26*, 31–67.

Grether, D., & Plott, C. (1979). Economic theory of choice and the preference reversal phenomenon. *American Economic Review 69*, 623–638.

Hanson, J. D., and Kyasar, D. A. (1999). Taking behavioralism seriously: Some evidence of market manipulation. *Harvard Law Review, 112*, 1420–1572.

Hsee, C. (1996). The evaluability hypothesis: An explanation for preference reversals between joint and separate evaluations of alternatives. *Organizational Behavior and Human Decision Processes, 67*, 247–257.

Jeffrey, R. (1987). Risk and human rationality. *The Monist, 70*, 223–236.

Kahneman, D. (1994). New challenges to the rationality assumption. *Journal of Institutional and Theoretical Economics, 150*, 18–36.

Kahneman, D., Knetsch, J., & Thaler, R. (1986). Fairness and the assumptions of economics. *Journal of Business, 59*, s285–s300.

Kahneman, D., Slovic, P., & Tversky, A. (1982). *Judgment under uncertainty: Heuristics and biases.* New York: Cambridge University Press.

Kahneman, D., & Tversky, A. (1979). Prospect theory: An analysis of decision under risk. *Econometrica, 47*, 263–291.

Lichtenstein, S., & Slovic, P. (1971). Reversals of preference between bids and choices in gambling decisions. *Journal of Experimental Psychology, 89*, 46–55.

Loomes, G., & Sugden, R. (1982). Regret theory: An alternative theory of rational choice under uncertainty. *Economic Journal, 92*, 805–824.

Machina, M. (1982). Expected utility analysis without the independence axiom. *Econometrica, 50*, 277–323.

March, J. (1978). Bounded rationality, ambiguity, and the engineering of choice. *Bell Journal of Economics, 9*, 587–608.

Raiffa, H. (1968). *Decision analysis: Introductory lectures to choices under uncertainty.* Reading, MA: Addison-Wesley.

Simon, H. A. (1956). Rational choice and the structure of the environment. *Psychological Review, 63*, 129–138.

Slovic, P. (2000, April). *Rational actors and rational fools: The influence of affect on judgment and decision making.* Paper presented at the Symposium on Rational Actors or Rational Fools? The Implications of Psychology for Products Liability, Bristol, RI.

Slovic, P., Finucane, M., Peters, E., & MacGregor, D. (in press). The affect heuristic. In T. Gilovich (Ed.), *Intuitive judgment: Heuristics and biases.* New York: Cambridge University Press.

Slovic, P., Griffin, D., & Tversky, A. (1990). Compatibility effects in judgment and choice. In R. M. Hogarth (Ed.), *Insights in decision making: Theory and applications* (pp. 5–27). Chicago: University of Chicago Press.

Thaler, R. (1980). Towards a positive theory of consumer choice. *Journal of Economic Behavior and Organization, 1*, 39–60.

Tversky, A., & Kahneman, D. (1981). The framing of decisions and the psychology of choice. *Science, 211*, 453–458.

Tversky, A., & Kahneman, D. (1986). Rational choice and the framing of decisions. *Journal of Business, 59*, 251–278.

Tversky, A., Slovic, P., & Kahneman, D. (1990). The causes of preference reversal. *American Economic Review, 80*, 204–217.

Ubel, P. A., & Loewenstein, G. (1995). The efficacy and equity of retransplantation: An experimental study of public attitudes. *Health Policy, 34*, 145–151.

Viscusi, W. K. (1989). Prospective reference theory: Toward an explanation of the paradoxes. *Journal of Risk and Uncertainty, 2*, 235–264.

Weisman, J. (1998, October 28). Reformer in unexpected struggle. *The Baltimore Sun*, p. A1.

West, P. (1998, September 27). U.S. public was fed misleading predictions. *The Baltimore Sun*, p. A1.

Whitcover, J. (1998, October 27). Boxer's attack ads tied to turnaround in polls. *The Baltimore Sun*, p. A1.

3   Cognition, Intuition, and Policy Guidelines

Eldar Shafir

Introduction

Intuition plays a central role in our ethical and moral judgments and, consequently, in the formulation of policy guidelines. Which benefits are worth what costs, which losses are tolerable and which not, and what are some of the more pressing societal issues are all problems that lend themselves to certain amounts of empirical research, but eventually they depend on people's values and intuitive judgment. Some of the most poignant policy debates of our time – for example, those surrounding active or passive euthanasia, abortion, or social welfare programs – rely on arguments (concerning the quality of life worth living, the difference between killing versus letting die, when life begins or ends, societal obligations to the less fortunate, etc.) whose main function is to appeal to moral intuition. The appeal to intuition is common, and often central to policy formulation and conduct. Nevertheless, human intuition can be fickle, and sometimes in predictable and systematic ways.

   This chapter is unabashedly descriptive in its treatment of intuition. It focuses on a number of systematic, well-documented aspects of the psychology that underlies people's intuition; it ignores philosophical quandaries such as whether there are moral facts or facts about rationality and whether we have intuitive, perceptual, or other privileged access to such facts. Of concern will be the systematic ways in which preferences and intuitions can change as a result of supposedly inconsequential differences in the manner in which problems are presented, and the implications that this has for the formulation and conduct of policy. People's intuitive judgments are shown to exhibit patterns that are often at odds with a normative treatment; empirical generalizations are then proposed to help explain the problematic patterns. An account of the psychology that underlies people's intuitions must be given serious consideration, even by those preoccupied mostly with normative concerns. To the extent that people's intuitions systematically conflict with principles considered normatively indispensable, these intuitions are likely to affect people's preferences and sense of well-being in ways that need to be taken into account in setting policy guidelines.

In what follows, selected findings from social psychology and the behavioral decision sciences are discussed, and psychological principles that underlie preference and evaluation are considered. In particular, we focus on systematic discrepancies that are observed between evaluations that are conducted in isolation, one alternative considered at a time, and choices that are observed in comparative settings when two or more alternatives are considered simultaneously. Typically, isolated evaluations are obtained in a *between-subject* design, where one person evaluates one scenario and another person evaluates another (or – although this is not the standard use of the term – when the same person evaluates the different scenarios at different points in time so as to avoid direct comparisons). Simultaneous evaluations are observed in a *within-subject* design when a person is presented with two or more scenarios concurrently and asked to compare them. The systematic discrepancy that emerges between these two modes of evaluation, it is suggested, has profound implications for policy and for the role of intuition in setting policy guidelines. Most of life's experiences take place in what can be thought of as a between-subject design – one person lives through one scenario; someone else lives through another. Normative intuitions, on the other hand, typically arise from within-subject introspection – a person entertains a scenario and its alternatives. The implications of this tension are explored (see also Kahneman, 1996; Hsee, Blount, Loewenstein, & Bazerman, 1997; Shafir, 1999).

In the following section, alternative elicitation methods are shown to give rise to differential weighting of dimensions and, consequently, to inconsistent decisions. Related phenomena are then reviewed in the realm of counterfactual evaluation and in contexts that explore people's feelings of sympathy, urgency, and indignation. The third section considers the advantages and disadvantages of separate versus comparative evaluation. Comparative processes, it is argued, can help make subtle differences discernible; on the other hand, they can cause some nuanced trade-offs to be dominated by general qualitative principles. Eyewitness identification procedures are then briefly considered, as they shed light on the role of evaluation procedures. Showup versus lineup identification procedures, it is suggested, trigger, respectively, separate versus concurrent evaluation. The observed differences between the two methodologies provide useful lessons for policy assessment. Concluding remarks comprise the last section.

Some Empirical Facts

Compatibility and Preference Reversals

Elicitation of Preferences. Preferences can be elicited through different methods. People can indicate which option they prefer; alternatively, they can be asked to price each option by stating the amount of money that is as valuable to them as the option. A standard assumption, known as *procedure invariance*, requires that logically equivalent elicitation procedures give rise to the same preference order. Thus, if one option is chosen over another, it is also expected to be priced higher. Procedure invariance is essential for the interpretation of both psychological and physical measurement. The ordering of physical objects with respect to mass, for example, can be established either by placing each object separately on a scale or by placing both objects on the two sides of a pan balance. Procedure invariance requires that the two methods yield the same ordering within the limit of measurement error. Analogously, the rational theory of choice assumes that an individual has a well-defined preference order that can be elicited either by choice or by pricing, giving rise to the same ordering of preferences.

Compatibility Effects. Despite its appeal as an abstract principle, people systematically violate procedure invariance. For example, people often choose one bet over another but price the second bet above the first. In a typical study, subjects are presented with two prospects of similar expected value. One prospect, the H bet, offers a high probability to win a relatively small payoff (e.g., 8 chances in 9 to win $4), whereas the other prospect, the L bet, offers a low probability to win a larger payoff (e.g., a 1 in 9 chance to win $40). When asked to choose between these prospects, subjects tend to choose the H bet over the L bet. Subjects are also asked, on another occasion, to price each prospect by indicating the smallest amount of money for which they would be willing to sell this prospect. Here many subjects assign a higher price to the L bet than to the H bet. One recent study that used this particular pair of bets observed that 71% of subjects chose the H bet, whereas 67% priced L above H (Tversky, Slovic, & Kahneman, 1990). This phenomenon, called *preference reversal*, has been replicated in experiments using a variety of prospects and incentive schemes; it has also been observed with professional gamblers in a Las Vegas casino (Lichtenstein & Slovic, 1973; Slovic & Lichtenstein, 1983) and in a study conducted in the People's Republic of China for real payoffs equal to several months' worth of the subjects' salary (Kachelmeier & Shehata, 1992).

Why do people assign a higher monetary value to the low-probability bet but choose the high-probability bet more often? It appears that the major cause of preference reversal is a differential weighting of probabilities and payoffs in choice and in pricing induced by the type of response required. In line with the general notion of compatibility that has long been recognized by students of perception and motor control, experimental evidence indicates that an attribute of an option is given more weight when it is compatible with the response format than when it is not (Tversky, Sattath, & Slovic, 1988; for review, see Shafir, 1995). Because the price that the subject assigns to a bet is expressed in dollars, the payoffs of the bet, which are also expressed in dollars, are weighted more heavily in pricing than in choice. As a consequence, the L bet (which has the higher payoff) is evaluated more favorably in pricing than in choice, which can give rise to preference reversals. (The foregoing account is further supported by the observation that the incidence of preference reversals is greatly reduced for bets involving nonmonetary outcomes, such as a free dinner at a local restaurant, where outcomes and prices are no longer expressed in the same units and are therefore less compatible; see Slovic, Griffin, & Tversky, 1990.)

The compatibility hypothesis does not depend on the presence of risk. It predicts a similar discrepancy between choice and pricing in the context of riskless options that have a monetary component. Consider a long-term prospect L, which pays $2,500 five years from now, and a short-term prospect S, which pays $1,600 in one and a half years. Subjects were invited to choose between L and S and to price both prospects by stating the smallest immediate cash payment for which they would be willing to exchange each prospect (Tversky et al., 1990). Because the payoffs and the prices again are expressed in the same units, compatibility suggests that the long-term prospect (offering the higher payoff) will be overvalued in pricing relative to choice. In accord with this hypothesis, subjects chose the short-term prospect 74% of the time but priced the long-term prospect above the short-term prospect 75% of the time.

These observations indicate that different methods of elicitation, such as choice and pricing, can induce different weightings of attributes, which, in turn, give rise to discrepant preferences.

Note that the pricing of an option involves independent evaluation and is typically used to assign worth in isolation. Choice, on the other hand, is an inherently comparative process, which requires concurrent presentation. When options are encountered one at a time, they can be priced or assigned other measures of attractiveness, but direct comparison is not feasible (except for special cases where an option is compared to a prototypical or remembered item). The relative weights that characterize our evaluations when these are conducted in isolation can differ in systematic ways from those that characterize comparative evaluation. When considering which of a number of options is preferable, ethicists and policymakers, as well as laypeople, typically resort to a concurrent evaluation, with the various options before their attention. The chosen or implemented option, on the other hand, is likely to be experienced in isolation. To the extent that the two evaluation formats – concurrent and in isolation – lead to differential focusing, there will be a systematic tendency for people to experience scenarios in isolation in ways that remain beyond the scope of within-subject introspection. Life presents us with one scenario at a time, whereas intuitions about relative worth tend to arise from comparative evaluations. As a result, the intuitive assessment of alternatives is often expected to differ from their eventual experience.

The Prominence Hypothesis and Reversals in Perceived Importance

People often feel that one attribute (e.g., safety) is more important than another (e.g., cost). Although the interpretation of such claims is not entirely clear, there is evidence that the attribute that is judged more important looms larger in choice than in independent evaluation, such as pricing (Slovic, 1975; Tversky et al., 1988). Known as the *prominence hypothesis*, this has been shown to lead to systematic violations of invariance.

An early demonstration of this phenomenon was provided by Slovic (1975), who was interested in how subjects choose between equally attractive options. To investigate this question, Slovic first had subjects equate pairs of alternatives, and later asked them to choose between the equally valued alternatives in each pair. One pair, for example, consisted of gift packages offering a combination of cash and coupons. In each pair, one component of one alternative was missing, as shown subsequently, and subjects were asked to determine the value of the missing component that would render the two alternatives equally attractive. (In the following example, the value supplied by the subject may be, say, $10).

	Gift package A	*Gift package B*
Cash	—	$20
Coupon book worth	$32	$18

A week later, subjects were asked to choose between the two equated alternatives. They were also asked, independently, which dimension – cash or coupons – they considered more important. Standard intuition assumes that the two alternatives – explicitly equated for value – are equally likely to be selected. In contrast, in the preceding choice between gift packages, 88% of the subjects who had equated these alternatives for value chose the alternative that was advantageous on the dimension they considered more important. (This pattern was replicated in numerous domains, including the choice between college applicants, auto tires, baseball players, and routes to work. For additional data and a discussion of elicitation procedures, see Tversky et al., 1988.)

These results indicate that people do not choose between the equated alternatives at random. Instead, they resolve the conflict by following a choice mechanism that is easy to explain and to justify: Selecting the alternative that is superior on the more important dimension provides a compelling reason for choice. Note that such tie-breaking procedures are likely to loom larger in choice situations where one option appears better than the other on a compelling dimension; they play a lesser role in evaluation, where the comparative advantage is less prominent. Naturally, this effect is likely to become all the more pronounced when the evaluation is conducted in a noncomparative setting, where each option is evaluated separately, as opposed to a choice setting, which is inherently comparative.

Consider, for example, the following study concerning people's responses to environmental problems (Kahneman & Ritov, 1994). Several pairs of issues were selected, one of which addresses human health or safety and the other concerns protection of the environment. Each issue included a brief statement of a problem, along with a suggested form of intervention, as illustrated.

Problem:	Skin cancer from sun exposure is common among farm workers.
Intervention:	Support free medical checkups for threatened groups.
Problem:	Several Australian mammal species are nearly wiped out by hunters.
Intervention:	Contribute to a fund to provide safe breeding areas for these species.

One group of respondents was asked to choose which of the two interventions they would rather support; a second group was presented with one issue at a time and asked to determine the largest amount they would be willing to pay for the respective intervention. Because the treatment of cancer in humans is generally viewed as more important than the protection of Australian mammals, the prominence hypothesis predicts that the former will receive greater support in direct choice than in independent evaluation. This prediction was confirmed. When asked to evaluate each intervention separately, respondents, who were predictably more moved by the hunted animals' plight than by mundane checkups, were willing to pay more, on average, for the safe breeding of Australian mammals than for free skin cancer checkups. However, when faced with a direct choice between these options, most subjects favored free checkups for humans over safe breeding for the mammals. As expected, the issue that is considered more important (human versus animal safety) acquired greater prominence in the choice condition, which allows for a direct comparison between issues, than in separate presentation, where each issue is evaluated in accord with its own generated emotions and with no direct metric for comparison. Irwin, Slovic, Lichtenstein, and McClelland (1993) report related findings in settings where improvements in air quality were compared with improvements in consumer commodities. In general, people may evaluate one alternative more positively than another when evaluating them independently, but they reverse their judgment in performing comparative evaluation, which tends to bring to prominence the more important attribute.

A related pattern can be observed in cases where an attribute is particularly difficult to gauge in isolation. Hsee (1996), for example, presented subjects with two alternative secondhand music dictionaries, one with 20,000 entries but a slightly torn cover, the other with 10,000 entries and a cover that was like new. Subjects had little notion of how many entries to expect in a music dictionary. Consequently, under separate evaluation, they expressed a willingness to pay more for the dictionary with the new cover than for the one with a slightly torn cover. When the two dictionaries were evaluated concurrently, however, most subjects obviously preferred the dictionary with twice as many entries, despite its inferior cover.

Intuitions about importance, worth, and gravity, as well as ethical propriety, are often obtained in comparative settings; we ask ourselves which issue, A or B, is more grave or more worthy of our attention? Which act, A or B, constitutes a greater ethical violation? In life, we often encounter the relevant scenarios one at a time; we might encounter scenario A today, and somebody else, or we at another time might encounter scenario B. To the extent that our encounter with such scenarios triggers sentiments and reactions that depend partly on their being experienced in isolation, some critical (and perhaps normatively appropriate) aspects of our response are likely to be misjudged by intuitions that arise from concurrent within-subject introspection.

Affect and Principles

In a study ostensibly intended to establish the amounts of compensation that the public considers reasonable, Miller and McFarland (1986) presented respondents with brief descriptions of victims who had applied for compensation and asked them to decide upon a monetary payment. Two such descriptions concerned a male victim who was described as having lost the use of his right arm as a result of a gunshot wound suffered during a robbery at a convenience store. Some respondents were told that the robbery happened at the victim's regular store. Others were told that the victim was shot at a store he rarely frequented, which he happened to go to because his regular store was closed. It was hypothesized that subjects would assign higher compensation to a person whose victimization was preceded by an abnormal event. This is because abnormal events strongly evoke a counterfactual undoing, which tends to raise the perceived poignancy of the outcome and the sympathy for their victims. (For more on the psychology of counterfactual thinking, see Kahneman & Miller, 1986; Roese & Olson, 1995.) Indeed, the victim who was shot at a store he rarely visited was assigned significantly greater compensation than the victim shot at his regular store. The difference in poignancy created by the normal-versus-abnormal manipulation translated into a $100,000 difference in compensation judged appropriate for the two cases.

The affective impact of events is often influenced by the ease with which an alternative event can be imagined. The death of a soldier on the last day of the war seems more poignant than the death of his comrade six months earlier. The fate of a plane crash victim who switched to the fatal flight only minutes before takeoff is seen as more tragic than that of a fellow passenger who had been booked on that flight for months. Whereas the affective impact of such distinctions is predictable and often strong, do people actually consider these distinctions relevant? Consider the earlier study about compensation to victims. Recall that the two versions of the robbery scenario – at the regular versus the unusual stores – were presented to separate groups of subjects. Their affective responses – stronger for the unusual than for the regular scenario – were thus obtained in isolation. In contrast, when respondents were presented with both versions concurrently, the great majority (90%) thought that the victims in the two cases should not be awarded different compensations (Kahneman, 1996). Evidently, despite the large difference in awards observed previously, most subjects considered the difference between the two scenarios irrelevant to compensation. In a within-subject evaluation that allows for direct comparison, rules about what is relevant seem easy to apply: We can decide, for example, that the victim's past frequency of visits to the store is immaterial. In between-subjects evaluation, on the other hand, the application of rules remains elusive: The affective reactions that guide our response in isolation need not conform to the principles that would be endorsed upon concurrent evaluation. Using data from the 1992 Summer Olympics, Medvec, Madey, and Gilovich (1995) showed that athletes who had won silver medals tended to be less satisfied than those who had won bronze medals. Apparently, the silver medalists compared themselves to the gold medal winners, whereas for the bronze medallists a natural counterfactual was not having won a medal at all. Presumably, if they had to choose, all athletes would prefer silver to bronze. Thus, the feelings of relief or disappointment that overwhelm individual experience would clearly be dominated by a preference for better placement upon direct comparison.

Feelings of satisfaction, empathy, or indignation, which arise in the context of specific experience, can be affected by nuanced factors. Principles of decision that help transcend some of these factors are often compelling in direct comparison but difficult to apply in isolated evaluation. This tension produces interesting philosophical questions. In one study (Tversky & Griffin, 1991), respondents were presented with two hypothetical job possibilities, one offering a higher yearly salary in a company where others with similar training earn more (You: $35,000; Others: $38,000) and the other offering a lower salary in a company where others with similar training earn even less (You: $33,000; Others: $30,000). Most of us tend to abide by a simple principle: We prefer outcomes that make us better off (particularly when others are thereby made better off as well). In fact, a majority of respondents chose the job with the higher absolute salary, despite the lower relative position. This simple principle, however, is hard to apply when the jobs are contemplated separately. In this condition, without the other job to compare to, earning a lower salary than comparable others brings forth sentiments that reduce our feelings of satisfaction. Indeed, contrary to the preference observed through direct choice, the majority of respondents who evaluated the two jobs separately anticipated higher satisfaction in the job with the lower salary and the higher relative position. A variant of this study was replicated with second-year MBA students, who were presented with two hypothetical job offers: In one, they would be paid $75,000 – the same as other starting MBAs; in the other, they would be paid $85,000, whereas some of the others would receive $95,000. As predicted, these students were more willing to accept the former than the latter job offer when these were evaluated in isolation, but they preferred the latter over the former when asked to choose between them (Bazerman, Schroth, Shah, Diekmann, & Tenbrunsel, 1994; see also Bazerman, White, & Loewenstein, 1995, for related discussion).

Separate or Comparative Evaluation?

Discernible Differences and Qualitative Rules

In light of the tension observed in the previous section between intuitions that arise in independent versus comparative evaluations, an obvious question arises: Which ought to be the preferred mode of evaluation, independent or comparative? As it turns out, there may not be a simple solution. Depending on the nature of the problem and on the psychological factors that enter into its evaluation, either mode of presentation may prove preferable to the other. Consistent with the preceding job offer studies, there appear to be situations in which the utilitarian worth of outcomes, which is often hard to gauge in isolation, plays a decisive role in comparative evaluations. Hsee, Blount, Loewenstein, and Bazerman (1997), for example, presented subjects with pictures of two servings of Haagen Dazs ice cream. One serving contained more ice cream but failed to fill a large cup; the other contained less ice cream that over-filled a smaller container. When the two pictures were evaluated jointly, subjects were willing to pay more for what was clearly a larger serving. In separate evaluation, however, when the precise amount of ice cream was hard to gauge, subjects tended to pay more for the overfilled cup than for the one that seems partly empty.

Simple principles of worth, merit, and entitlement, which can play a decisive role in comparative settings, often prove difficult to apply in independent evaluations. The compensation a victim is entitled to, the attractiveness of a job offer, or the value of a serving of ice cream can be hard to gauge when these occur in isolation. In these situations, other considerations, such as the emotional impact of the victim's plight, the sense of unfairness produced by a coworker's salary, or the amount of ice cream relative to the size of the container can significantly influence our evaluation. When such experiences involve sentiments and reactions that largely depend on their being evaluated in isolation, these aspects of our affective response are likely to be missed by well-articulated policies and compelling principles that are sometimes possible to apply only in concurrent within-subject evaluation.

To what extent we want to uphold or to avoid the sentiments that arise from isolated evaluation may depend on the particular problem. When evaluating the worth of a serving of ice cream, for example, it is unlikely that we would want to factor in the relative size of the container. In this case, there seems to be a decisive advantage to comparative evaluation. In fact, in many cases, limited sensitivity on our part is likely to render a comparative evaluation preferable. Thus, whereas in separate evaluation it is not clear that we would react differently to an airplane crash that kills 100 people versus one that kills 200, in comparative evaluation we would all agree that the latter is even worse (and thus, for example, justifies greater total compensation payments) than the former.

Comparative evaluation can help discern certain differences that we may not be sensitive to in separate evaluation. Furthermore, it high-lights the relevance of certain features, such as the size of a salary as opposed to its rank, that loom larger in comparative than in separate evaluation. As it turns out, however, it is not always clear that the greater weight accorded to features in comparative settings is preferable. Con-sider again the example of the competing job offers. If we acknowledge that earning a salary lower than comparable others triggers sentiments that reduce one's well-being, in what sense are people being utilitarian when they opt for the job with the higher absolute salary despite the lower relative position? Perhaps, upon direct comparison, higher pay seems more consequential and a more legitimate concern than relative rank, but the direct comparison ends when the choice is made; from then on, one is left with the sentiments and well-being that go with the job one has chosen. And if those prove inferior, in what sense was that the right choice? Young faculty looking at job offers sometimes face similar dilemmas. How much ought the school's prestige be weighted relative to a supportive environment accorded to young faculty? When comparing places of work, prestige may count more than it ought to, and certainly more than it is likely to matter when one gets up every morning to go to one's (only) job. Similar tensions may be found in purchasing decisions. Hsee et al. (1997) illustrate this with an example of a purchase at an audio store. Suppose that one pair of speakers has superior sound but is aesthetically unattractive relative to a second pair, which looks much better but has a slightly less impressive sound. At the store, with the two sets of speakers directly comparable, one is likely to opt for the better-sounding system, which, after all, one might reason, matters more than how it looks. But then, at home with the chosen speakers, the slight superiority in sound may prove inconsequential, whereas the unattractiveness of the speakers may loom large every day.

Principles that prove decisive in comparative settings may not always be those that ought to guide the decision. On occasion, they may overwhelm important considerations that lose their salience in the passage from separate to comparative evaluation. In an earlier example, subjects were seen to prefer programs intended to save Australian mammals over skin cancer tests for farm workers when these were evaluated in isolation, but then they reverted to supporting the tests for humans when these were directly compared. The notion that issues concerning human health should come before those concerning other animals played a decisive role in comparative evaluation but may not always be entirely defensible. Comparative evaluation emphasizes the application of qualitative principles, but these may often not be sensitive enough to variation in quantity or degree. In this vein, a cost-effectiveness analysis of various states of health conducted by Ubel, Loewenstein, Scanlon, and Kamlet (1996) found a large discrepancy between subjects' preferences derived from utility measures (obtained separately) and their rationing choices among alternative treatments obtained in comparative settings. When making a comparison between treatments, subjects overwhelmingly chose to treat the more severely ill even if the number of less severely ill patients who stood to benefit instead was hundreds of times greater than demanded by the exchange rate implied in separate evaluation. These subjects applied a simple rule in comparative evaluation that required treating more severely ill patients first, with relative disregard for the exchange rate with patients who were less severely ill. A plausible exchange rate, on the other hand, could be derived from separate utility evaluations, where the principle in favor of more severe cases could not be indiscriminately applied. Similar arguments have been made against government programs intended merely to augment the number of lives saved as opposed to, say, quality-adjusted life years (Zeckhauser & Shepherd, 1976) and against policies intended largely to minimize the number of deaths, with relative disregard for other death-related factors such as dread, lack of control, and involuntariness that make certain deaths particularly bad (Sunstein, 1997).

Baron (1994) presents a related critique of decision rules that have a consequentialist justification in some cases but then tend to be overgeneralized. Consider, for example, the distinction between killing versus letting die, which many view as justified in certain cases. Some have argued that this distinction is misapplied, for example by the American Medical Association (AMA), to instances involving active versus passive euthanasia, where they think it is invalid (Rachels, 1975). An interesting dilemma emerges regarding the appropriateness of such distinctions in separate versus comparative settings. Suppose the AMA's governing body concludes that from a simple consequentialist point of view there is, in fact, no justification for the distinction between active and passive euthanasia. On the other hand, we have seen that simple consequentialist considerations often loom larger in comparative than in separate evaluation. Those individuals who contemplate euthanasia will have to implement one version, active or passive, and not the other. Assume that in isolated experience, one version, say the active version, feels worse than the other does, even after all relevant medical facts have been thoroughly considered. Should the AMA then ignore the sentiments of most individuals in favor of an intuition that arises in comparative settings?

In general, which mode of evaluation, comparative or independent, ought to be preferred will depend on the nature of the problem and the purposes of the evaluation. When the main concern is an insufficient sensitivity to differences that really ought to count (such as the number of lives lost in a crash or the amount of ice cream purchased), a comparative evaluation is likely to help make those differences discernible. On the other hand, if the concern is with a general principle that may overwhelm otherwise valid distinctions (like the principle that severe illnesses should be taken care of first, regardless of the number of patients; or that people matter more than animals, regardless of the problem or its extension), then an independent evaluation may help trigger the correct sensitivities without the corrupting influence of the overarching principle.

Suspect Identification Procedures

In thinking about alternative policy recommendation procedures, the following may provide a useful metaphor. Two common procedures used by police for suspect identification by a witness are the *showup*, wherein the witness is presented with a single suspect at a time, and the *lineup*, in which the witness is asked to select the perpetrator from among a group of suspects. The former requires a separate evaluation (is this the person or not?), whereas the latter is partly a comparative procedure (which of these looks most like the perpetrator?).

Contrary to standard assumptions, empirical investigation suggests that witnesses at a lineup are less likely to say "not there" than are witnesses in a showup (Gonzalez, Ellsworth, & Pembroke, 1993; Lindsay et al., 1991). In a lineup, with several options available, the witness searches for the suspect who most closely resembles the remembered perpetrator. The witness thus comes to treat the task as identifying that suspect who best matches his or her recollection of the culprit (even if that match is not perfect) rather than as identifying the actual culprit (Gonzalez et al., 1993; Woocher, 1977). In this sense, the showup versus lineup may be seen as analogous to a true–false versus multiple-choice question. In the former, one presumably does not respond "true" unless the option exceeds a certain threshold; in the latter, one chooses the best answer, independent of threshold. In light of the fact that eyewitness misidentification appears to be the factor most often associated with wrongful conviction (Rattner, 1988), this can be consequential.

In general, independent versus comparative evaluations are likely to differ in the perceived task and, consequently, in the likelihood of finding a satisfying solution. When a proposed treatment or policy is considered in isolation, it is typically evaluated relative to some threshold. When various proposals are compared, on the other hand, all that is required is to determine which is better, independently of how good they may actually be. Consequently, in choosing evaluation formats, one may want to contemplate the specific goals or needs presented by the situation. If what we are looking for is an ideal (above threshold) solution, we ought to evaluate alternatives in isolation; if, on the other hand, we need to adopt some quick course of action "no matter what," then we may want to resort to a simple comparative evaluation. Occasionally, there may be effective ways of combining the two evaluation modes – first, say, by comparatively screening the options down to the acceptable few and then by evaluating them independently, one after another.

Concluding Remarks

Various psychological factors contribute to inconsistent sentiments, judgments, and preferences in isolated versus concurrent evaluations. First, different methods of elicitation, such as choice versus pricing, were seen to induce divergent weightings of attributes and thus give rise to inconsistent preferences. Next, dimensions that were considered more important, or harder to evaluate, were seen to acquire greater prominence in concurrent presentations, which allow for clearer contrast, than in isolated presentations. Similarly, rules of decision that favor some factors over others were seen to play a decisive role in direct comparisons but proved more difficult to apply in isolated evaluation. These phenomena, it was suggested, contribute to persistent discrepancies between the nature of everyday experience and the conditions that yield normative judgment. In life, people typically experience and evaluate things one at a time, as in a between-subject design, whereas normative intuitions typically result from concurrent within-subject introspection.

Intuition need not always arise from a purely concurrent mode of evaluation. Instead, a person may attempt to evaluate one alternative in isolation and then evaluate the second. The attempt at a sequential evaluation of isolated events, however, is likely to prove difficult and to meet with limited success, particularly when the desired intuition depends on the eventual comparison of the disparate evaluations. Furthermore, even if one were successful at predicting reactions to events in isolation, that would not resolve the conflict with intuitions that emerge from concurrent consideration.

Within-subject introspection provides insight into our normative intuitions. Those intuitions can be quite robust, generating compelling principles of ethics and rationality that many of us share. People's behavior, on the other hand, is often at variance with their own normative intuitions. When confronted with actual judgments or preferences that violate normative principles, people often wish to modify their behavior to conform with the principles. Evidently, both introspection and actual behavior capture important aspects of human competence: The first typically is the outcome of comparative within-subject deliberation whereas the second results from actual responses in specific situations. People often wish to adhere to normative principles born out of comparative evaluation, but these sometimes conflict in nontrivial ways with the impulses that arise in specific situations. Thus, for example, when these choices are directly compared, people may typically wish to contribute to the well-being of fellow humans before they help other animals, but when these choices are faced one at a time, the helpless animals often generate greater sentiments of pity and adoration than the humans, leading to a greater willingness to contribute to the former than to the latter.

The tension between introspective ideals and actual behavior is, of course, well known. People generally agree that one should contribute to worthy causes, be faithful to one's partner, refrain from lying, and avoid fatty foods, despite the fact that many do not always do so. Along similar lines, people believe they ought to pay or contribute more for things they prefer, but persistent preference reversals violate this belief in specific choices. The discrepancy between ideals and actual behavior is easier to predict when it stems from self-interest or a lack of self-control; it proves less intuitive when it is the result of cognitive operations.

Counterintuitive sentiments and decisions often need to be demonstrated through between-subject designs. Only in such contexts can we discover certain facts about our mental life that cannot be accessed by within-subject intuition. This has obvious implications for the study of normative, ethical, and societal problems and for the setting of policy guidelines. Consider, for example, the intuitive distinction most of us make between acts of omission and acts of commission, or between intentional versus nonintentional acts, or between different forms of allocation, distribution, or justice. In most of these cases, our intuitions arise from direct comparison and concurrent evaluation. It seems important to know to what extent these sentiments are maintained in a between-subject context when evaluated in isolation. In light of the previous findings, we should expect some systematic differences to emerge, and these could have nontrivial policy implications. Imagine that some distinctions that our intuition tells us are important disappear in between-subject evaluations, and that distinctions we did not previously entertain suddenly prove important. What should we do then? Should we strive for arrangements that improve things according to intuitions that emerge from concurrent evaluation, or should we instead, contrary to our intuition, strive to create a world that ameliorates experience in between-subject conditions? You can contemplate both of these possibilities; or, perhaps, you should consider one and ask someone else to entertain the other.

References

Baron, J. (1994). Nonconsequentialist decisions. *Behavioral and Brain Sciences, 17,* 1–42.

Bazerman, M. H., Schroth, H. A., Shah, P. P., Diekmann, K. A., & Tenbrunsel, A. E. (1994). The inconsistent role of comparison others and procedural justice in reactions to hypothetical job descriptions: Implications for job acceptance decisions. *Organizational Behavior and Human Decision Processes, 60,* 326–352.

Bazerman, M. H., White, S. B., & Loewenstein, G. F. (1995). Perceptions of fairness in interpersonal and individual choice situations. *Current Directions in Psychological Science, 4,* 39–43.

Gonzalez, R., Ellsworth, P. C., & Pembroke, M. (1993). Response biases in lineups and showups. *Journal of Personality and Social Psychology, 64,* 525–537.

Hsee, C. K. (1996). The evaluability hypothesis: An explanation of preference reversals between joint and separate evaluations of alternatives. *Organizational Behavior and Human Decision Processes, 67,* 247–257.

Hsee, C. K., Blount, S., Loewenstein, G. F., & Bazerman, M. H. (1997). *Preference reversals between joint and separate evaluations of options: A review and theoretical analysis.* Working paper, Graduate School of Business, University of Chicago.

Irwin, J. R., Slovic, P., Lichtenstein, S., & McClelland, G. H. (1993). Preference reversals and the measurement of environmental values. *Journal of Risk and Uncertainty, 6,* 5–18.

Kachelmeier, S. J., & Shehata, M. (1992). Examining risk preferences under high monetary incentives: Experimental evidence from the People's Republic of China. *American Economic Review, 82,* 1120–1141.

Kahneman, D. (1996). *The cognitive psychology of consequences and moral intuition.* Manuscript, Princeton University.

Kahneman, D., & Miller, D. T. (1986). Norm theory: Comparing reality to its alternatives. *Psychological Review, 93,* 136–153.

Kahneman, D., & Ritov, I. (1994). Determinants of stated willingness to pay for public goods: A study in the headline method. *Journal of Risk and Uncertainty, 9,* 5–38.

Lichtenstein, S., & Slovic, P. (1973). Response-induced reversals of preference in gambling: An extended replication in Las Vegas. *Journal of Experimental Psychology, 10,* 16–20.

Lindsay, R. C. L., Lea, J., Nosworthy, G., Fulford, J., Hector, J., LeVan, V., & Seabrook, C. (1991). Biased lineups: Sequential presentation reduces the problem. *Journal of Applied Psychology, 76,* 796–802.

Medvec, V. H., Madey, S., & Gilovich, T. (1995). When less is more: Counterfactual thinking and satisfaction among Olympic medalists. *Journal of Personality and Social Psychology, 69,* 603–610.

Miller, D. T., & McFarland, C. (1986). Counterfactual thinking and victim compensation: A test of Norm Theory. *Personality and Social Psychology Bulletin, 12,* 513–519.

Rachels, J. (1975). Active and passive euthanasia. *New England Journal of Medicine, 292,* 78–80.

Rattner, A. (1988). Convicted but innocent: Wrongful conviction and the criminal justice system. *Law and Human Behavior, 12,* 283–293.

Roese, N. J., & Olson, J. M. (Eds.). (1995). *What might have been: The social psychology of counterfactual thinking.* Mahwah, NJ: Erlbaum.

Shafir, E. (1995). Compatibility in cognition and decision. In J. R. Busemeyer, R. Hastie, & D. L. Medin (Eds.), *Decision making from the perspective of cognitive psychology: The psychology of learning and motivation* (Vol. 32, pp. 247–274). New York: Academic Press.

Shafir, E. (1999). Philosophical intuitions and cognitive mechanisms. In M. DePaul & W. Ramsey (Eds.), *Rethinking intuition* (pp. 59–74). Lanham, MD: Rowman and Littlefield.

Slovic, P. (1975). Choice between equally valued alternatives. *Journal of Experimental Psychology: Human Perception and Performance, 1,* 280–287.

Slovic, P. Griffin, D., & Tversky, A. (1990). Compatibility effects in judgment and choice. In R. Hogarth (Ed.), *Insights in decision making: Theory and applications* (pp. 5–27). Chicago: University of Chicago Press.

Slovic, P., & Lichtenstein, S. (1983). Preference reversals: A broader perspective. *American Economic Review, 73,* 596–605.

Sunstein, C. R. (1997). Bad deaths. *Journal of Risk and Uncertainty, 14,* 259–282.

Tversky, A., & Griffin, D. (1991). Endowment and contrast in judgments of well-being. In F. Strack, M. Argyle, & N. Schwarz (Eds.), *Subjective well-being* (pp. 101–118). New York: Pergamon Press.

Tversky, A., Sattath, S., & Slovic, P. (1988). Contingent weighting in judgment and choice. *Psychological Review, 95,* 371–384.

Tversky, A., Slovic, P., & Kahneman, D. (1990). The causes of preference reversal. *American Economic Review, 80,* 204–217.

Ubel, P. A., Loewenstein, G., Scanlon, D., & Kamlet, M. (1996). Individual utilities are inconsistent with rationing choices: A partial explanation of why Oregon's cost-effectiveness list failed. *Medical Decision Making, 16,* 108–116.

Woocher, F. D. (1977). Did your eyes deceive you? Expert psychological testimony on the unreliability of eyewitness testimony. *Stanford Law Review, 29,* 986–1030.

Zeckhauser, R., & Shepherd, W. (1976). Where now for saving lives? *Law and Contemporary Problems, 40,* 5–41.

Part II

Economic Applications and Contrasts

4   Policy Analysis and Design with Losses Valued More than Gains and Varying Rates of Time Preference

Jack L. Knetsch

The use of economics in the analysis and design of public policy has enjoyed considerable success and approval, particularly among economists, and the call has usually been for more such analyses. However, recent research findings demonstrate that some important behavioral assumptions that form the basis of much current economic and policy analysis often provide neither a very good description of people's preferences nor very useful predictions of their reactions to real choices.

Although little use is being made of these behavioral findings, on present evidence the consequences appear substantial. Many analyses based on conventional assumptions may provide distorted guidance, and policy design may be materially improved with what now seem to be better readings of people's preferences.

There are several areas in which recent results show people's behavior to be at variance with commonly accepted assumptions. Many are the result of the context dependence of people's valuations of entitlements or of outcomes. Two of these, both of which illustrate the importance and range of policy issues potentially affected by these behavioral findings, will be discussed here. The first is the widely reported finding that people commonly value losses much more than otherwise fully commensurate gains – the reference state, or endowment, effect. The second is the less well documented, and somewhat related, evidence that people have varied rates rather than a single rate of time preference that they use to value and choose among future outcomes. Each will be discussed, with illustrative examples of their policy implications, followed by an outline of an emerging more generic issue of the extent to which

This draws on research supported by Environment Canada and the U.S. Forest Service.

people may not hold stable preferences of the sort normally assumed in economic and policy analysis.

The Reference State Effect

Evidence

The economic value of a good or a change that affects people's welfare is what they are willing to sacrifice to obtain it or to accept its loss. In policy terms: "Benefits are measured by the total number of dollars which prospective gainers would be willing to pay to secure adoption, and losses are measured by the total number of dollars which prospective losers would insist on as the price of agreeing to adoption" (Michelman, 1967, p. 1214). There is wide agreement on this characterization of valuations, and the maximum willingness to pay (WTP) and the minimum willingness to accept compensation (WTA) remain the standard definitions of the monetary measures, respectively, of gains and losses.

The usual working assumption of economics and policy analysis has been that the two measures, the maximum WTP and the minimum WTA, are for all practical purposes[1] equivalent: "We shall normally expect the results to be so close together that it would not matter which we choose" (Henderson, 1941, p. 121). This remains the presumption of choice – "... there is no basis consistent with economic assumptions and empirical income effects for WTP and WTA to exhibit sizable differences" (Diamond, Hausman, Leonard, & Denning, 1993, p. 66).

The empirical evidence is sharply at variance with the conventional assertion of equivalence between the WTP and WTA valuations. The finding that people instead commonly value losses more than commensurate gains comes from a wide array of survey studies, real exchange experiments, and the choices made by individuals in their daily lives. The results of these studies have been widely reported in the professional literature – including all of the leading economics journals and those of related fields – over the past two decades. The earliest reports of reference effect disparities were based on survey studies and appeared in the early 1970s. For example, duck hunters said they would be willing to pay, on average, $247 to preserve a marsh area important to propagation of bird life but would demand $1,044 to agree to its destruction (Hammack & Brown, 1974). Studies in the years since have become more extensive in terms of the nature of entitlements valued, investigators and research methods used, populations studied, and realism of exchanges. For example, in an early study involving real as opposed to hypothetical exchanges, participants demanded a minimum of four times as much money to give up a lottery ticket than the maximum sum they were willing to pay to acquire a ticket (Knetsch & Sinden, 1984). In a later real exchange experiment, individuals were willing to pay, on average, $5.60 for a 50% chance to win $20, but these same individuals demanded an average of $10.87 to give up the identical entitlement (Kachelmeier & Shehata, 1992).[2] In more common nonexperimental decisions, the strong reluctance to give up a default automobile insurance option when an otherwise more attractive choice is readily available (Johnson, Hershey, Meszaros, & Kunreuther, 1993), the reluctance to realize a loss by selling securities that have declined in price relative to those for which prices have increased (Odean, 1998; Shefrin & Statman, 1985), the typically greater demands for regulation of new environmental risks than of equivalent old risks (Sunstein, 1993), and the greater legal protection accorded losses over foregone gains in judicial choices (Cohen & Knetsch, 1992) are further examples of the difference in valuations of gains and losses.

Other studies have demonstrated that the valuation disparity is pervasive; is usually large; is not a result of income effects, wealth constraints, or transaction costs; and does not appear to be eliminated by repeated valuations or repetitions of market exchanges (e.g., Kahneman, Knetsch, & Thaler, 1990). The buying (WTP) and selling (WTA) valuations of an embossed mug over six repeated trials, for example, are given in Table 4.1 (Knetsch, Tang, & Thaler, 1999). In this particular test there is evidence not only of a large disparity between the valuations of gains and losses, but also of divergence, not convergence, of values over subsequent repeated trials.

Table 4.1. *The Mean WTP and WTA Valuations of a Mug Over Six Repeated Auctions*

Measure of Value	Trial					
	1	2	3	4	5	6
WTP	$3.58	$2.89	$2.39	$2.00	$2.04	$1.23
WTA	8.40	9.00	9.09	9.50	8.99	9.16

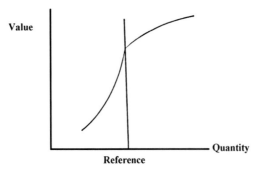

Figure 4.1. Gains and losses of welfare and the reference state.

Rather than being valued in terms of endpoints, as assumed by standard economic principles, the valuation of a change – the gain or loss of a good, or benefiting or losing from a policy – is instead typically made from the standpoint of changes from a reference position (Kahneman & Tversky, 1979). Most people, for example, weigh changes to their income or wealth as gains or losses to their current income or wealth, not as smaller or larger positive sums. As in the case of income or wealth, gains from the reference state of essentially all entitlements or holdings are valued less and losses from the reference state of these entitlements are valued more, as indicated by the functional relation illustrated in Figure 4.1.

One consequence of this valuation disparity is that the sacrifice that individuals are willing to make to receive or not lose a benefit, or to avoid or accept a loss – the economic value of the change – may well be substantially different, depending on the gain or loss domains of both the good being valued and the numeraire being used to measure the value. These resulting alternative measures of value can be illustrated as comparisons among four quadrants formed by a vertical axis indicating the gain or loss of an entitlement and a horizontal axis indicating the gain or loss of money (or another good or outcome used as the value numeraire), as in Figure 4.2.[3]

The expected pattern of differing valuations of entitlements is indicated by the results of a real exchange experiment involving three groups of participants who were all asked to value a mug, but to do so in three ways. The valuations of one group were expressed in terms of how much they would pay to gain a mug, those of the second group by how much money they would demand to give up a mug, and those of the third group by how much money they would need to receive

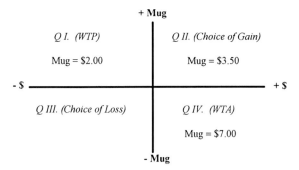

Figure 4.2. Combinations of gains and losses and the median value of mugs.

rather than receive a mug – a choice between two gains (Kahneman et al., 1990). The results are indicated in Figure 4.2.

The value of a gain is appropriately measured by the maximum sum an individual would pay to receive an entitlement. This WTP is in the domain of gains for the good and losses for money, indicated by the Quadrant I measure. As gains are expected to be worth less than losses for both the good and the numeraire, money, people would presumably be willing to pay relatively less for the good, and this measure can therefore be expected to yield the lowest monetary value. This was confirmed by the lowest valuation of the mug, $2.00.

In the same way, the value of a loss is appropriately measured by the compensation required to leave the individual as well off as he or she would be without the change. This is the WTA measure of Quadrant III. As losses carry relatively more weight, this means that the compensation would need to be larger to accept a loss and this measure can therefore be expected to yield the largest monetary value. This result was evident in the $7.00 valuation of the mug in this context.

Quadrants II and IV represent choice measures.[4] Quadrant II is a choice between a gain of a good and a gain of money, and Quadrant IV is a choice between a loss of the good and a loss of money. As such, they are both opportunity cost measures of value, the amount of money forgone to receive a gain of a good and the amount of money lost to avoid the loss of a good. The opportunity cost measures can only be expected to provide estimates of values intermediate between the gain (WTP) and loss (WTA) values of Quadrants I and III – as given by the $3.50 valuation of the mug in the choice of gains context; they do not provide appropriate measures of economic sacrifice or value. Although the choices between two gains (Quadrant II) or two losses (Quadrant IV) might be of some interest as indications of preferences between alternatives, they remain opportunity cost measures rather than direct measures of sacrifice.

In sum, there is often not a single value of an entitlement but instead different values, depending on whether the entitlement is being gained or lost. The negative value to a community of losing a park will be greater than the value of gaining the same amenity; losing jobs will be more aversive than the benefits of gaining like numbers of jobs, and initiating a new fee will likely provoke more negative feeling than the positive impact resulting from eliminating a charge.

Policy Relevance of the Valuation Disparity

The pervasive existence of the disparity between the values people attach to gains and losses raises an initial question of whether or not such differences should be taken into account in the analysis and design of policy. Should, for example, a loss be weighed more than forgoing a benefit in considering the benefits and costs of a change, or should reducing a loss be weighed more heavily than providing an otherwise commensurate gain? Should, in other words, the difference in people's valuations of losses and gains be incorporated into the assessments of the social worth of policy or other changes?

In the standard models of rational economic preferences and choices, which form the basis of most policy analyses, there is little or no allowance for deviations from the prescribed dictates and axioms. While individual actions are widely acknowledged to sometimes depart from such "rational" behavior, these are traditionally taken to be random events of little consequence that will "average out" over larger populations and will generally be corrected, or at least reduced, by the discipline of markets and exchange.

The treatment of people's systematic biases in making decisions and choices is by and large generally similar to the prescription for random errors. It is becoming increasingly appreciated that individuals rely on heuristics and are subject to such biases as availability of recall, insensitivity to base rates or to sample sizes, anchoring, and the confirmation trap (e.g., Bazerman, 1998). Rather than be counted as revealing preferences, these are generally viewed as mistakes, the results of which are not to be taken into account in normative prescriptions or in policy analyses and design. They are regarded as faults to be avoided or corrected by training.

There is also a view, common in textbooks, that takes this further by proclaiming essentially all departures from traditional rational choice models as involving irrational behavior and therefore not to be taken into account in any policy analysis. By this reckoning, such behavior should be the subject of debiasing therapy rather than the basis for formulating policy.[5] Hence, all choices and valuations that are not consistent with conventional behavioral assumptions are declared as irrational and largely due to cognitive pathologies, and are therefore not to be counted in the design of policies.

There is, however, an alternative view that holds that while some behaviors and choices may be based on biases or other mistakes and therefore should not be counted in policy analyses, other behaviors and choices that diverge from the standard behavioral models reflect real preferences and consequently should be taken into account. Thus, in the case of differing perceptions of the seriousness of various risks, Pildes and Sunstein (1995), for example, suggest:

> If lay assessments rest on factual misinformation, or on cognitive distortions in the way inferences are drawn from the known facts, they need not be credited. But to the extent that they reflect different valuations of risk, such as concern for how equitably distributed a risk is, or whether the processes by which the risk is imposed and managed are fair, they are the kind of citizen preferences, backed up by legitimate reasons and values, that democracies should take seriously. (p. 73).

Similarly, the finding that people may be willing to spend three times as much to prevent a cancer death as to prevent other premature deaths is, in this view, a difference that should be taken into account in policy analysis and allocation decisions (Pildes & Sunstein, 1995). To the extent that this assessment of the importance of premature deaths from different causes reflects real preferences, the difference indicates that reducing cancer deaths is valued more than reducing deaths from other causes and that this disparity should guide allocations. Much the same would be true of allocations for safety measures that favor reducing premature deaths from air travel rather than those from road travel, a response in keeping with people's known greater aversion to the possibility of air deaths, even if it means that more total premature deaths may result from shifting resources away from road safety, where they might well be more effective in reducing accidents and premature deaths.

The case of the disparity between valuations of gains and losses appears to be far more one of reflecting real preferences and not one of mistake. The evidence of differences is not only pervasive, with essentially no contrary observations, but it has been found in studies of repeated valuations and in everyday decisions of individuals – circumstances in which people have many opportunities to learn and motivation to discipline their decisions (Kahneman, Knetsch, & Thaler, 1991).

Analogous to the cases in which people value prevention of accidents or premature deaths from cancer or air travel more than from other diseases or automobile travel, they give every indication of simply valuing a loss more than a commensurate gain. There is, in standard economic principles, no questioning of people's valuing successive units of a good less and less – of the near-universal observation of diminishing marginal utility. Indeed, diminishing returns, or values, forms a major foundation of theories of rational economic behavior and, not incidentally, of prescriptive policy analysis. And there is similarly little questioning of marginal utilities for some goods diminishing faster than those for other goods. So in this sense the supposed shape of people's utility or value functions, in which marginal utility diminishing at various rates is a major characteristic, is universally agreed to be taken fully into account in economic and policy analyses.

However, if values from the presumed function showing decreasing returns are to be counted, then there would seem to be little reason for not counting values as they appear on an empirically shaped function indicating that people value entitlements from a reference state, with losses valued more than gains (as indicated in Figure 4.1). Not only is the claim of a better reading of people's preferences enhanced by the empirical evidence, but it does not seem in any meaningful way irrational to weigh losses from a reference point more than gains beyond it.

In sum, the available empirical evidence points to pervasive and large endowment effects. In many circumstances, including many cases of values affected by alternative policies, people value losses much more than gains. And to the extent that this is the case, these differences should be taken into account in most policy analyses.

The Reference State

The economic value of a change will in most cases differ not only in being a positive or negative move, but it will also often vary, depending on the reference state from which individuals assess the change. Positive changes can be either a gain or a reduction in a loss. Such positive changes beyond the reference point seem best to be regarded as gains, and those short of the reference as reductions of losses. Negative changes can be either losses or forgone gains; those detracting from the reference level are clearly losses, and ones beyond the reference seem best to be considered as forgone gains. Therefore, depending on how a change is viewed relative to the reference state, different measures for positive changes and different measures for negative changes may be appropriate.

The distinction is important because of the strong evidence that the value function (Figure 4.1) is commonly much steeper in the domain of losses than in the domain of gains, implying a large difference in values. Consequently, a given change will likely have a greater or lesser impact on the welfare of an individual, depending on whether it is viewed by the individual as being a loss or a gain. A positive change that results in reducing a loss will be considered more valuable than one that provides a gain. A negative change that imposes a loss is more aversive than one that results in forgoing a gain.

The well-recognized payment for gains and compensation for losses definition of economic value, and the distinction between the frames corresponding to domains of gains and losses, suggest clear criteria for selecting an appropriate measure of the value of a policy change. Those that bring about a change that is regarded as being in the domain of gains – obtaining gains and forgoing gains – are generally best measured in terms of how much people would be willing to pay either to obtain the benefit or keep a gain that they consider to be beyond the reference (Quadrant I of Figure 4.2). In like fashion, changes in the domain of losses short of the reference are generally best assessed in terms of the minimum compensation measure: how much people would require to accept a loss or how much compensation they would demand to forgo a reduction of a loss (Quadrant III of Figure 4.2).

These criteria make it important not just to distinguish between gains and losses, but also to differentiate between positive changes as being gains or reductions in losses and negative changes as being losses or forgone gains. Reducing pollution levels, for example, is likely valued more, and more likely to be economically justified, if viewed by people as reducing the harm caused by pollution than as a gain in environmental quality.

This discrimination between gains and reduction of losses, and between losses and forgone gains, appears to turn largely on the reference state from which changes are judged. The reference is in most cases obvious, but in some cases it may be far less so. Reference levels appear to be mostly a matter of what people regard as the expected or normal state (Kahneman & Miller, 1986). They may often be the status quo, but not always.

Reference states also appear largely not to be a matter of legal entitlement (Knetsch, 1997). Legal entitlements determine what claims receive recognition by the community and support a cause of action (usually injunctive relief or damage payments) of an injured party against a neighbor. They presumably reflect not only efficiency, but also equity, fairness, and other justice goals of the community, taking account of asymmetries in avoidance costs and costs of enforcement and compliance. The choice of economic measure concerns another issue, that of choosing a measure that best reflects actual changes in welfare in particular cases. The extent of welfare loss associated with various injuries may well be influenced by the assignment of specific legal entitlements – as rules presumably evolve to provide greater protection against more important losses. To this extent, and largely in accord with this direction of causality, property rights are related to losses.

The dependence of the reference on what is regarded as normal or expected is indicated by Leowenstein's (1988) perceptive example of biological references sometimes being a function of time, whereby the positive change of acquiring food may be perceived as a gain under normal circumstances but would be viewed as a reduction of a loss after long periods of deprivation. Similarly, the finding that people believe restoration of environmental quality and human health to historic levels to be more valuable and worth doing than making equivalent changes from the status quo suggests that the reference condition may also be a function of past deterioration (Gregory, Lichtenstein, & MacGregor, 1993). Further evidence of the variability of the reference, depending on people's expectations of normal, is provided by the findings that people expect increasing wages over their working lives and therefore regard an interruption of these increases in earnings as a loss, but consider decreases in health with age as the expected course and consequently do not regard such normal deterioration as a loss (Chapman, 1996).

Current practice is overwhelmingly to treat any positive change as an improvement for which the WTP is used as the measure of its value. This is legitimate for gains, but not for changes that people are more likely to regard as a reduction of a loss. Containing an oil spill might be considered an improvement, for example, but it seems more likely that most people would regard it more realistically as an action to reduce a loss, for which the minimum compensation they would accept not to have the spill contained would measure the value of the action. Similarly, framing the saving of lives by reducing discharges of noxious pollutants as an improvement implies the strong empirical assertion that people would consider "exposure to a pollutant, often a cancer-causing one" (Cropper, Aydede, & Portney, 1994, p. 243), as a neutral reference state and therefore would regard an intervention that reduces the number of people dying from this cause as an improvement. People might instead regard being exposed to a cancer-causing pollutant as being put in the domain of losses, and an action to reduce the exposure would then be taken as reducing a loss rather than an improvement. Given that the value of an improvement would be measured in terms of WTP and the value of reducing a loss by people's WTA, an intervention to cut the pollution is more likely to be economically justified in the latter case than in the former. As the differences are likely to be large, the distinction has substantial practical importance, and ignoring it seems likely to lead to many inappropriate policy choices.

Policy Implications of the Disparity Between Measures

The continuing use of the WTP measure of economic value to assess losses, for which it is not the agreed-on measure, on such dubious advice as "the willingness to pay format should be used instead of the compensation required because the former is the conservative choice" (U.S. NOAA Panel, 1993, p. 4608), has little justification. The reported differences of WTA values, from two to five or more times WTP measures, are too large to defend this practice on grounds of prudence. Further, the implications of the differences in valuations of gains and losses extend far beyond formal analyses of costs and benefits, present values of future outcomes, and the like. They also importantly include the way in which issues and problems are thought about and discussed – the habit of mind that can so greatly influence social judgments and policy proposals. Contemplating the negative consequences of a proposed action or policy in terms not of how much individuals would pay to avoid them, but in terms of how much compensation would be required for them to accept the losses, is likely to evoke quite different and more behaviorally accurate feelings and responses.

The current practice of using the WTP measure, rather than the appropriate WTA measure, for losses and for reductions of losses will in most cases give rise to systematic understatements of their value. This will lead to undue encouragement of activities with negative impacts such as pollution and risks to health and safety, as such losses will be underweighed. Similarly, compensation and damage awards may be too small to provide proper restitution and deterrence; and inappropriately lax standards of protection against injuries will be set, as assessments of added costs of further harm will be heavily biased. Too few resources will be devoted to avoiding environmental and other forms of community deterioration, as the efficiency of alternative allocations will be biased against avoiding losses, and full accounting and appropriate pricing of resources with nonpecuniary value, such as environmental amenities, will be frustrated.

A further illustrative example of a likely bias toward inefficient policies resulting from a failure to take a more realistic account of people's preferences is the frequently recommended choice of compensation payments over mitigation measures as a preferred remedy for harms. This preference stems from the usual economic assumption that presumes that people favor receiving money over efforts to reduce the impacts of the injury because a money award permits injured parties to substitute other goods for the loss, whereas mitigation measures restrict their remedy to reducing the particular injury. This reasoning turns on the well-known textbook presumption that a monetary award will yield greater welfare gains than an equal sum in the form of a particular good; the usual demonstration allegedly shows the superiority of money over housing allowances or food vouchers.

The finding of losses being valued more than gains points to the possibility that mitigation, rather than being an inferior choice, may be a preferred option. This arises because mitigation actions might be valued more as they reduce losses and compensation awards might be heavily discounted by people as they fall in the domain of gains. Further, findings of what people regard as fair and unfair suggest that tying a relief action to the injury, as with the acceptance of passing on directly related costs in the form of price increases (Kahneman, Knetsch & Thaler, 1986), increases the acceptability of the mitigation remedy. The limited available empirical evidence is consistent with this view of preferences for mitigation measures (Knetsch, 1990).

In much the same way that people often prefer mitigation measures to monetary compensation for an injury, they also commonly want funds collected as user fees or other special-purpose levies used for a purpose related to the levy, rather than have such monies put into general or consolidated revenue accounts. The use of such dedicated funds, or *earmarking* of funds, is widely denounced in public finance texts and handbooks, and is frequently discouraged by official policies on roughly the same grounds as favoring compensation over mitigation, the alleged greater efficiency of putting the money into central coffers to be used for whatever purpose is judged most valuable rather than directed to a single, possibly less valued, purpose.

The valuation disparity can, however, give rise to net gains from the use of some forms of dedicated funds. Feelings of loss may be reduced if the funds are seen to be spent for actions related to the purpose for which the money was taken. Park entry fees, for example, are usually far more acceptable to park users if they know the money will go to the maintenance and improvement of the park rather than to general government revenue accounts. Similarly, pollution charges and probably even carbon taxes might be more acceptable if the resulting revenues were allocated to environmental purposes rather than to government support, lower taxes, or even international redistribution efforts.

The disparity between gain and loss values also has implications for the operations of markets, and consequently for policies aimed at facilitating or controlling such exchanges. If people's WTA values were equal to their WTP values, if buy prices were equal to sell prices for each individual, then costless market exchanges would be expected to exhaust all gains from trade and shift entitlements to those individuals willing to pay the most for them. However, a consequence of the valuation disparity is that the sell prices will generally be much higher than the buy prices of individuals, thereby reducing the possible gains available from exchanges. The smaller gains will result in smaller numbers of Pareto-efficient trades that would take place even in costless markets. Also, the final allocations will not be independent of the initial entitlements and, depending on the original distributions of these entitlements, market exchanges will likely not shift goods to those willing to pay the most for them.

Limited simulation tests using real buy and sell values of individuals show that when these actual preferences are taken into account, not only will final allocations vary, depending on initial assignments of entitlements, but the magnitude of possible gains that can be realized from voluntary exchanges are perhaps less than half of the gains that are assumed to be available with the traditional assumption of valuation. The number of trades that will take place in such markets is less than half of the number that would be expected with traditional assumptions; and completion of all possible Pareto-efficient exchanges fails by a wide margin to shift entitlements to those willing to pay the most for them (Borges & Knetsch, 1998).

These findings suggest that the disparity may be a significant cause of market stickiness, which is independent of transaction costs. They also indicate that the shortfalls from traditionally assumed trade numbers and gains may not be trivial. They should also give further pause to assertions of the irrelevance of initial distributions of exchangeable entitlements, such as pollution rights, fishing quotas, broadcast licenses, and other resource permits, and to predictions of the number of expected trades and the likely gains from their exchange.

The commonplace nature of the greater valuation of losses is evident in most editions of daily newspapers. The anguish of job losses and disruptions to people's lives command far more attention than the gains others receive. And although they further motivate special pleadings, they also signal a legitimate policy concern.

Time Preferences

The disparity between people's valuations of gains and losses is also a major contributing factor to the pattern of time preferences that are frequently observed – patterns that again differ substantially from those assumed in traditional economic and policy analyses. And to the extent that future outcomes are valued differently than is commonly assumed, this has significant implications for policy analysis and for the design of acceptable and effective institutions to deal with gains and losses accruing in differing time periods.

The economic and policy model of any standard textbook assumes that people adjust their varying intertemporal preferences for present and future outcomes to a market interest rate through borrowing and saving. Consequently, the rate of time preference between the present and future will be the same for all individuals at the margin. In the absence of transaction costs, risks, and other such considerations, the trade-off between a dollar of present consumption and a dollar of future consumption will, for example, be given by the risk-free market interest rate. This is analogous to the assumption that all consumers will adjust their consumption patterns to market prices so that the marginal value of another unit of any good will be the same for all individuals and will be given by its relative price.

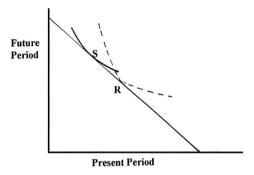

Figure 4.3. Traditional two-period model of intertemporal choice.

The traditional model of people's intertemporal choices – commonly used for purposes of explanation, prediction, and policy design – is usually considered in terms of individuals making trade-offs between present and future consumption or income. This two-period model is illustrated by an opportunity or cost line connecting the possible income distributions in the two periods and smooth indifference curves indicating relative preferences of different allocations of income between the two periods, as in Figure 4.3. Given the expected income in each of the periods before any borrowing or lending, represented by point R, all other possible distributions of income between the two periods available through borrowing and lending are given by the cost/opportunity line through R that reflects the rate of interest; a steeper slope indicates higher rates that reward savings by yielding larger future income and penalize borrowing by taking more from present income. The preferred position is indicated by the tangency with the indifference curve (indicating all equally valued combinations of present and future income), in this case point S, indicating that at this interest rate this individual would give up some present income to enjoy a larger future income; the opposite would be suggested by a tangency below the initial reference state R.

With given intertemporal preferences, borrowing and saving or investment decisions are usually taken to be very largely functions of the prevailing rates of interest or return. The initial, or reference point R, is given no particular status or standing over any other point along the cost curve – except that if there are any differences in borrowing and savings rates facing the individual, it would then be the point of a kink in the cost curve reflecting such differences.

The disparity between gains and losses – the reference effect – suggests, however, that reference states may play a very large and additional role in intertemporal choices. For example, the expected incomes over the present and future period, given by point R in Figure 4.3, might well be taken as a reference state from which changes are weighed as gains or losses to and from this point. Saving may then be viewed as giving up present income – a loss – in order to obtain a larger future income – a gain. In terms of Figure 4.2, this is a Quadrant I "purchase" option for which people can be expected to be willing to pay less money to secure the gain – as in the case of people paying less to gain mugs in Figure 4.2 – implying the need for a high rate of return to induce saving. Given the same reference state, borrowing may then be viewed as losing a portion of the reference future income in order to obtain more present income, a Quadrant III "sell" option for which people can be expected to demand a larger present gain to make up for the future loss – implying that borrowing would be viewed favorably only at low interest rates.

The expected difference in the implied rates of time preference between gains now and losses in the future, or the reverse – Quadrant I or Quadrant III – also has implications for the measure used to weigh the value of future gains and future losses in policy analyses. An individual's rate of discount for the same entitlement change over the same time period can be expected to differ greatly, depending on the nature of the change relative to the reference state – a difference evident, for example, in the finding that a group of high school students required compensation of $1.09 to delay the use of a $7 gift certificate by seven weeks but were willing to pay only $0.52 to speed up its use by the same amount of time (Loewenstein, 1988). The choice of which measure should be used for valuing any particular future outcome is not a matter of convenience or indifference. Instead, it is one that is consistent with the valuation of all entitlements. Just as the value of an immediate gain is the maximum amount a person would pay now to receive it, the present value of a future gain is appropriately measured by the maximum sum the individual would sacrifice now to receive an entitlement to the future benefit – the WTP measure. Similarly, just as the value of a current loss is correctly measured by the minimum compensation demanded to accept the adverse outcome, the present value of a future loss is the compensation that would leave the individual as well off as without the change – the WTA measure.

The different measures are likely to reflect different rates of time preference. For example, one half of a group of undergraduate students were asked for "the largest sum of money you would pay today to receive $20 a year from now," and the other half of the respondents were asked for "the smallest sum of money you would accept today to give up receiving $20 a year from now." The rate used to discount the future gain was, on average, about three times higher than the rate used to discount the future loss. Because of such expected differences, the distinction between measures has the important implication of a likely need to depart from the conventional practice of using a single rate to discount all future outcomes attributable to a program or project. Instead, it may be reasonable and efficient to assess future gains by what people are willing to pay now to receive future benefits, which itself may vary with the length of delay and other characteristics of the gain, and assess future costs using a likely lower rate reflecting what people demand now to accept a future loss (Harvey, 1994).

The expected greater weight accorded losses over commensurate gains might also be expected to lead to both a reluctance to save and a similar reluctance to borrow. This is illustrated by the kinked intertemporal preference indifference curve centered on point R of Figure 4.3. Given such a kink, an individual might well be expected to both not borrow and not save over perhaps a wide range of interest rates, even in the absence of transactions costs. Such insensitivity of individuals' borrowing and savings behavior to interest rates appears consistent with widely observed behavior indicating that the level of interest rates is less important – "Most studies are unable to reject the hypothesis that the elasticity of personal saving with respect to the interest rate is zero" (Thaler, 1994, p. 186).

This does not mean that people do not borrow or save. They clearly do. However, pervasive endowment effects may well lead to far less saving and borrowing than is suggested by traditional models that ignore this characteristic of people's behavior. Further, much of the borrowing and saving that are observed may well be due to what might usefully be thought of as reference state effects. That is, many decisions that people make with respect to how much they save and borrow may be less dependent on the going rates of interest they face, and more dependent on what is institutionally or socially considered as normal or expected. These expectations will likely determine reference states, and to the extent that these will differ from ones such as point R in Figure 4.3, these shifts will be major determinants of saving and borrowing.

In many countries, the reference may well include normal or expected provision for pensions or other forms of retirement income. Devoting a fixed proportion of income to old-age security is widely seen as prudent in many societies, and this allocation then becomes the reference from which a reluctance to undertake further borrowing and saving might be observed. For large portions of savings for old age, the sums set aside out of current income are insensitive to interest rates. They are instead set by government programs, a form of forced saving, and by fixed percentage employee and employer contributions to pension schemes. Individuals can sometimes alter these proportions, but these decisions too seem largely to be made with little or no consideration of rates of return. Even contributions to various retirement funds that benefit from tax deferments appear to be based largely on contribution limits and cash available to households rather than on interest rate considerations – shifts in reference states more than responding to changing slopes of cost curves. And such contributions tend to be strongly habitual, with contributions in one year following ones made in preceding years, again consistent with a reference consideration rather than one dependent on shifting rates of return.

Similarly, borrowing decisions may be motivated by shifts in reference positions. A likely example is a reference that includes provision for home mortgages. Given that people normally finance home purchases out of future income, the resulting allocation of income across periods is then likely seen as the expected arrangement, and this becomes the reference from which the value of gain and loss movements in either direction is judged. Such a shift appears analogous to the finding that people typically frame payments of insurance premiums differently from most other expenditures, because insurance is considered an expected and prudent monetary outlay rather than a loss, and therefore consider other gains and losses from a reference point that incorporates this cost (Slovic, Fischhoff, & Lichtenstein, 1982).

The location of the reference point may also be a significant policy variable – in contrast to the view that the rate of return is the only policy lever influencing consumer decisions. For example, to the extent that pension schemes can be implemented in ways that people view such intertemporal reallocations as desirable self-control mechanisms, they may be expected to be viewed as shifts in reference positions rather than as losses of present income to gain future income. Another example is provided by the British Columbia, Canada, property tax deferment program, by which homeowners 60 years of age and older have this local tax paid by the provincial government, to be repaid, at a very favorable rate of interest, when the house is eventually sold by the owner or by the estate. Yet although this program is widely known, and offers a cash flow supplement to owners and a financially attractive opportunity, fewer than 3% of eligible home owners participate. The reason for this extremely low rate is widely known to be the reluctance to take on debt – to gain current income but lose a future return. A possible way to increase the participation rate might be to change the repayment responsibility from the seller, or estate, to the eventual buyer[6] – a policy manipulation that is unlikely to change the actual incidence of the future liability, but would likely change the reference position of many owners.

The incorporation of some forms of saving and borrowing into reference states suggests that saving and borrowing decisions can be influenced in a variety of ways that induce changes in reference positions. This may well turn on people's viewing intertemporal financial arrangements as prudent, expected, or acceptable. To the extent that purchases of consumer durables, for example, are successfully framed as normally and acceptably financed by borrowing against future income, this may induce a change in purchasing and borrowing for such purposes. In analogous ways, decisions can also be influenced by differentiating between lump-sum and periodic payments. Similarly, by reframing changes in asset holdings as rearrangements of current and future asset yields rather than losses and gains, a reverse mortgage might be more favorably viewed as an arrangement to provide a present and future stream of income rather than one of losing equity for a present gain.

Reference states and shifts in reference positions might provide strong motivations in savings and lending decisions that are largely independent of interest rates and transactions costs. Although interest rates, transactions costs, perceptions of risk, and capital market imperfections are no doubt important factors, they have been the nearly exclusive focus of attention in explaining saving and borrowing decisions. Recognition of the likely impact of the reference effect appears to provide further explanatory variables that may be useful in understanding observed behavior, predicting the impact of changes, and designing better financial instruments.

In addition, the influence of the reference effect on rates of time preferences can be of substantial importance in creating socially beneficial policy alternatives. It can also be important in designing more appropriate policy instruments to deal with such issues as mitigation of long-term environmental change, future tax liabilities, and arrangements for old-age security.

Valuations and the Stability of Preferences

Although it seems clear that people's valuations of present and future outcomes will likely vary with the nature of the gain and loss at issue, as per the quadrants of Figure 4.2, the available evidence also suggests that there is likely to be substantial variation among values nominally within the same class. For example, receiving a future benefit, postponing a future loss, and speeding up a future gain may all be future benefits the present value of which is measured by people's willingness to pay now for the future outcome. But it seems unlikely that an individual would express the same rate of time preference for all three opportunities even in the absence of any other difference in the arrangements.

Although nominally equivalent, and treated so in most policy analyses, people's judgments and decisions may often differ, depending on the framing or the context of an option. For example, judgments of the relative attractiveness of a series of gambles were found to be much more sensitive to differences in the probability of winning than to the size of the payoffs, in spite of the quite obvious equivalence in determining their expected values (Slovic & Lichtenstein, 1968). Also, many preference reversals have been demonstrated in which people prefer some good A over another good B when offered a choice between them, but indicate that they value B more than A when evaluated separately. For example, 83% of subjects in one experimental study chose to receive $2,500 in 5 years rather than receive $3,550 in 10 years; but only 29% expressed the same preference when asked in separate questions how much compensation they would require to give up each of these payments (Tversky, Slovic, & Kahneman, 1990). Similar changes, or instabilities, in preferences take place when goods or outcomes vary in what may be thought of as their evaluability: A large music dictionary with a torn cover was given a lower valuation when the lack of a comparative dictionary focused attention on the defective cover, but its large number of entries was brought to prominence and resulted in a higher valuation when an alternative smaller dictionary was also offered (Hsee, 1996). Another example, which also illustrates how different attributes of an outcome can have unexpected impacts, concerns medical patients ascribing greater discomfort to a shorter unpleasant medical procedure than to a longer one that includes the shorter procedure plus an added final segment at a reduced level of discomfort; the preference for more pain over less was due to lack of sensitivity to the length of the procedure and the importance of a less unpleasant ending (Kahneman, Wakker, & Sarin, 1997). These are but examples of many that have been reported in recent years, demonstrating that many preferences "... are remarkably labile, sensitive to the way a choice problem is described or 'framed' and to the mode of response used to express the preference" (Slovic, 1995, p. 365).

The traditional view that individuals hold specific stable preferences that they reveal through their behavior seems increasingly at odds with the evidence. The latter seems more in accord with the notion that many judgments and valuations vary widely with differing contexts and, especially in some instances, are more realistically constructed or "assembled" during the decision process than revealed by it (Payne, Bettman, & Johnson, 1992; Slovic, 1995). People's preferences may be less well defined and consequently malleable to context, description, transaction procedure, and means of assessment. Although direct evidence is scanty, this lack of well-defined and stable preferences might be less characteristic of common routinely purchased goods and more so with public goods and policy alternatives (Payne, Bettman, & Schkade, 1999).

Many judgments appear to be made on the basis of attitudes or valuations that are sensitive to the salience of particular attributes, and this sensitivity may not correspond to the traditional view of the contribution of these attitudes to their value. For example, the size or quantity dimension of an entitlement plays an important role in determining its economic value – more of a good is worth more than less. Yet in many cases people's attitude about a change of entitlements, which motivates their response, is fairly insensitive to this characteristic (Kahneman, Ritov, & Schkade, 1999). A program that saves smaller areas of a wildlife habitat, for example, may be considered nearly the equal of one that saves much larger areas – people's focus of attention being on the benefit of saving habitat to the near exclusion of how much is being saved. In the case of the reference effect, individuals appear to focus largely on the gain or loss characteristic causing this attribute to greatly influence the value people place on the good – a mug, or whatever, is more valuable when it is given up than when one anticipates its acquisition. In a similar way, perceptions of dread and anticipation may largely undo any symmetry between the benefits of moving a gain closer to the present and a loss further into the future.

Although much is known about judgments and decisions and the role of context and attitudes, little has been applied to questions of policy. The evidence suggests that well-known anomalies, preference reversals, varying sensitivities to the characteristics of an outcome, and the weaknesses of jury conclusions and contingent valuations might be more explicable with some relaxation of the conventional stable preference assumption (Sunstein, Kahneman, & Schkade, 1998). A better understanding of preferences and preference formation could contribute greatly to more productive policy analysis and design.

Conclusions

The results of a vast array of tests have provided consistent evidence that people value losses more than commensurate gains and use widely varying rates to discount different kinds of future outcomes. The implications for economic and policy analysis appear substantial, and a more accurate accounting of people's behavior gives promise of much improved designs of policy instruments.

Given the pervasive presence and size of the reference effect and its commensurate impact on different measures of change and on people's time discount rates, the decision of which measure to use for specific applications becomes an important practical issue. If there were little or no difference in the value of gains and losses, there would then be little or no difference in the assessment of gains and losses or of time preference rates that would result from alternative measures, and, as a practical matter, little or no reason for favoring one measure over another. However, this appears not to be the case: The differences are large, and the wrong choice of measure can therefore seriously mislead.

Behavioral findings can provide useful insights into policy analysis and design, as they have for economics, finance, law, and the decision sciences generally (Jolls, Sunstein, & Thaler, 1998). The discussion here has centered on gains, losses, and future outcomes; however, these are but indicative of the implications of a wider array of behavioral insights (Rabin, 1998). The evidence further suggests that search energies could now usefully be employed in both expanding our understandings and finding further applications of what is known.

Notes

1 They are equivalent except for an income or wealth effect, which is normally demonstrably very small and commonly is taken to be of little or no consequence.

2 There is a curious result of a low correlation (of about 0.30) between the WTP and WTA bids and offers of the participants in this experiment, which also appears in the results of other within-subject disparity studies (Borges & Knetsch, 1998). These low correlations suggest that individuals' WTP valuations may not be very closely related to their WTA valuations.

3 Daniel Kahneman suggested this illustrative scheme in joint work on preliminary analyses of early endowment effect findings.

4 Although this valuation was not included in the mug experiment, a reasonable prediction based on the ratios of the Quadrant II to the Quadrant I values and the Quadrant III to the Quadrant II values would be around $4.

5 This issue is discussed in, for example, Laibson and Zeckhauser (1998) and Sunstein (1998).

6 This was originally suggested in a private discussion of the issue by John Chant.

References

Bazerman, M. (1998). *Judgment in managerial decision making*. New York: Wiley.

Borges, B. F. J., & Knetsch, J. L. (1998). Tests of market outcomes with asymmetric valuations of gains and losses: Smaller gains, fewer trades, and less value. *Journal of Economic Behavior and Organization, 33*, 185–193.

Chapman, G. B. (1996). Expectations and preferences for sequences of health and money. *Organizational Behavior and Human Decision Processes, 67*, 59–75.

Cohen, D., & Knetsch, J. L. (1992). Judicial choice and disparities between measures of economic values. *Osgoode Hall Law Journal, 30*, 737–770.

Cropper, M. L., Aydede, S. K., & Portney, P. R. (1994). Preferences for life saving programs: How the public discounts time and age. *Journal of Risk and Uncertainty, 8*, 243–265.

Diamond, P. A., Hausman, J. A., Leonard, K. L., & Denning, M. A. (1993). Does contingent valuation measure preferences? Experimental evidence. In J. Hausman (Ed.), *Contingent valuation: A critical assessment* (pp. 41–90). Amsterdam: Elsevier Science.

Gregory, R., Lichtenstein, S., & MacGregor, D. (1993). The role of past states in determining reference points for policy decisions. *Organizational Behavior and Human Decision Processes, 55*, 195–206.

Hammack, J., & Brown, G. M., Jr. (1974). *Waterfowl and wetlands: Toward bio-economic analysis*. Baltimore: Johns Hopkins University Press.

Harvey, C. M. (1994). The reasonableness of non-constant discounting. *Journal of Public Economics, 53*, 31–51.

Henderson, A. M. (1941). Consumer's surplus and the compensation variation. *Review of Economic Studies, 8*, 117–121.

Hsee, C. M. (1996). The evaluability hypothesis: An explanation for preference reversals between joint and separate evaluations of alternatives. *Organizational Behavior and Human Decision Processes, 67*, 242–257.

Johnson, E. J., Hershey, J., Meszaros, J., & Kunreuther, H. (1993). Framing probability distortions and insurance decisions. *Journal of Risk and Uncertainty, 7,* 35–51.

Jolls, C., Sunstein, C. R., & Thaler, R. H. (1998). A behavioral approach to law and economics. *Stanford Law Review, 50,* 1471–1550.

Kachelmeier, S. J., & Shehata, M. (1992). Examining risk preferences under high monetary incentives: Experimental evidence from the People's Republic of China. *American Economic Review, 82,* 1120–1140.

Kahneman, D., Knetsch, J. L., & Thaler, R. H. (1986). Fairness as a constraint on profit seeking: Entitlements in the market. *American Economic Review, 76,* 728–741.

Kahneman, D., Knetsch, J. L., & Thaler, R. H. (1990). Experimental tests of the endowment effect and the Coase theorem. *Journal of Political Economy, 98,* 1325–1348.

Kahneman, D., Knetsch, J. L., & Thaler, R. H. (1991). The endowment effect, loss aversion, and status quo bias. *Journal of Economic Perspectives, 5,* 193–206.

Kahneman, D., & Miller, D. T. (1986). Norm theory: Comparing reality to its alternatives. *Psychological Review, 93,* 136–153.

Kahneman, D., Ritov, I., & Schkade, D. (1999). Economic preferences or attitude expressions?: An analysis of dollar responses to public issues. *Journal of Risk and Uncertainty, 19,* 220–242.

Kahneman, D., & Tversky, A. (1979). Prospect theory: An analysis of decisions under risk. *Econometrica, 47,* 263–291.

Kahneman, D., Wakker, P. P., & Sarin, R. (1997). Back to Bentham?: Explorations of experienced utility. *Quarterly Journal of Economics, 112,* 375–405.

Knetsch, J. L. (1990). Environmental policy implications of disparities between willingness to pay and compensation demanded measures of value. *Journal of Environmental Economics and Management, 18,* 227–237.

Knetsch, J. L. (1997). Reference states, fairness, and choice of measure to value environmental changes. In M. Bazerman, D. Messick, A. Tenbrunsel, & K. Wade-Benzoni (Eds.), *Environment, ethics, and behavior* (pp. 13–32). San Francisco: Lexington Press.

Knetsch, J. L., & Sinden, J. A. (1984). Willingness to pay and compensation demanded: Experimental evidence of an unexpected disparity in measures of value. *Quarterly Journal of Economics, 99,* 507–521.

Knetsch, J. L., Tang, F. F., & Thaler, R. H. (1999). *The endowment effect and repeated market trials: Is the Vickrey auction demand revealing?* Working paper, University of Chicago.

Laibson, D., & Zeckhauser, R. (1998). Amos Tversky and the ascent of behavioral economics. *Journal of Risk and Uncertainty, 16,* 7–47.

Loewenstein, G. F. (1988). Frames of mind in intertemporal choice. *Management Science, 34,* 200–214.

Michelman, F. I. (1967). Property, utility and fairness: Comments on the ethical foundation of just compensation law. *Harvard Law Review, 80,* 1165–1258.

Odean, T. (1998). Are investors reluctant to realize their losses? *Journal of Finance, 53,* 1775–1798.

Payne, J. W., Bettman, J. R., & Johnson, E. (1992). Behavioral decision research: A constructive processing perspective. *Annual Review of Psychology, 43,* 87–132.

Payne, J. W., Bettman, J. R., & Schkade, D. A. (1999). Measuring constructed preferences: Towards a building code. *Journal of Risk and Uncertainty, 19,* 243–271.

Pildes, R. H., & Sunstein, C. R. (1995). Reinventing the regulatory state. *University of Chicago Law Review, 62,* 1–129.

Rabin, M. (1998). Psychology and economics. *Journal of Economic Literature, 36,* 11–46.

Shefrin, H., & Statman, M. (1985). The disposition to sell winners too early and ride losers too long: Theory and evidence. *Journal of Finance, 40,* 777–790.

Slovic, P. (1995). The construction of preference. *American Psychologist, 50,* 364–371.

Slovic, P., Fischhoff, B., & Lichtenstein, S. (1982). Response mode, framing and information processing effects in risk assessment. In R. M. Hogarth (Ed.), *New directions for methodology of social and behavioral science: Question framing and response consistency* (pp. 21–36). San Francisco: Jossey-Bass.

Slovic, P., & Lichtenstein, S. (1968). Relative importance of probabilities and payoffs in risk taking. *Journal of Experimental Psychology Monographs, 78*(3, pt. 2).

Sunstein, C. R. (1993). Endogenous preferences, environmental law. *Journal of Legal Studies, 22,* 217–254.

Sunstein, C. R. (1998). Selective fatalism. *Journal of Legal Studies, 27,* 799–823.

Sunstein, C. R., Kahneman, D., & Schkade, D. (1998). Assessing punitive damages (with notes on cognition and valuation in law). *Yale Law Journal, 107,* 2071–2153.

Thaler, R. H. (1994). Psychology and savings policies. *American Economic Review (Papers and Proceedings), 84,* 186–192.

Tversky, A., Slovic, P., & Kahneman, D. (1990). The causes of preference reversal. *American Economic Review, 80,* 204–217.

U.S. NOAA Panel. (1993). Report of the NOAA panel on contingent valuation. *U.S. Federal Register, 58,* 4602–4614.

5   Comparing Micro and Macro Rationality

Robert J. MacCoun

Are people rational economic actors? Perhaps to a very rough first approximation, but not as a rule because the algorithms of rational choice don't describe how we actually make judgments and decisions. We are rarely irrational in a random, erratic sense. Rather, most of us manage to cope reasonably well most of the time, using a variety of "cold" cognitive processes (the psychophysics of perception, the associative nature of memory, our finite attention span) and "hot" cognitive processes (the effects of motivation and emotion) that can easily lead us astray in situations that are complex, or are simple but subtly different from the norm. As the chapters in this book attest, these psychological biases have potentially profound implications for economic theory and policy.

But what if various aggregate-level processes (group discussion, market transactions, the social diffusion of ideas) attenuate or compensate for these individual-level biases, as many critics contend (e.g., Kagel & Roth, 1995; Page & Shapiro, 1992)? If so, individual failures of rationality would tell us little about aggregate or collective rationality – about mass markets, public opinion trends, voting behavior, social movements, fashion, crowd behavior, congressional decision making, jury verdicts, and so on. Even seemingly individual decisions of considerable import – for example, presidential decisions – are usually made after much consultation with advisors, committees, and increasingly, data from polls and focus groups.

Recent experiments by social psychologists and experimental economists have begun to examine whether interaction with others attenuates individual biases, sustains them, or amplifies them. Are groups more or less biased than individuals? Unfortunately, no simple conclusion has emerged from this research (see reviews by Kerr, MacCoun, & Kramer, 1996a; Tindale, 1993). Some studies find a clear reduction of bias at the aggregate level, whereas others find that groups are significantly more biased than individuals acting alone.

To clarify discrepant research findings, my colleagues Norb Kerr, Geoff Kramer, and I (Kerr, MacCoun, & Kramer, 1996a, 1996b) have conducted theoretical "thought" experiments that identify some of the conditions that determine *relative bias* (group bias − individual bias). Our work suggests that relative bias is a function of the type of bias, the applicable social combination process, group size, and the distribution of individual opinions prior to interaction or exposure to others. At the core of our work is a stochastic modeling approach called *social decision scheme analysis* (Davis, 1973; Stasser, Kerr, & Davis, 1980).

Social Decision Scheme (SDS) Modeling

The social decision scheme approach (Davis, 1973; Stasser et al., 1980) models group decisions as a product of two different processes, a sampling process and a social combination process. The sampling process models the likelihood of groups starting with various initial distributions of opinion; the social combination process models the likelihood of each possible decision for each possible starting point.

Sampling Process

Following Davis (1973), let:

$n \equiv$ number of decision alternatives/response options ($a_1, a_2, \ldots a_j, \ldots a_n$);

$r \equiv$ number of group members (i.e., r_j is the number of members supporting alternative j); and

$p \equiv (p_1, p_2, \ldots p_n) =$ distribution of individual decisions across n alternatives.

The number of possible distributions of the r group members across the n alternatives is then

$$m = \binom{n+r-1}{r} = \frac{(n+r-1)!}{r!(n-1)!} \tag{1}$$

If the groups are composed randomly (an assumption I relax later in this chapter), then it follows from the multinomial distribution that the probability that the group will begin deliberation with the ith possible distribution, $(r_{i1}, r_{i2}, \ldots r_{in})$, is

$$
\begin{aligned}
\pi_i &= \begin{pmatrix} r \\ r_{i1}r_{i2}\ldots r_{in} \end{pmatrix} p_1^{r_{i1}} p_2^{r_{i2}} \cdots p_n^{r_{in}} \\
&= \left[\frac{r!}{(r_{i1}!r_{i2}!\ldots r_{in}!)} \right] p_1^{r_{i1}} p_2^{r_{i2}} \cdots p_n^{r_{in}}
\end{aligned}
\tag{2}
$$

Decision Process

The key theoretical component of the SDS approach is the *social decision scheme*, D, an $m \times n$ transition matrix, where element d_{ij} specifies the probability that a group beginning deliberation with the ith possible distribution of member preference will ultimately choose the jth decision alternative. These D's are frequently misunderstood to represent formal or explicit voting or decision rules, perhaps because many have labels like "simple majority scheme." In actuality, these matrices simply summarize the net effect of all the many cognitive, sociopolitical, procedural, and coordinational processes (see Kerr et al., 1996a) that combine to integrate the judgments of individual members into a group decision – processes that may not even be recognized by the group members. SDS modeling is a useful theoretical framework – an "environment" for thinking through the consequences of alternative theoretical processes – rather than a specific theory per se (see Stasser et al., 1980).

Table 5.1 presents five D's that have been shown to have either broad empirical support in particular task domains (e.g., Simple Majority, Truth Supported Wins, Reasonable Doubt) or utility as theoretical baselines (Proportionality, Truth Wins) (see Stasser et al., 1980). The table assumes a particular example, a six-person jury trial with two verdict options, Guilty (G) and Not Guilty (NG).

Proportionality Scheme

This scheme reproduces exactly at the group level what was observed at the individual level, providing a useful "asocial" theoretical baseline. The probability of a particular faction prevailing is equal to the relative frequency of that faction; that is, $d_{ij} = r_{jj}/r_i$. A faction with half of the members will prevail half of the time; a faction with a third of the members will prevail a third of the time. Hence, in this scheme, factions are no more or less than the number of their members.

Table 5.1. *Selected Social Decision Schemes*

Initial Split		Proportionality		Simple Majority		Truth Wins[a]		Truth-Supported Wins		Reasonable Doubt[b]	
G	NG	G	NG	G	NG	G	NG	G	NG	G	NG
6	0	1.00	0.00	1.00	0.00	1.00	0.00	1.00	0.00	1.00	0.00
5	1	0.83	0.17	1.00	0.00	0.00	1.00	1.00	0.00	1.00	0.00
4	2	0.66	0.33	1.00	0.00	0.00	1.00	0.00	1.00	0.67	0.33
3	3	0.50	0.50	0.50	0.50	0.00	1.00	0.00	1.00	0.19	0.81
2	4	0.33	0.66	0.00	1.00	0.00	1.00	0.00	1.00	0.06	0.94
1	5	0.17	0.83	0.00	1.00	0.00	1.00	0.00	1.00	0.00	1.00
0	6	0.00	1.00	0.00	1.00	0.00	1.00	0.00	1.00	0.00	1.00

[a] In this instance, alternative NG is the true response.
[b] The 4:2, 3:3, and 2:4 entries are taken from meta-analysis in MacCoun and Kerr (1988); the 5:1 and 1:5 entries are taken from Kerr and MacCoun (1985).

Simple Majority Scheme

This is one representative of a family of D's in which there is disproportionate "strength in numbers." Formally, if MC = a majority criterion, then for $r_{ij} >$ MC, $d_{ij} > r_{ij}/r$. In the Simple Majority D, MC = .5, and the alternative favored by more than half of the members will be selected as the group decision; that is, if $r_{ij}/r_i > .50$, then $d_{ij} = 1.0$; if $r_{ij}/r_i < .50$, then $d_{ij} = 0.0$. (Majority D's require a subscheme to handle ties where r is an even number; here I assume equiprobability in the case of a tie.) Thus, a majority faction is more than the sum of its member votes because the minority faction is less than the sum of its member votes – minority members "cave in" to the majority. The simple majority scheme or slight variants have been shown to do a good job of summarizing group judgments in a very broad array of decision tasks, settings, and populations, particularly in judgmental situations where there is no normative algorithm for defining or deriving a correct answer.

Truth Wins Scheme

This is one of a large class of schemes in which factions favoring one particular alternative have greater drawing power. In this particular scheme, if $r_{iT} > 1$, then $d_{iT} = 1.0$; otherwise, $d_{ij} = r_{ij}/r_j$. (In Table 5.1, I assume that for the task in question, NG is the correct verdict. Note, however, that the same logic might apply to a *Bias Wins* scheme, in which NG is the incorrect verdict.) The Truth Wins scheme is of special interest because it depicts the optimal case in which there is a normatively correct decision and the group selects it so long as at least one member finds it.

Truth-Supported Wins Scheme

Empirically, the Truth Wins model does a poor job of describing actual group behavior, even in tasks with a demonstrably correct answer according to a broadly shared normative framework (e.g., deductive logic). At best, *Truth-Supported Wins* – that is, the member finding the solution needs at least some initial social support or the group will often fail to adopt the correct solution; specifically, if $r_{iT} > 2$, then $d_{iT} = 1.0$; otherwise, $d_{ij} = r_{ij}/r_j$. In this model, truth-finding is a social process. Solving a problem is rarely sufficient; you need to convince others of your solution. The history of science is replete with examples of solutions that went unnoticed for decades (e.g., Bayes's theorem, Mendel's genetics). Empirical evidence on group performance tends to fall somewhere between the Simple Majority scheme (in more purely judgmental tasks) and the Truth-Supported wins scheme (in tasks with a mathematical, logical, or algorithmic solution) (see Laughlin, 1996; Stasser et al., 1980).

Reasonable Doubt Scheme

The final example in Table 5.1 is another asymmetrical scheme. This one was not derived theoretically but rather estimated empirically from a meta-analysis of about a dozen experimental studies of criminal mock juries (MacCoun & Kerr, 1988). The scheme shows that in criminal juries, there is an asymmetry such that, ceteris paribus, 50:50 splits generally result in an acquittal, and two-thirds majorities favoring acquittal tend to fare better than two-thirds majorities favoring conviction. MacCoun and Kerr (1988) present evidence that this asymmetry reflects the rhetorical advantages provided by the reasonable doubt standard of proof in criminal trials.

How do these decision schemes translate the initial distribution of opinions into a final group decision? The probability of group outcome j is

$$P_j = \Sigma \pi_i d_{ij}, \text{ or in matrix notation, } P = \pi D \tag{3}$$

where $\pi = (\pi_1, \pi_2, \ldots \pi_m) =$ the distribution of starting points for group

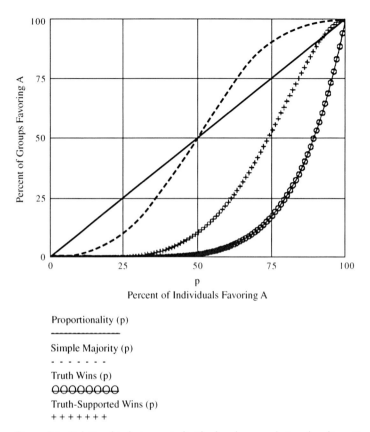

Figure 5.1. Relationship between individual and group choices for alternative social decision schemes.

deliberation, and $P = (P_1, P_2, \ldots P_n) =$ the distribution of group decisions across the n alternatives. Figure 5.1 shows the relationship between p (the probability that an individual will favor option G – in this case, wrongly convicting an innocent defendant) – and P (the probability that the group will select option G) for four of the six decision schemes. The proportionality scheme produces a 45-degree baseline against which to compare the disproportionate strength in numbers of the Simple Majority and the asymmetrical drawing power of the NG option in the Truth Wins and Truth Supported Wins schemes.

Comparing Judgmental Biases in Individual and Groups

When will groups be more, less, or equally biased as individuals? Norb Kerr, Geoff Kramer, and I used the basic SDS framework to analyze the implications of various theoretically interesting or empirically well-validated D's for this question. Our approach is fairly complex and can only be summarized here (see Kerr et al., 1996a, 1996b).

The family of biases I examine here are *sins of commission* (what Hastie and Rasinski, 1988, call "using a bad cue"), where exposure to some information influences judgment, despite the fact that a relevant normative model (e.g., logic, probability theory, a legal rule of evidence) would treat that information as irrelevant or inappropriate.[1] Examples include effects of decision framing (e.g., describing the same situation in terms of relative gains vs. relative losses; Kahneman & Tversky, 1984), preference reversals (e.g., choosing among options vs. ranking options; Tversky, Sattath, & Slovic, 1988), and the effects of extraevidentiary information that is clearly irrelevant (e.g., an automobile-theft defendant's physical attractiveness; MacCoun, 1990).

Note that we are discussing bias, not noise (random error). It is trivially true that, thanks to the law of large numbers, statistical aggregation will tend to cancel out random errors in individual judgment. Aggregation will also largely (but not always completely) cancel out *heterogeneous biases* – idiosyncratic biases that are randomly or at least heterogeneously distributed in the population (see Davis, Spitzer, Nagao, & Stasser, 1978; Kerr & Huang, 1986). Examples include impulsiveness versus cautiousness, leniency versus harshness, political liberalism versus conservatism, and so on. But the present analysis focuses on *homogeneous biases* – cases where all group members are exposed to or vulnerable to the biasing stimulus, though they needn't manifest the bias equally. Most of the biases identified in the behavioral decision research tradition are of this sort; they are believed to be basic cognitive tendencies common to all or most people (including experts) – possibly for evolutionary reasons – that are readily triggered by certain types of stimuli in certain situations.

To motivate the analysis, consider a mock jury experiment in which there are $n = 2$ decision alternatives: Guilty (G) versus Not Guilty (NG). Let $p =$ the probability that any given individual will vote "guilty" either prior to or in the absence of group deliberation. Assume that we are experimentally manipulating extraevidentiary bias (e.g., exposure to pretrial publicity that misleadingly implicates the defendant) using two conditions. In the High Bias (H) condition, the biasing information (e.g., the publicity) is either present, highly salient, or otherwise extreme. In the Low Bias (L) condition, the biasing information is either absent, less salient, or at a low level. (We can ignore the specifics of the manipulation for the purpose of generality across types of bias.) Jurors are unbiased to the extent that $p_H \approx p_L$ and biased to the extent that $p_H > p_L$; the magnitude of individual bias is then

$$b = p_H - p_L, \quad \text{where} \quad |p_H - p_L| > 0 \tag{4}$$

and group bias is defined as

$$B = P_H - P_L = (\pi_H D_H - \pi_L D_L), \quad \text{where} \quad |P_H - P_L| > 0 \tag{5}$$

In the sin of commission case examined here, *relative bias* (*RB*, the degree to which groups are more or less biased than individuals) is then defined as

$$RB = B - b \tag{6}$$

In the analyses that follow, group size is held constant at 6.

Following Kerr et al. (1996a), I will use three-dimensional surface plots and their corresponding two-dimensional contour plots to depict the magnitude of *RB* at any given combination of p_H (the response tendency in the High Bias condition) and p_L (the response tendency in the Low Bias condition). These plots get rather complicated; as a guide, Figure 5.2 shows the "floor" of these plots and the *x* and *y* axis labels that

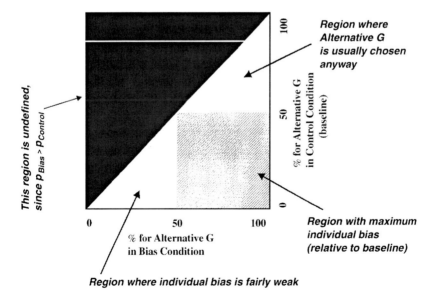

Figure 5.2. Relative bias under varying bias conditions.

apply to all subsequent plots. (Except where indicated, the vertical z axis in the surface plots depicts RB, where higher values represent greater group bias relative to individual bias.) Note that half of the parameter space is undefined; by definition, p_L can never exceed p_H.

For clarity, I have demarked three regions of the remaining space – though their properties actually vary gradually, not discretely. The lower left triangle (in white) is a region where the individual bias ($b = p_H - p_L$) favoring G is fairly weak. The upper right triangle (also in white) is a region where G would most likely be chosen anyway, even in the absense of bias – that is, there's a ceiling effect. The gray square is the region of greatest interest. This is the region of maximum individual bias; G is favored in the High Bias condition but rarely in the Low Bias condition. This diagram provides a graphical illustration of a point made by Funder (1987): A bias will not inevitably produce a mistake; it is possible to be influenced by the bias and still make the right decision or to avoid the bias and still make a blunder.

Figure 5.3 presents three pairs of surface plots and contour plots, corresponding to the Simple Majority, Truth Wins, and Truth-Supported Wins decision schemes (see Kerr et al., 1996a, for a similar analysis of groups of size 11 and a somewhat different set of decision schemes). In all the contour plots, positive numbers refer to locations where groups are more biased than individuals, and negative numbers indicate locations where groups are less biased than individuals. Not shown are the plots for the Proportionality scheme; recall that this scheme simply reproduces individual judgment probabilities at the group level; hence the surface plot is a flat plane at the $RB = 0$ level. It is helpful to imagine that plane as a baseline against which to compare the surface plots – just as the Proportionality scheme provided a 45-degree baseline in the two-dimensional plot of p-to-P in Figure 5.1.

Recall that the Simple Majority scheme and its variants are the modal empirical pattern in judgment tasks where there is no widely shared algorithm for determining correct answers. This category encompasses many, if not most, real-world judgments (purchasing decisions, voting decisions, aesthetic judgments, etc.). The most striking feature of the top panel of Figure 5.3 is that in the region of maximal individual bias, *groups generally can be expected to amplify rather than correct individual bias* (mean $RB = 4.67$). Recall from Figure 5.1 that a simple majority scheme tends to amplify majority views near the .75 (pro-G majority) and .25 (pro-NG majority) regions. In the middle region of the parameter space, High Bias groups have their pro-G majority view amplified, but Low

Simple Majority Decision Scheme:

Truth Wins Decision Scheme:

Truth Supported Wins Decision Scheme:

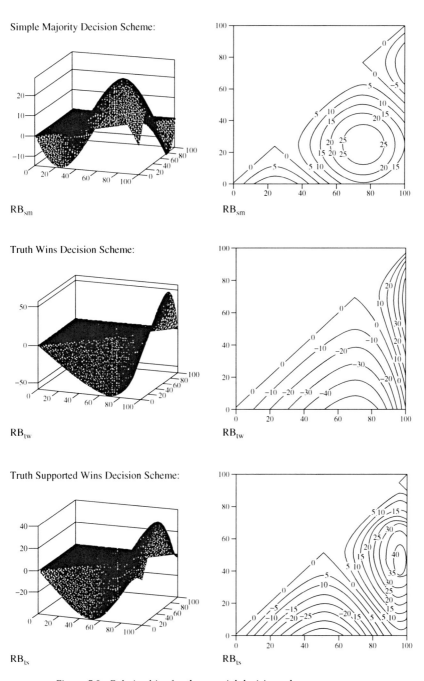

Figure 5.3. Relative bias for three social decision schemes.

Bias groups have their pro-NG majority view amplified. The net result is a striking High–Low difference.

Only in those regions where the bias is either weak or affects judgments near the ceiling can groups be expected to be less biased than individuals, so long as some form of disproportional strength in numbers process is occurring. Near the lower left corner, any pro-G bias in High Bias *groups* is washed out by the pro-NG majority amplification; *individuals* in the High Bias condition miss this correction and show the weak (around .10 to .30) bias relative to their Low Bias counterparts. Near the upper right corner, High Bias groups are near the 1.0 ceiling and experience little amplification, yet Low Bias groups are near the .75 mark and their pro-G tendency does get amplified. The net (High − Low) result is negligible *group* bias in a region where *individuals* show a small but nonzero bias. MacCoun (1990; Kerr et al. 1996a) notes that unfortunately, it is in just these regions that earlier investigators had inadvertently looked for evidence that "jury deliberation corrects juror biases"; later studies examining close cases (where the base rate was near .50) reached just the opposite conclusion. And we should take little comfort from the relative advantage of groups over individuals in these regions; arguably, these are the two regions where biases seem least likely to produce actual mistakes – that is, wrong decisions where right decisions would otherwise have been made (cf. Funder, 1987).

Happily, under a Truth Wins scheme (the middle panel of Figure 5.3), groups will be less biased than individuals under a very large range of parameter space (mean $RB = -5.83$). Only at the most extreme levels of High Bias will groups do as badly as or worse than individuals – the region where relatively few groups can be expected to have any advocates of the correct, unbiased option. Thus, when truth wins, collective judgments can indeed be expected to better approximate the rational actor of normative models. Unhappily, as noted earlier, the evidence suggests that, at best, Truth-Supported Wins, and then only for tasks where arithmetic, basic logic, or some other normative scheme is widely shared among group members (Laughlin, 1996). As seen in the lower panel of Figure 5.3, under a Truth-Supported Wins process, the region of amplified bias expands relative to the Truth Wins scheme, for groups are less likely to begin with two correct members than one correct member. The net result of this social support requirement is that unlike Truth Wins, Truth-Supported Wins generally amplifies individual biases, although the net effect is quite weak (mean $RB = 1.17$).

What If Exposure to Bias Changes the Group Process?

The examples thus far all share a key psychological assumption: Exposure to biasing information doesn't alter the processes that influence the individual-to-group transition; that is, the same D matrix applies to both High Bias and Low Bias conditions. The inputs differ across conditions, but the processes that produce the output stay the same. Kerr et al. (1996a, 1996b) cite various empirical examples where that assumption is violated. Here I extend that discussion by explicitly modeling a situation where a different D is applicable to each condition. MacCoun and Kerr (1988) cite considerable evidence that in criminal juries, the reasonable doubt criterion promotes an asymmetric D (see Table 5.1). MacCoun (1990) and Kerr et al. (1996a) present evidence that some extraevidentiary biases (defendant unattractiveness, pretrial publicity that is biased against the defendant) seem to eliminate that asymmetry. In essence, the jury no longer gives the defendant the benefit of the doubt.

Figure 5.4 depicts such a situation. The decision scheme in the Low Bias condition is the asymmetric Reasonable Doubt D shown in Table 5.1 – the typical pattern for criminal mock juries. The decision scheme in the High Bias condition is the Simple Majority D. Figure 5.4 shows that the net pattern of relative bias (mean $RB = 3.30$) falls somewhere between the Simple Majority pattern (top panel of Figure 5.3) and the Truth-Supported Wins pattern (bottom panel of Figure 5.3) (mean $RB = 4.67$ and 1.17, respectively). When both the prosecution's case and

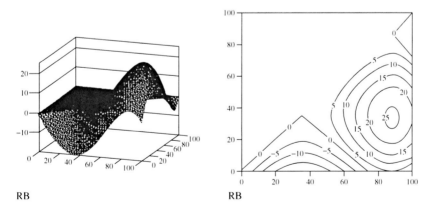

RB   RB

Figure 5.4. Reasonable doubt D in the control condition; simple majority D in the bias condition.

the antidefendant bias are weak, juries still provide fairer verdicts than jurors. But when the antidefendant bias is strong, juries are considerably more biased than jurors.

Other situations where exposure to bias changes the group process seem plausible; for example, one can imagine groups *anchoring and adjusting* (see Kahneman, Slovic, & Tversky, 1982) on a numerical value when one is provided (e.g., "let's take the plaintiff's requested award and reduce it by a third") but constructing a quantitative estimate more systematically when no anchor is available (e.g., "let's award lost wages plus medical bills plus future expenses plus something for pain and suffering"). Tindale (1993) presents some evidence for the operation of a Bias Wins decision scheme, but this seems plausible only in cases where a heuristic or bias, once voiced, is so compelling to others that they are willing to change their preferences, without any recognition that the stated argument reflects a bias.

The notion that biasing manipulations might change the group process is of considerable interest to those of us concerned with the interface between cognitive and social psychology; where it occurs, it suggests a social aspect of otherwise cognitive biases. Nevertheless, I suspect that most real-life examples will occupy the region of parameter space bounded by Strength-In-Number majority schemes at one extreme and the asymmetrical Truth-Supported Wins scheme at the other (i.e., Figure 5.3, top and bottom panels). To the extent that biases change the group process, they seem likely to do so by amplifying either Strength-In-Numbers (shifting the group from an asymmetric scheme toward a majority scheme) or Strength-In-Arguments (shifting the group from a majority scheme toward an asymmetric scheme). If so, identifying process-altering biases and explicating their effects is unlikely to alter fundamentally the basic patterns illustrated here and in Kerr et al. (1996a, 1996b).

What Happens When Groups Fail to Form or Fail to Decide?

Empirical SDS applications – and most individual versus group bias studies – generally use procedures of quasi-random sampling of participants and randomly assign participants to groups. (A few empirical studies have composed groups nonrandomly for experimental purposes, e.g., MacCoun & Kerr, 1988.) Thus, our earlier SDS analyses (here and in Kerr et al., 1996a) assumed randomly sampled group composition for a given individual $p(A)$ in the population. And for simplicity, our thought experiments assumed that all groups, once formed, reach a judgment. Here I explore some consequences of relaxing those assumptions.

The random composition assumption is sensible for addressing the theoretical question: Does the group decision process amplify or attenuate individual-level bias? It is less appropriate for addressing the more applied question: Are the group decisions that we observe in the world more or less biased than those of individuals in the population? A problem with the random composition assumption is that realistically, not all possible groups will have the opportunity to form; not all groups that have the opportunity to form will form; and not all groups that form will reach a judgment. There is a continuum of possibilities:

1. *No opportunity*: A given configuration will have a lower probability of encountering each other than predicted by random sampling.
2. *Failure to form*: A given configuration will fail to group even when given the opportunity.
3. *Disintegration*: A given configuration will fall apart before reaching a group decision.
4. *Fragmentation*: A given configuration will splinter into smaller, more homogeneous groups.
5. *Deadlock*: A given configuration will decide not to decide or fail to reach a decision (e.g., hung juries).
6. *Nonunanimity*: A given configuration will form and reach decisions by overriding the objections of minority faction members – or the latter will overtly consent but covertly disagree with the group's decision (as indicated by postdeliberation private questionnaire responses).
7. *Unanimity*: A given configuration will group and reach a unanimous decision, either by preexisting agreement or through genuine conversion of minority faction members.

Scenarios 5, 6, and 7 are modeled by traditional SDS analyses (see Stasser et al., 1980). Note that in the unanimity scenario, one need not assume that groups were required to reach a unanimous decision; D is a representation of the group process (or, rather, a summary of the consequences of that process), not a formal decision rule. The empirical success of simple majority D's – the strength in numbers effect – occurs because minority factions either tend to join the majority or are overridden in a nonunanimous group decision.

Scenario 4 is both plausible and interesting, but I will not explore it in any detail here. In short, a given population capable of producing, say, k six-person group decisions will instead produce more than k group decisions, many from groups of fewer than six members. These groups will be smaller but more homogeneous. If a Simple Majority scheme is operative, the proportionality near .50 in large, heterogeneous groups will give way to majority amplification near .25 and .75 in the smaller homogeneous groups.

Scenarios 1, 2, and 3 can be modeled separately, but since they have similar consequences, I model them identically by introducing a simple weighting function, λ, which equals *the proportion of group members belonging to the largest group faction*. The idea is that if a minority faction is proportionately large enough, there is some probability that the groups won't form, will form but then fall apart, or will remain intact but fail to reach a decision on certain topics. In *forced composition* situations (e.g., military units), it is unlikely that heterogeneous groups will fall apart; instead, it is more likely that small minorities will be ostracized (Mac-Coun, 1996). But in unforced situations, it is probable that heterogeneous groups are less likely to form in the first place.

Several lines of research on group formation, composition, and cohesion suggest that this is plausible (see Levine & Moreland, 1998; Mac-Coun, 1996). These studies are often limited by convenience sampling, and for logistical and economic reasons, they rarely examine the full range of possible groupings in a population. Perhaps most directly relevant for present purposes are cellular automata models of social influence processes (e.g., Axelrod, 1997; Epstein & Axtell, 1996; Latané, 1996), which show that under a variety of plausible assumptions, social influence processes will result in a clustering of opinion members across social space. If so, "interior" members will have less opportunity to group with members of outgroups than predicted by random sampling; only "border" members may end up in overlapping groups. (Alternatively, people may group based on one issue then find less agreement on a second issue.)

The analysis to be presented is fairly limited. I applied the lambda (λ) weighting function to only one decision scheme (Simple Majority). Lambda is surely an oversimplification of the myriad processes by which groups fail to form, fall apart, or fail to reach a decision.[2] Nevertheless, this seems to be a useful starting point for an analysis of the effects of nonrandom groupings on relative bias.

Table 5.2. *Effect of Lambda Weighting for Six-Person Groups, Assuming That Baseline $p = .66$*

Initial Split	π_i	λ_i	$\pi_i\lambda_i$	Simple Majority d_i	$\lambda_i d_i$	P_i (i.e., $\pi_i\lambda_i d_i$)
6, 0	0.08	1.00	0.08	1.00	1.00	0.08
5, 1	0.26	0.83	0.21	1.00	0.83	0.21
4, 2	0.33	0.67	0.22	1.00	0.67	0.22
3, 3	0.23	0.50	0.11	0.50	0.25	0.06
2, 4	0.09	0.67	0.06	0.00	0.00	0.00
1, 5	0.02	0.83	0.01	0.00	0.00	0.00
0, 6	0.00	1.00	0.00	0.00	0.00	0.00
Sum	1.00	N/A	0.69	N/A	N/A	0.57

Because the adjusted P_i equals $p_i\lambda_i d_i$, one can conceptualize λ in two different ways: as a weighting of the sampling process (i.e., $\pi_i\lambda_i$, as in Scenarios 1 and 2) or as a weighting of the decision process (i.e., $\lambda_i d_i$, as in Scenario 3). Table 5.2 illustrates this weighting for the case of six-person criminal juries where $p = .66$. Note that because of *attrition*, the weighted probabilities of a group of a given initial split ($\pi_i\lambda_i$) no longer sum to 1.00 in Scenarios 1 and 2. Similarly, the weighted transition probabilities ($\lambda_i d_i$) no longer sum to 1.00 in Scenario 3. Of course, one could normalize these product terms to make them sum to 1.00, but this would be beside the point in the present inquiry, which is to examine the effect of this attrition on the individual–group comparison.[3]

Figure 5.5 shows the probabilities of reaching either of two alternative decisions (A and B) for individuals (p) and groups (P) when the Simple Majority group process is vulnerable to attrition, as modeled by the lambda weights. It is instructive to compare this figure to Figure 5.1. Relative to the unweighted Simple Majority process, the weighted process yields lower probabilities of group majorities prevailing – for either decision. The hump-shaped curve shows the probability that groups will fail to form or fail to reach a decision; that is, the attrition that results from the weighting process.

This weighting process seems both simple and innocuous, but it has some rather counterintuitive consequences. The top panel of Figure 5.6 repeats the Simple Majority analysis of the top panel of Figure 5.3, but with lambda weighting to represent group attrition. Americans tend

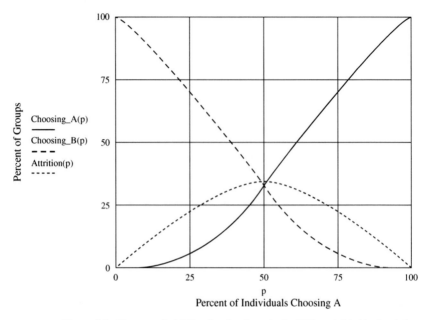

Figure 5.5. Group probabilities for simple majority SDS, weighted by lambda.

to believe that an important advantage of group decision making is the diversity of viewpoints it brings to bear on a decision (MacCoun & Tyler, 1988), and this belief is not unfounded (Nemeth, 1986). Nevertheless, the top panel of Figure 5.6 suggests that, if anything, the loss that occurs when heterogeneous groups fail to form, or fail to reach a decision, makes the relative bias of groups versus individuals *appear to behave surprisingly like groups operating under the Truth-Supported Wins scheme*, despite the fact that a basic majority-amplification process is actually operative. The lambda-weighted simple majority scheme still produces greater relative bias – mean $RB = 2.33$ versus 1.17 in the Truth-Supported Wins case – but the patterns are qualitatively quite similar.

Does this mean that those groups that actually form in the world are frequently *less* biased than individuals? Well, yes and no. No, if the question is: Is the group decision-making *process* less biased than individual decision making? The reason is that the apparent benefits depicted at the top of Figure 5.5 result not from improved decision making, but from attrition due to the group decisions that don't occur. Much of this

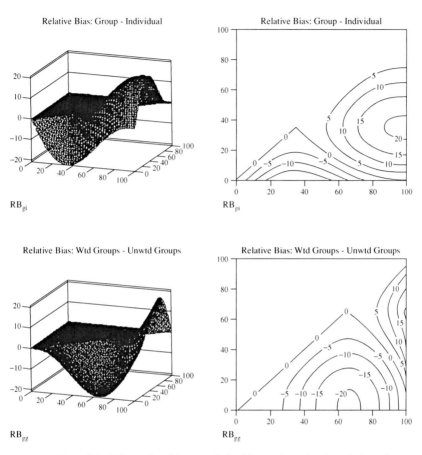

Figure 5.6. Effects of attrition on relative bias under a simple majority scheme.

attrition occurs in a region where *majority amplification would otherwise make groups more biased than individuals*. This is apparent in the bottom panel of Figure 5.6, where I compare the decisions produced by this weighted group process, not to those of individuals but to those produced by unweighted groups; that is, I subtract the surface at the top of Figure 5.3 from that at the top of Figure 5.5.

Table 5.3 illustrates the effect of attrition, the loss of group outcomes modeled by the weighting function, at three different regions of the parameter space. In the first region (the upper right corner of Figure 5.6), High Bias = .90 and Low Bias = .60. Here there is little relative bias in the unweighted case. But weighting eliminates many of the Low Bias groups that would have shifted in the direction of G, making

Table 5.3. *Effects of Weighting Function in Selected Regions*

Condition	p	b	Unweighted Case			Weighted Case			$RB_{difference}$ (Wtd-Unwtd)
			P	B	RB	P	B	RB	
High Bias	.90	.30	.99	.31	.01	.90	.42	.12	+.11
Low Bias	.60		.68			.48			
High Bias	.33	.23	.20	.19	−.04	.12	.12	−.11	−.07
Low Bias	.10		.01			.00			
High Bias	.60	.50	.68	.67	.17	.48	.48	−.02	−.19
Low Bias	.10		.01			.00			

groups look more biased (relative to individuals) than in the unweighted case.

In the second region, High Bias = .33 and Low Bias = .10. Unweighted groups significantly reduce this bias because of a shift in both conditions toward the NG majority. The weighting process has no effect on this shift; the probability of a G verdict drops simply because some groups fail to form or reach decisions.

In the third region, High Bias = .60 and Low Bias = .10. The lower panel of Figure 5.6 suggests that this is where the most profound effects of weighting occurred. In this region, individuals are quite biased but groups (in the unweighted case) are much less so, mostly because the individuals who start out at .10 end up in groups shifting toward .01. Weighting preserves the latter phenomenon, but the loss of many High Bias groups creates a reduction in G decisions (48% instead of 67%), resulting in relative bias near 0. Thus, weighting in this region has significantly reduced total group bias.

Note that it isn't that attrition has encouraged more groups to reach the unbiased NG decision than would otherwise be the case. The lambda weighting function is symmetrical and does not influence the direction of the group decisions that actually get made. Rather, attrition has weeded out groups from many bias-enhancing regions.

What if the question is: How does the *population* of group decisions that occur in the world differ from the *population* of individual decisions? From that perspective, the analysis presented here suggests the intriguing hypothesis that, in an indirect and almost perverse fashion, something approximating Truth-Supported Wins might describe the distribution of group decisions that actually occur, even in purely judgmental tasks where groups tend to follow a Majority-Wins process. Truth wins to the extent that attrition attenuates majority amplification processes that would have pushed groups into greater bias. The apparent benefits of attrition occur by eliminating many diverse groups where minorities would have caved in to their biased majority counterparts. The remaining population of groups is more homogeneous, and underrepresents some regions of parameter space where majority amplification would otherwise have a deleterious effect.

This may seem counterintuitive. Americans often see heterogeneity as a desirable attribute of decision-making groups (e.g., MacCoun & Tyler, 1988; cf. MacCoun, 1996) – it enhances their legitimacy, curbs extremism, and increases the likelihood of a fair, thorough consideration of relevant points of view. Yet the analysis presented here suggests that perhaps we should be grateful that not all groups that might be formed do get formed – not because diversity is undesirable, but because diverse viewpoints that might be expressed individually too frequently get swallowed up by the enormous social influence of group majorities.

Notes

1 Many but not all of the judgmental biases described in this book are of this sort. Kerr et al. (1996a) also analyze the category of *sins of omission* (what Hastie & Rasinski, 1988, call "failure to use a good cue"), situations where people fail to use normatively relevant information. Examples include the underutilization of base rate information in predictive and diagnostic judgments (Kahneman et al., 1982) or the failure to take into account strong situational pressures on an actor when attributing causation and responsibility for his or her actions (for a review, see Gilbert & Malone, 1995).

2 I've tested the fit of lambda to Kerr and MacCoun's (1985) data on hung jury rates for 12-, 6-, and 3-person mock criminal jury deliberations ($N = 167, 158,$ and 158 deliberations, respectively). At each group size, I computed three indices: (1) the average discrepancy between lambda and the observed proportion reaching a verdict given each distinct initial split, (2) the correlation between lambda and observed decision rates, and (3) a chi-squared goodness of fit using lambda to compute expected cell frequencies – i.e., the null hypothesis is that the lambda model is correct. Lambda fit the data quite well by all three indices for six-person deliberations; the average discrepancy was -0.03, with a correlation of .90, and $\chi^{2(6)} = 5.90$, $p = .43$. For three-person groups, the correlation was high (.96) and the average discrepancy was $-.09$, but lambda tended to underpredict the probability of reaching a decision among 2,1 and 1,2 splits; $\chi^{2(3)} = 15.38$, $p < .01$. This is understandable because at very small group sizes, absolute faction size matters more than relative faction size (Kerr & MacCoun, 1985), a fact that lambda ignores. Fit was poorest for 12-person deliberations; the average discrepancy was 0.05, the correlation was .74, and $\chi^{2(11)} = 39.25$, $p < .01$. In these larger groups, lambda underpredicted the probability of reaching a verdict when initial majorities favored acquittal

(3:9 and 2:10) and overpredicted the probability of reaching a verdict for groups with initial majorities favoring conviction (10:2, 9:3, 8:4, and 7:5). This is also understandable because lambda is symmetrical and does not reflect the fact that in criminal juries, factions favoring acquittal have extra drawing power (MacCoun & Kerr, 1988). The lambda formulation could be modified to account for such asymmetries and absolute group size effects, but the version used here provides a reasonable balance between accuracy and parsimony or generality.

3 Normalizing the product terms produces a weighted pi that correlates strongly (e.g., .96 in the case shown in Table 5.2) with its unweighted counterpart, pi. Similarly, the normalized weighted d correlates .88 with the unweighted d. The resulting relative bias plots differ only subtly from their unweighted counterparts.

References

Axelrod, R. (1997). *The complexity of cooperation*. Princeton, NJ: Princeton University Press.

Davis, J. H. (1973). Group decision and social interaction: A theory of social decision schemes. *Psychological Review, 80*, 97–125.

Davis, J. H., Spitzer, C. E., Nagao, D. H., & Stasser, G. (1978). Bias in social decisions by individuals and groups: An example from mock juries. In H. Brandstatter, J. H. Davis, & H. Schuler (Eds.), *Dynamics of group decisions* (pp. 33–52). Beverly Hills, CA: Sage.

Epstein, J. M., & Axtell, R. (1996). *Growing artificial societies*. Washington, DC: Brookings Institution Press.

Funder, D. C. (1987). Errors and mistakes: Evaluating the accuracy of social judgment. *Psychological Bulletin, 101*, 75–90.

Gilbert, D. T., & Malone, P. S. (1995). The correspondence bias. *Psychological Bulletin, 117*, 21–38.

Hastie, R., & Rasinski, K. A. (1988). The concept of accuracy in social judgment. In D. Bar-Tal & A. W. Kruglanski (Eds.), *The social psychology of knowledge* (pp. 193–203). Cambridge: Cambridge University Press.

Kagel, J. H., & Roth, A. E. (Eds.). (1995). *The handbook of experimental economics*. Princeton, NJ: Princeton University Press.

Kahneman, D., Slovic, P., & Tversky, A. (Eds.). (1982). *Judgment under uncertainty: Heuristics and biases*. New York: Cambridge University Press.

Kahneman, D., & Tversky, A. (1984). Choices, values, and frames. *American Psychologist, 39*, 341–350.

Kerr, N. L., & Huang, J. Y. (1986). How much difference does one juror make in jury deliberation? *Personality and Social Psychology Bulletin, 12*, 325–343.

Kerr, N. L., & MacCoun, R. J. (1985). The effects of jury size and polling method on the process and product of jury deliberation. *Journal of Personality and Social Psychology, 48*, 349–363.

Kerr, N. L., MacCoun, R. J., & Kramer, G. P. (1996a). Bias in judgment: Comparing individuals and groups. *Psychological Review, 103*, 687–719.

Kerr, N. L., MacCoun, R. J., & Kramer, G. P. (1996b). When are N heads better (or worse) than one? Biased judgment in individuals vs. groups. In E. Witte & J. H. Davis (Eds.), *Understanding group behavior*, Vol. 1: *Consensual action by small groups* (pp. 105–136). Hillsdale, NJ: Erlbaum.

Latané, B. (1996). Strength from weakness: The fate of opinion minorities in spatially distributed groups. In E. Witte & J. H. Davis (Eds.), *Understanding group behavior*, Vol. 1: *Consensual action by small groups* (pp. 193–219). Hillsdale, NJ: Erlbaum.

Laughlin, P. R. (1996). Group decision making and collective induction. In E. Witte & J. H. Davis (Eds.), *Understanding group behavior*, Vol. 1: *Consensual action by small groups* (pp. 61–80). Hillsdale, NJ: Erlbaum.

Levine, J. M., & Moreland, R. L. (1998). Small groups. In D. T. Gilbert & S. T. Fiske (Eds.), *The handbook of social psychology*, (Vol. 2, pp. 415–469). Boston: McGraw-Hill.

MacCoun, R. J. (1990). The emergence of extralegal bias during jury deliberation. *Criminal Justice and Behavior, 17*, 303–314.

MacCoun, R. J. (1996). Sexual orientation and military cohesion: A critical review of the evidence. In G. M. Herek, J. B. Jobe, & R. Carney (Eds.), *Out in force: Sexual orientation and the military*. Chicago: University of Chicago Press.

MacCoun, R. J., & Kerr, N. L. (1988). Asymmetric influence in mock jury deliberation: Jurors' bias for leniency. *Journal of Personality and Social Psychology, 54*, 21–33.

MacCoun, R. J., & Tyler, T. R. (1988). The basis of citizens' perceptions of the criminal jury: Procedural fairness, accuracy and efficiency. *Law and Human Behavior, 12*, 333–352.

Nemeth, C. J. (1986). Differential contributions of majority and minority influence. *Psychological Review, 93*, 23–32.

Page, B. I., & Shapiro, R. Y. (1992). *The rational public: Fifty years of trends in Americans' policy preferences*. Chicago: University of Chicago Press.

Stasser, G., Kerr, N. L., & Davis, J. H. (1980). Influence processes and consensus models in decision-making groups. In P. Paulus (Ed.), *Psychology of group influence* (2nd ed., pp. 431–477). Hillsdale, NJ: Erlbaum.

Tindale, R. S. (1993). Decision errors made by individuals and groups. In N. J. Castellan (Ed.), *Individual and group decision making: Current issues* (pp. 109–124). Hillsdale, NJ: Erlbaum.

Tversky, A., Sattath, S., & Slovic, P. (1988). Contingent weighting in judgment and choice. *Psychological Review, 95*, 371–384.

6 Bounded Rationality versus Standard Utility-Maximization: A Test of Energy Price Responsiveness

Lee S. Friedman

Introduction

Over the past decade, there has been a growing and fruitful debate over the applicability of various models of limited or bounded rationality to economic decision making. In particular, in a wide variety of situations the claim is frequently made that the standard model of utility-maximization (SUM) provides an inadequate explanation for observed behavior and that some alternative behavioral model provides a better explanation. However, SUM models continue to guide applied economic research in market settings. There have not been, to my knowledge, any empirical studies of actual market decision making that specify two competing models (one SUM and one based on an alternative behavioral model) and test their relative strengths. This study contributes such a test in the context of residential energy consumption.

The alternative behavioral models emphasize the difficulty or the impossibility of obtaining and processing the information required to maximize utility. Although some maintain the concept of utility-maximization, they impose information and transactional constraints that alter the predicted behavior. Other models reject the concept of utility-maximization and substitute some form of simplifying decision routine.[1] For short I shall refer to each class of models, respectively, as *limited utility-maximization* (LUM) and *bounded rationality* (BR). A full review of both classes of alternative models is beyond the scope of this study.[2]

I am grateful to the San Diego Gas and Electric Company for making its MIRACLE IV database available and to the University of California Energy Institute, whose support has made this research possible. I have benefited from the advice and assistance of many people, including Carl Blumstein, Karl Hausker, Ted Keeler, Daniel Khazzoom, John Quigley, Herb Simon, and Chris Weare.

138

Two of their attributes are particularly relevant to note here. First, the existing tests of the alternative models almost always rely on data that are not normally observable in market settings. Second, within the alternative models, it can be exceedingly difficult to test a LUM model against a BR model: The decision rules a consumer follows can often be thought of as *if* they are derived from LUM, even if they are not.[3]

Perhaps for these reasons, a surprising amount of the literature in economics relevant to this debate focuses on tests that can reject SUM but that cannot reject some alternative model. For example, there are many studies that show subjects in laboratory experiments behaving inconsistently with utility-maximization but that do not test any other specific theory.[4] To make intellectual progress, it is important to consider and test the relative strengths of alternative predictive models.

Furthermore, there are few tests that take place in actual market settings as opposed to in the laboratory or from the analysis of survey responses. Indeed, most of the chapters in this volume report on research based on the latter methods. Particularly in the case of the formal experiment, there is much to be said in favor of the methodology. I have already mentioned the ability to plan treatments (or, in the case of the survey, ask questions) and observe the responses to them that may be difficult or impossible to observe in natural market settings. The evidence concerning preference reversals is a good example.

But what about situations in which one can observe important evidence in the actual market? This is particularly relevant for public policy research because the effect of actual policies in the marketplace is paramount. Another important advantage of the experiment is the ability, through random assignment of subjects to experimental and control groups, to determine highly precise treatment effects. That is, the variation in decisions across groups is fully attributable to the designed treatment differences among the groups, save for some small statistical noise. By contrast, the use of natural (nonexperimental) decisions in the marketplace (like this study) requires the analyst to account for all of the factors that may explain systematic differences in choices among individuals. Such studies are always subject to the criticism that important factors besides the "treatment" of interest have not been sufficiently controlled, possibly leading to biased estimates of the treatment effect.

For example, suppose we wish to know how consumers respond to a price increase for a given product. The experimentalist will assign people randomly to a treatment group that will face the higher price and a control group that will not. The experimentalist will conclude, subject to normal statistical inference, that the price increase causes the difference in average consumption between the two groups.

The analyst who uses nonexperimental market data, however, will first have to make sure that the data include the consumption of both individuals who have and who have not experienced the price increase. Typically, this will involve time-series data from one geographic area, or geographic cross-sectional data within a given time period, or a combination. If, say, the price difference occurs across regions, then the analyst must make sure to control for nonprice regional factors that may cause differences in consumption (e.g., if studying home energy consumption, control for climate, wealth, and residence size differences). Similarly, there may be nonprice factors that cause changes in consumption over time (e.g., weather, occupancy changes). The list of nonprice factors may be large, and the ability to get data that measure each of these differences accurately may be limited. And, of course, the treatment studied – the size of the price increase – is limited to what has actually happened rather than chosen by experimental design.

Why, given the complication and imperfection of studying nonexperimental market decisions, would the researcher ever prefer to study them? There are several important reasons. If the alternative is a nonexperimental survey, then it is well recognized that *survey responses are not always reliable indicators of how people behave when making actual decisions*. This uncertainty makes it valuable to know if survey-based findings are consistent with what can be observed in actual market settings. Indeed, experimentalists value this as well, because *there are also varying degrees of undesirable artificiality in experiments*. To clarify this, let us note the important distinction between a laboratory experiment, which is the predominant mode for BR and LUM research, and a social experiment. The laboratory experiment may have as subjects university students who differ from the actual market decision makers, and it almost always takes place in an environment or setting that is quite unlike the actual market. The social experiment, by contrast, studies the actual market decision makers in an actual market setting. In principle, the earlier criticisms of the nonexperimental market study can be avoided by the social experiment.

But *few social experiments are conducted because they are expensive, difficult to arrange, and time-consuming*. If these costs were no object, almost all experimentalists would prefer to conduct a social rather than a laboratory experiment to understand the choices observable in the marketplace. However, given the limited resources available for research, it is possible to conduct social experiments only in rare circumstances.

These usually involve high public policy stakes that make the cost of the social experiment seem small in comparison.

Even when social experiments are conducted, important elements of artificiality often remain. For example, an experimental price increase is often regarded by participants as more temporary than a naturally occurring market price increase. This can affect the investment choices of subjects. In negative income tax social experiments, subjects whose real wage rates increased through lower taxes might have invested more in income-producing education if the increase was permanent. In our energy price increase example, fewer new energy-efficient furnaces will be bought under a temporary social experiment than under an actual market price increase of equal size.

Another source of artificiality in the social experiment is that the experimental population, although consisting of real market participants, may not be representative of the broader population to which the treatment may be administered. A rigorous social experiment that recruits volunteer participants who are randomly assigned to experimental and control groups may not tell us much about the effects of the same treatment when applied to those who did not volunteer. Similarly, the environment in which the social experiment takes place can have important effects: The response of participants in a suburb might be quite different from the response of an otherwise identical group located in a large city.

All of these sources of artificiality can, in principle, be removed (or at least reduced) by larger, more inclusive, and longer-duration social experiments. But then we run into the cost issue again. Once one recognizes that the costs prohibit us from routinely doing the ideal social experiment, we have several different ways of lowering costs. Some of them retain the experimental design, but they move from larger to smaller social experiments and then down to laboratory experiments, with each step increasing the artificiality and reducing the generalizability of the observed decision making. Alternatively, we can move away from the experiment but retain some of the comprehensiveness of time, place, and population studied by using the nonexperimental research design.

Imagine research efforts of both types that have equal (and relatively low) costs. It is not at all clear which is preferable. One must judge the extent of artificiality in the experiment against the quality and comprehensiveness of the data available for the nonexperimental design. Because each method has different strengths and weaknesses, it is valuable when possible to know if the findings are consistent across them.

The decisions that I study here would be difficult to simulate in a laboratory experiment. They involve consumer responses to energy price schedules, but also more than that. A key part of the actual decision environment is the long period of time, perhaps several years, during which the consumer forms a routine by making a series of (daily) decisions with infrequent and limited (monthly) feedback about the consequences. The lag between the decisions and feedback is (perhaps) long enough to forget important circumstances that framed the original decisions, and long enough so that the circumstances for the next series of decisions may have changed substantially from those of the prior series.

Smith (1989) noted that in the market consumers may learn their utility-maximizing choices by repetitive trials over time, even if they do not actually arrive at them by explicit maximizing calculations.[5] Although I remain open to the cleverness of experts in the design of laboratory experiments to test this in the home energy context, I believe that it is worthwhile to study the actual decisions with nonexperimental methods. This conclusion is reinforced by the unusual comprehensiveness of the available data, as well as the direct policy relevance of evidence on the effects of rates set by regulatory commissions.

This study is of a market decision by households concerning the consumption of natural gas. There are some good reasons why consumers might use simplified decision routines in this setting. I suggest that the use of one particular one with a common rate structure would cause a systematic departure from the conventional utility-maximizing choice.

I postulate a specific BR model (although the same systematic departure could be predicted by a LUM model, and I do not claim to distinguish these). Using only the type of data normally used to estimate SUM models, I estimate both and I pit the BR model against the SUM model. The results might be summarized as follows: The SUM model is not terrible, but the BR model is better. In the market examined, the welfare and policy implications are likely to be significant. Furthermore, the consumer decision routine specified may be applied with the same flaws (deviations from SUM) and similar implications in other contexts (and could be further tested in these settings). The rest of the chapter explains the basis for these conclusions.

The Two Competing Hypotheses for Residential Consumption of Natural Gas

The context I will focus on is that of short-run consumption choices, holding the stock of natural-gas-using appliances constant.[6] The equilibrium quantity of each model will be assumed to depend on the appliance stock (including characteristics of the dwelling unit itself), price of natural gas, household income, wealth and demographic features, and weather and climate conditions. When it comes to specification, the only difference between the two models will be the manner in which the rate structure affects the predicted equilibrium quantity. I will next lay the groundwork for this analysis.

The standard economic hypothesis is that the household will choose its utility-maximizing quantity of natural gas. With the SUM model, the household is assumed to be able to calculate this quantity and to select it. *The alternative BR hypothesis is that the household is characterized by a total bill sensitivity*, responding to the total monthly expenditure on natural gas (not the actual price) as well as the other nonprice factors mentioned earlier. This sensitivity is not assumed to be derived from any explicit calculation, but it parameterizes the household's adjustment function.

If the rate structure for natural gas consisted of a simple *uniform* price (independent of the quantity consumed), the BR model is assumed to have an equilibrium identical to that of the standard model.[7] This research focuses on the consumer response to a *nonlinear* rate structure. Almost all utility companies employ block rate structures, where the price per unit changes as the consumption level reaches the end of one specified block and begins another. With nonlinear rate structures for this good, the BR equilibrium will diverge from the SUM equilibrium.

Under the BR hypothesis, the household finds it easier to choose a sensitivity to the total natural gas bill rather than use a decision routine that has more explicit accounting for the price per unit consumed. Reasons why this might occur are as follows: (1) Consumers have imperfect information about the current rate structure (fuel cost adjustments, seasonal changes, and rate case decisions often cause frequent changes in price per block and in block sizes as well). (2) Even the information on a bill about the prior month is generally quite incomplete (many utilities simply list the total bill and the quantity consumed, without information on the block sizes or rates). (3) It is extremely difficult to purchase any particular quantity even if one was decided on (the actual quantity consumed results from a complicated interaction of exogenous weather conditions and daily household use of numerous natural-gas-using appliances like furnaces, hot water heaters, dryers, dishwashers, and swimming pool heaters).

Facing the previous decision difficulties, the household may simply consider if it is satisfied with its choice based on the prior month's outcome. If it feels that it overconsumed, for example, it can take a few actions to reduce consumption for the coming month (e.g., lowering the thermostat, closing the drapes at night, conserving on hot water usage, covering the swimming pool). Anthropologists Kempton and Montgomery (1982) provide some supporting evidence for this behavior based on interviews with householders.

To clarify the expected divergence in equilibrium between the SUM and BR models, I proceed in two steps. The first step is to define equilibrium and assume that under a *uniform* rate structure the equilibria of both models are the same. In the second step, the *nonlinear* rate structure will be introduced and shown to cause a systematic divergence between the equilibria. In addition, the BR equilibrium under nonlinear rates will be seen as identical to that of a particular LUM model, and thus the empirical tests that follow have the potential only for distinguishing SUM from the other two (BR and its LUM relative). I prefer the BR interpretation rather than LUM on grounds of a priori plausibility, but this is a matter of judgment and cannot be tested here.

Step One. The BR model of total bill sensitivity is described by an adjustment function:

$$Q_{t+1} = D(E_t, Z)$$

where Z represents a vector of all factors other than the total natural gas bill, E_t is total natural gas expenditures in time t, and Q_{t+1} is consumption quantity in time $t+1$. Except for relying on the total bill rather than the price, the adjustment function is assumed to be normal and well behaved. Let us define an equilibrium quantity as one from which the household would make no further adjustments (holding exogenous conditions constant):

$$Q_{t+1} = Q_t = D(E_t, Z)$$

Let us also define the total bill sensitivity α as the elasticity of equilibrium output Q with respect to E (dropping t subscripts since we are focusing on equilibrium):

$$\frac{\partial D}{\partial E} * \frac{E}{Q} = \alpha$$

Let us assume for a given household that in the *uniform* price case the BR equilibrium is identical to that of SUM.[8] In this case, total bill sensitivity α is equivalent to an ordinary price elasticity of $\alpha/(1-\alpha)$. I show this by making use of the chain rule. In the uniform case, total natural gas expenditure $E_t = P_t * Q_t$ by definition. Applying the chain rule to the equilibrium BR quantity:

$$\frac{\partial Q}{\partial P} = \frac{\partial D}{\partial E} * \frac{\partial E}{\partial P}$$

Note from the definition of total bill sensitivity that

$$\frac{\partial D}{\partial E} = \alpha * \frac{Q}{E} = \alpha * \frac{Q}{P * Q} = \frac{\alpha}{P}$$

Substituting this expression in the chain rule and differentiating $\partial E / \partial P$:

$$\frac{\partial Q}{\partial P} = \left(\frac{\alpha}{P}\right) \left(Q + \left[P * \left\{\frac{\partial Q}{\partial P}\right\}\right]\right)$$

Solving for $\partial Q/\partial P$ and multiplying both sides by P/Q results in the ordinary price elasticity:

$$\frac{\partial Q}{\partial P} * \frac{P}{Q} = \frac{\alpha}{1 - \alpha}$$

Step Two. Imagine the household in equilibrium, and now let the rate structure change to be one of two or more blocks, but with the expenditure at the initial equilibrium quantity unchanged. The BR household, sensitive only to the bill total, remains in equilibrium and will make no adjustments.

The SUM household, however, is no longer in equilibrium. Its marginal rate of substitution of natural gas for other things equals the old uniform price (equal to the current average price), which is no longer the marginal price. If the marginal price exceeds the average price (as with increasing block rates), the SUM consumer will act to reduce consumption. If the marginal price is below the average price (as with decreasing block rates), the SUM consumer will increase consumption.

An interesting interpretation of the BR equilibrium under nonlinear rates can be offered. Note that by definition expenditure equals *average* price (P_A) times quantity. Then the same manipulation done earlier, replacing P with P_A, reveals that *the BR household is responding as if it is a faulty utility-maximizer, making the error of perceiving the marginal price as the average price.* It does not actually make this calculation, but it acts as if it does. Put differently, for any given E and Z the equilibrium of a BR household with bill sensitivity α will be identical to the equilibrium of an LUM household using average rather than marginal price and with price elasticity $\alpha/(1 - \alpha)$.

Two important implications follow from the preceding illustration. First, the nature of the errors caused by this type of bounded rationality becomes clear: The household responding only to the total bill will overconsume if the average price at the true utility-maximum is below the marginal price and will underconsume if the average price at the true utility-maximum is above the marginal price.[9] In general, the BR household will overconsume with an increasing block rate structure and underconsume with a decreasing block rate structure (except when the true utility-maximum is in the first block). Second, empirical tests based on predicted equilibria cannot distinguish between the BR model and its LUM relative (since both predict the same equilibrium).

How common are the circumstances that may lead to behavior described? One characteristic important to the model here is a nonlinear budget constraint, and the other is consumer uncertainty about their locations relative to it. Similar situations characterize most other utility services: electricity, water, and telephones.[10] A quite different but important market concerns the labor–leisure choices of welfare recipients, particularly those qualifying for more than one assistance program (e.g., food stamps, Supplemental Security Income, Medicaid). The return on investment or savings decisions depends on the individual's income tax brackets, and many of these decisions may be made when the consumer is unaware of the relevant brackets. Similarly, depreciation and other rules governing net tax assessments may imply nonlinearities that are not clearly understood at the time of an investment.[11]

A more general application of this BR model, not requiring nonlinear prices, can be imagined. Suppose consumers follow common advice for household budgeting, with fixed proportions of income allocated to major expenditure categories (food, housing, etc.). The consumer's response to a price change for a specific item may occur only through its effect on the total expenditure for the category in which that item is a component. If the consumer's response is the same no matter which specific item prices in the category have increased, then that consumer is behaving in accordance with the same total bill sensitivity model described here. The plausibility of this situation increases with the difficulty of identifying the specific sources of change. For example, consumers may be less aware of the prices of specific items in a supermarket marked only for electronic scanning.

In short, there may be many areas of economic decision making where consumers adopt this type of simplified decision routine. The simplification is to make decisions based on an easy-to-utilize monetary total instead of its difficult-to-utilize components. A variety of cognitive difficulties, as illustrated in the preceding examples, trigger the use of this routine.

Let us summarize this discussion of the two hypotheses in a format that bridges the intuitive exposition and the formal econometric modeling to come. A SUM demand function relating the equilibrium quantity Q_U to the nonlinear rate structure with $i = 1, 2, \ldots, n$ segments and other factors may be represented as follows[12]:

$$Q_U = D_U(P_1, \ldots, P_N, B_1, \ldots B_N, Z)$$

where

> $P_i =$ the price per unit on segment i of the rate structure
> $B_i =$ the virtual budget size for segment i, where B_1 is the consumer's actual budget and B_i is B_1 plus the sum of the differences between P_i and the actual price for all units on preceding segments
> $Z =$ the vector of all nonrate structure variables that influence consumption

We have seen that the BR equilibrium may be described as if it results from faulty utility-maximizing with the error of using the average price P_A. That is:

$$Q_{BR} = D(E, Z) = D_U(P_A, \ldots, P_A, B_1, \ldots, B_1, Z)$$

Thus the equilibrium quantity under the BR hypothesis may be represented by the same functional form (but different rate structure variables) used to predict the SUM quantity. In the BR version, price and budget levels are represented as uniform over the segments and are equal to the average price and the actual budget level B_1, respectively. It remains an empirical question which of the two models is closer to the truth. We turn now to the empirical work of specifying the Z variables, selecting a functional form, and testing the relative strength of the two models.

Econometrics

This section describes the database and the procedures used to specify and estimate models based on the competing behavioral hypotheses.

The following section describes the estimation results and the tests made to evaluate the two models.

The San Diego Gas and Electric Company
MIRACLE IV Database

The MIRACLE IV file contains usable monthly consumption and billing data from more than 6,863 households in the service area for 53 months beginning in February 1979 and ending in June 1983.[13] Each household in the file was randomly selected from the company's service area and surveyed in late 1979 or early 1980 to provide detailed microdata on the physical characteristics of the dwelling unit, the appliances in it, and socioeconomic characteristics of the household itself. The service area contains nine separate weather districts, and a weather tape with the daily high and low temperatures in each district for the 53-month period was used in constructing an observation set. During this period, the rate structure consisted of three blocks. The blocks were increasing in price: The second block price per unit was 15 to 51% above the first block price, and the third block price varied from 15 to 53% above the second block price.

For estimation purposes, a random 5% sample was drawn from these households. Observations were not used if they had important missing data (e.g., square footage) or contained detectable coding errors.[14] This left a sample with 11,775 monthly observations used for this study.

The rate structure during this period was one of increasing blocks, and there was substantial variation in it. In nominal terms, the rate on the first block was 19 cents per therm at the start of the period and rose to 51 cents per therm at the end. This represented a 238% increase in nominal rates, or 184% in real rates based on the Consumer Price Index. Thirteen discrete rate changes occurred during the period. The upper block rates changed at these times as well and relative block rates varied, with block two ranging from 15 to 51% above block 1 and block three ranging from 15 to 53% above block two. In addition, block sizes changed twice each year for seasonal reasons.

Consumption at the sample geometric mean was 44.3 therms. Such consumption does not lead to high average bills; in 1983, for example, the average winter bill was about $45 and the average summer bill was only $20. However, the average masks considerable variation. In winter months, the lifeline (first) block was 81 therms, and the top quartile of the sample consumed 94 therms or more. In any year, more than half of the households exceed the lifeline block for one or more months. If there is power to the BR hypothesis, it ought to be detectable with the variation in rates and consumption that characterizes this database.

Econometric Procedures

In this section, I discuss model specification procedures: variable definitions, simultaneity, pooling time series and cross-sectional data, and functional form.

Precise definitions of the variables used in this study are contained in Table 6.1. There are 35 nonprice and nontemporal variables used to describe the physical characteristics of the dwelling unit, the natural-gas-using appliances in it and other appliances that may substitute for them, weather and climate indicators, and socioeconomic characteristics of the household. I will describe these briefly.

Most physical characteristics of the dwelling unit affect energy consumption in conjunction with a specific appliance for space heating or space cooling. These characteristics include the square footage of the house, the presence of an attic, the amount of wall and ceiling insulation, and the age of the house. They enter the model in conjunction with a natural gas main heating system, and the latter four are defined as dummy variables in Table 6.1. The only house characteristic interacted with gas cooling is the house size.[15] I also include the overall size of the house as a noninteracted independent variable. This is because it may be the best proxy for the general wealth level of the household, as well as a correlate of other unmeasured gas-using appliances (e.g., the number of hot water outlets).

The basic gas-using appliances in a dwelling unit, other than main heating, are water heaters, stoves, and clothes dryers. Dishwashers and washing machines are also included as control variables if the water heater runs on gas. Additionally, some households have jacuzzis that use gas-heated water, and these, too, are included as control variables. Each of these appliance variables is interacted with the number of people in the household. Some households also report having an extra space heater that runs on natural gas, and this is included as a simple dummy variable.

Two nongas appliances are included as control variables: microwave ovens and extra space heaters. These secondary appliances permit some substitution of services from the main gas-using appliances by using alternative energy sources. However, they may also reflect general

Table 6.1. *Definition of Variables*

Dependent

SGAS: The monthly number of billed therms divided by the number of billing days multiplied by 365/12

SGASBC: SGAS divided by its geometric mean, Box–Cox transformation (see XBC)

Demographic

EDUC: The educational background of the household head, scaled from 1 to 8 as follows:

$1 = 0$–7 years; $2 = 8$ years; $3 = 9$–11 years; $4 = 12$ years; $5 = 12 +$ noncollege; $6 =$ college, no BS; $7 =$ college, BS; $8 =$ college advanced

PREBOOM: $= 1$ if there are persons aged 35–44 in the household; $= 0$ otherwise

MIDDLE: $= 1$ if there are persons aged 45–54 in the household; $= 0$ otherwise

MATURE: $= 1$ if there are persons aged 55–64 in the household; $= 0$ otherwise

ELDER: $= 1$ if there are persons aged 65 or more and if the preceding three variables $= 0$; $= 0$ otherwise

BABY: $= 1$ if there are persons aged 5 or under; $= 0$ otherwise

NUM: $=$ the total number of persons in the household is defined as follows: $= 1$ if one person; $= 2$ if two people; $= 3.5$ if three or four; $= 5.5$ if five or six; $= 7.5$ if seven or eight; $= 10$ if nine or more

INLAND: $= 1$ if the climate zone is categorized as inland

$= 0$ if the climate zone is categorized as maritime or coastal

SFHOME: $= 1$ if the dwelling unit is single family;

$= 0$ if apartment, duplex, triplex, condominium, or other

Temporal Terms

JAN: $= 1$ if the observation is from January; $= 0$ otherwise
Similarly for FEB–DEC

YR79: $= 1$ if the observation is from 1979; $= 0$ otherwise
Similarly for YR80-YR83

Interaction Term with Some Appliances

N at the end of a variable name means that the variable is multiplied by NUM, defined under DEMOGRAPHIC

Appliances

STOV: $= 1$ if cooking range uses natural gas; $= 0$ otherwise

DRY: $= 1$ if clothes dryer uses natural gas; $= 0$ otherwise

WAT: $= 1$ if water heater uses natural gas; $= 0$ otherwise

JAC: $= 1$ if there is a jacuzzi or hot tub; $= 0$ otherwise

WASH: $= 1$ if WAT $= 1$ and there is a washing machine; $= 0$ otherwise

DISHWSH: $= 1$ if WAT $= 1$ and there is a dishwasher; $= 0$ otherwise

EXHT: $= 1$ if there is an additional room heater using natural gas; $= 0$ otherwise

SUBHEAT: $= 1$ if main heating is natural gas and an additional room heater not natural gas; $= 0$ otherwise

MICRO: $= 1$ if STOV $= 1$ and there is a microwave oven; $= 0$ otherwise

HEATDY: if there is gas main heating and the month is November–May
$=$ the square footage of the dwelling unit multiplied times HMAX; $= 0$ otherwise

HEATNT:		if there is gas main heating and the month is November–May, = the square footage of the dwelling unit multiplied times HMIN; = 0 otherwise
POOLDY:		if there is a natural gas swimming pool heater, = the average daily high temperature for the month; = 0 otherwise
POOLNT:		if there is a natural gas swimming pool heater = the average daily low temperature for the month; = 0 otherwise
COOLDY:		if there is natural gas air conditioning and the month is May–October, = the square footage of the house multiplied times CMAX; = 0 otherwise

Interaction Terms with Main Heating and Swimming Pool Heaters

HMAX:	=	the number of degrees by which 68 exceeds the average daily high temperature for the month; = 0 if 68 does not exceed the average daily high
HMIN:	=	the number of degrees by which 68 exceeds the average daily low temperature for the month; = 0 if 68 does not exceed the average daily low
CMAX:	=	the number of degrees by which the average daily high for the month exceeds 68; = 0 if the average daily high does not exceed 68
NWHTDY:	=	HEATDY if the dwelling unit age is 5 years or less; = 0 otherwise
NWHTNT:	=	HEATNT if the dwelling unit age is 5 years or less; = 0 otherwise
FA:	= 1	if gas main heating system is forced air; = 0 otherwise
AT:	= 1	if there is an attic; = 0 if no or partial attic
CI:	= 1	if at least 2 in. of ceiling insulation; = 0 otherwise
WI:	= 1	if wall insulation; = 0 if no or partial wall insulation

Economic Variables (All Prices Are Deflated to February 1979 Using the Monthly Consumer Price Index)

SQFT:	=	the square footage of the dwelling unit
INCM:	=	total household income
PAP:	=	the predicted average price
PMP:	=	the predicted marginal price
PLS:	=	the predicted lump sum subsidy, which equals the minimum of $1.00, or the sum of the differences between the prices of the marginal unit and each intramarginal unit minus the fixed connection charge
PAPHEAT:	=	the predicted average price if there is a gas main heating system; = 0 otherwise
PMPHEAT:	=	the predicted marginal price if there is a gas main heating system; = 0 otherwise

Transformation of Economic Variables

XBC:	=	$(X^\lambda - 1)/\lambda$, where X is an economic variable and $0 < \lambda \leq 1$
PAPHTBC:	=	PAPBC if there is gas main heating and the month is November–May; = 0 otherwise
PMPHTBC:	=	PMPBC if there is gas main heating and the month is November–May; = 0 otherwise

wealth effects (the microwave) or an inefficient main gas-heating system (the extra nongas heater).

Three of the gas-using home appliances are expected to be heavily dependent on weather conditions: main heating, main cooling, and swimming pool heaters. Given the general climate of the area, it is reasonable to constrain the main heating to be off from June through October and the main cooling to be off from November through April. In other months, indices of heating and cooling requirements with reference to a 68°F base are constructed. Because the daily temperature variation may be large, averaging 20°F differences between high and low for some months, we construct one index based on the average daily high (daytime requirements) and another based on the average daily low (nighttime requirements).

The day heating requirement index is defined as zero if the average daily high exceeds 68°F for that month, and equals the difference between the average daily high and 68°F otherwise. The night heating requirement is defined similarly, substituting the average daily low for the average daily high. The day cooling requirement index is defined analogously: zero if the average daily high is below 68°F and the difference between the high and 68°F otherwise.[16]

Finally, the gas space heating and cooling indices are defined as the relevant temperature index times the square footage of the house whenever the dwelling unit contains gas main heating or cooling (and the month is not one in which the appliance is constrained to be off). The day and night space heating indices are included independently and in interaction with several other dummy variables: the type of gas heating (forced air or other) and the house insulation variables mentioned earlier. The swimming pool heating indices are defined simply as the average daily high and low temperatures for the month whenever a gas pool heater is present.

The additional control variables in the model can be simply described. A regional dummy variable is included to discriminate between inland and coastal or maritime areas. Another dummy variable is included to distinguish single-family dwellings from others. Dummy variables are also used to indicate the age brackets (e.g., 45–54 or 55–64) of the adults and whether a young child (5 years of age or less) is present. Additional variables representing socioeconomic characteristics are included: the number of people in the household, the educational level of the head (measured on a scale of 0 through 8), and the income level of the head. The last was estimated by using the midpoints of the first 9 income brackets identified by the survey, and through an auxiliary regression based on Pareto's Law to estimate the mean income in the 10th and highest bracket of $50,000 and over.[17]

Let us turn now to the econometric procedures. One problem is how to deal with the simultaneity problem. There are both demand and supply functions that relate price (or cost) and quantity. The demand function is observed with errors, whereas the supply function is not. This suggests that ordinary least squares (OLS) estimates will be biased toward the supply parameters. To deal with this, I use an instrumental variable approach used by Hausman and Wise (1976) for labor supply and later used by Hausman, Kinnucan, and McFadden (1979) for residential energy demand.[18] An unbiased estimate of predicted quantity is made by regressing all of the exogenous variables on actual quantity. This predicted quantity is then used with the known rate schedule to determine the predicted average price (for the BR hypothesis), as well as the predicted marginal price and predicted lump sum subsidy (the latter two for the SUM hypothesis).[19] These series are then used with the other model variables to estimate the structural demand equations associated with each of the two behavioral hypotheses.

Another econometric problem to contend with concerns the pooling of time series and cross-sectional data. Using a Cobb–Douglas functional form, the data determine temporal groupings through a series of structural homogeneity (Chow) tests. I sought the fewest equations possible in order to reduce the chances for ambiguous results of the main tests of the behavioral hypotheses. I began with one equation (for each hypothesis) using all 53 months of data with month and year temporal dummies, and tested it for homogeneity against two equations in which the 6 summer months per year and 6 winter months per year were estimated separately. Structural homogeneity was rejected, and I continued the process (next testing each of the 6-month equations against two 3-month equations, etc.). The result was four stable monthly groupings, each including all years, as shown at the top of Tables 6.2 and 6.3.

An important finding of this testing is that there is a great deal of stability over the years: All of the monthly equations are stable (i.e., homogeneity cannot be rejected) over the 4.5-year period. Relative to 1979, consumption in the later years either decreased or changed insignificantly; there is only one case (May–June 1980) where consumption increased significantly. This suggests that any uncontrolled changes

Table 6.2. *Bounded Rationality Model Estimates (Asymptotic t-Statistics in Parentheses)*

Variable	Feb.–Apr.	May–June	July–Oct.	Nov.–Jan.
INTERCEPT	−2.11226	−2.47123	−1.74154	−1.25908
	(5.66)	(5.34)	(7.45)	(4.13)
EDUC	−.02145	−.02527	−.01075	−.00917
	(4.58)	(4.26)	(2.22)	(1.66)
PREBOOM	−.05342	−.01433	.02341	−.04248
	(2.28)	(.48)	(.98)	(1.53)
MIDDLE	.08394	.07120	.13947	.13699
	(4.24)	(2.82)	(6.74)	(5.79)
MATURE	.15355	.09504	.04671	.24057
	(6.90)	(3.41)	(2.07)	(9.01)
ELDER	.15081	.11203	.10218	.15858
	(5.02)	(2.97)	(3.28)	(4.46)
BABY	−.03487	.04212	.15286	.03389
	(1.12)	(1.06)	(4.75)	(.91)
NUM	−.03640	−.04482	−.02615	−.03479
	(2.78)	(2.73)	(1.90)	(2.20)
INLAND	.08967	.10305	−.00499	−.03109
	(3.84)	(3.46)	(.21)	(1.12)
SFHOME	.11598	.01768	−.00178	.11746
	(3.91)	(.49)	(.06)	(3.40)
STOVN	.00957	.03034	.05940	.01291
	(1.54)	(3.83)	(9.33)	(1.74)
DRYN	.03202	.02817	.03878	.02576
	(6.00)	(4.15)	(7.10)	(4.08)
WATN	.02517	.06408	.03229	.01984
	(1.52)	(3.08)	(1.90)	(1.00)
JACN	.02021	.00729	.02760	.02496
	(1.82)	(.53)	(2.53)	(1.90)
WASHN	.03070	.00913	.00295	.05119
	(2.45)	(.58)	(.23)	(3.46)
DISHWSHN	.00429	.00690	.02302	.00035
	(.68)	(.86)	(3.59)	(.05)
EXHT	.29875	−.25303	−.41563	.17326
	(3.42)	(2.29)	(4.57)	(1.66)
SUBHEAT	.03038	−.00554	−.06352	−.01754
	(1.62)	(.24)	(3.46)	(.78)
MICRO	.04715	.07874	.11806	.08560
	(1.75)	(2.32)	(4.36)	(2.67)
HEATDY	−.10052	−.05048	—	.14588
	(.72)	(.12)		(.87)
HEATNT	.00297	−.02023	—	−.01247
	(.18)	(.62)		(.67)

Variable	Feb.–Apr.	May–June	July–Oct.	Nov.–Jan.
NWHTDY	−.07330	.28229	—	−.05798
	(.62)	(.87)		(.44)
NWHTNT	−.04953	−.05825	—	−.04623
	(6.00)	(3.00)		(5.57)
FAHEATDY	.57262	.44781	—	.36238
	(4.21)	(1.10)		(2.40)
FAHEATNT	.01351	−.00292	—	.01427
	(1.57)	(.13)		(1.60)
ATHEATDY	.04167	.08997	—	.16969
	(.38)	(.27)		(1.46)
ATHEATNT	−.00210	−.00355	—	−.02192
	(.29)	(.20)		(2.88)
CIHEATDY	−.34138	.64391	—	−.42346
	(2.52)	(1.63)		(2.91)
CIHEATNT	.00852	.05385	—	.02371
	(.88)	(2.28)		(2.33)
WIHEATDY	−.05285	−.15612	—	−.04512
	(.48)	(.48)		(.36)
WIHEATNT	.03630	.04234	—	.01066
	(4.98)	(2.37)		(1.41)
POOLDY	.01403	.00810	.02131	.01925
	(2.82)	(1.84)	(6.33)	(4.13)
POOLNT	−.02655	−.01507	−.03122	−.03568
	(3.75)	(2.57)	(6.87)	(4.93)
COOLDY	—	.08888	.06307	—
		(3.06)	(4.11)	
YR80	−.17285	.14516	−.07638	−.10879
	(4.41)	(2.93)	(3.32)	(3.58)
YR81	−.19917	−.06206	−.14163	−.25568
	(3.77)	(.80)	(5.70)	(7.80)
YR82	−.13535	.05382	−.04660	−.10263
	(2.11)	(.55)	(1.08)	(1.82)
YR83	−.11774	.24893	—	−.10905
	(.99)	(1.53)		(1.21)
JAN.	—	—	—	.21508
				(5.23)
FEB.	.28879	—	—	—
	(13.02)			
MAR.	.13812	—	—	—
	(7.10)			

(continued)

Table 6.2 *(continued)*

Variable	Feb.–Apr.	May–June	July–Oct.	Nov.–Jan.
MAY	—	.11402	—	—
		(2.11)		
JULY	—	—	.02044	—
			(.78)	
AUG.	—	—	−.04845	—
			(2.09)	
SEP.	—	—	−.07977	—
			(3.52)	
NOV.	—	—	—	−.47429
				(17.92)
SQFTBC	.02986	.01824	.01854	.03500
	(9.95)	(9.11)	(12.32)	(9.32)
INCBC	.00454	.00235	.00178	.00412
	(8.72)	(5.97)	(5.66)	(6.73)
PAPBC	−.43923	−1.20395	−.70913	.45076
	(1.32)	(2.75)	(2.73)	(1.40)
PAPHTBC	−.10008	−.04493	—	−.17153
	(2.06)	(.74)		(2.72)
n	3163	2263	3599	2750
λ	.35	.40	.40	.35

over the time of the sample are an unlikely source of bias. This would apply, for example, to changes in the appliance stock of households over this period. Furthermore, a bill formatting change implemented during 1981 to provide some additional information (but not the complete rate structure) seems to have had an insignificant impact (one would expect consumption to increase if the BR hypothesized here was reduced; the trend, however, was in the opposite direction).

The Goldfeld–Quandt tests were used to check for heteroskedasticity, and the hypothesis of homoskedasticty was maintained. Finally, the Box–Cox technique was used to determine a precise functional form. The dependent variable (divided by its geometric mean for normalization) and those identified as the economic variables in Table 6.1 were subjected to the Box–Cox transformation, choosing the minimum sum of squared errors (SSE) within the range for the transformation parameter λ of $0 < \lambda \leq 1$. The transformation parameters were estimated at .35 for two equations and .40 for the other two (the same across the competing behavioral specifications); since the 95% confidence interval in each

Table 6.3. *Utility-Maximization Model Estimates (Asymptotic t-Statistics in Parentheses)*

Variable	Feb.–Apr.	May–June	July–Oct.	Nov.–Jan.
INTERCEPT	−1.34111	−1.00308	−1.14238	−1.70339
	(2.83)	(3.94)	(4.78)	(6.17)
EDUC	−.02228	−.02708	−.01209	−.00907
	(4.74)	(4.58)	(2.49)	(1.64)
PREBOOM	−.05977	−.01734	.02197	−.04268
	(2.55)	(.58)	(.92)	(1.54)
MIDDLE	.08896	.07452	.14837	.13417
	(4.45)	(2.95)	(7.14)	(5.71)
MATURE	.16220	.10012	.05147	.23698
	(7.11)	(3.58)	(2.28)	(8.96)
ELDER	.15923	.11842	.10110	.15999
	(5.23)	(3.13)	(3.22)	(4.47)
BABY	−.04146	.04594	.16218	.03164
	(1.32)	(1.16)	(5.04)	(.86)
NUM	−.03735	−.04616	−.02984	−.03319
	(2.85)	(2.80)	(2.17)	(2.10)
INLAND	.09514	.12557	.00199	−.03198
	(4.09)	(4.32)	(.08)	(1.14)
SFHOME	.12077	.03032	.00145	.10928
	(4.15)	(.84)	(.05)	(3.19)
STOVN	.00973	.03062	.06025	.01305
	(1.56)	(3.85)	(9.28)	(1.76)
DRYN	.03391	.03031	.03916	.02546
	(6.34)	(4.48)	(7.13)	(4.04)
WATN	.02636	.06971	.03607	.01776
	(1.59)	(3.37)	(2.13)	(.89)
JACN	.02178	.01037	.02643	.02595
	(1.96)	(.75)	(2.42)	(1.97)
WASHN	.03266	.00695	.00366	.05142
	(2.59)	(.44)	(.29)	(3.46)
DISHWSHN	.00507	.00688	.02376	.00029
	(.80)	(.85)	(3.68)	(.04)
EXHT	.32296	−.23120	−.46814	.16801
	(3.68)	(2.09)	(5.26)	(1.61)
SUBHEAT	.03096	−.00253	−.06343	−.01791
	(1.65)	(.11)	(3.44)	(.80)
MICRO	.05095	.08999	.12220	.08312
	(1.89)	(2.66)	(4.45)	(2.61)
HEATDY	−.09356	−.12221	—	.13114
	(.67)	(.29)		(.79)

(continued)

Table 6.3 *(continued)*

Variable	Feb.–Apr.	May–June	July–Oct.	Nov.–Jan.
HEATNT	.00288	−0.2387	—	−0.1430
	(.17)	(.73)	—	(.78)
NWHTDY	−.08008	.24248	—	−.04544
	(.68)	(.75)		(.35)
NWHTNT	−.05135	−.05776	—	−.04696
	(6.19)	(2.91)		(5.62)
FAHEATDY	.57013	.47852	—	.36594
	(4.20)	(1.17)		(2.43)
FAHEATNT	.01482	.00104	—	.01437
	(1.72)	(.05)		(1.61)
ATHEATDY	.04501	.12329	—	.16931
	(.41)	(.36)		(1.46)
ATHEATNT	−.00137	−.00291	—	−.02105
	(.19)	(.16)		(2.77)
CIHEATDY	−.35015	−.64429	—	−.42761
	(2.58)	(1.63)		(2.93)
CIHEATNT	.00861	.05147	—	.02347
	(.89)	(2.18)		(2.31)
WIHEATDY	−.03755	−.12527	—	−.05346
	(.34)	(.39)		(.42)
WIHEATNT	.03704	.04110	—	.01154
	(5.09)	(2.27)		(1.53)
POOLDY	.01397	.00836	.02321	.01843
	(2.81)	(1.90)	(7.01)	(4.02)
POOLNT	−.02688	−.01589	−.03409	−.03432
	(3.79)	(2.71)	(7.68)	(4.84)
COOLDY	—	.08953	.06109	—
		(3.08)	(3.93)	
YR80	−.25741	.02636	−.07173	−.09960
	(6.13)	(.69)	(3.03)	(3.22)
YR81	−.33014	−.28920	−.16539	−.23402
	(5.09)	(5.90)	(6.61)	(6.82)
YR82	−.28987	−.25233	−.14442	−.03070
	(3.62)	(3.90)	(3.69)	(.57)
YR83	−.40709	−.26249	—	.00531
	(2.68)	(2.96)		(.07)
JAN.	—	—	—	.175220?
				(5.59)
FEB.	.31350	—	—	—
	(15.05)			
MAR.	.14556	—	—	—
	(7.37)			

Variable	Feb.–Apr.	May–June	July–Oct.	Nov.–Jan.
MAY	—	.16266	—	—
		(3.03)		
JULY	—	—	−.05342	—
			(2.27)	
AUG.	—	—	−.03934	—
			(1.69)	
SEP.	—	—	−.07956	—
			(3.50)	
NOV.	—	—	—	−.45977
				(18.66)
SQFTBC	.03162	.01969	.01970	.03491
	(10.82)	(10.15)	(13.43)	(9.57)
INCBC	.00477	.00244	.00184	.00416
	(8.92)	(6.11)	(5.763)	(6.70)
PLSBC	−.03410	−.01420	.02311	.00893
	(1.14)	(.50)	(.59)	(.39)
PMPBC	.27396	.18203	−.02136	.01549
	(.73)	(.92)	(.11)	(.07)
PMPHTBC	−.10956	−.05857	—	−.16157
	(2.43)	1.05)		(2.93)
n	3163	2263	3599	2750
λ	.35	.40	.40	.35

case is approximately ±.04, both Cobb–Douglas ($\lambda = 0$) and linear ($\lambda = 1$) forms must be rejected.[20]

Estimation Results

The estimates of the resulting structural demand equations are shown in Table 6.2 (for the BR hypothesis) and Table 6.3 (for the SUM hypothesis), and the regression means of the variables are shown in Table 6.4. For the noneconomic variables, there are only minor differences in the estimated coefficients and asymptotic standard errors across the behavioral models.[21] Among the demographic variables, education has the expected negative sign, and is clearly significant in three equations and marginally significant ($t = 1.65$) in the other. To illustrate its effect, an increase from 5 to 6 in education level (to some college beyond high school) implies just over a one therm reduction from the February–April

Table 6.4. *Means of Variables*

Variable	Feb.–Apr.	May–June	July–Oct.	Nov.–Jan.
SGASBC	.05730	.06963	.07112	.07683
EDUC	5.78185	5.76491	5.78327	5.78182
PREBOOM	.21499	.21167	.21756	.21455
MIDDLE	.29592	.29386	.29536	.29709
MATURE	.24850	.24967	.24979	.24727
ELDER	.12646	.12638	.12170	.12655
BABY	.10117	.10164	.10169	.09964
NUM	2.83070	2.82346	2.83857	2.82782
INLAND	.15839	.15952	.16088	.15891
SFHOME	.86374	.86213	.86079	.86073
STOVN	1.35093	1.36036	1.36774	1.36436
DRYN	1.31552	1.30137	1.32870	1.31236
WATN	2.63468	2.62329	2.66032	2.63636
JACN	.22321	.21807	.22048	.22218
WASHN	2.41827	2.40544	2.44248	2.42054
DISHWSHN	1.61650	1.60384	1.62656	1.61727
EXHT	.00885	.00884	.00889	.00873
SUBHEAT	.36390	.36058	.35621	.36073
MICRO	.13405	.13257	.13365	.13455
HEATDY	.07969	.01622	—	.08657
HEATNT	2.58693	.84917	—	3.01011
NWHTDY	.02120	.00471	—	.02453
NWHTNT	.59913	.19452	—	.69472
FAHEATDY	.07969	.01280	—	.06754
FAHEATNT	2.58693	.62565	—	2.22417
ATHEATDY	.05599	.01168	—	.06014
ATHEATNT	1.76510	.57727	—	2.05753
CIHEATDY	.05893	.01192	—	.06521
CIHEATNT	2.04061	.66683	—	2.39086
WIHEATDY	.02948	.00644	—	.03153
WIHEATNT	.82451	.27293	—	.95553
POOLDY	5.85686	6.41361	6.97102	6.03764
POOLNT	4.09583	4.79992	5.18052	3.88838
COOLDY	—	.04067	.07319	—
YR80	.21530	.19841	.24535	.25382
YR81	.21530	.20415	.25507	.24582
YR82	.21562	.19973	.25452	.25018
YR83	.21910	.20548	—	.08364
JAN.	—	—	—	.33636
FEB.	.28612	—	—	—
MAR.	.35694	—	—	—

Variable	Feb.–Apr.	May–June	July–Oct.	Nov.–Jan.
MAY	—	.50155	—	—
JULY	—	—	.25035	—
AUG.	—	—	.24423	—
SEP.	—	—	.25063	—
NOV.	—	—	—	.32982
SQFTBC	33.64066	43.49570	43.53626	33.61666
INCBC	92.31331	135.01849	135.20256	92.10303
PAPBC	−1.01527	−.97226	−.93193	−.98888
PAPHTBC	−.94061	−.45895	—	−.91583
PLSBC	.50407	.03297	−.09317	−.06892
PMPBC	−1.01698	−1.00041	−1.01942	−1.06751
PMPHTBC	−.93909	−.48308	—	−.98618

monthly mean of 55 therms. From this same mean, the difference between the least and most educated households is 8.6 therms.

Among the other demographic variables, household consumption generally increases with the age of the head. The negative coefficient on the number of people in the household is a bit misleading; the number of people is also interacted with most of the natural-gas-using appliances, all of which have the right sign and some of which all households have. Increases in number at the mean have the expected positive effects on consumption. Those households located inland generally use more energy than others, and single-family homes generally use more energy than other dwellings.

All of the appliances have the correct signs with two minor exceptions. Having an extra (natural-gas-using) heater seems to reduce consumption in May through October, and having a microwave oven (assumed to be a substitute for a natural-gas-using appliance) is associated with increased gas consumption.[22]

The effects of the main home heating appliance are not transparent because they work through 12 complex variables. Nevertheless, new homes are more efficient than older ones, and insulation does reduce consumption. For example, dwelling units with attics enjoy an average reduction of consumption of between 3 and 4 therms per month during the November–January period, or about 7% of mean consumption.

Swimming pool heaters do not have strong effects in this sample; the two variables measuring high and low temperatures for residences with pool heaters are each significant but together largely offsetting.

Nevertheless, the estimates suggest, as expected, that higher temperatures (e.g., a 1°F increase in both the high and the low temperature) tend to reduce consumption. Finally, homes with air conditioners powered by natural gas do have substantially higher consumption in May through October.

To sum up, the estimated effects of the noneconomic variables are in accord with expectations. Almost all of them are significant, with the expected signs and coefficients of plausible magnitudes.

The economic variables represent wealth, income, and price factors. The square footage variable, interpreted here as a wealth proxy, is strongly significant in all equations. The elasticity of consumption with respect to wealth is approximately constant across the estimated equations from .34 in the July–October period to .38 in February–April. The income elasticity is also positive and significant in all equations, from .10 in July–October to .15 in February–April. Both of these are quite inelastic, as one should expect when the appliance stock is being held constant.

Turning to the price variables, it now becomes important to consider the estimates from the competing models separately. Under the BR hypothesis, there are seven price variables in the four equations. Four of these variables are negative and significant, two are negative but not significant, and one is positive but not significant. The elasticities associated with these estimates at the sample geometric means are shown in Table 6.5. Over a year, the average short-run elasticity is −.25 for residences with natural gas heating and −.19 for those without natural gas heating. These estimates certainly are close to what one would expect a priori.

Table 6.5. *Summary of Price Elasticity Estimates from the Box–Cox Estimations*

Period	Residences w/o Gas Heating		Residences with Gas Heating		Therms at Sample Geometric Means
	BR	SUM	BR	SUM	
Feb.–Apr.	−.28	+.08	−.34	+.10	55.12
May–June	−.72	+.11	−.74	+.07	31.16
July–Oct.	−.43	−.01	−.43	−.01	21.59
Nov.–Jan.	+.29	+.01	+.18	−.09	49.20
Monthly average	−.19	+.08	−.25	+.02	44.32

Under the SUM hypothesis, there are seven marginal price variables analogous to the average price variables discussed previously. Five of the seven variables are not significant, two with negative signs and three with positive signs. Two are negative and significant. Table 6.5 shows the implied elasticities at the means. Over the year, the average short-run elasticity is slightly positive, .02 for gas-heated residences and .08 for others. These estimates are somewhat disappointing if the underlying theory is valid; they imply that consumers are simply not detectably sensitive to price in the short run. Although some consumers may in fact be insensitive, one would hope that in a sample as detailed as this one, with the length of time and magnitude of price changes covered, a detectable negative response would be identified.

In addition to the seven marginal price variables of this specification, there are four lump-sum subsidy variables. These are all insignificant, two with negative signs and two with positive signs. Although a strict interpretation of the theory implies that these variables should have effects identical to those of the income variables, I do not find the insignificance disturbing. After all, the size of the lump-sum subsidy is almost always under $20, and the expected effect of this on therm consumption (given the sample incomes and income elasticities reported earlier) is so small that it would strain credulity to believe it could be reliably detected.

Finally, I note that there may be an interpretable seasonal pattern to the BR price elasticity estimates reported in Table 6.5. Bills are highest in the February–April period, which may heighten sensitivity in the following May–June period. As bills decrease due to seasonal factors, price sensitivity decreases with a lag. Responding to the lowest bills in July–October, consumers display the least price sensitivity during November–January. But then bills increase sharply, and price sensitivity grows again in February–April. One cannot offer this interpretation under the SUM hypothesis, where the estimates suggest a constant insensitivity.

Hypothesis Testing

There are three types of tests I use to evaluate the two competing hypotheses. The first one is not really a formal test and has already been described: the plausibility of the estimated price effects under each hypothesis. Although this "test" is by its nature and with respect to actual results hardly definitive, the only plausible inference is that the results discussed earlier favor somewhat the BR hypothesis. The degree to which it is favored depends on the strength of convictions concerning the detectability of small, negative price effects. Virtually all prior econometric studies of home energy consumption in the short run, unconcerned with the hypotheses under examination here, have maintained the expectation of detecting small, statistically significant negative price effects. By extension, one ought to maintain that expectation here as well, and therefore the results favor the BR hypothesis.

The second and third tests are more formal. The second test consists of a series of *J*-tests on the estimated demand equations. The *J*-test is appropriate when there are two competing models and one data set used to explain the same dependent variable. It essentially adds to the model being tested an additional right-hand-side variable of predicted consumption based on the alternative model; if this additional variable is significant based upon its *t*-statistic, then one rejects the model being tested in favor of the alternative (see Ram, 1986, for another example).

Column 2 of Table 6.6 reports the results of the tests with the null hypothesis that the BR model is true and the SUM model is false. Column 3 reports the results of testing the reverse null hypothesis that SUM is true and BR is false. Columns 4 and 5 summarize the results. At the 1% level, the BR hypothesis is supported in two of four periods (the lower consumption periods), and SUM is not supported in any period. This unambiguously favors BR. At the weaker 5% level, however, some ambiguity is introduced: There is no additional support for BR, but SUM is now supported in three of the four periods (the higher-consumption

Table 6.6. *J-Tests of Estimated Equations (T-Ratios)*

Period	H_0: BR Is True and SUM Is False	H_0: SUM Is True and BR Is False	Supported Hypothesis (Level = .01)	Supported Hypothesis (Level = .05)
Feb.–Apr.	2.42*	.34		SUM
May–June	2.54*	3.91**	BR	BR, SUM
July–Oct.	1.95	3.39**	BR	BR
Nov.–Jan.	2.06*	.54		SUM

*$t > 1.97$, the 5% level.
**$t > 2.60$, the 1% level.

periods). Since it is difficult to argue that there is one "right" testing level for making the comparison, I conclude that the *J*-tests by themselves do not show which hypothesis should be preferred.

These results may not be very surprising. It is tempting to offer the interpretation that consumers pay more attention to their bills in the higher-consumption months (i.e., behave closer to SUM) and less in the lower-consumption months (i.e., behave closer to BR). If one relates these tests to the estimated price elasticities, this conclusion is reasonable for November–January. It is the one period in which the elasticities from both models for gas-heated residences are insignificant, with the wrong sign for BR and the right sign for SUM. However, the results for February–April do not really support this interpretation. The *J*-test offers weak support for the SUM model with an insignificant but positive price elasticity of .10 for gas-heated residences, but not for the BR model with a significant and negative elasticity of −.34.

The third test is designed to be the most important: comparing the predictions of the two models on an independent sample. A new 1% sample was drawn from the master tape, with the restriction that only residences with square footage exceeding 1,050 be selected. This restriction served two purposes: (1) it ensured that the distribution of the random sample would not be identical to the distribution of the estimating sample; and (2) recalling that the two hypotheses had the greatest predictive difference for households with consumption exceeding the lifeline amount, it tilted the test sample toward those households.

There are 2,738 monthly observations in this sample, and the results of the prediction tests are shown in Table 6.7. For each of the structural equations, predicted consumption is compared with actual consumption and the root mean square is calculated. In three of the four equations,

Table 6.7. *Prediction Accuracy on New Sample with SQFT > 1,050 (Root Mean Squares)*

Period	n	BR	SUM	Supported Hypothesis
Feb.–Apr.	732	27.88	28.76	BR
May–June	528	21.83	22.07	BR
July–Oct.	845	13.65	13.84	BR
Nov.–Jan.	633	26.74	26.49	U-Max
Total	2738	22.86	23.16	BR

Table 6.8. *Summary Table of Three Tests*

Period	Significant Negative Price Effects	J-Test .01 Level	J-Test .05 Level	Predictive Accuracy
Feb.–Apr.	BR		SUM	BR
May–June	BR	BR	BR, SUM	BR
July–Oct.	BR	BR	BR	BR
Nov.–Jan.	SUM		SUM	SUM
Overall	BR	BR	?	BR

BR has lower root mean squares and is thus more accurate than SUM. SUM does better only in the November–January period, and recall that it is the one period for which a comparison of the estimated price effects does not favor BR. For the overall prediction test, shown in the last row of Table 6.7, the BR model is more accurate.

In Table 6.8, I attempt to summarize the results of each test for each structural equation. Each cell in the table reports the hypothesis favored by a particular test. Column 2 reports the favored hypothesis based on the expectation of negative price effects, columns 3 and 4 based on the J-test, and column 5 based on predictive accuracy. The first four rows represent the four structural equations, and the final row is an overall assessment. It is clear that in three of the four periods, and overall, the preponderance of the evidence favors the BR model.

Concluding Observations

The tests reported here are designed to answer one question about residential energy consumption under block rate pricing structures. The question is: If we are to choose one of two alternative behavioral models to represent household behavior, which one is best? For this study, the answer is the Bounded Rationality (BR) model: Household behavior is better explained and predicted by the model, assuming that households respond simply to the total bill, compared to the SUM model, which assumes that households maximize utility subject to the actual block rate structure.

What other questions are raised by the results reported here? Just how poorly does the SUM model fare? In the November–January period, the standard model works better. This makes one wonder if perhaps consumers put more effort into their decision making as the stakes go up. Perhaps, by extension, consumers in the San Diego area, due to its moderate climate, are not typical of consumers living in less moderate climates. This is certainly worth exploring, although the results reported here do not fully support this idea: The stakes here are highest in February–April, and in this period the BR model generates more plausible price elasticities and better predictions.

The preceding idea sticks with the notion of households characterized by identical decision-making processes; the precise routine used for any particular situation varies with the importance of the situation. Of course, households need not all be characterized by the same type of decision making. It is certainly possible that one could better explain and predict behavior (holding the decision-making environment constant) by classifying each household into one of the two models and using both. That is, one could imagine concluding that the SUM model works best for, say, 30% of the population and the BR model is best for the other 70%. Again, this is certainly worth exploring, but it does work against the objective of model simplicity that has characterized economic research heretofore.

Are the welfare implications of these results important for energy allocation? I believe the answer is yes, primarily because it is so common to observe large price differences (of 50 to 100%) across blocks, and under BR such differences create large errors. Take the example of a household with short-run price elasticity of −.25 facing a rate structure with a 50% price increase for the second block and consuming a modest 20% above the first block size (such a household is near the average in northern California). If this consumption choice is due to BR, then the overconsumption is about 8%, the overexpenditure is about 12%, and the net loss from the consumer's perspective is about 2% of expenditure.[23] These figures become substantially larger if the behavior extends to long-run decision making, where price elasticities are thought to be in the elastic range. Thus it is certainly worthwhile to consider whether or not there are cost-effective policies by which one might reduce these errors.

One can imagine trying to reduce the errors through two types of strategies: information provision and changes in the rate structure. For example, each bill might include a message of the following sort: "10% less consumption would have saved you $8.20." However, if such information provision has effects similar to those generally reported in studies of information provision, it is unlikely to eliminate the majority of errors and thus a substantial problem will remain.[24]

Thus one might consider alterations in the rate design itself. Of course, economists have long advocated changes to bring rates more in line with marginal costs. It is interesting to note that the two-part tariff idea, with rates uniform at marginal costs and a fixed customer charge assessed to raise the rest of the utility's revenue requirement, has good potential for solving the BR problem as well. If the fixed charge could be assessed separately from the monthly consumption charges, substantial efficiency gains would be predicted (for different reasons) by both models compared to the block rate structures now in common use.

Finally, the results reported here raise the issue of whether similar behavior may be found in other areas. It would, of course, be natural to explore the BR hypothesis for other difficult consumption choices subject to block rate structures, like that of commercial and even industrial energy customers, or for other services like telephones or water delivery. More intriguing still is the question of whether this behavior characterizes other choices made under nonlinear price structures, like the labor-leisure choices of those eligible for income-support programs, or choices made nonlinear by complex tax rules such as child-care expenditures or many investments. And the possibility exists, as suggested by the earlier example of household budgeting in general, that this behavior may characterize certain difficult choices under normal price structures.

Notes

1 Herbert Simon has been a long-time proponent of these models. See, for example, Simon (1959, 1979). More recently, Richard Thaler (1980, 1985) has made numerous modeling contributions in this vein.

2 A good discussion of these is contained in Lesourne (1977). See also Machina (1987, 1989) and Camerer and Kunreuther (1989). Much of the debate has focused on individual responses to uncertainty, particularly low-probability events like the reliability of electricity (see Hartman, Doane, & woo, 1991), or insurance purchases in earthquake- or flood-prone areas (see Kunreuther, 1976, and Brookshire, Thayer, Tschirhart, & Schulze, 1985). Sometimes the debate in this context is described as relevant only to utility-maximization, although Grether and Plott (1979) and Tversky, Slovic, and Kahneman (1990) make it clear that the debate extends to utility-maximization more generally.

3 For a discussion of testing difficulties, see Roth (1989).

4 See Smith (1989) for an introduction to and a summary of this literature. The same generalization can be applied to the public goods literature studying actual preference revelations more "honest" than those expected by conventional theory; see, e.g., Marwell and Ames (1981).

5 The effect of repetitive trials has also been considered in the public goods literature; see, e.g., Isaac, McHugh, and Plott (1985).

6   In the long run, the appliance stock would itself change in response to fuel prices. The short-run focus here avoids this issue.

7   In such a case, one still might be interested in the difficult problem of understanding the adjustment process. This research tests the central tendencies rather than the nature of adjustment around them. Research to test the nature of the adjustment process itself can potentially be useful for distinguishing LUM from BR models, which this research does not attempt. Such research would examine trial-and-error learning, and might distinguish between optimal and suboptimal trials.

8   Most BR models do not have a unique equilibrium, but rather a set of outcomes that satisfice and adjustments triggered only by outcomes outside of the satisficing range. Further assumptions would be required to specify such behavior here, and the main testable implication of a divergence in equilibrium between BR and SUM would be the same: The shift to a nonlinear rate structure has no effect on the midpoint of the set of satisficing points, although it does affect the SUM equilibrium.

9   *Overconsumption* and *underconsumption*, as used here, refer to deviations from the utility-maximizing choice, not to a social perspective. Evaluating the latter requires linking actual rates to true social costs, which is beyond the scope of this study.

10 Little attention has been given to the possibility of this type of consumer in the empirical literature on utility services. For electricity, there was an early debate (reviewed in Bohi, 1982) on the use of average versus marginal prices, but this was motivated by an entirely different issue: how to represent a block rate structure when each observation was an *aggregate* of consumers (many facing different marginal prices and each assumed to be utility-maximizing). Similarly, Taylor (1975) considered the use of average price to represent the income effect of intramarginal tiers relevant to a utility-maximizing consumer, although Nordin (1976) pointed out that this is incorrect and that the lump-sum subsidy must itself be calculated. Parti and Parti (1980) did use the average price as perceived by each household rather than the marginal price. However, the focal point of their work was not to debate or theorize about consumer behavior or price specification, but to construct their conditional demand model, which allows separate demand equations for each appliance to be inferred from the overall household demand equation. Keane and Aigner (1982) considered the possibility of bounded rationality in a different way. Using aggregate data with cities as the unit of observation they tested whether jointly billed customers (i.e., those with one bill for both natural gas and electricity) responded differently to price than other customers and found no significant differences. An interesting debate at the theoretical level occurred in the journal *Land Economics*, in which several authors raised the possibility that water consumers (facing block rates) respond to average price and discussed possible tests. See, for example, Opaluch (1984).

11 An excellent survey by Moffitt (1990) of estimation problems with nonlinear budget constraints did not discuss the type of bounded rationality problem under consideration here.

12 Nordin (1976) describes the theoretical treatment of the nonlinear rate structure.

13 The original tape contains an unfortunate but detectable compilation error that corrupts the consumption and billing data for 45% of the original 12,379

households. I am grateful to Steve Slezak for calling this to my attention. No important differences were found between the included and excluded observations in terms of demographics or physical characteristics of the dwelling unit; there are concentrations of excluded observations in a few geographic portions of the service area. The error was detectable because in each case the household time series had a few missing observations and then continued by repeating identically the earlier consumption and billing data.

14 Coding errors were presumed if the reported quantity combined with the rate structure for that time was inconsistent with the reported billing amount.

15 There are a small number of air conditioning systems run centrally on natural gas (1.7% of households in the master file), and potentially the insulating characteristics would also affect the energy required for cooling. However, in the sample we use here, such air conditioners are negligible in number and thus do not permit these interaction terms.

16 The sample had no positive observations with an analogously defined night cooling index, so no variable for it was included.

17 Pareto's Law states that the number of households (N) with incomes (Y) greater than the mean income of the population may be approximated as

$$N = \alpha Y^\beta$$

with parameters $\alpha > 0$ and $\beta < 0$. From this we may derive a simple expression for the total income contributed by households with income greater than $50,000. First, note that the (negative) change in the number of households as Y increases can be expressed as the derivative:

$$\frac{\partial N}{\partial Y} = \beta \alpha Y^{\beta-1}$$

The contribution of this incremental group to total income is simply the negative of the preceding expression multiplied by Y:

$$-Y\left(\frac{\partial N}{\partial Y}\right) = -\beta \alpha Y^\beta$$

The integral of the preceding expression from $Y = \$50,000$ to $Y = \infty$ is the total income contributed by households with incomes in excess of $50,000.

$$\int_{Y=\$50,000}^{Y=\infty} -\beta \alpha Y^\beta \, dy = \frac{\beta \alpha (50,000)^{\beta+1}}{\beta + 1}$$

This expression can be used with the sample data to estimate the mean income level in the $50,000 and up bracket. The mean income in the original survey was reported as $21,800. In a preliminary sample drawn from the master tape, there were 90 households with income greater than $30,000, 28 households exceeding $40,000 in income, and 17 households reporting income in excess of $50,000. These four observations were used to estimate the parameters α and

β from the basic Pareto equation by regression in logarithmic form (t-statistics in parentheses):

$$\ln N = \ln \alpha + \beta \ln Y$$
$$= 29.31977444 - 2.44917816 \ln Y$$
$$\quad (36.90) \qquad\qquad (-32.26) \qquad R^2 = .998$$

Taking the antilog of the first term to solve for α, and then plugging the estimates of α and β into the equation for the value of the integral, we estimate that households with incomes of $50,000 or greater have a total income of $1,417,980.12 among them. Since there were 17 such households in the sample, we estimate the mean income for this group at $83,411.

18 An alternative method with two error components, introduced by Burtless and Hausman (1978) and reviewed by Moffitt (1990), has advantages for dealing with observations at the kink points. This method is not used here for several reasons. First, one of the error components represents optimization error, which implies that observed behavior cannot be taken as utility-maximizing and is thus inconsistent with the purpose of this study. Second, the observations in this sample are very widely dispersed over the budget constraint, and do not cluster at the kink points where the alternative method gains its advantages.

19 A utility-maximizing equilibrium with a nonlinear constraint is described in terms of two effects: the effect of the marginal price and the income effect of the lump-sum subsidy caused by not charging the marginal price for the intramarginal units. See Nordin (1976).

20 An approximate 95% confidence interval for λ is found by solving for the two values of λ for which $\ln \text{SSE}(\lambda) - \ln \text{SSE}(\lambda) = 3.84/\text{d.f.}$, where 3.84 is from the chi-square distribution table with 1 degree of freedom and $p = .05$. See, e.g., Box and Draper (1987, pp. 289–291).

21 Tables 6.2 and 6.3 report asymptotic t-ratios: those approached as error due to the use of price instruments, estimated G's, and uncontrolled household preference effects vanish.

22 These are minor because it is, of course, possible to use the extra heater as a substitute for the main heating and to use the microwave as a complement to other gas cooking appliances.

23 It is important to distinguish this net loss calculation from the standard measures of relative efficiency. Due to the nature of utility regulation, there is no reason to assume that the actual marginal price faced by a consumer has any relation to the social cost of providing the marginal unit. This calculation is simply a measure of the importance of the household's error from its own perspective. The importance of these errors to efficiency depends on the relationships between actual rates and marginal social costs of electricity. The calculations are approximations made using a constant elasticity demand function and are similar for a linear function.

24 See, for example, the discussion of this point in Friedman and Hausker (1988) and the studies on energy consumption reviewed in Stern (1986). I have argued elsewhere (Friedman, 1991) that the effectiveness of other rate design policies in electricity pricing, such as interruptible service and time-of-day rates (and

its extension to continuous or real-time pricing), depends on the information provided about them and the ease with which consumers can understand and respond to them.

References

Bohi, D. (1982). Price elasticities of demand for energy: Evaluating the estimates. EPRI EA-2612. Palo Alto, CA: Electric Power Research Institute.

Box, G. E. P., & Draper, N. R. (1987). *Empirical model-building and response surfaces.* New York: Wiley.

Brookshire, D. S., Thayer, M., Tschirhart, J., & Schulze, W. (1985). A test of the Expected Utility Model: Evidence from earthquake risks. *Journal of Political Economy, 93,* 369–389.

Burtless, G., & Hausman, J. (1978). The effect of taxation on labour supply: Evaluating the Gary negative income tax experiment. *Journal of Political Economy, 86,* 1103–1130.

Camerer, C. F., & Kunreuther, H. (1989). Decision processes for low probability risks: Policy implications. *Journal of Policy Analysis and Management, 8,* 565–592.

Friedman, L. S. (1991). Energy utility pricing and customer response: The recent record in California. In R. Gilbert (Ed.), *Regulatory choices: A perspective on developments in energy policy* (pp. 10–62). Berkeley: University of California Press.

Friedman, L. S., & Hausker, K. (1988). Residential energy consumption: Models of consumer behavior and their implications for rate design. *Journal of Consumer Policy, 11,* 287–313.

Grether, D. M., & Plott, C. R. (1979). Economic theory of choice and the preference reversal phenomenon. *American Economic Review, 69,* 623–638.

Hartman, R. S., Doane, M. J., & Woo, C. K. (1991). Consumer rationality and the status quo. *Quarterly Journal of Economics, 106,* 141–162.

Hausman, J., Kinnucan, M., & McFadden, D. (1979). A two-level electricity demand model: Evaluation of the Connecticut time-of-day pricing test. *Journal of Econometrics, 10,* 263–289.

Hausman, J., & Wise, D. (1976). The evaluation of results from truncated samples: The New Jersey income maintenance experiment. *Annals of Economic and Social Measurement, 5,* 421–445.

Isaac, R. M., McHugh, K. F., & Plott, C. R. (1985). Public goods provision in an experimental environment. *Journal of Public Economics, 26,* 51–74.

Keane, D., & Aigner, D. J. (1982). Testing the joint billing effect hypothesis. *The Energy Journal, 3,* 113–128.

Kempton, W., & Montgomery, L. (1982). Folk quantification of energy. *Energy, 7,* 817–827.

Kunreuther, H. (1976). Limited knowledge and insurance protection. *Public Policy, 24,* 227–261.

Lesourne, J. (1977). *A theory of the individual for economic analysis.* New York: North-Holland.

Machina, M. J. (1987). Choice under uncertainty: Problems solved and unsolved. *Journal of Economic Perspectives, 1,* 121–154.

Machina, M. J. (1989). Dynamic consistency and non-expected utility models of choice under uncertainty. *Journal of Economic Literature, 27*, 1622–1668.

Marwell, G., & Ames, R. E. (1981). Economists free ride, does anyone else? Experiments on the provision of public goods, IV. *Journal of Public Economics, 15*, 295–310.

Moffitt, R. (1990). The econometrics of kinked budget constraints. *Journal of Economic Perspectives, 4*, 119–139.

Nordin, J. A. (1976). A proposed modification of Taylor's demand analysis: Comment. *Bell Journal of Economics, 7*, 719–721.

Opaluch, J. J. (1984). A test of consumer demand response to water prices: Reply. *Land Economics, 60*, 417–421.

Parti, M., & Parti, C. (1980). The total and appliance-specific conditional demand for electricity in the household sector. *Bell Journal of Economics, 11*, 309–321.

Ram, R. (1986). Government size and economic growth: A new framework and some evidence from cross-section and time-series data. *American Economic Review, 76*, 191–203.

Roth, T. P. (1989). *The present state of consumer theory.* Lanham, MD: University Press of America.

Simon, H. (1959). Theories of decision-making in economics and behavioral science. *American Economic Review, 49*, 223–283.

Simon, H. (1979). Rational decision making in business organizations. *American Economic Review, 69*, 493–513.

Smith, V. L. (1989). Theory, experiment and economics. *Journal of Economic Perspectives, 3*, 151–169.

Stern, P. (1986). Blind spots in policy analysis: What economics doesn't say about energy use. *Journal of Policy Analysis and Management, 5*, 200–227.

Taylor, L. D. (1975). The demand for electricity: A survey. *Bell Journal of Economics, 6*, 74–110.

Thaler, R. H. (1980). Toward a positive theory of consumer choice. *Journal of Economic Behavior and Organization, 1*, 39–60.

Thaler, R. H. (1985). Mental accounting and consumer choice. *Marketing Science, 4*, 199–214.

Tversky, A., Pal Slovic, P., & Kahneman, D. (1990). The causes of preference reversal. *American Economic Review, 80*, 204–217.

Part III

Applications to Political and Legal Processes and Institutions

7 Judgmental Heuristics and News Reporting

Sharon Dunwoody and Robert J. Griffin

A kind of cultural folklore has grown up around the practice of news reporting to explain how journalists do their job. It's a vibrant and enduring set of stories, spurred largely by the intersection of two factors. One is that, although news products are ubiquitous features of the cultural landscape, the processes that underlie these products are hidden from the users. Despite the fact that viewers can often see the newsroom looming behind well-groomed anchor people during TV newscasts, they are never permitted to see news actually being constructed. The second is that our culture (as well as others) regards the effects of media messages as both powerful and problematic. That is, we are much more likely to worry about the negative impacts of media messages than to celebrate the positive ones. Legends build rapidly around any process that combines mystery with the potential for evil.

These folkloric explanations are summoned to provide reasons for what people see when they attend to news. More specifically, they serve to rationalize people's perceptions that their media diet is awash in flawed accounts. Here are a few of the explanations that we hear from friends and family:

- Generating the largest audience possible is the primary goal of a journalist, and he or she will accomplish this by selecting stories that pander to the "lowest common denominator."
- Entertaining is more important than educating, so journalists will "sensationalize" information with few moral qualms.
- Social responsibility will always play second fiddle to the economic bottom line; journalists are out to "sell newspapers," not to provide a public service.

Like all folklore, these tales contain bits of truth. But they offer a very blunt instrument with which to trace the contours of news judgment and practice. Put another way, they don't explain much of the variance in what we see in our daily newspapers or on our television news programs.

In this chapter, we offer another set of tools that we think does a much better job of accounting for variance in news making. Our argument is that any single news story is the product of a host of small, individual-level decisions: selecting a story topic, choosing the story angle, deciding who will serve as a source, making sense of the streams of information that come the reporter's way. Further, we argue that the occupation of journalism employs some standardized strategies to make those decisions, judgmental shortcuts that closely resemble the heuristics used by most individuals to negotiate daily life. Permit us to emphasize this last point: These heuristics are not unique to the news business; rather, journalistic practice reinforces reporters and editors for using heuristics that are integral to problem solving for all of us, for better or worse. In the course of this chapter, we will discuss some of these heuristic devices and will offer a case study from the realm of environmental reporting to illustrate our points. Finally, we will speculate about the potential effects of such heuristic decision making on news and, ultimately, on the audiences for news products.

A Couple of Caveats

The reader should be aware that, although we will rarely use the term *behavioral decision theory* in this chapter, our focus on heuristic decision making places us squarely within that psychological domain. Where we may depart from some of our colleagues is that we do not, a priori, define heuristic decision making as necessarily deficient or irrational. Heuristic decisions are indeed superficial ones, as they rely on assessing only one or a handful of variables in a multivariate environment. But if an individual selects an important subset of variables on which to ground his or her decision, that may produce a respectable outcome most of the time. The heuristics promoted by journalism are often so grounded. And although journalists may utilize evidentiary strategies that occasionally make systematic analysts wince, their ways of making sense of the world resonate strongly with those of their audiences. One explanation of the power of the media, in fact, may be that mass media accounts amplify – rather than contradict – cultural sense-making.

This position is consonant with that of scholars of judgment and decision making who have followed on the heels of economist Herbert Simon (1982), who posits that individuals make judgments through a process of *satisficing*, that is, by selecting the first reasonable course of action instead of evaluating a larger set of options more systematically. Such a strategy is an adaptation, argues Simon, both to one's cognitive abilities and to the environment in which a given decision must be made. And it's an adaptation that suffices in most instances.

The psychologist Gerd Gigerenzer has built on Simon's work. He suggests that *one-reason decision making*, although indeed violating the tenets of classical rationality, is effective. In one recent study, Gigerenzer and Goldstein (1996) held a computer-simulation competition between one-reason decision making and more effortful inference procedures and found that the former consistently matched or outperformed the latter.

A final word of caution: Although this chapter will dwell on psychological processes, it will be important for the reader to resist concluding that one can account for 100% of the variance in news making at this level. Studies of journalistic work over the decades have found important determinants at the cultural (Coleman, 1995; Glasser & Ettema, 1989; Silverstone, 1985), occupational/professional (Dunwoody and Griffin, 1993; Fishman, 1980; McManus, 1991; Tuchman, 1978), and organizational (Breed, 1955; Dunwoody, 1979; Soloski, 1989) levels. In fact, our argument in this chapter is, in part, that the *occupation* of journalism works to privilege some judgmental shortcuts over others. Like all individuals, reporters are creatures of their social environment. Our job in this chapter is not to ignore the impact of that environment but rather to examine the influence of judgmental heuristics as they are brought into play within those sociocultural and organizational boundaries.

Journalistic Judgments

Journalistic work is characterized by speed, particularly in the world of daily news gathering. Products must emerge daily, even hourly; it is inconceivable to decide to skip, say, the Wednesday issue of a daily newspaper because reporters need more time to report complex stories. And new channels such as the World Wide Web are, if anything, ratcheting up the need for speed. An Internet news site may be updated on a minute-by-minute basis, raising legitimate questions about the social value of raw information.

In a world of rapidly recurring deadlines, journalists cannot afford to engage in systematic information processing. Instead, the occupation rewards those who can make quick decisions about "what's news" and decide rapidly how to cobble together a story. Extremely fast decisions are, perforce, heuristic ones. Thus, journalism is unapologetically a world of heuristic decision making.

To accomplish its work, journalism employs the kinds of judgmental shortcuts used in other walks of life; it has not constructed unique heuristics or even necessarily improved on existing ones. Part of the reason for the use of "mainstream" shortcuts is that the occupation has historically resisted the notion that one needs specialized training to become a journalist. Individuals are welcomed into the occupation from a variety of backgrounds, making it necessary for them to rely on a common subset of heuristics.

But perhaps more importantly, stories that employ the kinds of heuristic decision making likely to be used by members of the audience get a sympathetic reading from that audience. Readers may immediately see the relevance of vivid anecdotal information in a story and thus be more likely to learn from such information than from more systematic – but more pallid – evidence. Perversely, journalists may be most effective in influencing audiences when they employ the kinds of heuristic strategies that may be least effective in producing high-quality information.

Although there are many ways to categorize heuristic decision making, we will divide the heuristics used by journalists into two groups – those employed in topic selection and those used to make decisions about evidence in the course of reporting and writing a story. In the following sections, we provide examples from each category.

What's News?

Although news is a reconstruction – not a reflection – of reality, journalists rely heavily on environmental cues to signal when news is occurring. A journalist cannot create a topic from whole cloth; reporters who make up events or who interview nonexistent sources run afoul of their employers if discovered. (For the account of one promising young journalist who met his end by fabricating, see Bissinger, 1998.) Thus, journalists must monitor events and processes around them and select from those myriad possibilities a small subset of happenings to define as "news." Given the welter of possible news cues, reporters are quickly socialized to attend to a subset. Here are three of the more important cues:

Journalists Pay Attention When Things Go Wrong, Not When Things Go Right. The folkloric version of this heuristic is that journalists emphasize the negative, not the positive. And indeed, the typical daily newspaper or TV news report does seem to wallow in accounts of things going awry. A scientist whose fraudulent behavior is revealed will get much more press than one who plays by the rules. A convicted felon who, upon release from prison, commits another crime will get far more attention than will the former criminal who lives a respectable life after release.

Although individuals in our society routinely disparage this journalistic emphasis on the negative, it is a popular mainstream heuristic (Shoemaker, 1996). We all attend more closely to aberrant, usually negative happenings than to ordinary events in our environment. These negative occurrences are so salient that we routinely assign them a greater weight than we do positive ones. Slovic and colleagues have found that when people confront an array of evidence in the course of making a decision, a positive attribute does not count as much as a negative one (Slovic, 1992). In trying to decide how to react to a novel technology, for example, the presence of a small likelihood of coming to harm (negative) may outweigh numerous proposed benefits, leading an individual to reject the technology.

Another acknowledgment of the social importance of this heuristic is people's tendency to use the mass media as a surveillance device, as a way of keeping track of events in their environment (Shoemaker, 1996). It is apparently far more important to spot catastrophe looming than it is to be reminded of social regularity. Thus, the mass media typically characterize their societal role as that of serving as society's watchdog. That they honor this role more in the breach than in daily practice (see, e.g., Donohue, Tichenor, & Olien, 1995) does not detract from its importance as an occupational or cultural norm.

Events Are More Newsworthy Than Processes. The world of deadlines presents journalists with a major interpretive challenge. How does one give meaning to long-running natural and social processes, the warp and woof of daily life, when the goal is to produce independent dollops of information – stories – on a weekly, daily, or hourly basis? Sociologist Gaye Tuchman responds that journalism has established routines to help it anticipate, categorize, and package these processes. The result is a reconceptualization of the process as a series of discrete events. Says Tuchman, "The way in which newsmen classify events-as-news decreases the variability of the raw material processed by news organizations and facilitates routinization" (1997, p. 174).

The event is a ubiquitous feature of the news, so much so that sources have learned to stage events – press conferences, meetings, ceremonies of all kinds – to increase their public visibility. Journalists grumble about such overt management attempts but turn them into stories anyway. For example, even though the *Los Angeles Times* science writing staff reacted skeptically when the University of Utah arranged a press conference in 1989 to herald the achievement of room-temperature fusion, the newspaper covered the event. Noted science editor Joel Greenberg:

> It seemed like a textbook case of a story to avoid. The claim, particularly using such a technique, seemed fantastic. The research paper had yet to be published in a refereed journal. And no one at Princeton or anywhere else where fusion research had been pursued for many years had come close to such a result. Most science writers knew this was a sensational story that almost certainly would prove to be not true, at least not to the point of the university's claims.
>
> Nevertheless, the results emanated from a respected university and from two scientists . . . who, as far as anyone could tell, were legitimate members of the research community. And finally, whether we covered it or not, it was obvious that this was a story destined to lead the television news and make the covers of *Time* and *Newsweek* (which it did). To ignore it would have been a mistake. (Greenberg, 1997, p. 100)

Reinterpreting a process as a cascade of events is a spectacularly successful heuristic device. It allows journalists to survey their terrain rapidly for event markers and to prioritize those markers by some criterion for importance. Events have easily discernible beginnings and endings, simplifying the construction of narratives. Events' ready availability in the environment encourages both journalists and society to interpret journalistic work as the process of mirroring – not reconstructing – reality. And, as with so many of the heuristics employed by journalists, this preference for events is shared by audiences, who also find it much easier to grapple with concrete happenings than with diffuse processes.

But the debits of this heuristic are substantial. The notion that events are features of the landscape that can readily be seen and selected forces journalists to ignore great swaths of process that cannot be easily packaged in event narratives. Journalists' failure to represent abstract concepts and linkages in their stories leads some critics to argue that journalistic training robs reporters of the ability to think conceptually. Reporters "do not conceptualize their own experience or place particular, concrete facts into broader theoretical frameworks," argues one such critic. "Journalists are nontheoretic knowers who depend upon instinctive, concrete, first-hand 'acquaintance with' events, not formal, systematic 'knowledge about'events" (Phillips 1977, p. 70).

Equally problematic, reliance on events discernible in the environment promotes a kind of journalistic reactivity that allows sources much greater control over what becomes news than they otherwise might have. McManus (1994) and others find that only a fraction of daily news stories can be traced back to journalistic efforts to conceptualize and write independently about issues and problems, a process called *enterprise reporting* in the business. Rather, the bulk of a day's news depends heavily on the flow of information *into* the newsroom, much of that information packaged by sources specifically to gain the attention of reporters and editors.

News Values. Journalists are routinely confronted by too much news. Put another way, of the vast array of happenings in the environment available to a journalist on a given day, most must be set aside. And that decision must be made in a matter of seconds. There is simply no time for thoughtful deliberation, for extended discussions with journalistic colleagues about how to approach an issue or about whether a particular topic warrants coverage. Editors and subeditors will engage in regular story conferences, but discussions there focus less on what to cover and more on such production issues as where in a newspaper or newscast to situate a story.

The speed with which news selections are made requires journalists to employ a set of heuristic judgments to categorize the world around them. Called *news values*, these judgments are usually unspoken, operating at an almost unconscious level. But they are reinforced at all levels, from journalism classrooms in universities to the newsroom itself. What are these criteria that allow a thin trickle of information through the news "gate" while keeping much of the rest of the world at bay? Here are a few of those values:

- Size matters. Large-scale happenings are much more likely to be noticed and covered than are small-scale happenings. In a recent study of media coverage of environmental hazards, for example, Freudenburg and colleagues (1996) found that the best predictor of media attention was magnitude: the number of casualties or the level of damage caused by the hazard. Below a certain size threshold, events were essentially invisible.

- The closer, the better. Given two similar events, the more geographically proximate one will get far more media attention than the more distant event. And more proximate sources will be preferred to more distant ones. This focus on proximity helps illuminate a number of otherwise puzzling patterns – for example, the tendency of a reporter attending an international meeting or a national political convention to cover the speeches and comments of the hometown delegates, often to the exclusion of more visible, more impactful sources.

- Once a topic has become news, it tends to remain newsworthy. That is, once a story has crossed the news threshold, subsequent, related events are much more likely to be defined as newsworthy regardless of their relative importance at the time. To return to the cold fusion story by way of example, once the University of Utah press conference had put the topic on the national – nay, international – news agenda, reporters returned to it time and time again, despite the fact that cold fusion was never demonstrated to occur in a laboratory.

News criteria have been the subject of much study over the years, with results generally supporting the ubiquity of these heuristic devices across time, across countries, and across types of media organizations. Frequency of production is a major predictor of news criteria use: The more frequently you publish, the more likely you are to utilize these judgmental shortcuts. One of the more seminal studies, by Galtung and Ruge (1965), remains an excellent conceptual guide to these criteria.

It bears repeating that the selection criteria employed by journalists to decide what's news closely resemble the heuristic devices that people use every day to make sense of their world. Thus, one could argue that although news is indeed a product of relatively superficial judgments, those judgments bear a close resemblance to decisions that most folks make about what deserves their time and attention. In that sense, then, journalistic decision making may mirror the priorities of the culture within which it is embedded. We all love to hate our local newspaper or our local TV news team. But there's a good chance that, given the Cinderella opportunity to trade places with a reporter for a day, we'd make our news selections in ways quite similar to those of our ridiculed journalistic colleagues.

Sifting and Winnowing the Evidence

Deciding what's news is only a start, however. Topic in hand, the journalist must turn that topic into an actual story; she or he must decide what that story is about. That decision involves not only selecting the narrative focus of a story – its angle – but also selecting sources, gathering information from them, and then deciding how to represent that information in the story itself. Such decisions can be extremely complex. But once again, the speed of the journalistic process requires that reporters opt for an array of judgmental shortcuts. We have selected a few judgmental shortcuts from the panoply to illustrate our point.

Objectivity. One of the frustrations of journalism is that, although it is given the responsibility of "covering" the world around it and helping citizens to make reasoned choices about that world, it can rarely determine what's true. Both the speed of production and the occupation's tendency to eschew specialized training make it extremely difficult for a reporter to have either the time or the skill to evaluate competing truth claims. Thus, there is some chance that what becomes news may simply not be true.

Journalists have adopted a couple of heuristics to handle this validity problem and the social criticism that accompanies it. Objectivity is one. The practice of objectivity rewards a journalist not for figuring out what's true but, in the absence of such analysis, for accurately reflecting the voices of others. If you can't tell if someone is telling the truth, in other words, at least you can make sure that you are accurately transmitting the person's message.

The cold fusion story is a good example of this heuristic in action. Many science writers doubted the validity of the two scientists' claim, in 1989, that they had achieved room-temperature fusion. But these journalists were in no position to render a definitive judgment about the truth of that claim. Thus, they felt they had no choice but to cover the claim and to concentrate on reproducing it as accurately as possible. Achieving objectivity in the cold fusion debate, in other words, was good journalism.

This heuristic offers a number of advantages for reporters. Even specialists in a field understand the difficulty of making and defending validity judgments. Science, for example, is replete with challenges to validity; there is rarely a consensus on what's true. In such a climate, it would be disastrous for less specialized individuals to try to ascertain the truth, as their judgments would carry little credibility. An emphasis on accuracy is thus much safer than an emphasis on validity.

But this privileging of accuracy can have negative consequences. Although a manageable goal, objectivity has become a journalistic ritual (Tuchman, 1972) that actually encourages journalists to eschew responsibility for making validity judgments. Journalistic training has never included the kinds of systematic analytical tools that members of other occupations often utilize for validity purposes. And those reporters who actually attempt to make a distinction between more or less likely truth claims often find themselves in a kind of no-man's land, bereft of support from either their sources or their journalistic peers (see, e.g., Crewdson, 1993; Fragin, 1998).

Balancing Contrasting Accounts. A second heuristic that allows journalists to eschew validity judgments is the practice of balancing contrasting points of view. Since many arenas contain competing truth claims, this heuristic dictates that, in the absence of knowing what's true, a journalist should offer the audience the whole array of possible claims. Thus, this judgmental shortcut asks journalists to be responsible for knowing about the extent of variance in truth claims, not about the validity of those claims.

Typically, this heuristic gets operationalized in a story by providing two competing claims, each meant to demarcate a contrasting domain of beliefs. So, for example, if a journalist is writing a story about one group of scientists'claim to have found fossilized life in a Martian meteorite, the reporter is responsible for seeking a point of view at the other end of the belief continuum. The story is not complete, in other words, until it contains comments by a scientist who is skeptical of the claim.

Again, this heuristic encourages the journalist to accomplish a manageable evidentiary task: identifying variance in rather than validity of points of view. But the ritualistic practice of balance is often reduced to selecting points of view situated at the ends of a belief continuum and then giving those (sometimes rather extreme) beliefs equal space.

Interestingly, journalists continue to endorse the concept of balance even when they have some evidence suggesting that a belief is *not* true. For example, Dearing (1995) examined coverage of three controversial science issues that featured less than believable assertions offered by individuals considered to be scientific mavericks. One was the 1989 cold fusion announcement. The second was the claim by a self-trained climatologist, in 1990, that there was a 50-50 chance that a severe earthquake (the so-called New Madrid quake, which never occurred) would shake the lower Midwest by a specific date. And the third was a well-known biologist's long-running assertion that the human immunodeficiency virus (HIV) virus cannot be the cause of acquired immune deficiency syndrome (AIDS).

Dearing found that, in all three cases, despite the fact that journalists believed the extreme claims were wrong, they not only included these claims in their stories but also, in the interest of balance, provided the information in ways that lended legitimacy to them. Thus, he argued, balancing truth claims sent the message to readers that these scientific mavericks were as likely to be right as the mainstream scientific sources on the other side of the issue.

Preference for the Vivid Anecdotal Account. Psychologists argue that most people prefer to make inferences on the basis of vivid anecdotal information rather than utilizing systematic or consensus data (Nisbett & Ross, 1980). That is, we opt for the concrete over the abstract.

This heuristic tendency is exacerbated in journalism. Journalistic training expressly privileges self-reported data by encouraging reporters to gather information in face-to-face interview settings. Systematic data are relegated to the position of backup information, available to flesh out a story but not intended as primary information on which a story can be hung. And when systematic data are indeed the focal point of a story – as is often the case when journalists are writing about newly published scientific research – reporters will often seek out anecdotal information to make the story more "readable."

For example, when a scientific study some years ago suggested a relationship between drinking coffee and the risk of pancreatic cancer, the research made front-page headlines around the country. But many journalists felt the need for a more vivid, concrete dimension to the tale. Some asked the researchers about any changes they might have made in their own coffee-drinking habit as a result of the study. Others went to locations such as restaurants to confer with coffee drinkers about their reactions to the study (Ryan, Dunwoody, & Tankard, 1991).

This focus on the anecdotal has a distinct storytelling advantage. Audiences are more likely to get caught up in vivid personal stories than in accounts that rely only on systematic data gathering. But there is a risk that both journalist and audience will mistake the personal tale as a marker for a larger pattern. We turn to that possibility in the following case study about an event in Wisconsin that offered journalists both anecdotal and systematic data. The resulting media coverage of the state's attempt to introduce reformulated gas into daily use serves as a useful illustration of the kinds of heuristic devices popular among journalists.

The Reformulated Gas Controversy in Wisconsin

As a consequence of the Clean Air Act Amendments of 1990, gasoline stations in certain urban corridors of the United States have been required by the U.S. Environmental Protection Agency (EPA) to sell a reformulated gas mixture designed to cut down significantly on the levels of automobile-related smog. The additives in reformulated gas are ethyl- or ether-based compounds, chief among them methyl tertiary-butyl ether (MTBE).

The Milwaukee area, a large urban region in Wisconsin on the shores of Lake Michigan, was one of the metropolitan areas required to use reformulated gas, and Milwaukee gas stations began selling the fuel in late fall 1994. Local media reports in early 1995 fueled a growing awareness of the gas, and people began contacting state and federal offices to complain that pumping reformulated gas was making them sick. Calls eventually mounted into the thousands. Wisconsin finally directed its state epidemiologists to conduct an investigation of the possible health impacts of reformulated gas, a study that was completed in June 1995 (Wisconsin Department of Health and Social Services, 1995).

We became interested in media coverage of this controversy because the issue confronted journalists with a challenging array of evidence. On the one hand, the early stages of the issue were dominated by vivid anecdotal testimonials. Individuals who felt that they had become ill from exposure to the gas contacted governmental officials and media organizations to complain and demand redress. Even the state's governor got into the act, eventually traveling to Washington, DC, to urge the U.S. EPA to renege on its requirement that Milwaukee area motorists use reformulated gas, a plea that was ultimately unsuccessful.

But although all this anecdotal information conveyed the perception that reformulated gas was causing problems such as nausea and flulike symptoms, the state's investigation of those claims offered systematic data that painted a very different picture. The state's study was conducted in four parts:

    1. Researchers monitored the air near the pumps dispensing reformulated gas to see if substances to which individuals were

exposed were any more toxic than normal (any gasoline is made of a soup of chemicals, some of which are linked to cancer).

2. They contacted the health departments of other states using reformulated gas to learn if these other locations were also experiencing health disruptions.
3. They compared the composition of the reformulated gas being pumped in Milwaukee with that of reformulated gas elsewhere.
4. Finally, researchers conducted a random digit dial phone survey to compare the rate of occurrence and correlates of health complaints in three areas: metropolitan Milwaukee; metropolitan Chicago, where reformulated gas also was in use; and other regions of Wisconsin where reformulated gas was not available.

State epidemiologists found that a much greater proportion of Milwaukee gasoline users reported becoming ill than did those surveyed in other areas, including Chicago, where the same type of reformulated gas was being used. But neither the availability of reformulated gas nor the chemical constituents of the gas in Milwaukee predicted the illness reports. Rather, the state found that the best predictors of the likelihood of feeling ill were (1) having had a cold or the flu and (2) an awareness of the possibility that reformulated gas might be a health threat. To put that latter predictor in a more colorful context, media coverage of the reformulated gas controversy was making people sick.

Once the systematic data became available in September 1995, we asked: How would Milwaukee media organizations cope with the array of evidence now available to them? The reformulated gas issue was certainly news, as it had led to local TV newscasts several times earlier in the winter, when anecdotal evidence poured in about the possible health effects. So the new epidemiological study would be readily defined as newsworthy. But would media organizations continue to privilege the earlier anecdotal accounts in the face of strong evidence that Milwaukee residents were not becoming ill from exposure to reformulated gas? And, given the existence of carefully gathered, systematic data, would journalists still feel the need to balance the findings of state epidemiologists with information skeptical of the new information?

To answer these questions, we videotaped the reformulated gas news stories aired by the three Milwaukee television stations for several days after release of the state epidemiological report. We also attended to stories written by journalists working for *The Milwaukee Journal Sentinel*, the city's daily newspaper. (A more detailed analysis of these findings is available in Trumbo, Dunwoody, & Griffin, 1998.)

Preference for the Vivid

Although all news organizations began their stories with the announcement that the state's study had found no health effects that could be linked to the use of reformulated gas, reporters typically headed to nearby gas stations to ask individuals for their reactions to that news. Ultimately, those anecdotal interviews took up equal or more time in the stories than did reporters'efforts to explain the study's findings. Thus, it was clear that journalists did not feel that the systematic evidence could stand on its own; they needed to either bolster or contradict it with anecdotal accounts.

But another possible indicator of the power of the anecdotal account lay in the obvious skepticism that journalists brought to the state's findings. Recall that journalists had been bombarded for months by individual testimonials of illness, a pattern reinforced by actions of state officials to convince the U.S. EPA to ban reformulated gas in the state. Confronted with a systematic study that debunked the cause-and-effect assertions, many journalists reacted cautiously, even skeptically.

For example, when an anchor at one of the Milwaukee television stations introduced a story about the survey findings by saying, "The state says the facts are in and the new gas we are required to use is not a health problem," her coanchor responded: "*Not* a health problem? Thousands of people have complained about the reformulated gasoline, saying it makes them sick" (from transcript in Trumbo et. al., 1998, p. 257).

Another anchor, after sitting through an account of the epidemiological findings, ended the news segment by remarking: "Makes you wonder if 15,000 [sic] people could all be wrong" (from transcript in Trumbo et al., 1998, p. 262).

Yet another station embedded the skepticism in its lead-in for the story. Said the anchors: "While it runs your car, will it ruin your health? A new report on reformulated gas says no. [The two anchors identify themselves.] But some people are still hesitant to reformulate an opinion on that gas" (from transcript in Trumbo et al., 1998, p. 258).

One possibility is that reporters had found the earlier anecdotal evidence persuasive, making it difficult for them to interpret the new, systematic data as offering a higher-quality interpretation of reality. Stocking and Gross (1989), in a monograph that examines cognitive bias in news making, reflect on how reporters – like all folks – tend to adopt a set of beliefs and then define subsequent information that supports their original theory as more valid than information that doesn't. In this case, the state survey stood in stark contrast to the anecdotal accounts, making it easy prey to those reporters who had become convinced by the earlier accounts of health problems.

The Persistence of Balance

If reporters indeed were reacting warily to the new study results, that wariness would have reinforced occupational pressure to balance the study findings with points of view that contradicted it. And that's what we found in the television reports. The epidemiological study was never allowed to stand unchallenged. Rather, journalists worked to find points of view from the other side of the continuum. Some journalists went seeking comments from the state's governor, who had earlier gone on the record as opposing the use of reformulated gas in the state. (The governor, incidentally, reacted with "no comment.") Others gave space to a congressperson who, inexplicably, railed against the validity of using survey research to accomplish the ends sought by the study.

In the most extreme instance of balancing, a reporter from one of the stations learned that a scientist asked to evaluate the state's study as part of a consensus panel had refused to endorse the study's conclusion that it had found no link between reformulated gas and reported health problems. The reporter tracked down the researcher, put him on the air, and literally badgered him into dissenting:

Reporter voice over: Just [an] hour and a half ago, in a satellite interview from Raleigh, (name) told me he never signed off on the study because, he said, it's riddled with problems. (Cut to side-by-side shots of the reporter and the scientist.)
Scientist: You simply can't make that statement . . .
Reporter: The study is flawed, is what you're saying, the study *is* flawed.
Scientist: Well, the study . . . yea, the study's got a lot of problems, too . . . (cut off mid-sentence). (From transcript in Trumbo et al., 1998, p. 260)

And Now for Something Completely Different

A very different account of the state's findings appeared in *The Milwaukee Journal Sentinel*. Written by the environmental reporter, Don Behm (1995), the story clearly privileged the epidemiological work over the earlier anecdotal accounts. In fact, it included no anecdotal material at all, concentrating instead on explaining the study's goals and methods and reflecting the views of a variety of individuals regarding the meaning of the findings.

Efforts to balance contrasting viewpoints were also missing from this story. A reader would have to have made it to the very bottom of the story (which by this time has "jumped" to an inside page) to learn that some individuals were taking issue with the state's study. The story offered a one-sentence critique by a Wisconsin congressperson who referred to the study as "bogus." In this account, then, heuristic strategies that dominated other accounts were abandoned.

What lies behind the rather dramatic difference between the newspaper and television accounts? One possibility is differential production stresses. In addition to its insatiable need for visuals, television can be more physically demanding than a daily newspaper. For example, television reporters may have to package the same issue two or three times in a given day (the noon, early evening, and late evening news shows), so time may be even more scarce than at the typical newspaper. When time is scarce, heuristic devices blossom.

A second possible factor accounting for the variance is reporter expertise. Years of reporting on complex environmental issues have enabled *Milwaukee Journal Sentinel* reporter Don Behm to become more adept at systematic evaluation of evidence. Specialty reporters, who can spend entire careers covering a particular information domain, are among the few reporters who are encouraged to develop in-depth knowledge. But specialty beats are rare in television – certainly at the local level, where reporters are few and equipment costs are high. Thus, most TV reporters are generalists, unable to develop expertise and rewarded, instead, for speed and reliability.

The reformulated gas story is a case study in how journalists may mistake anecdotal evidence as markers of larger patterns. This is a familiar cycle for all of us, from the scientist who has an unpleasant experience with a journalist and concludes that all journalists are bad to the employer who insists that she can determine the potential of an applicant on the basis of an interview alone. In the course of coverage of the reformulated gas controversy, it is possible that Milwaukee television journalists readily defined anecdotal evidence as reflections of a larger pattern, that they interpreted the many public complaints about the health repercussions of pumping reformulated gas as sufficient evidence of a cause-and-effect relationship. Their skeptical reactions to the subsequent state epidemiological study certainly bolster this interpretation.

Discussion

In this chapter we have put forward an argument on behalf of journalism as an occupation that has institutionalized heuristic decision making. Without the ability to make extremely quick decisions, daily journalism as we know it could not exist. Although some components of the journalism world – magazines, television and radio documentaries, nonnews sections of newspapers – allow reporters to be more reflective, the bulk of what counts as journalism demands split-second decisions.

To accommodate this fact of life, journalism has commandeered a host of garden-variety judgmental shortcuts and made them its own. Although some have been given occupational labels – the use of news values, for instance, or the concept of objectivity – they function within the occupation in ways quite similar to their use in daily life.

That resonance with daily practice may be one of the reasons that journalism has evolved to play such an important role in human culture. We may rely on journalistic accounts not because they are of high quality in an evidentiary sense but because journalists *think like us*. News choices validate our own priorities. Journalists' search for cause and effect parallels our own. It is culturally reassuring to see such consonance out and about in the land.

Policymakers, too, have picked up on that social consonance. They are among the most intense users of media information not only to keep abreast of the behaviors of other policymakers (Price, 1992) but also, presumably, to take advantage of the tendency of mass media channels to mirror common cultural judgmental processes. To that extent, then, the kinds of heuristic judgments reflected in media accounts provide valuable clues for policymakers about popular ways of thinking.

The Problems with "Thinking Like Us"

But the tendency of journalists to rely on shortcut decision-making strategies is also problematic, for at least a couple of reasons. First, consumers and policymakers tend to believe that news stories indeed reflect the more important social occurrences in our environment. Although we may have smiled when Walter Cronkite signed off his newscast each evening with "Well, that's the way it is" back in the 1960s and 1970s, *we believed him!* One of the most important functions of journalistic work seems to be its role in legitimating some forms of reality over others.

By way of illustration, a group of sociologists (Phillips, Kanter, Bednarczyk, & Tastad, 1991) tested the legitimizing ability of media coverage on a very difficult audience indeed: scientists. The scholars isolated two groups of research reports from the prestigious *New England Journal of Medicine* that differed on one important variable: One group of studies had generated stories in the *New York Times* and the other group had not. The sociologists controlled for a host of other confounding variables and then looked at how frequently the studies got cited *in the scientific literature* in the ensuing years.

To their astonishment, those studies that got *New York Times* attention received 73% more citations in the peer-reviewed literature than did the equally good but less publicly visible studies. The investigators concluded that the *New York Times* was playing a role in establishing the importance and legitimacy of particular research efforts even for other specialists within these scientists'own fields.

Admittedly, few media organizations have the legitimizing clout of the *New York Times*. But even *Times* reporters must rely on judgmental shortcuts to select those topics to which they will attend, to make judgments about sources, and the like. Thus, relatively superficial heuristics may play a disproportionate role in constructing reality for media consumers.

Policymakers seem to fall prey to this legitimizing function of the media just as easily as do other inhabitants of American culture. Although the ability of the mass media to help establish public notions of what's important has been amply demonstrated across time and topic, evidence grows that media content may have even more powerful effects on policymakers'agendas. For example, in one study of the agenda-setting influence of mass media coverage of global warming during the 1980s and early 1990s, Trumbo (1995) found that media accounts had little influence on lay audiences' judgments of the importance of this environmental topic but profoundly affected policymakers' judgments. Even more interesting, the effect formed a kind of feedback loop:

Actions by policymakers produced media stories, which in turn served as catalysts for further policy action.

A second possible debit of the ubiquity of shortcut decision making in daily journalism is that journalistic practices may encourage heuristic thinking among members of the audience. It is likely that we all utilize judgmental shortcuts for most decision-making needs. But we are routinely enjoined to resort to systematic thinking whenever possible, certainly when important decisions loom. Confronted with a complicated medical situation, we are urged to seek a second opinion. Faced with a long but somewhat unpredictable earnings life, we are advised to learn about different kinds of savings options and to make multivariate plans for a secure economic future. Information processing that seeks and evaluates alternatives is difficult, however. And most of us are, quite simply, bad at it.

Although journalism exists ostensibly to help individuals make reasoned decisions about the world around them, the heuristic base that buttresses the business offers up to information consumers the same kinds of judgmental shortcuts to which those consumers themselves may fall prey. Thus, a search for information that includes a heavy reliance on media accounts may reinforce individuals in their own hurried heuristic habits. The confluence of a complex medical situation *and* a newspaper story about it may encourage a reader to contact the medical center featured in the story, no questions asked. Similarly, an individual at sea regarding her financial future may latch onto a financial adviser whose ad appears in a local magazine. From such heuristic judgments is the edifice of advertising built.

When policymakers encounter topics in the news that are near and dear to their hearts, we would expect those individuals to be more resistant to the potential media reinforcement of heuristic thinking strategies. Although policymakers are indeed heavy users of mass media, they come to these channels with well-developed belief systems about specific topics and issues. Such belief systems make individuals more likely to be information *constructors* than information *ingesters*. That is, such persons are less likely to be influenced by message content than they are to "rewrite" that content to fit their prevailing mental maps.

On the other hand, when policymakers encounter media information for which they don't have well-developed beliefs, they may be subject to the same reinforcement effect that may bedevil the public itself. That is, they may naively conclude that if it's in the newspaper, it must be true.

Effecting Change

Although daily journalism is unavoidably an occupation dominated by heuristic judgments, occupants of other journalistic niches may have the time and resources to think more systematically and make more careful decisions about who and what. Magazine articles, broadcast documentaries, and newspaper series are often the product of weeks or months of thought, reflection, information gathering, and writing. Journalists who are equipped to view the world more systematically should be able to flourish in these modes.

But are journalists so equipped? Whereas the typical journalist of 19th- and early-20th-century America entered the occupation via an apprenticeship system, today's journalists increasingly get their basic training in university journalism programs (Weaver and Wilhoit, 1996). Those programs urge on their students a bifurcated education: On the one hand, the programs work to instill basic professional skills and values; on the other, they push their young charges to attain a traditional liberal arts education. A typical ratio of coursework would be one skills course to every two or three courses elsewhere in the university.

Unfortunately, neither of those educational goals gives young journalists systematic information processing skills in today's university. Most schools fail either to define such skills as part of an individual's basic competencies or, even if they do identify the ability to process information systematically as an important tool, to offer courses that give students basic training in it. Journalism courses are no different.

This means that journalists will continue to make relatively superficial judgments about the world around them. Most of those judgments will be reasonably good ones, and we information consumers will be well served, all told. But the business of journalism is simply not equipped to turn a sustained, systematic eye to an issue in ways that illuminate that issue's basic assumptions. As one historian put it many years ago, journalism is "history on the run." A dead run does not offer a good venue for systematic thinking.

References

Behm, D. (1995, June 2). Symptoms not linked to fumes, study says. *Milwaukee Journal Sentinel*. pp. A1, A7.

Bissinger, B. (1998, September). Shattered glass. *Vanity Fair, 457*, 176–190.

Breed, W. (1955). Social control in the newsroom. *Social Forces, 33*, 326–55.

Coleman, C. L. (1995). Science, technology and risk coverage of a community conflict. *Media, Culture & Society, 17*, 65–79.

Crewdson, J. (1993). Perky cheerleaders. *Nieman Reports, 47*, 11–16.

Dearing, J. W. (1995). Newspaper coverage of maverick science: Creating controversy through balancing. *Public Understanding of Science, 4*, 341–361.

Donohue, G. A., Tichenor, P. J., & Olien, C. N. (1995). A guard dog perspective on the role of media. *Journal of Communication, 45*, 115–132.

Dunwoody, S. (1979). News-gathering behaviors of specialty reporters: A two-level comparison of mass media decision-making. *Newspaper Research Journal, 1*, 29–39.

Dunwoody, S., & Griffin, R. J. (1993). Journalistic strategies for reporting long-term environmental issues: A case study of three Superfund sites. In A. Hansen (Ed.), *The mass media and environmental issues* (pp. 22–50). Leicester, UK: Leicester University Press.

Fishman, M. (1980). *Manufacturing the news*. Austin: University of Texas Press.

Fragin, S. (1998). Flawed science at the *Times*. *Brill's Content, 1*, 104–115.

Freudenburg, W. R., Coleman, C. L., Gonzales, J., & Helgeland, C. (1996). Media coverage of hazard events: Analyzing the assumptions. *Risk Analysis, 16*, 31–42.

Galtung, J., & Ruge, M. H. (1965). The structure of foreign news. *Journal of International Peace Research, 1*, 64–90.

Gigerenzer, G., & Goldstein, D. G. (1996). Reasoning the fast and frugal way: Models of bounded rationality. *Psychological Review, 103*, 650–669.

Glasser, T. L., & Ettema, J. S. (1989). Investigative journalism and the moral order. *Critical Studies in Mass Communication, 6*, 1–20.

Greenberg, J. (1997). Using sources. In D. Blum & M. Knudson (Eds.), *A field guide for science writers* (pp. 94–101). New York: Oxford University Press.

McManus, J. (1991). How objective is local television news? *Mass Comm Review, 18*, 21–30, 48.

McManus, J. (1994). *Market-driven journalism: Let the citizen beware?* Thousand Oaks, CA: Sage.

Nisbett, R., & Ross, L. (1980). *Human inference: Strategies and shortcomings of social judgment*. Englewood Cliffs, NJ: Prentice-Hall.

Phillips, D. P., Kanter, E. J., Bednarczyk, B., & Tastad, P. L. (1991). Importance of the lay press in the transmission of medical knowledge to the scientific community. *New England Journal of Medicine, 325*, 1180–1183.

Phillips, E. B. (1977). Approaches to objectivity: Journalistic versus social science perspectives. In P. M. Hirsch, P. V. Miller, & F. G. Kline (Eds.), *Strategies for communication research* (pp. 63–77). Thousand Oaks, CA: Sage.

Price, V. (1992). *Public opinion*. Newbury Park, CA: Sage.

Ryan, M., Dunwoody, S., & Tankard, J. (1991). Risk information for public consumption: Print media coverage of two risky situations. *Health Education Quarterly, 18*, 375–390.

Shoemaker, P. J. (1996). Hardwired for news: Using biological and cultural evolution to explain the surveillance function. *Journal of Communication, 46*, 32–47.

Silverstone, R. (1985). *Framing science: The making of a BBC documentary*. London: BFI Publishing.

Simon, H. A. (1982). *Models of bounded rationality*. Cambridge, MA: MIT Press.

Slovic, P. (1992). Perception of risk: Reflections on the psychometric paradigm. In S. Krimsky & D. Golding (Eds.), *Social theories of risk* (pp. 117–152). Westport, CT: Praeger.

Soloski, J. (1989). News reporting and professionalism. *Media, Culture & Society,* *11*, 207–228.

Stocking, S. H., & Gross, P. H. (1989). *How do journalists think?* Bloomington, IN: ERIC Clearinghouse on Reading and Communication Skills.

Trumbo, C. (1995). Longitudinal modeling of public issues: An application of the agenda-setting process to the issue of global warming. *Journalism & Mass Communication Monographs*, No. 152.

Trumbo, C., Dunwoody, S., & Griffin, R. J. (1998). Journalists, cognition, and the presentation of an epidemiologic study. *Science Communication, 19*, 238–265.

Tuchman, G. (1972). Objectivity as a strategic ritual: An examination of newsmen's notions of objectivity. *American Journal of Sociology, 77*, 660–679.

Tuchman, G. (1978). *Making news*. New York: The Free Press.

Tuchman, G. (1997). Making news by doing work: Routinizing the unexpected. In D. Berkowitz (Ed.), *Social meaning of news* (pp. 173–192). Thousand Oaks, CA: Sage.

Weaver, D. H., & Wilhoit, G. C. (1996). *The American journalist in the 1990s*. Mahwah, NJ: Erlbaum.

Wisconsin Department of Health and Social Services. (1995). *An investigation of health concerns attributed to reformulated gasoline use in southeastern Wisconsin*. Unpublished manuscript.

8   A Behavioral Approach to Political Advertising Research

Jeffrey C. Fox and Rick Farmer

Introduction

Political candidates in the United States spend hundreds of millions of dollars each election year on political ads designed to influence voters' judgments about and choices among candidates. Campaign ads are so important that some campaigns spend up to two thirds of their budgets on ad production and airtime. Political advertising is an especially good communication tool because it reaches a wide audience and allows candidates to control the information content voters obtain, whereas the news media may "filter, alter, distort or ignore altogether" the candidate and his or her message (Ansolabehere, Behr, & Iyengar, 1993, p. 1). Ads are so pervasive that they now constitute a significant portion of the candidate information voters receive.

As the prevalence of televised political advertising has grown, so has concern about the content and effects of political ads. Citizens routinely complain about the nastiness and negativity of political ads. Negative advertising alienates the voting public and may even decrease voter turnout (Ansolabehere & Iyengar, 1995; Ansolabehere, Iyengar, & Simon, 1999; Ansolabehere, Iyengar, Simon, & Valentino, 1994; Kahn & Kenney, 1999; Lau, Sigelman, Heldman, & Babbitt, 1999; Wattenberg & Brians, 1999).

News organizations are most concerned about the accuracy of information in ads. The media use "Ad Watches" to scrutinize the veracity of ads because they are convinced that ads are manipulative and misleading. Ironically, Ad Watches have also helped legitimate the use of political ads as the dominant form of campaign communication (Kaid, Gobetz, Garner, Leland, & Scott, 1993).

Scholars, meanwhile, have been primarily concerned about the irrationality of the issue discourse in ads. Research on the content of political ads has been consumed by the fruitless search for rational issue dialogue. Scholars believe that ads lack the specific issue information voters need to make informed choices.

Almost everyone – scholars, pundits, and the public – agree that campaign ads would be better if their content more closely approximated the normative ideal: issue dialogue that is positive, forward-looking, and specific. Compared to the normative ideal, political advertising is seen as inadequate at best, and possibly harmful to the political system because it manipulates as much as it informs. Popular disgust with negative ads has led some to call for greater regulation of ads. For example, some believe that requiring candidates to appear and speak in their ads will make ads less negative (Gans, 1991; West, 1992). North Carolina passed a law in 1999 that requires candidates to appear in their ads and disclose the identity of the ad sponsor in the hope of decreasing the negativity of campaigns (Associated Press, 1999).

Normative theory, which assumes citizen rationality, has been the dominant theoretical lens for research and discussion of political ads. This view has dominated despite research in psychology and experimental economics that has long questioned whether the normative model accurately depicts real-world judgment and choice. We believe that the dominance of the normative perspective has artificially restricted political advertising research and debate by ignoring cognitive processes that are crucial in understanding the effects of political advertising.

In this chapter we will explore the implications of behavioral decision theory for our understanding of ad content and effects. Where appropriate, we will report our own empirical research on television advertising in U.S. Senate races. Our goals in writing this chapter are to expand the theoretical debate about the effects of political ads in the political system and to propose a refined research agenda informed by behavioral decision theory.

Competing Models of Judgment and Decision Making

Past research on campaign discourse has been guided by the tenets of normative theory, a rationalistic model of judgment and choice. Normative theory assumes that people make judgments based on full (or at least extensive) information and that each piece of information is weighted in proportion to its utility – its effect on desired goals and outcomes. People make judgments and choices by calculating the respective utilities of various alternatives, ordering them from best to worst, and choosing the option that maximizes their perceived utility.

Democratic theory shares these idealistic assumptions about human behavior. Democratic theory envisions a political system where candidates provide specific issue information to attentive voters so that they can make fully informed, rational decisions. Then, and only then, they say, can an attentive and interested electorate obtain the information they need to make informed judgments and choices about policies and candidates.

With the lofty normative standard in mind, scholars naturally conclude that 30-second ads fail to inform the public adequately or provide much information that voters can use to make informed choices. With such a dearth of information, the argument goes, televised spot advertisements do nothing more than sell a candidate, just as advertisers sell soap or toothpaste (Bennett, 1992; Dionne, 1991; McGinnis, 1969; Page, 1978; West, 1992; Wyckoff, 1968). We, too, have written from this perspective because the concerns and expectations of normative theory have dominated previous political advertising research.

It is easy to see that the normative ideal does not exist in modern campaigns and elections (Lau & Redlawsk, 1997). It is nearly impossible to conduct a rational dialogue in 30-second ads, or even a series of them, that would rise to the lofty heights of the normative ideal. Thirty-second ads simply do not provide enough information to allow people to be true utility maximizers. In fact, no venue exists in modern politics that can provide such in-depth information (except possibly debates, which are questionable as well). None exists because no one except scholars wants it. Candidates don't want to be too specific, and voters don't necessarily want or use in-depth issue information.

People do not necessarily follow the rational model when they make decisions. There are numerous cases in which people deviate systematically from the assumptions and conclusions of the normative model. These empirical findings are collectively labeled *behavioral decision theory* (BDT). BDT views people not as rational utility maximizers but as *cognitive misers*, who exert minimal effort to acquire and process political information. Suedfeld and Tetlock (1992) argue that people are *cognitive managers* who minimize cognitive effort on less important issues, but consider more rationally information about topics that they are interested in or that have important personal effects. People use cognitive shortcuts when decisions are less important, when choices affect individuals rather than groups, when decisions need not be justified to others, when information is scarce, and when the decision maker is uninformed or unable or unwilling to consider other information (Levy, 1992; Suedfeld & Tetlock, 1992). Some behavioral researchers question whether voters seek or use detailed information even when it is available. The assumption that more information leads to better choices has been shown to be false in certain instances (see Lupia & McCubbins, 1997, and Suedfeld & Tetlock, 1992, for reviews).

Nevertheless, the normative model still dominates. William Riker (1995) argues that BDT adds little or nothing to normative insights about human behavior. Nevertheless, even he admits that

[d]oubtless there are cases in which [normative theory] does not work and some other method of calculations must be hypothesized. But not many such cases have as yet been identified. The only one I feel uneasy about in politics is negative appeal of campaigns, which, as I have already indicated, probably applies only to a small proportion of the voters, those who are uninformed and marginal between parties. (p. 33)

But this is no small admission, as political scientists know. The "small proportion of voters" Riker mentions is far from small. Uninformed voters constitute a majority of the electorate, and independents constitute about one third of all voters (Nie, Verba & Petrocik, 1979; Wattenberg, 1994). Independents are especially important in American politics because they constitute the crucial swing vote that often decides elections. Research has also shown that there is a great imbalance in the cognitive weight of positive and negative information (Lau, 1982, 1985; Richey, Koenigs, Richey, & Fortin, 1975). Thus, we cannot afford to dismiss any of these issues as easily as Riker suggests.

Judgment and Choice in a Low-Information Environment

Political campaigns are low-information, low-interest decision-making environments (Dye & Zeigler, 1984; Lupia & McCubbins, 1997). Most Americans cannot answer basic questions about the structure of the political system, discuss current issues, or even name their congressional representatives (Lau & Redlawsk, 1997; Page & Shapiro, 1992). Marginally informed voters constitute a majority of the electorate, and are dependent on the media and campaigns for their political information (Ansolabehere & Iyengar 1993, p. 331; see also Lupia & McCubbins, 1997; Neuman, 1986; Niemi & Weisberg, 1993).

People are generally uninformed about political matters because it is irrational to spend too much time gathering political information and considering political choices (Downs, 1957). Instead, most voters operate under "low-information rationality" (Popkin, 1991). Political ads expose voters to political information in small, easily digestible portions while they watch their favorite television programs. Voters can gain information with no conscious effort of their own.

People with minimal political information must still make judgments and choices, but must do it based on the bits and pieces of information they have available, which makes those pieces more important in their decision processes. Ansolabehere and Inyengar (1993) explain that people

have a limited store of political information, and since, that information is of dubious value outside the act of voting, they are unlikely to put much effort into predicting political events. . . . It is likely, therefore, that others will resort to rules of thumb to compute statistical expectations and that their calculations will be susceptible to a variety of biases, depending on the manner in which information is presented. (p. 326)

The cognitive processes involved in the processing, and recall of political information from the news media and political ads can significantly influence opinion formation and candidate evaluation (Lodge & McGraw, 1995; Kahn & Geer, 1994; Rosenberg, Bohan, McCaffrey, & Harris, 1986), issue salience (Kinder & Iyengar, 1987), and voting preferences (Ansolabehere & Iyengar, 1995; Campbell, Converse, Miller, & Stokes, 1960; Kinder, 1986; Popkin, 1991; Quattrone & Tversky, 1988).

BDT has great potential to aid our understanding of the content and effects of political advertising precisely because its effects are greatest in low-information environments like political campaigns. And political ads are one of the main sources of campaign information voters receive. In the remainder of this chapter we will briefly define some of the important components of BDT and relate them to our current understanding of political advertising in campaigns.

Applications of BDT in Political Advertising

Information Cues and Heuristics

People often make reasonable judgments and choices on the basis of limited information by using cognitive shortcuts, or heuristics (Tversky

& Kahneman, 1974). Partisan and ideological labels are two key short-cuts people utilize in the political domain. Political ad researchers have shown a special interest in partisan and ideological labels because they believe them to be good indicators of the candidates' political positions. Our research, and that of other observers, however, finds that candidates rarely use partisan labels in television advertising (Joslyn, 1981; Kaid & Davidson, 1986; West, 1993). For example, less than 10% of 420 Senate ads we sampled used partisan labels. Ideological labels (*liberal* and *conservative*) were used even more sparingly at around 7% (Hale, Fox, & Farmer, 1995; Joslyn, 1987).

Candidates do not use these labels much because they do not want to be overtly partisan. Research shows that U.S. Senate candidates moderate their issue stances in campaigns to appeal to moderate voters (Wright & Berkman, 1986). They do so in ads as well. Most ads are designed to appeal to independent or leaning swing voters, not the party faithful (Flanigan & Zingale, 1994; Nie, Verba, & Petrocik, 1976; Page, 1978; Wattenberg, 1994; Wright & Berkman, 1986). Candidates simply dislike providing too much partisan or ideological information, except perhaps where their party makes up a large majority of the registered voters in an electoral district.

Using their normative lenses, scholars lament the absence of these labels, believing that their absence deprives voters of a reliable voting cue. However, Ansolabehere and Iyengar (1995) found that overt partisan and ideological labels are not necessary for voters to make correct judgments about a candidate's political ideology and party. Rather, *issue cues* signal a candidate's party to voters without using overt labels. How does this work? Candidates from each party tend to focus on issues that "belong" to their party (Ansolabehere et al., 1993). For example, Democrats produce more ads that express concern for health care, education, jobs, and the environment. Meanwhile, Republicans are more likely to emphasize taxes, values, and character (Farmer & Fox, 1996). Thus, candidates signal their party and ideology by speaking to issues that appeal to their base constituency (Ansolabehere & Iyengar, 1995). People pick up on these cues and correctly judge the political positions of the candidates. This finding is important because scholars searching only for evidence of rational issue dialogue overlook issue cues. This may lead us to understate the amount of useful information in ads and the ability of voters to ascertain partisanship and ideology.

In a similar vein, Lau and Redlawsk (1997) find that three quarters of people in their campaign simulations "vote correctly," using only a few information cues contained in campaign communication. They find that people with limited information make the same judgments and choices as they would make if they had significantly more information. This again suggests that ads may provide more useful information than researchers in search of rational issue discourse would detect. We would not even suspect that these effects might exist without the insights of BDT.

There are numerous other heuristics and cues in political ads that affect judgment and choice. Political consultants purposely use cues and symbols to create impressions and affect judgment. Symbols, props, computer graphics, music, slow motion, physical settings, humor, slogans, endorsements, references to recorded votes, newspaper comments, group ties, guilt or credit by association, and so on are all cues carefully packaged to influence voter impressions of candidates (Biocca, 1991; Kaid & Davidson, 1986). BDT shows us that each of these can have important effects on judgment and choice. These subtle cues have been the subject of some important scholarly work, but deserve even greater attention in the future because they are the very foundation of *symbolic politics* (Combs & Nimmo, 1993; Edelman, 1988).

Prospect Theory

Prospect theory is one of the most prominent components of BDT. Utility theory posits that gains and losses with the same net change in utility should be weighted equally. Prospect theory, in contrast, posits that people are risk averse when presented with gains but risk seeking when facing equivalent losses. This systematic tendency violates the assumption of invariance in utility theory.

Prospect theory has several important implications for understanding political ads. Quattrone and Tversky (1988) have shown that people generally like their representatives and reelect them year after year. Around 85% of senators and 95% of representatives are reelected in any given year. However, prospect theory predicts (and Quattrone and Tversky find) that when people *perceive* an impending loss, such as economic decline, they will throw the incumbent out and "risk" voting for an unknown challenger.

Prospect theory also helps explain *when* candidates and their consultants use negative advertising. Ansolabehere and Iyengar (1993) suggest that prospect theory could provide insight into this question. "As yet, however, there is no theory of spatial competition that predicts when candidates will attack each other rather than merely promote them-selves" (p. 334). Our research, however, shows that prospect theory provides a plausible foundation for understanding the strategy of ad use in campaigns.

Campaign operatives know that negative advertising can be an effective tool against opponents. But they also know that negative ads bring the risk of a backlash against the sponsor because they are so unpop-ular (Garramone, 1985). Therefore, almost all campaigns use a mix of negative and positive ads – with most ads being positive.

It is surely rational for candidates to use some negative ads – but how many? And when? The normative model predicts that the utility of ads, either positive or negative, is constant. Prospect theory, on the other hand, predicts that candidates with a higher probability of losing, or in the domain of loss, are more likely to use attack ads to avert the loss. Challengers usually trail incumbents, so they are most often in the loss domain. So, on average, they should be more likely to take the risks as-sociated with attack advertising. Meanwhile, in competitive races, both candidates face an impending loss, so we would expect both candidates to use more negative ads. Meanwhile, incumbency advantage decreases incumbents' risk of losing, so they should generally use less negative ads than challengers. Finally, we may expect that candidates in heavily populated states would use attack ads more often because Senate races in such states are more competitive.

We tested these hypotheses using a sample of 420 U.S. Senate ads sampled primarily from the University of Oklahoma Political Commer-cial Archive. We constructed a mulitvariate LOGIT equation predicting the likelihood of producing a negative ad. The independent variables were competitiveness, state size, and candidate status. Competitiveness was measured using *Congressional Quarterly* ratings (Safe Democrat and Safe Republican = 1, Democrat Favored and Republican Favored = 2, Leans Democrat and Leans Republican = 3, No Clear Favorite = 4). Population size was measured using the number of House seats in each state. Candidate type (1 = challenger, 0 = nonchallenger) and cam-paign type (1 = open seat, 0 = nonopen seat) were measured as dummy variables.

The resulting LOGIT equation is presented in Table 8.1. The coef-ficients for candidate type, competitiveness, and population size are all statistically significant, showing that each of these variables ex-erts an independent impact on the probability that an ad will be negative.

Table 8.1. *LOGIT Analysis of Negative Ad Use*

	Negative Ads	Standard Errors
Competitiveness	.304*	.138
Population	.022*	.008
Challengers	.623*	.234
Open seats	.259	.264
Constant	−1.737	
N	420	
χ^2	$p < .001$	
Percent correctly classified	60%	

Note: The table presents LOGIT maximum likelihood estimators.
* Significant at the $p < .05$ level.
Source: Adapted from Hale, Fox, and Farmer (1996).

Table 8.2 shows the estimated probability of negative ad use in specific contexts. Here we see clearly that negative ad use follows the predictions of prospect theory. We expected challengers, being in the loss domain, to produce more negative ads. In fact, challengers are 14% more likely to produce negative ads than incumbents. In highly competitive races, both candidates face an impending loss. Indeed, candidates in competitive races are 22% more likely to produce negative ads than

Table 8.2. *Probability of Negative Ad Use If All Other Variables Are Set Equal to Their Means*

	Negative Ads
Competitiveness = 1	.30
Competitiveness = 4	.52
House seats = 1	.30
House seats = 30	.45
Challengers = 0	.31
Challengers = 1	.45
Open seats = 0	.30
Open seats = 1	.35

Note: Computed from logit coefficients in Table 8. 1.
Source: Adapted from Hale, Fox, and Farmer (1996).

those in noncompetitive races. Finally, candidates in large states usually draw strong opposition, so we would expect candidates in such states to produce more negative ads. Again, we see this is true. Candidates in large states were 15% more likely to produce negative ads than those in small states (Hale, Fox, & Farmer, 1996).

In sum, challengers and candidates in competitive races use negative ads most often. Candidates increase their attacks when they are in the loss domain, that is, when the probability of losing is heightened. Meanwhile, front-runners, usually incumbents, can "take the high road" and run more positive ads. If the race gets close, however, the front runner will feel the need to use attack ads, which campaigns believe are more effective.

Framing and Reference Point Effects

An important implication of prospect theory is that subtle differences in the presentation of the same information can produce different evaluations and choices. For example, information is perceived differently depending on whether it is framed negatively or positively; health risks are judged differently when presented as lives saved or lives lost; and the prices of goods are evaluated differently when framed as discounts or surcharges (see Kahneman & Tversky, 1979; Nelson, Oxley, & Clawson, 1997; Shafir, this volume). People's evaluations change when they compare the same information against different reference points. Thus, the reference point greatly influences perception and evaluation.

Framing is an important part of political discourse in ways that go beyond loss or gain frames. Candidates and parties portray facts and events in ways that benefit their candidates or policies. The goal is to define for voters "what it is they are deciding" by defining relevant reference points and values to be considered (Magleby & Patterson, 1998; Nelson, Clawson, & Oxley, 1997).

One example of framing was seen in the 1992 presidential campaign. Bill Clinton argued that the economy was underperforming compared to historical, expected growth rates and that President George Bush was doing little to fix the problem. Meanwhile, Bush argued that compared to the rest of the world, the United States was doing relatively well; it was outperforming every other country in the world, including Europe and Japan. In each case, the facts remained the same. But each campaign used different reference points (past performance versus current world conditions) to get voters to draw opposite conclusions: The growth rate was either worse than or better than expected. The true art of popular politics is to sell or "spin" the frame that benefits your cause. In this case, George Bush was slow to make his argument and was unable to convince many voters that his was the better interpretation of events.

As one might expect, party labels appear to decrease framing effects on policy choices (Druckman, 1999). People often judge policies and candidates as good or bad based upon party affiliation alone. But as mentioned before, party labels are rarely used in ads, so in practice, party labels are not a very effective check on framing effects in ads.

Certainty Effects

Another tenet of BDT is a bias toward certain outcomes, also known as the *certainty effect*. People prefer certainty to gambles, even when gambles have a larger net change in utility (see Baron, 1994, pp. 358–361, for a discussion). Certainty effects are especially appealing in policy debates because many people tend to be risk averse – they want guarantees. They want to eradicate risk, not just decrease its probability; they want problems solved, not merely addressed.

Campaign ads are a perfect forum for exploiting certainty effects. Candidates want to provide the illusion that they will bring certainty and security by using terms such as *never, never again, always,* and so on throughout their ads. A candidate may make sweeping promises to "never allow x to happen again," "make sure you get x," or some other similar promise. Virtually all ads utilize these types of messages.

The second way candidates exploit the certainty effect is by focusing on *easy issues* (Carmines & Stimson, 1980). Easy issues are those that appear to have certain solutions. They elicit people's gut reactions and require little discussion of the complexities of policy issues. For example, Republicans advocate policies like "three strikes and you're out," term limits, capital punishment, and "no new taxes," whereas Democrats may "guarantee" social welfare, universal health care, and absolutist interpretations of individual liberties.

From a normative perspective, "certain" issue discussion is good because it is specific. Of course, too much specificity can also have negative side effects. First, easy, specific issue positions may impede compromise in the law-making process. President Bush learned this hard lesson with his "no new taxes" pledge in 1988. Second, "certain" policy positions are simple to understand but are destined to produce unrealistic and therefore less effective policies. The public will inevitably be disappointed with the performance of government when politicians fail to deliver on their unrealistic promises and/or the policies are ineffective because they are oversimplified. For example, "zero tolerance" policies are popular among decision makers of all stripes, but they often have unintended outcomes. One boy was expelled from school for four months after a search turned up a carving knife in his school locker. He put it there after confiscating it from a suicidal friend, but that fact could not be considered in deciding his punishment. (After all, if it was considered, it would no longer be zero tolerance.) In short, the issues discussed in ads are generally the major issues on each candidate's issue agenda. If only easy issues are discussed in ads, then tough, complex issues may get short shrift on the nation's political agenda.

Priming

Another goal of political advertising is to prime voters to focus on a candidate's issue agenda. People care about many issues, but only a few issues can occupy the national political agenda at any given time. Priming is an attempt to set the agenda and to "isolate particular issues, events, or themes . . . as criteria for evaluating politicians" (Ansolabehere & Iyengar, 1993; Kinder & Iyengar, 1987; Kinder & Krosnick, 1990; McCombs & Shaw, 1972).

Candidates use ads to raise the salience of "their" issues and qualifications in the minds of voters (Ansolabehere & Iyengar, 1995; Ghorpade, 1986). Campaign ads highlight and raise the profile of key issues, which will hopefully raise their salience on the political agenda. In 1992, President Clinton's campaign overwhelmingly stressed the economy ("It's the economy stupid"), knowing that people would be more likely to reject an incumbent president if voters focused on the failing economy. He also helped put health care front and center on the national agenda.

Priming is possible because people cannot simultaneously consider all of the issues in existence; therefore, they must rely on "those bits and pieces of political memory that are accessible" to decide which issues should occupy the national agenda (Kinder & Iyengar, 1987, p. 4). Elite actors, politicians, the news media, and campaigns all help create these preferences. Political ads do not exclusively decide the national agenda, but the ads can have a great influence. They highlight the major campaign themes that dominate political discourse. This area of ad effects deserves further attention because power rests with those who control the political agenda (Schattschneider, 1975).

Availability

The availability heuristic is the tendency to judge probabilities by the extent to which salient examples are easily recalled (Tversky & Kahneman, 1974). One of the main goals of ads is to increase the availability of certain information in voters' minds so that they can recall it when they walk into the polling booth. For example, ads often repeat a candidate's name and office in order to increase name recognition.

Availability has many potential applications to political advertising. Availability may help explain why people mistakenly believe that negative ads are more numerous than positive ads. Content analyses of ads have show that this perception is wrong – most ads are positive. We find that 43% of all Senate ads are negative, and the percentage of negative ads actually aired appears to be only slightly higher (Freedman & Goldstein, 1999). Other types of races have even lower proportions of negative ads, as low as 23% (Hale et al., Farmer, 1995; Johnson-Cartee & Copeland, 1991; Joslyn, 1986; Kaid & Johnston, 1991; Sabato, 1981). The fact that negative ads are more memorable (Basil, Schooler, & Reeves, 1991; Lau 1982, 1985) may inflate the prevalence of negative information in the minds of voters, leading them to overestimate the percentage of negative ads produced and aired. If voters overestimate negativity, it may contribute to lower voter turnout (Ansolabehere & Iyengar, 1995), increase their dissatisfaction, and further deflate their confidence in the political process.

Memorable negative ads may also influence whether a candidate is considered a negative campaigner. The "Willie Horton" ad is a perfect example. This ad has become synonymous with George Bush's 1988 presidential campaign. Extensive media coverage of the ad increased its availability and caused people to view President Bush as a negative campaigner. But this judgment is not entirely correct. First, the ad was not produced or aired by the Bush campaign; rather, it was sponsored independently by Bush supporters. Second, content analyses of presidential ads showed that Dukakis produced significantly more negative ads than Bush that year (Kaid, 1993). The label also stuck in 1992 when George Bush ran against Bill Clinton. People generally presumed that

Bush was the more negative candidate at precisely the same time that Bill Clinton was producing the highest percentage of negative ads of any presidential candidate in history to that point (Kaid, 1993).

Discussion and Conclusion

In this chapter, we highlighted only a few of the ways in which behavioral decision theory can illuminate our understanding of political advertising. As we suggest throughout this chapter, these applications have great potential to enrich our understanding of candidate behavior, voter decision making, and the operation of the larger political system. More specifically, prospect theory may help us better understand the context in which *candidates and campaigns* decide to attack, and also explain when voters are more likely to vote against incumbents. BDT's findings may also illuminate previously ignored ad effects on *voters*, such as framing effects, issue priming, issue cues, heuristics, and the like. Finally, voters' perception of ads can influence their perceptions of the political system, which in turn have repercussions on voter turnout, trust in government, and the nature of the issue agenda.

We should reiterate our observation that the cognitive mechanisms outlined by BDT can have both positive and negative effects on voters. Unwarranted inferences, misleading or incomplete information, personal attacks, and the like all have potentially troublesome effects on human judgment. But BDT reminds us that ads can contain helpful cues as well. In some ways, ads may be more helpful than was previously assumed. Further study is needed to determine the full scope of these effects, both positive and negative.

We have shown throughout this chapter how BDT provides a useful framework for studying political advertising content and its effect on voters and the political system. In return, political campaigns provide an ideal milieu in which to further test and refine behavioral theories. Nevertheless, we advise the cautious application of BDT. Humans are not solely cognitive beings. Neither normative nor cognitive theories are sufficient to fully understand human thought and behavior. Emotion, affect, elite and group connections, and various contextual variables are also important (Just, Crigler, & Neuman, 1996; Kern, 1989). Furthermore, cognitive effects appear to be context dependent (see Levy, 1992; Swoyer, this volume) and challenging to test empirically (Levy, 1992; Shafir, 1992). All of these factors together determine how people make judgments and choices with the limited information that they have.

No doubt most people will continue to worry about the dark side of campaigns – the manipulation of decision processes by politicians and consultants – and continue to ponder how to improve campaign communication. We suggest that one way to minimize manipulation is to increase ad competition, so that one candidate cannot dominate the issue agenda or issue frame (Lau & Redlawsk, 1997). In a competitive information environment, competing information, cues, frames, agendas, and so on mitigate the effect of the opponent's messages. The key to competition, however, is often money. Unequal campaign spending will create unequal ad competition where manipulative ad effects are more likely to arise.

Ultimately, we do not believe that we can improve campaigns by feeding people more information in more rationalistic formats. Rather, we should accept that people are not ideal decision makers and view people's judgment and choice processes as givens rather than as mistakes. If we accept this fact, we reconceptualize the nature of the problem, as well as its proposed solutions. Ads are one of the most ubiquitous and useful sources of information for voters. The cues and signals in them are not necessarily useless or irrational, but are often very useful to voters. Therefore, increasing their number and balance may be as helpful as improving their quality (normatively speaking). We believe Samuel Popkin (1991) had it right when he said:

If voters look for information about candidates under streetlights [easily available sources of information like media and ads], then that is where candidates must campaign, and the only way to improve elections is to add streetlights. Reforms can only make sense if they are consistent with the gut rationality of voters. Ask not for more sobriety and piety from citizens, for they are voters, not judges; offer them instead cues and signals which connect their world with the world of politics. (p. 236)

References

Ansolabehere, S., Behr, R., & Iyengar, S. (1993). *The media game: American politics in the television age*. New York: Macmillan.

Ansolabehere, S., & Iyengar, S. (1993). Information and electoral attitudes: A case of judgment under uncertainty. In S. Iyengar & W. J. McGuire (Eds.), *Explorations in political psychology* (pp. 321–327). Durham, NC: Duke University Press.

Ansolabehere, S., & Iyengar, S. (1995). *Going negative*. New York: Free Press.

Ansolabehere, S., Iyengar, S., & Simon, A. 1999. Replicating experiments using aggregate and survey data: The case of negative advertising and turnout. *American Political Science Review, 93*, 901–909.

Ansolabehere, S., Iyengar, S., Simon, A., & Valentino, N. (1994). Does attack advertising demobilize the electorate? *American Political Science Review, 88,* 829–838.

Associated Press. (1999, August 13). Hunt signs campaign reform bill. *The Salisbury Post,* p. A 6.

Baron, J. (1994). *Thinking and deciding.* Cambridge: Cambridge University Press.

Basil, M., Schooler, C., & Reeves, B. (1991). Positive and negative political advertising: Effectiveness of ads and perceptions of candidates. In F. Biocca (Ed.), *Television and political advertising: Psychological processes* (Vol. 1, pp. 245–262). Hillsdale, NJ: Erlbaum.

Bennett, W. L. (1992). *The governing crisis: Media, money and marketing in American elections.* New York: St. Martin's Press.

Biocca, F. (1991). *Television and political advertising: Signs, codes and images,* Volume 2. Hillsdale, NJ: Erlbaum.

Campbell, A., Converse, P., Miller, W., & Stokes, D. (1960). *The American voter.* Ann Arbor: University of Michigan Press.

Carmines, E. G., & Stimson, J. A. (1980). The two faces of issue voting. *American Political Science Review, 74,* 78–91.

Combs, J. E., & Nimmo, D. (1993). *The new propaganda.* New York: Longman.

Diamond, E., & Bates, S. (1992). *The spot.* Cambridge, MA: MIT Press.

Dionne, E. J., Jr. (1991). *Why Americans hate politics.* New York: Simon & Schuster.

Downs, A. (1957). *An economic theory of democracy.* New York: Harper & Row.

Druckman, J. N. (1999, November). *Do party cues limit framing effects?* Paper presented at the annual meeting of the Southern Political Science Association, Savannah.

Dye, T. R., & Zeigler, L. H. (1984). *The irony of democracy.* Monterey, CA: Brooks/ Cole.

Edelman, M. (1988). *Constructing the political spectacle.* Chicago: University of Chicago Press.

Farmer, R., & Fox, J. C. (1996, August). *Public policy issues in U.S. senate ads: 1984–1994.* Paper presented at the annual meeting of the American Political Science Association, San Francisco.

Flanigan, W. H., & Zingale, N. H. (1994). *Political behavior of the American electorate* (8th ed.). Washington, DC: Congressional Quarterly, Inc.

Freedman, P., & Goldstein, K. (1999). Measuring media exposure and the effects of negative campaign ads. *American Journal of Political Science, 43,* 1189–1208.

Gans, C. B. (1991). Yes – campaign commercials should be regulated. In G. L. Rose (Ed.), *Controversial issues in presidential selection* (pp. 133–142). Albany, NY: SUNY Press.

Garramone, G. M. (1985). Effects of negative political advertising: The roles of sponsor and rebuttal. *Journal of Broadcasting and Electronic Media, 29,* 2 147–159.

Ghorpade, S. (1986). Agenda setting: A test of advertising's neglected function. *Journal of Advertising Research, 26,* 23–27.

Hale, J. F., Fox, J. C., & Farmer, R. (1995, March). *The content of Senate advertising: 1984–1994.* Paper presented at the annual meeting of the Southwestern Political Science Association, Dallas.

Hale, J. F., Fox, J. C., & Farmer, R. (1996). Negative advertising in U.S. Senate campaigns: The influence of campaign context. *Social Science Quarterly, 77,* 329–343.

Johnson-Cartee, K. S., & Copeland, G. A. (1991). *Negative political advertising: Coming of age.* Hillsdale, NJ: Erlbaum.

Joslyn, R. A. (1981). The content of political spot ads. *Journalism Quarterly, 57,* 92–98.

Joslyn, R. A. (1986). Political advertising and the meaning of elections. In L. L. Kaid, D., Nimmo, & K. R. Sanders (Eds.), *New perspectives on political advertising* (pp. 139–183). Carbondale, IL: Southern Illinois University.

Joslyn, R. A. (1987). Liberal campaign rhetoric in 1984. In J. P. Vermeer (Ed.), *Campaigns in the news: Mass media and congressional elections* (pp. 31–50). New York: Greenwood Press.

Just, M. R., Crigler, A. N., & Neuman, W. R. (1996). Cognitive and affective dimensions of political conceptualization. In A. N. Crigler (Ed.), *The psychology of political communication* (pp. 133–148). Ann Arbor: University of Michigan Press.

Kahn, K. F., & Geer, J. (1994). Creating impressions: An experimental investigation of political advertising on television. *Political Behavior, 16,* 93–116.

Kahn, K. F., & Kenney, P. 1999. Do negative campaigns mobilize or suppress turnout? Clarifying the relationship between negativity and participation. *American Political Science Review, 93,* 877–889.

Kahneman, D., & Tversky, A. (1979). Prospect theory: An analysis of decision under risk. *Econometrica, 47,* 263–291.

Kaid, L. L., & Johnston, A. (1991). Negative versus positive television advertising in U.S. presidential campaigns, 1960–1988. *Journal of Communication, 41,* 53–64.

Kaid, L. L. (1993). Political advertising in the 1992 campaign. In R. E. Denton, Jr. (Ed.), *The 1992 presidential campaign: A communication perspective* (pp. 111–127). Westport, CT: Praeger.

Kaid, L. L., & Davidson, D. (1986). Elements of videostyle: A preliminary examination of candidate presentation through television advertising.

Kaid, L. L., Gobetz, R., Garner, J., Leland, C., & Scott, D. (1993). Television news and presidential campaigns: The legitimization of televised political advertising. *Social Science Quarterly, 74,* 274–285.

Kern, M. (1989). *30 second politics: Political advertising in the eighties.* New York: Praeger.

Kinder, D. (1986). Presidential character revisited. In R. R. Lau & D. O. Sears (Eds.), *Political cognition* (pp. 233–256). Hillsdale, NJ: Erlbaum.

Kinder, D., & Iyengar, S. (1987). *News that matters.* Chicago: University of Chicago Press.

Kinder, D., & Krosnick, J. A. (1990). Altering the foundation of support for the president through priming. *American Political Science Review, 84,* 497–512.

Lau, R. R. (1982). Negativity in political perception. *Political Behavior, 4,* 353–378.

Lau, R. R. (1985). Two explanations for negativity effects in political behavior. *American Journal of Political Science, 29,* 119–138.

Lau, R. R., & Redlawsk, D. P. (1997). Voting correctly. *American Political Science Review, 91,* 585–598.

Lau, R. R., Sigelman, L., Heldman, C., & Babbitt, P. (1999). The effects of negative political advertisements: A meta-analytic assessment. *American Political Science Review, 93,* 851–875.

Levy, J. (1992). Prospect theory and international relations: Theoretical applications and analytical problems. *Political Psychology, 13,* 283–310.

Lodge, M., & McGraw, K. (1995). *Political judgment*. Ann Arbor: University of Michigan Press.

Lupia, A. W., & McCubbins, M. D. (1997). *The democratic dilemma: Can citizens learn what they need to know?* Cambridge: Cambridge University Press.

Magleby, D., & Patterson, K. (1998). Consultants and direct democracy. *PS: Political Science and Politics, 31*, 160–169.

McCombs, M., & Shaw, D. (1972). The agenda-setting function of the mass media. *Public Opinion Quarterly, 36*, 176–187.

McGinnis, J. (1969). *The selling of the president, 1968*. New York: Trident Press.

Nelson, T. E., Clawson, R. A., & Oxley, Z. M. (1997). Media framing of a civil liberties conflict and its effect on tolerance. *American Political Science Review, 91*, 567–583.

Nelson, T. E., Oxley, Z., & Clawson, R. A. (1997). Toward a psychology of framing effects. *Political Behavior, 19*, 221–246.

Neuman, W. R. (1986). *The paradox of mass politics: Knowledge and opinion in the American electorate*. Cambridge, MA: Harvard University Press.

Nie, N., Verba, S., & Petrocik, J. R. (1976). *The changing American voter*. Cambridge, MA: Harvard University Press.

Niemi, R., & Weisberg, H. (1993). *Controversies in voting behavior*. Washington, DC: Congressional Quarterly.

Page, B., & Shapiro, R. (1992). *The rational public*. Chicago: University of Chicago Press.

Page, B. I. (1978). *Choices and echoes in presidential elections: Rational man and electoral democracies*. Chicago: University of Chicago Press.

Popkin, S. (1991). *The reasoning voter*. Chicago: University of Chicago Press.

Quattrone, G. A., & Tversky, A. (1988). Contrasting rational and psychological analyses of political choice. *American Political Science Review, 82*, 719–736.

Richey, M. H., Koenigs, R. J., Richey, H. W., & Fortin, R. (1975). Negative salience in impressions of character: Effects of unequal proportions of positive and negative information. *Journal of Social Psychology, 97*, 223–241.

Riker, W. H. (1995). The political psychology of rational choice theory. *Political Psychology, 16*, 23–44.

Rosenberg, S. W., Bohan, L., McCaffrey, P., & Harris, K. (1986). The image and the vote: The effects of candidate presentation on voter preference. *American Journal of Political Science, 30*, 108–127.

Sabato, L. (1981). *The rise of political consultants*. New York: Basic Books.

Schattschneider, E. E. (1975). *The semisovereign people*. Hinsdale, IL: Dryden Press.

Shafir, E. (1992). Prospect theory and political analysis: A psychological perspective. *Political Psychology, 13*, 311–329.

Suedfeld, P., & Tetlock, P. E. (1992). Psychological advice about political decision making: Heuristics, biases, and cognitive defects. In P. Suedfeld & P. E. Tetlock (Eds.), *Psychology and social policy* (pp. 51–70). New York: Hemisphere.

Tversky, A., & Kahneman, D. (1974). Judgment under uncertainty: Heuristics and biases. *Science, 211*, 453–458.

Wattenberg, M. (1994). *The decline of American political parties, 1952–1992*. Cambridge, MA: Harvard University Press.

Wattenberg, M., & Brians, C. 1999. Negative campaign advertising: Demobilizer or mobilizer? *American Political Science Review, 93*, 891–899.

West, D. M. (1992). Reforming campaign ads. *PS: Political Science & Politics, 25,* 74–77.

West, D. M. (1993). *Air wars: Television advertising in election campaigns, 1952–1992.* Washington, DC: Congressional Quarterly.

Wright, G. C., Jr., & Berkman, M. B. (1986). Candidates and policy in U.S. Senate elections. *American Political Science Review, 80,* 567–590.

Wyckoff, G. (1968). *The image candidate: American politics in the age of television.* New York: Macmillan.

9 Toward Behavioral Law and Economics

Cass R. Sunstein

Following the success of behavioral economics, behavioral law and economics has recently generated a great deal of new analysis of the legal system and now promises to become a field of its own (Jolls, Sunstein, & Thaler, 1998; Langevoort, 1998; Sunstein, 2000). The starting point here is that a great deal of empirical research requires qualifications of rational choice models (Bazerman, Messick, Tenbrunsel, & Wade-Bensoni, 1997; Conlisk, 1996; Thaler, 1994b). Those models are often wrong in the simple sense that they yield inaccurate predictions. Cognitive errors and motivational distortions may press behavior far from the anticipated directions; normative accounts of rational choice should not be confused with descriptive accounts (Tversky, 1996). But it does not follow that people's behavior is unpredictable, systematically irrational, random, rule-free, or elusive to social scientists.

On the contrary, the qualifications can be described, used, and sometimes even modeled. Those qualifications, and the resulting understandings of decision and choice (Kahneman & Tversky 1979; Loomes & Sugden, 1982), are playing a large and increasing role in many fields within economics and law. A large question is how analysis of the legal system might be altered if people are understood to be quasi-rational agents displaying bounded willpower, bounded self-interest, and bounded rationality (see Jolls et al., 1998; Sunstein, 1999).

Much behavioral work suggests that preferences and values are sometimes constructed rather than elicited by social situations (Slovic, 1995). "[O]bserved preferences are not simply read off some master list; they are actually constructed during the elicitation process. . . . Different elicitation procedures highlight different aspects of options and suggest alternative heuristics, which give rise to inconsistent responses" (Tversky, 1996, p. 186). People do not generally consult a free-standing

218

"preference menu" from which selections are made at the moment of choice; preferences can be a product of procedure, description, and context at the time of choice. "Alternative descriptions of the same choice problems lead to systematically different preferences; strategically equivalent elicitation procedures give rise to different choices; and the preference between x and y often depends on the choice set within which they are embedded" (Tversky, 1996, p. 186). What has been learned about human behavior and choice should be linked, at the theoretical and empirical levels, with analysis of the legal system.

The legal system is pervasively in the business of constructing procedures, descriptions, and contexts for choice. Of course, the legal system creates procedures, descriptions, and contexts in the course of litigated cases. For example, the alternatives (selected to be) placed before the jury or judge may matter a great deal; liability or conviction on some count A may very much depend on the nature of counts B, C, and D. In this respect, the preferences and values of judges and juries may well be constructed, not elicited, by the legal system. Certainly this is true for the award of damages, where special problems may arise; the plaintiff's initial demand, for example, may "anchor" the judgment of the jury or judge. But similar points also hold outside of the courtroom. The allocation of legal entitlements, and the structures created for exchange (or nonexchange) by law, may well affect both preferences and values. Thus law can construct rather than elicit preferences internally, by affecting what goes on in court, and externally, by affecting what happens in ordinary transactions, market and nonmarket.

For purposes of analysis, we might distinguish three different tasks: positive, prescriptive, and normative. *Positive work* is concerned with predictions. If, contrary to conventional assumptions, people dislike losses far more than they like equivalent gains, predictions will go wrong insofar as they rest on conventional assumptions. As we will shortly see, this point has important implications for positive analysis of law.

Prescriptive work is concerned with showing how society might actually reach shared goals; this is a central purpose of economic analysis of law. Consider the following information campaigns, which conventional analysis deems equivalent. (1) If you use energy conservation methods, you will save $X per year. (2) If you do not use energy conservation methods, you will lose $X per year. It turns out that information campaign (2) is far more effective than information campaign (1) (Aronson, 1996). Some features of human judgment, properly understood, undermine conventional economic prescriptions about what will work best; they help explain, to take just one example, precisely why the public service advertising slogan "Drive defensively; watch out for the other guy" is particularly ingenious. (In a nutshell: The slogan attempts to counteract optimistic bias, whereby the vast majority of people believe that they are safer drivers than average.)

Normative work is concerned with what the legal system should do. Recent revisions in understanding human behavior greatly unsettle certain arguments against paternalism in law. They unsettle those arguments by showing that people are prone to error and sometimes do not promote their own interests. Behavioral law and economics does not make an affirmative case for paternalism, but it supports a form of anti-antipaternalism (see Jolls et al., 1998). If, for example, people use heuristic devices that lead to systematic errors, their judgments about how to deal with risks may be badly misconceived. Thus the literature on heuristics and biases helps support Supreme Court Justice Stephen Breyer's analysis favoring technocratic assessments of risk (Breyer, 1993); it also helps support cost-benefit analysis on psychological rather than cognitive grounds (Sunstein, 1999). If people are unrealistically optimistic, they may run risks because of a factually false belief in their own relative immunity from harm, even if they are fully aware of the statistical facts. And if people's choices are based on incorrect judgments about their experience *after choice*, there is reason to question whether respect for choices, rooted in those incorrect judgments, is a good way to promote utility or welfare. None of these points makes a firm case for legal paternalism, not least because bureaucrats may be subject to the same cognitive and motivational distortions as everyone else (Viscusi, 1993). But they suggest that objections to paternalism should be more empirical and pragmatic, having to do with the possibility of education and likely failures of government response, rather than a priori in nature.

Now let me offer a few details, tracing some of the principal findings that emerge from behavioral research and showing how they bear on positive, prescriptive, and normative work in law.

Loss Aversion

People are especially averse to losses (Kahneman, Knetsch, & Thaler, 1990; Kahneman & Tversky, 1979; Knetsch, 1997). They are more displeased with losses than they are pleased with equivalent gains – roughly speaking, twice as displeased. Contrary to economic theory, people do not treat out-of-pocket costs and opportunity costs as if they were equivalent.

Loss aversion has important implications for positive analysis of law. It means, for example, that the Coase theorem is in one respect quite wrong (Kahneman et al., 1990). The Coase theorem holds that when transaction costs are zero, the allocation of the legal entitlement will not matter; parties will bargain their way to the same result in any case. The theorem is wrong because the allocation of the legal entitlement may well matter in the sense that those who are initially allocated an entitlement are likely to value it more than those without the legal entitlement. Thus workers allocated a (waivable) right to be discharged only for cause may value that right far more than they would if employers were allocated a (tradable) right to discharge at will; thus breathers of air may well value their (tradable) right to be free from air pollution far more than they would if polluters had been given a (tradable) right to emit polluting substances into the air. The legal entitlement creates an *endowment effect*, that is, a greater valuation stemming from the mere fact of endowment. This effect has been observed in many contexts (Sunstein, 1997).

There is a further point. People are averse to losses, but whether an event "codes" as a loss or a gain depends not on simple facts but on a range of contextual factors, including how the event is framed. The status quo is usually the reference point, so that losses are understood as such by reference to existing distributions and practices (Samuelson & Zeckhauser, 1988); but it is possible to manipulate the frame so as to make a change code as a loss rather than a gain, or vice versa. Consider a company that says *cash discount* rather than *credit card surcharge*; or a parent who says that for behavior X (rather than behavior Y) a child will be rewarded, as opposed to saying that for behavior Y (rather than for behavior X) a child will be punished; or familiar advertisements to the effect that "you cannot afford not to" use a certain product. In environmental regulation, it is possible to manipulate the reference point by insisting that policymakers are trying to "restore" water or air quality to its state at time X; the restoration time matters a great deal to people's choices (Gregory, Lichtenstein, & MacGregor, 1993).

For present purposes, the most important source of a reference point is the law – where has the legal system placed the initial entitlement? Much research remains to be done on the effects of this initial allocation. It bears, for example, on the distinction between *subsidies* and *penalties* that has proved so crucial to the law governing unconstitutional conditions (Stone, Seidman, Sunstein, & Tushnet, 1998); that distinction can be understood as responsive to the phenomenon of loss aversion, and framing effects very much affect different judgments about whether someone has been subsidized or instead penalized.

Loss aversion also raises serious questions about the goal of the tort system. Should damages measure the amount that would restore an injured party to the status quo ante, or should they reflect the amount that an injured party would demand to be subject to the injury before the fact? Juries appear to believe that the amount that would be demanded preinjury is far greater than the amount that would restore the status quo ante (McCaffery, Kahneman, & Spitzer, 1995). The legal system appears generally to see the compensation question as the latter one, though it does not seem to have made this choice in any systematic way.

The disparity has large implications for the choice between liability rules (allowing property to be taken on payment of damages) and property rules (allowing property to be taken only pursuant to voluntary contract). Property rules allow a taking only via *willingness to accept*; liability rules frame the question in terms of *willingness to pay*. The economic literature on the choice between the two generally does not recognize that the resulting valuations may be dramatically different (see Kaplow & Shavell, 1996; Knetsch, this volume). But there is evidence that the endowment effect is larger and indeed may exist at all only when the interest is protected by a property rule (see Rachlinsk & Jourden, 1998).

Extremeness Aversion

People are averse to extremes. Whether an option is extreme depends on the stated alternatives. Extremeness aversion gives rise to *compromise effects*. Between given alternatives, people seek a compromise. In this as in other respects, the framing of choice matters; the introduction of (unchosen, apparently irrelevant) alternatives into the frame can alter the outcome. When, for example, people are choosing between a small radio A and a midsize radio B, most may well choose A; but the introduction of a third, large radio C is likely to lead many people to choose B instead (Kelman, Rottenstreich, & Tversky, 1996). Thus the introduction of a third, unchosen (and in that sense irrelevant) option may produce a switch in choice as between two options. Almost everyone has had an experience of switching to (say) the second most expensive item on some menu of options, and of doing so partly because of the presence of the (very) most expensive item. Compare this to the phenomenon of *trade-off contrast*: The introduction of a third alternative – including a charge introduced to a judge or jury – may make some characteristic of the choice especially salient and thus affect judgment.

Extremeness aversion suggests that a simple axiom of conventional economic theory – involving the irrelevance of added, unchosen alternatives – is wrong (Kelman et al., 1996; Sen, 1993). It also has large consequences for legal advocacy and judgment, as well as for predictions about the effects of law. How can a preferred option best be framed as the compromise choice? When should a lawyer argue in the alternative, and what kinds of alternative arguments are most effective? This should be a central question for advocates to answer. Juries and judges may well try to choose a compromise solution, and what codes as the compromise solution depends on what alternatives are made available. And in elections, medical interventions, and policymaking, compromise effects may matter a great deal.

Self-Serving Bias, Unrealistic Optimism, and Overconfidence: Negotiation Breakdown and Risk Regulation

As we will see, people care about being fair and about being treated fairly, and sometimes they are willing to sacrifice their material self-interest for the sake of fairness. This point has considerable importance to law. But note also that people's judgments about fairness are self-serving, and people tend to be both unrealistically optimistic and over-confident about their judgments (Kahneman & Tversky, 1995). In any random couple, it is highly likely that the addition of answers to the question "What percentage of the domestic work do you do?" will produce a number greater than 100%.

The point bears on the otherwise largely inexplicable phenomenon of bargaining impasses. Why aren't more cases settled? Why does the legal system spend so much on dispute settlement? Part of the answer lies in the fact that self-serving bias – a belief that one deserves more than other people tend to think – affects both parties to a negotiation, and this makes agreement very difficult (Babcock & Loewenstein, 1997; Kahneman & Tversky, 1995).

Unrealistic optimism and self-serving biases also bear on individual risk-bearing, and hence on the role of the regulatory state, especially in the area of dangers to life and health. Even factually informed people tend to think that they are less at risk than others. Thus there is systematic overconfidence in risk judgments, as the vast majority of people believe that they are less likely than others to be subject to automobile accidents, acquired immune deficiency syndrome (AIDS), heart attacks, asthma, and many other health risks (Weinstein, 1989). In one survey, for example, 90% of automobile drivers considered themselves to be above-average drivers (Taylor, 1989). In another survey, students asked to envision their future said that they were far less likely than their classmates to be fired from a job, to have a heart attack or to get cancer, to be divorced after a few years of marriage, or to have a drinking problem (Taylor, 1989).

Reflecting illusions about their own practices, gay men appear to underestimate systematically the chance that they will get AIDS, even though they do not lack information about the risk of AIDS in general (Bauman & Siegel, 1987). Older people similarly underestimate the likelihood that they will be in a car accident or contract major diseases. Unrealistic optimism appears to characterize people in most social categories (Bauman & Siegel, 1987). People systematically underestimate the extent to which they are at risk, and perceptions of relative invulnerability affect preventive health practices (Bauman & Siegel, 1987). A random communitywide survey of attitudes toward health risks found a systematic belief of above-average immunity from risk (Weinstein, 1986).

Unrealistic optimism and self-serving biases are relevant to the positive and prescriptive tasks of law. Efforts to educate people about risk may run afoul of unrealistic optimism; hence mere statistical knowledge may fail to produce adequate information. Moreover, efforts to increase consensual solutions must take account of self-serving bias; problems with negotiated rule making, one of the most popular new developments in administrative law, may have self-serving bias at their roots.

Unrealistic optimism also creates a distinctive problem for conventional objections to paternalism in law. If people tend to believe that they are relatively free from risks, they may lack accurate information even if they know statistical facts. Moreover, such evidence greatly complicates the widespread view that people often overstate low-probability events. It is true that people may think that low-probability events have a higher probability than they in fact do. But many individual agents think that they are peculiarly immune from such events, which may mean that they err in the other direction.

Decision Utility versus Experience Utility

In economics it is often assumed that the utility of experience is best measured by the anticipated utility shown by people's decisions. But a good deal of recent research shows that *there may well be systematic differences between the utility expected at the time of a decision and the utility actually experienced as a result of a decision* (Kahneman, 1996; Loewenstein & Schkade, 1999). People's judgments about their experience at the time of a decision can be mistaken, in the sense that they have a hard time assessing what the experience will actually be like.

There are many examples. From the phenomenon of loss aversion we can infer that people value goods more when they own them than when they do not. This effect – the endowment effect – has been observed in many settings (Thaler, 1994b). But in recent experiments, people have been unable to predict the endowment effect and thus unable to predict their own tastes (Loewenstein & Schkade, 1999). This finding is paralleled by many studies showing that people do not accurately predict the consequences of (for example) winning the lottery or becoming paraplegic. (Winning the lottery produces much lower hedonic gains than expected, and people adjust to becoming paraplegic much more easily than expected.) An especially important example comes from studies dealing with human immunodeficiency virus (HIV) testing. People are quite terrified of their reaction if they find that they are HIV positive; they predict a high degree of panic and depression. But a recent study suggests that people are able to adapt fairly well to the bad news, and their panic and depression are far less severe than they thought ex ante (Sieff, Dawes, & Loewenstein, 1999). We might expect that people would therefore *undertest*; they are likely to be especially averse to undergoing a process of which they are very fearful. It might follow that regulatory approaches – education, persuasion, financial incentives, conceivably coercion – would make a good deal of sense.

Economists have stated that people have adequate information about the risks of smoking and that additional regulation is therefore inappropriate (Viscusi, 1993). And it does seem that people know many of the basic facts. But a study of high school students suggests a problem (Slovic, 1998). About one-third of adolescent smokers believed that there was no risk from smoking a pack of cigarettes daily for the first years after starting to smoke. Young people who smoked believed that they had a below-average risk from smoking. And 85% of high school teenagers who smoked believed that they would not be smoking in five years, whereas a follow-up study showed that only 58% had quit and 37% had actually increased their consumption. About 32% of those who smoked one pack believed that they would quit in five years, but only 13% did so.

When people mispredict their future experiences, a common argument for paternalism, it is no longer plausible for ordinary people to choose what will promote their welfare. With further research perhaps, it will ultimately be possible to be systematic about issues of this kind – to know exactly when people's decisions produce bad experiences.

Cooperation, Fairness, and the Appearance of Fairness

Economists sometimes assume that people are self-interested. This may well be true, and often it is a useful simplifying assumption. But people also may want to act fairly and, equally important, they want to be seen to act fairly, especially but not only among nonstrangers. For purposes of understanding law, what is especially important is that people may sacrifice their economic self-interest in order to be, or to appear, fair.

Consider, for example, the ultimatum game (Kagel & Roth, 1995). The people who run the game give some money, on a provisional basis, to the first of two players. The first player is instructed to offer part of the money to the second player. If the second player accepts that amount, he can keep what is offered, and the first player gets to keep the rest. But if the second player rejects the offer, neither player gets anything. Both players are informed that these are the rules. No bargaining is allowed. Using standard assumptions about rationality, self-interest, and choice, economists predict that the first player should offer a penny and the second player should accept. But this is not what happens. Offers usually average between 30% and 40% of the total. Offers of less than 20% are often rejected. Often there is a 50-50 division. These results cut across the level of the stakes and also across diverse cultures.

The results of the ultimatum game are highly suggestive. Perhaps people will not violate norms of fairness, even when doing so is in their economic self-interest, at least if the norm violations will be public. What offers are made in bankruptcy negotiations? Do companies always raise prices when circumstances create short-term scarcity? For example, are there social constraints on price increases for snow shovels after a snowstorm or for umbrellas during a rainstorm? It may well be that contracting parties are reluctant to take advantage of the misfortunes of another, partly because of social constraints on self-interested behavior.

Here there is much room for future work. Experimental work also shows a high degree of cooperation in prisoners' dilemma situations, especially when people are speaking with one another (Kagel & Roth, 1995). The implication is that at least in some contexts, law may not be necessary to solve collective action problems. Norms will do the work of law.

The same point bears on the question of how a legal system might produce compliance without much enforcement. In some contexts, compliance is widespread even with little enforcement activity; people tend not to park in handicapped zones, they do not smoke in public places, they clean up after their dogs, and they pay their taxes much more regularly than economic theory would predict. At the same time, some laws are regularly flouted; consider bans on consensual sexual activity. An understanding of cooperation and fairness, and of the psychological preconditions for disregard of material self-interest, may help illuminate one of the great ill-understood phenomena in law.

Heuristics

People make judgments about probability on the basis of heuristic devices, responsive perhaps to the high costs of inquiry and decision that may often work well in many cases but that tend also to lead to systematic errors (Camerer, 1995). This work bears on the demand for (and hence also the supply of) government services, including regulation. It also has implications for assessment of the jury system – suggesting that juries are likely to make many mistakes in terms of probability assessments and that correction of those mistakes is a large task of the legal system. Here is a very brief description of several heuristics of particular relevance to law.

Availability, with a Note on Social Influences, Dupes, Freeloaders, and Cascades

People tend to think that events are more likely if an example is readily called to mind or *available*. If pervasive, the availability heuristic will produce systematic errors. For example, assessments of risk will be pervasively biased in the sense that people will think that some risks (of a nuclear accident, for example) are high, whereas others (of a stroke, for example) are relatively low. There is evidence that people's judgments about risk levels are much affected by the availability heuristic (Baron, 1994). The availability heuristic appears to affect the demand for law, especially in the area of risk regulation (Jolls et al., 1998; Kuran & Sunstein, 1999; Noll & Krier, 1991).

Of course, the availability heuristic operates in an emphatically social environment, and social influences may amplify the effects of the heuristic in a way that helps account for much behavior, including behavior that produces the supply of and demand for law (Kuran & Sunstein, 1999). People often think what (they think) other people think. Sometimes they do what (they think) others do. Partly this is because when a person lacks much personal information, he or she will sensibly rely on the information of others. If you don't know whether pesticides cause cancer or whether hazardous waste dumps are a serious social problem, you may as well follow what other people seem to think. And partly this is because of reputational influences. If most people think that hazardous waste dumps are a serious social problem or that laws should ban hate crimes, you might go along with them so that they do not think that you are ignorant, malevolent, or callous.

For the most part, an emphasis on informational and reputational influences is, of course, entirely consistent with conventional economics, though it has implications that have not been sufficiently exploited. An analyst attuned to informational and reputational influences might predict, for example, that people are more likely to vote if they think that most people are voting; that tax compliance is more likely if people think that most people comply; that college students are more likely to drink heavily, or to use unlawful drugs, if they think that this is what most college students are doing; and that teenagers in poor neighborhoods are more likely to join gangs if they think that most teenagers are gang members (Perkins, 1997). Behavioral economics and behavioral decision theory add two points. The first is an understanding of how the availability heuristic interacts with these influences; sometimes a salient event or anecdote can interact with informational and reputational forces so as to create cascade effects. In addition, behavioral economics emphasizes the role of reciprocity in producing these effects. People do not want to be either dupes or freeloaders, and hence they are most likely to contribute to some social goal if they believe that others are doing so as well.

These points have a wide range of implications for the content of law. They help explain the supply of and the demand for government regulation. *Availability cascades* help drive law and policy in both fortunate and unfortunate directions. They can eliminate public torpor by drawing attention to problems that, although serious, have long been overlooked.

On the other hand, they can produce public concern or outrage about problems that have little claim to the public fisc. An important task for the legal system is to decide, therefore, how to promote better priority setting.

Anchoring, with Special Reference to Damage Awards

Often people make judgments about appropriate numbers, including probabilities, on the basis of an initial value, or *anchor*, from which they make insufficient adjustments. When people lack information, this may be the best that they can do. The problem is that the initial value may have an arbitrary or irrational source. When this is so, the probability assessment may go badly wrong. Jury judgments about damage awards, for example, are likely to be based on an anchor; this can produce a high level of arbitrariness. There is considerable experimental evidence to this effect; in particular, the plaintiff's demand makes a great deal of difference in the process of "the more you ask for, the more you get." If the plaintiff's demand influences jury awards, it is possible that the legal system should take corrective steps by, for example, allowing appellate courts to exercise greater control in the interest of preventing unjustified unequal treatment or by preventing the jury from hearing demands that are legally unacceptable, for constitutional or other reasons. It is quite possible that an unlawfully high demand from the plaintiff will greatly inflate the resulting award, and even if that award is itself within legal limits, there is something troublesome about allowing such a demand to be its anchor or basic source. A great deal of work remains to be done on the real-world effects of anchors when juries and judges are dealing with dollar amounts.

Case-Based Decisions and Decision Costs

Legal reasoning is pervasively analogical in character; judges often reason by reference to past cases. Conventional economics can offer some explanations; analogical reasoning, or at least respect for the past, can increase predictability and at the same time reduce decision costs for judges. But conventional approaches have yet to explain why reasoning by analogy is so pervasive.

Behavioral law and economics provides some insight into why this might be so. If decision costs are put to one side, expected utility theory is demanding simply because it is difficult to calculate the expected costs and benefits of alternatives. People often simplify their burdens by reasoning from past cases and by taking small, reversible steps. Economists have offered an account, behavioral in spirit but independent of law, of an alternative to expected utility theory: case-based decision theory (Gilboa & Schmeidler, 1995). The account should be counted as a genuine (though apparently inadvertent) contribution to jurisprudence. Those who reason from past cases can reduce the burdens of thinking problems through from the ground up, and in a way that may minimize the sum of error costs and decision costs. An understanding of behavioral economics may in this sense illuminate some important aspects of legal reasoning.

Probability-Related Tastes

Here we are dealing not with simple factual errors, but with *tastes* or preferences that lead people to favor certain approaches to risk. Probability-related tastes present harder questions for the policy analyst. These tastes matter to law insofar as they bear on the demand for legal regulation and insofar as they are highly likely to affect judgments of both juries and courts.

"All or Nothing." People do not weight probabilities in a linear fashion. Most important, they greatly prefer the elimination of a risk over the diminution of a risk. Thus it appears that people would much rather see a risk of .001 reduced to zero than a risk of .002 reduced to .001 (Redelmeier, Rozin, & Kahneman, 1993). It is not clear whether this preference should be characterized as irrational. Perhaps people receive a great deal of peace of mind from an eliminated risk, and a risk of reduced probability still creates residual fear. The point appears to be reflected in law. Thus the Clean Air Act speaks in terms of ensuring safe levels of air quality, admittedly a highly misleading way to set up the problem.

Ambiguity Aversion. A closely related taste is the avoidance of ambiguity (Fox & Tversky, 1995). At least when they lack relevant knowledge, and know that they do, people prefer situations of uncertainty (in which probabilities can be assigned to outcomes) over situations of risk (in which probabilities cannot be assigned). Thus people are averse to situations of uncertain probability and try to avoid choices that place them in such situations. Often risk regulation is, of course, undertaken when probabilities cannot be assigned. If people are averse to ambiguities, they may produce an incoherent pattern of regulation, perhaps based on an illusory perception, related to all-or-nothing judgments, that some things are safe and others are dangerous.

Status Quo Bias. As noted, people evaluate situations largely in accordance with their relation to a certain reference point; gains and losses from the reference point are crucial. An ordinary reference is the status quo, which produces status quo bias. The legal system is certainly responsive to this kind of bias (Sunstein, 1997).

Mental Accounting

A simple and apparently uncontroversial assumption of most economists is that money is *fungible*. Indeed, if anything is fungible, money is. But the assumption appears to be false, at least some of the time. As Thaler suggests, many people act as if their money resides in compartments (Thaler, 1994a). In other words, people create *frames* that result in mental accounts through which losses and gains, including losses and gains in simple monetary terms, are not fungible with each other. To some extent, mental accounting can be viewed as a response to, and an example of, myopia. Frequently mental accounting works as a method by which people can overcome their own impulsiveness or their tendency to overlook the long term.

A glance at ordinary practice shows that people often organize decisions in terms of separate budgets and accounts, and they often segment these accounts. Thus some money is for retirement; some is for vacation; some is for college tuition; some is for mortgage or rental payments. Mental accounting is an important aspect of financial self-control; it can be understood as a kind of precommitment strategy.

What are the implications of mental accounting for law and policy? There appears to be a demand for publicly created mental accounts, perhaps as a self-control strategy, as for example with Social Security and other programs with an apparent paternalistic dimension. One reason for mental accounting is to alleviate the possible problem of self-control, and people may enlist law in this endeavor. If so, it is hard to object to the resulting enactments as paternalistic. The better view would be that they reflect a form of autopaternalism. Some statutes that appear to prevent people from making choices as they wish may be best understood as responsive to the widespread desire to have separate mental accounts.

Of course, there are private mechanisms for accomplishing this goal; lawyers will not understand those mechanisms well unless they see that money itself is not fungible.

The practice of mental accounting suggests that that government may be able to create certain mental accounts by creative policymaking. If government wants to encourage savings, for example, it may seek to give distinctive labels to certain accounts so as to discourage people from dipping into those accounts too readily. This idea suggests the possibility of restructuring Social Security, not by abolishing any effort to promote savings for old age but by facilitating the creation of specified private accounts, perhaps accompanied by penalties for current use.

The practice of mental accounting also suggests that redistributive legal rules may be more effective than they seem (Jolls, 1998). Christine Jolls suggests that although taxes operate "as a direct charge against incomes," the costs of redistributive rules "may be viewed as expenditures out of income . . . and heightened expenditures out of income may produce fewer work disincentives than direct charges against income" (Jolls, 1998, p. 1670). If this is so, those who receive money (from tort law or taxation) and those who give money (from tort law or taxation) may respond differently, depending on whether tort law or taxation is responsible. Those who are taxed may face a stronger work disincentive than those who are faced with a redistributive legal rule.

Most behavioral work involving mental accounting deals with money. But the phenomenon is far broader. In the moral domain, for example, there is reason to think that people engage in a form of accounting as well, treating actions of which they are ashamed or proud as falling in distinct compartments, and possibly as requiring a kind of compensation from future acts in the same compartment. Someone who has acted uncharitably toward a student or a friend might, for example, act quite generously to another student or friend so as to even out the account. This effect can be felt at the social level as well, as the demand for law reflects a desire to produce sensible accounts (by, for example, going slow on clean water legislation after having gone quickly on clean air legislation). Of course, much more work would be necessary to turn these speculations into something more systematic.

Because people are myopic, and have high and sometimes hyperbolic discount rates, it may be necessary to rethink conventional economic analysis of the criminal law (see Jolls et al., 1998, pp. 1538–1541). If criminals do not concern themselves with the future and focus on the short term, a system of reliable but relatively lenient punishments may have far more deterrent power than a system of infrequently enforced but stringent punishments. And for young people who greatly discount the future, an increase in punishment from, say, 20 years to 25 or 30 years may have little effect at all on the level of criminal activity.

The Difficulty, Outside of Markets, of Mapping Normative Judgments Onto Dollars

Often the legal system requires judges or juries to make judgments of some kind and then to translate those judgments into dollar amounts. How does this translation take place? Can it be done well? Behavioral evidence suggests that in many contexts, normative judgments of a sort are both predictable and nonarbitrary (Sunstein, Kahneman, & Schkade, 1998). With respect to bad behavior that might produce punitive damages, for example, people come up with relatively uniform judgments on a bounded numerical scale. At least it can be said that the judgment of any group of 12 people is a good predictor of the judgments of other groups of 12 people. Similar findings have been made for environmental amenities in the context of contingent valuation (Kahneman, Schkade, & Sunstein, 1998). But the act of mapping those normative judgments onto an unbounded dollar scale produces considerable noise and arbitrariness. When people are asked how much a defendant should be punished for reckless conduct leading to personal injury, the numbers they generate are highly variable, and the decision of any particular group of 12 people cannot well predict the judgments of other groups of 12 people. This finding has been confirmed for deliberating juries, where the relevant effects are extremely pronounced (Schkade, Sunstein, & Kahneman, 2000).

Insofar as this problem infects the award of damages, conventional economists need not be troubled; but many economists are enthusiastic about the process of contingent valuation, where similar problems have been shown to arise. When people are asked how much they are willing to pay to protect 2,000 birds, or 200 birds, the same kind of arbitrariness has been found (Kahneman & Ritov, 1994). The apparent reason is that people have great trouble *scaling without a modulus*, that is, they are not in a good position to generate predictable dollar amounts when they are not given a modulus, or standard, to compare with the case at hand. The problem of scaling without a modulus occurs in many areas in which juries (and judges) are asked to generate dollar amounts. It appears in areas not involving dollars as well. Consider, for example, the Americans with Disabilities Act, which makes it necessary to decide whether a suggested accommodation is reasonable and whether it creates an undue hardship. There is great deal of variability in the law, not least because it is extremely hard to decide whether a particular accommodation is reasonable, or a particular hardship undue, without a modulus to cabin the inquiry. (Cost-benefit analysis would work as well.) Or consider the question of whether an occupational hazard creates a significant risk within the meaning of judicial interpretations of the Occupational Safety and Health Act. Without some kind of modulus, the bare idea of *significance* is a recipe for arbitrariness.

The legal system, however, frequently relies on the resulting highly variable and unreliable measures. Thus the award of damages for libel, sexual harassment, and pain and suffering is infected by severe difficulties, as is the award of punitive damages in general. A great deal of empirical work remains to be done on this problem, and an understanding of those difficulties may well lead to concrete reform proposals.

Related research by Daniel Kahneman, Ilana Ritov, and David Schkade has found *valuation reversals* in two contexts of special importance to the legal system: contingent valuation and punitive damage awards (Kahneman, Ritov, & Schkade, 1999). The punitive damage cases involved, respectively, financial harm and personal injury. When the cases were viewed in isolation, people were willing to support higher awards for the financial harm case, partly because of the relatively higher compensatory award in those cases. (The compensatory award thus worked as an anchor.) But when the two cases were considered together, about three-quarters of people assessed larger awards for the personal injury case, "resulting in a dramatic reversal in median awards" (Kahneman & Ritov, 1994, p. 220). Similar reversals of judgment were observed not only for dollars but also for ratings, on a bounded numerical scale, of both outrage and punitive intent. Related findings were observed for contingent valuation problems, where it is likely that people's judgments will be quite different if cases are studied together rather than separately.

Kahneman and his coauthors believe that in many settings, dollar responses to public questions express attitudes rather than preferences, and also that attitudes have distinctive properties, including a tendency toward valuation reversals (Kahneman et al., 1999). If true, this claim has important implications for many legal contexts, including not only jury judgments in general, but also criminal sentencing and expenditures in the regulatory state. A possible implication is that judgments of cases and problems in isolation – and isolation is typical of the legal system – will lead to many problems. Isolated judgments may produce more global or systematic irrationality, as jurors (and perhaps judges and representatives) reach conclusions that do not cohere with other judgments, simply because cases are examined in isolation. In any case, the constructed nature of judgments about dollars, and the potential for judgment reversals, bears much further study (Sunstein et al., 1998).

From Quasi-Rationality to Rationality?

A central objection has to do with the domain of behavioral law and economics. Might it not be the case that markets, for example, will turn quasi-rational agents into fully rational agents? Work on the endowment effect has shown that there is no such effect for tokens (Kahneman et al., 1990). The point suggests that where goods are fully fungible – as in ordinary markets? – the endowment effect may be irrelevant. It is also clear that markets will tend to counteract some of the tendencies that we have discussed. It might seem, for example, that people who are unrealistically optimistic, or who are readily manipulated, will not do well in managing large companies.

In some circumstances, market forces are indeed strong enough to make behavioral economics irrelevant for predictive purposes. Then the question becomes whether it is possible to identify those circumstances. This is a large question, and we lack authoritative answers. When there are repeated decisions, and when people have an opportunity to learn, the conventional approach is most likely to be successful. But this statement leaves many questions unanswered, and as suggested earlier, behavioral economics has a role to play in markets and marketlike settings as well. A great deal of work remains to be done on this topic.

Debiasing and Institutional Solutions

An equally important question involves the extent to which education or other debiasing strategies can counteract cognitive and motivational distortions so as to eliminate some of the effects described earlier. Is it possible for those involved in law to push people toward greater rationality, and in the process, perhaps, lengthening human lives? What institutions work best to reduce the effects of biases? Would a broader understanding of behavioral economics produce learning and thus make it less necessary to use behavioral economics?

Some work has been done on these questions (Babcock et al., 1997). Unfortunately, the relevant work tends to show that quasi-rationality is robust and that it is hard to do much about it. Even experts are susceptible to most of the effects discussed here. With respect to debiasing, it does not do much good to ask people to read and consider both sides of an argument; once people know what side they are on, their view seems entrenched, and a reading of competing views seems only to strengthen their conviction (in a form of *confirmatory bias*). The only intervention that seems to work is to require people to make their own arguments for the other side (Babcock et al., 1997). The good news is that some of these effects, such as a taste for fairness, should not be characterized as distortions. On the contrary, such tastes may help solve prisoners' dilemmas, and it is striking to see that economics majors are less likely to adhere to fairness norms that produce solutions (Frank, Gilovich, & Regan, 1993). (Perhaps economics majors and law students immersed in conventional economics need to be "debiased"!)

If debiasing generally does not work, we might think that social forces, market and nonmarket, might press individuals and institutions in the direction of meta-decisions, or second-order decisions, that will make it more likely that things will go well. We might expect, for example, boundedly rational agents to come up with institutions that will overcome their own bounded rationality. They might, for example, make a second-order decision in favor of rules so as to reduce the errors produced by on-the-spot decisions. We might expect social institutions to help counteract some of the relevant problems; certainly an evolutionary account would so suggest.

There is some affirmative evidence here. For example, the legal system contains mechanisms to reduce the problems associated with hindsight bias (Rachlinski & Jourden, 1998). It also appears responsive to the difference between out-of-pocket costs and opportunity costs (Cohen & Knetsch, 1992). Many legal institutions might be investigated in an effort to see whether and how they overcome some of the difficulties discussed here. Such an investigation might even reveal an implicit understanding of behavioral economics on the part of those involved in the legal system.

The Future

Behavioral law and economics remains in its early stages, perhaps not so different from that of conventional law and economics in, say, 1971.

No treatise organizes the field, and a great deal of further research, theoretical and empirical, remains to be done. For example, there is no systematic work on the relationship between damage awards and the various ingredients of cases involving libel, sexual harassment, and intentional infliction of emotional distress. There is only preliminary work on the role of anchors in awards by juries and judges. Nor is there much work on the relationship between legal rules and reciprocity, and on the important question of whether and how legal rules might solve prisoners' dilemmas without requiring large levels of public enforcement activity. Under what circumstances does a legal provision (e.g., one that bans smoking or requires recycling) become self-enforcing? We lack much information about whether and how legal rules change preferences themselves; this is a promising area for both experimental and empirical work. Nor do we know a great deal about the effects of social institutions in overcoming cognitive and motivational limitations.

There can be no question that human beings care about fairness, that they can be myopic, and that they exhibit bounded rationality. The questions for the future are whether an understanding of the underlying phenomena can lead to better predictions about the effects of law, more reliable prescriptions about how law might promote social goals, and more refined judgments about when the legal system should respect or reject individual choices.

References

Aronson, E. (1996). *The social animal* (6th ed.). New York: W. H. Freeman.
Babcock, L., & L[eo]wenstein, G. (1997). Explaining bargaining impasse: The role of self-serving biases. *Journal of Economic Perspectives, 11,* 109–126.
Babcock, L., Loewenstein, G., & Issacharoff, S. (1997). Creating convergence: Debiasing biased litigants. *Law and Social Inquiry, 22,* 913–925.
Baron, J. (1994). *Thinking and deciding.* Cambridge: Cambridge University Press.
Bauman, L., & Siegel, K. (1987). Misperception among gay men of the risk for AIDS associated with their sexual behavior. *Journal of Applied Social Psychology, 17,* 329–350.
Bazerman, M., Messick, D., Tenbrunsel, A., & Wade-Bensoni, K. (Eds.). (1997). *Environment, ethics, and behavior.* San Francisco: Lexington Press.
Breyer, S. (1993). *Breaking the vicious circle.* Cambridge, MA: Harvard University Press.
Camerer, C. (1995). Individual decision making. In J. Kagel & A. Roth (Eds.), *Handbook of experimental economics* (pp. 587–616). Princeton, NJ: Princeton University Press.
Cohen, D., & Knetsch, J. (1992). Judicial choice and disparities between measures of economic values. *Osgoode Hall Law Journal, 30,* 737–770.

Conlisk, J. (1996). Why bounded rationality? *Journal of Economic Literature, 34,* 669–700.

Fox, C., & Tversky, A. (1995). Ambiguity aversion and comparative ignorance. *Quarterly Journal of Economics, 110,* 585–603.

Frank, R., Gilovich, T., & Regan, D. (1993). Does studying economics inhibit cooperation? *Journal of Economic Perspectives, 7,* 159–171.

Gilboa, I., & Schmeidler, D. (1995). Case-based decision theory. *Quarterly Journal of Economics, 110,* 605–639.

Gregory, R., Lichtenstein, S., & MacGregor, D. (1993). The role of past states in determining reference points for policy decisions. *Organizational Behavior and Human Decision Processes, 55,* 195–206.

Jolls, C. (1998). Behavioral economics analysis of redistributive legal rules. *Vanderbilt Law Review, 51,* 1653–1677.

Jolls, C., Sunstein, C., & Thaler, R. (1998). A behavioral approach to law and economics. *Stanford Law Review, 50,* 1471–1550.

Kagel, J. H., & Roth, A. E. (Eds.). (1995). *Handbook of experimental economics.* Princeton, NJ: Princeton University Press.

Kahneman, D. (1996). New challenges to the rationality assumption. In K. Arrow, E. Colombatto, M. Perlman, & C. Schmidt (Eds.), *The rational foundations of economic behaviour* (pp. 203–219). London: Macmillan and the International Economic Association.

Kahneman, D., Knetsch, J., & Thaler, R. (1990). Experimental tests of the endowment effect and the Coase theorem. *Journal of Political Economy, 98,* 1325–1348.

Kahneman, D., & Ritov, I. (1994). Determinants of stated willingness to pay for public goods: A study in the headline method. *Journal of Risk & Uncertainty, 9,* 5–37.

Kahneman, D., Ritov, I., & Schkade, D. (1999). Economic preferences or attitude expressions?: An analysis of dollar responses to public issues. *Journal of Risk and Uncertainty, 19,* 203–236.

Kahneman, D., Schkade, D., & Sunstein, C. (1998). Shared outrage and erratic awards: The psychology of punitive damages. *Journal of Risk & Uncertainty, 16,* 49–86.

Kahneman, D., & Tversky, A. (1979). Prospect theory: An analysis of decision under risk. *Econometrica, 47,* 263–291.

Kahneman, D., & Tversky, A. (1995). Conflict resolution: A cognitive perspective. In K. J. Arrow, R. H. Mnookin, L. Ross, A. Tversky, & R. B. Wilson (Eds.), *Barriers to conflict resolution* (pp. 44–60). New York: W. W. Norton.

Kaplow, L., & Shavell, S. (1996). Property rules and liability rules: An economic analysis. *Harvard Law Review, 109,* 713–790.

Kelman, M., Rottenstreich, Y., & Tversky, A. (1996). Context-dependence in legal decision making. *Journal of Legal Studies, 25,* 287–318.

Knetsch, J. (1997). Reference status, fairness, and choice of measure to value environmental changes. In M. Bazerman, D. Messick, A. Tenbrunsel, & K. Wade-Bensoni (Eds.), *Environment, ethics, and behavior* (pp. 13–32). San Francisco: Lexington Press.

Kuran, T., & Sunstein, C. (1999). Availability cascades and risk regulation. *Stanford Law Review, 51,* 683–768.

Langevoort, D. (1998). Behavioral theories of judgment and decision making in legal scholarship: A literature review. *Vanderbilt Law Review, 51,* 1499–1540.

Loewenstein, G., & Schkade, D. (1999). Wouldn't it be nice? Predicting future feelings. In E. Diener, N. Schwartz, & D. Kahneman (Eds.), *Hedonic psychology: Scientific approaches to enjoyment, suffering, and well-being* (pp. 85–105). New York: Russell Sage Foundation.

Loomes, G., & Sugden, R. (1982). Regret theory. *The Economic Journal, 92,* 805–824.

McCaffery, E., Kahneman, D., & Spitzer, M. (1995). Framing the jury. *Virginia Law Review, 81,* 1341–1420.

Noll, R. G., & Krier, J. L. (1991). Some implications of cognitive psychology for risk regulation. *Journal of Legal Studies, 19,* 747–79.

Perkins, H. W. (1997). College student misperceptions of alcohol and other drug norms among peers. In *Designing alcohol and other drug prevention programs in higher education* (pp. 177–206). Newton, MA: Higher Education Center for Alcohol and Other Drug Prevention.

Rachlinski, H., & Jourden, F. (1998). Remedies and the psychology of ownership. *Vanderbilt Law Review, 51,* 1541–1582.

Redelmeier, D., Rozin, P., & Kahneman, D. (1993). Understanding patients' decisions. *Journal of the American Medical Association, 270,* 72–76.

Samuelson, W., & Zeckhauser, R. (1988). Status quo bias. *Journal of Risk & Uncertainty, 1,* 7–59.

Schkade, D., Sunstein, C., & Kahneman, D. (2000). Deliberating about dollars: The severity shift. *Columbia Law Review, 100,* 1139–1176.

Sen, A. (1993). Internal consistency of choice. *Econometrica, 61,* 495–521.

Sieff, E., Dawes, R., & Loewenstein, G. (1999). Anticipated versus actual reaction to HIV test results. *American Journal of Psychology, 112,* 297–312.

Slovic, P. (1995). The construction of preference. *The American Psychologist, 50,* 364–371.

Slovic, P. (1998). Do adolescent smokers know the risks? *Duke Law Journal, 45,* 1133–1145

Stone, G. R., Seidman, L. M., Sunstein, C. R., & Tushnet, M. (1998). *Constitutional law.* Boston: Aspen Law and Business.

Sunstein, C. (1997). Endogenous preferences, environmental law. In C. Sunstein. (Ed.), *Free markets and social justice* (pp. 245–270). New York: Oxford University Press.

Sunstein, C. (1999). Behavioral law and economics: A progress report. *American Law and Economics Review, 1,* 115–157.

Sunstein, C. (Ed.). (2000). *Behavioral law and economics.* New York: Cambridge University Press.

Sunstein, C., Kahneman, D., & Schkade, D. (1998). Assessing punitive damages. *The Yale Law Journal, 107,* 2071–2153.

Taylor, S. (1989). *Positive illusions: Creative self-deception and the healthy mind.* New York: Basic Books.

Thaler, R. (1994a). The psychology and economics conference handbook. In R. Thaler (Ed.), *Quasi-rational economics* (pp. 189–195). New York: Russell Sage Foundation.

Thaler, R. (Ed.). (1994b). *Quasi-rational economics.* New York: Russell Sage Foundation.

Tversky, A. (1996). Rational theory and constructive choice. In K. Arrow (Ed.), *The rational foundations of economic behaviour* (pp. 185–197). London: Macmillan and the International Economic Association.

Viscusi, W. K. (1993). *Smoking: Making the risky decision*. New York: Oxford University Press.

Weinstein, N. (1986). Unrealistic optimism about susceptibility to health problems: Conclusions from a community-wide sample. *Journal of Behavioral Medicine, 10,* 481–500.

Weinstein, N. (1989). Optimistic biases about personal risks, *Science, 246,* 1232–1233.

Part IV

Other Policy Applications

10 Enhancing the Effectiveness of Innovative Policy Instruments: The Implications of Behavioral Decision Theory for Right-to-Know Policies

Rajeev Gowda

Introduction

The turn of the millennium has provided an occasion for scholars to step back from the hurly-burly of policy action to indulge in historical assessments of progress in knowledge and to make prognostications on policy trends. In one such exercise, Paul Portney, the president of the influential think tank Resources for the Future, considered what might emerge in environmental policy during 2000–2050. After applauding the acceptance of economic incentives-based approaches such as emissions trading, Portney hailed the emergence of information provision as an instrument of environmental policy and predicted that programs utilizing this technique would soon proliferate. He suggested that

> experience has shown that when firms are required to make public their emissions, they feel pressure to reduce them, even when the levels of emission are perfectly legal. . . . So long as citizens are able to make sense of this information, programs like this are not only democratic but also efficiency-enhancing. (Portney, 2000, p. 201)

The first sentence of the quote captures the essence of the information provision or right-to-know approach. Information provision is a remarkably simple policy instrument. Rather than trying to persuade citizens and firms toward some behavioral response, it merely mandates that information about risks be placed in the public domain. People and firms can then respond to this information in any manner they choose, though the expectation is that they will make better-informed decisions, particularly about risk management and self-protective behavior (Hadden, 1989). Information provision corrects a market failure – that of incomplete information. Firms will choose the level of emissions that is

243

acceptable to a concerned public, even if that level goes beyond that required by regulators. The attention paid to people's preferences actually makes the end result more completely efficiency enhancing than a perfectly tuned regulatory standard that only considers the technical risks involved. More fundamentally, enhancing the public's right to know is politically empowering and achieves the desired policy outcomes.

The preceding quote also points to the key caveat affecting the question of whether information provision is an efficiency-enhancing policy innovation. To address this issue, it is critical for policy analysts to understand how people make sense of the information provided. For information provision to be efficiency enhancing in the sense accepted by economists, it is important that people react rationally to this information. This would mean that people should behave in accordance with expected utility theory, a model of behavior that economists regard as both normatively appropriate because it leads individuals to maximize their utility, and more important, descriptively accurate because people do behave in this manner.

But do people actually behave in a manner consistent with expected utility theory? If their behavior deviates significantly in practice, does it mean that people are irrational? Regardless of normative judgments about rationality, we argue that policy designers and analysts must pay attention to how people actually behave rather than how they ideally should behave. We therefore turn to fields of research such as behavioral decision theory and risk analysis with the expectation that these will serve as better guides to realistic policy analysis. These bodies of literature are working toward a model of human decision making that is based on empirical research, conducted mainly in the cognitive psychology laboratory in the case of behavioral decision theory, and conducted mainly on the front lines of real-world conflicts over risk in the case of risk analysis. We need to build on these research findings to better understand the workings of right-to-know laws, and to suggest improvements in their design and implementation.

Behavioral decision theory and risk analysis are based on findings that suggest that humans behave in a manner that is more complex than, and sometimes flawed when compared to, the standard of economically rational behavior. This implies that the impact of information provision as a policy instrument is also more complex and may potentially be counter to the enhancement of economic efficiency. Thus the end results of a right-to-know policy may deviate substantially from its explicit goals. Such policies, instead of inducing efficient responses on the part of risk generators, may instead lead them to leave the market itself. And the information provided under the right-to-know policy may also end up being put to various political uses by interest groups and the media, with outcomes far different from the goals of the framers of the policy.

In this chapter, I explore the implications of behavioral decision theory and risk analysis for information provision policies. I examine a number of areas where the information provision approach is being utilized and will consider potential complications in policy implementation suggested by behavioral decision theory. I also explore the notion that proponents and opponents of right-to-know legislation are arguably aware of potential behavioral responses to risk-related information. Therefore, I suggest that information provision should not be considered a neutral instrument of policy, but rather a political tool and a potent weapon in battles over risk regulation. The findings of behavioral decision theory and risk analysis may provide insights into the nature and direction of such battles.

Insights from Behavioral Decision Theory and Risk Analysis for Information Provision

Information has long been a key public policy instrument. It has been used as a policy tool in public information campaigns where governments attempt to change people's behavior through one-way messages (Weiss & Tschirhart, 1994). Information is critical in the areas of product labeling and hazard warnings aimed at consumers and workers; here information is provided in particular formats, and consumers and workers are expected to process it and make their own risk-management decisions (Magat & Viscusi, 1992). Information is also a key component of risk communication efforts aimed at resolving risk-related conflicts. Leiss (1996) discusses the various phases of risk communication research and describes how risk communication practice has moved from one-way education efforts to inclusive, participatory, information-sharing processes aimed at consensual risk reduction.

Fischhoff, Riley, Kovacs, and Small (1998) suggest that policy designers, in designing information provision programs, need to (1) identify the information most critical to helping people understand how risks can arise and how they can be controlled; (2) assess people's current beliefs and knowledge about those risks; (3) develop messages aimed at filling critical gaps in people's knowledge; (4) test and evaluate these messages; and (5) develop processes that are capable of drawing the attention of people to these risk-related messages. As we shall see, in many of the cases where information provision is now being implemented, these steps may not have been followed, and information is merely made available to the public. It is then left to interest groups to process this information in a way that potentially enhances and empowers the target audience. For example, the Environmental Defense Fund empowers the public through an Internet web site (*www.scorecard.org*) that provides commentary on emissions and also provides opportunities to citizens to convey their views immediately to the appropriate member of Congress and to corporate officials (Portney, 2000).

Scholars examining information provision also recognize that it can have negative or unintended effects. In the case of public information campaigns, there is great potential for propagandization (Weiss & Tschirhart, 1994). In the case of product labels and hazard warnings negative effects may arise because of erroneous or unexpected reactions from consumers and workers arising from cognitive limitations in how they process risk-related information (Magat & Viscusi, 1992); and in the risk communication case, through both these factors and also through adverse reactions to the process of communication itself. In the case of warnings, Fischhoff et al. (1998) point out that it is important for policymakers to remember that there will be a level of misunderstanding associated with warning information, and that a crucial policy choice involves what level of misunderstanding is acceptable to society.

Given the possibility of negative or unintended effects, it is important that scholars understand people's reactions to risk-related information, particularly in complex areas such as those involving environmental, health, and crime risks. Researchers must inform the policy debate through integrating their insights about how to improve the workings of right-to-know laws. These findings generally arise from behavioral decision theory and from research on risk perception and risk communication.

Behavioral decision theory focuses on how people respond to risk-related information. The normative standard often considered in answering this question is derived from economics: People consider the risk-related information fully and systematically and then make appropriate risk-benefit trade-offs that maximize their expected utility. But this ideal response remains in the realm of theory. In practice, behavioral decision theory's findings show that people (1) use shortcuts when processing information and (2) rely on inherent preferences that are significantly different from those assumed in expected utility or rational choice, the economic standard of behavior. Thus individuals deviate from the rational choice standard of rationality in ways that are "persistent and large" and "systematic rather than random" (Knetsch, 1995, p. 75; see generally Kahneman, Slovic, & Tversky, 1982).

The use of shortcuts, or heuristics, is sometimes efficient in that they facilitate judgments without tremendous information-processing costs. Some heuristics can lead to inefficient or suboptimal outcomes that people would reject if confronted with a detailed analysis utilizing statistical arguments. Heuristics are termed *biases* when they lead to suboptimal outcomes from the normative standpoint of economic rationality (Camerer, 1995). However, in the realm of choice, where people have to make decisions rather than arrive at judgments about probabilities, their preferences are significantly different from those considered rational by expected utility theory. This is made clear in prospect theory, a descriptive theory of choice advanced by Kahneman and Tversky (1979) that is a key component of behavioral decision theory.

Among the key deviations from rational choice in judgment that affect people's response to risk-related information are the availability heuristic and the representativeness heuristic. The availability heuristic states that people "assess the frequency of a class or the probability of an event by the ease with which instances or occurrences can be brought to mind" (Tversky & Kahneman, 1974, p. 1127). In other words, if people can readily think of examples of events, they will inflate their estimates of the likelihood of their occurrence. People may base their estimates of a risk on media coverage, which may lead to exaggerated risk perceptions, given that the media have an incentive to focus on sensational or attention-grabbing events rather than the whole range of risks to which people are exposed. For example, this can lead people to rate accidents as causing as many deaths as diseases, even though diseases kill more than 10 times as many people (Slovic, Fischhoff, & Lichtenstein, 1979). Availability can lead to adverse public health consequences if people adopt only accident-avoidance measures and pay less attention to disease-prevention measures.

The effects of the availability heuristic may be accentuated by the representativeness heuristic, which states that people judge probability or likelihood "by the degree to which A is representative of B, that is, by the degree to which A resembles B" (Tversky & Kahneman, 1974, p. 1124). For example, people ascribe characteristics to groups or subgroups based on their experiences with or perceptions of members of a group (Tversky & Kahneman, 1982). When an individual's experiences with members of a population are not representative of that population, the individual might incorrectly ascribe the characteristic to the entire population. Another instance of the use of the representativeness heuristic arises when people believe that some sequence of events is more likely because it seems more believable than another sequence of events. The representativeness heuristic could affect people's willingness to support risk management policies (e.g., flood risk-reduction measures) if the adduced sequence of future events leading to such disasters does not seem believable. Working in tandem with the availability heuristic, the representativeness heuristic may lead people to make incorrect extrapolations from media coverage of particular risk-related issues.

Thus people rely on several important and systematic shortcuts when they make judgments about the probabilities of events. Although such errors in judgment could theoretically be ameliorated through education, deviations from rationality in the realm of choice are caused by factors other than rational laziness. People stand by inferior or irrational choices even after they are made aware of their mistakes. This is because when individuals make choices, their heuristics may be derived more from intuition than from cognition, that is, they represent true preferences, whereas errors in judgment result from correctable mistakes in the thought process; errors in choice stem from fundamental violations of the assumptions of expected utility theory (Tversky & Kahneman, 1986). This has led scholars to search for dimensions of choice that are not traditionally included in rational models of decision making.

One such deviation in choice is the certainty effect and its corollary, the zero risk bias. This bias states that people prefer small benefits that are certain to larger benefits that are uncertain (Baron, 1994). For example, people tend to place a higher value on reducing the probability of a negative outcome from 5% to 0% than reducing the probability of another, perhaps more serious, danger from 30% to 20%. People may generally support moves that promise to eliminate risk, regardless of the financial and social costs of these measures. Politicians seem to understand the certainty effect well and often offer "certain" solutions such as eliminating all carcinogenic food additives (Gowda, 1999) or three-strikes-and-you're-out laws in the criminal justice context. Voters, meanwhile, seem to expect clear and certain solutions, and politicians propagate the myth that they exist by continuing to promise them. Although incorporating certainty is a worthy aspiration, it may be inefficient from an economic perspective and impossible in terms of the real world, given diminishing returns.

The insights from behavioral decision theory discussed previously seem to suggest that people's reactions to risk-related information are characterized by flaws. Indeed, this was one of the key issues debated during the development of the field of risk analysis, as psychologists attempted to examine how behavioral decision theoretic features affected people in the context of real-world risk issues. These psychologists and other scholars working in the area of risk analysis came to the conclusion that the public, far from being ignorant and irrational, seeks to improve risk regulation (Hadden, 1991; Slovic, 1987, 1992). Slovic (1987, p. 285) lucidly captures the essence of this argument: "Lay people sometimes lack certain information about hazards. However, their basic conceptualization of risk is much richer than that of the experts and reflects legitimate concerns that are typically omitted from expert risk assessments." The concerns affecting the public include qualitative factors such as voluntariness, catastrophic potential, and impact on future generations, which experts typically ignore by restricting their focus to quantitative factors such as expected mortality and morbidity (Slovic, 1992). In addition, trust and other values, such as equity, and people's own ideological dispositions also play a significant role in affecting how they perceive and react to risks (Pidgeon & Beattie, 1998). As Leiss (1992) points out, the public's perceptions of risk have also been affected by its awareness of the historical record of risks being underestimated by governments and industries.

Kunreuther and Slovic (1996) therefore advocate a *contextualist* view of risk, in which its quantitative, qualitative, and values aspects are all considered but with different emphases in different contexts. They then call for risk management strategies that involve "more public participation [in] both risk assessment and risk decision making to make the risk-decision process more democratic, improve the relevance and quality of technical analysis, and increase the legitimacy and public acceptance of the resulting decisions" (p. 123). This is perhaps the way information provision policies should be considered – as efforts that in their own complex way attempt to help people protect themselves in as workable a manner as possible.

However, there are two more relevant considerations from risk analysis research that yield insights into the dynamics of information provision laws. One of these considerations is the systematic ways in which people respond to risk-related information developed by a large body of literature on risk communication. Unfortunately, most of these insights seem to have escaped the purview of proponents of right-to-know legislation in recent years. The other aspect considers the not-in-my-backyard (NIMBY) phenomenon characteristic of many risk-related disputes.

A large body of literature and experience in the field of risk communication demonstrates that mere provision of information is not enough to ensure that people take appropriate risk-reducing and self-protective behavior. Nordenstam and DiMento (1990, p. 346) describe how and where problems can arise and affect information processing. The range of problems includes "source problems (who says it), message problems (what is said), channel problems (how it is said), and receiver problems (to whom it is said)." Although these comments refer to actively delivered messages, they suggest the need for research into how passively provided information may generate a variety of reactions, and for research into how different channels, including the Internet, may affect how people react to information provision.

Information-providing entities need to heed the lessons of risk communication research because "a demonstrated commitment to responsible risk communication by major organizational actors can put pressure on all players in risk management to act responsibly" (Leiss, 1996, pp. 90–91). If right-to-know laws are not carefully designed to evoke responsible reactions and careful risk management, but are instead utilized for quick political gains, this will lay the stage for a further diminution of trust in various institutions in the future.

The other major consideration from risk analysis relevant to information provision policies is the NIMBY phenomenon. NIMBY is one of the key contributions of risk analysis research to the world of acronyms. It refers to a phenomenon that typically arose in the context of siting of facilities where host communities rejected siting proposals, often through significant grassroots mobilization. A NIMBY response arises for a variety of reasons: It is partly triggered by cognitive psychological features: People may misperceive the extent of the risks due to availability and representativeness, and may demand zero risk in their backyards due to the certainty effect and the zero risk bias. It is partly triggered by value conflicts, for example between the technically oriented rationales of siting or law enforcement agencies and the process and equity-oriented rationales of lay publics. Finally, it is triggered by rational self-interest, where communities would rather have the risk transferred to an alternative location. Central results from risk analysis suggest that NIMBY concerns can be rational because they may stem from worries that a location will be stigmatized (Slovic, 1992) and may lead to a loss of property values and other economic losses, even in areas relatively far away from the risk-imposing facility (Kasperson, 1992).

NIMBY reactions are regarded by some commentators as failures of the democratic process, but commentators drawn from the communitarian perspective, such as Williams and Matheny (1995), who regard the NIMBY phenomenon favorably, support the development of information provision–type laws. They argue that NIMBY is an example of empowerment at the local level that raises consciousness and impresses "upon nascent citizen-activists the connection between information about the risks they live with and, lacking access to that information, their powerlessness to affect those risks" (p. 169). Their view would address "the information problem by redrawing the boundaries among market, government, and community. [The right-to-know approach] envisions information as a public right rather than a private or privileged commodity" (p. 170). This argument emphasizes the importance of empowering citizens, and the underlying implication is that if any inefficiencies ensue, they are of less concern. Our aim, through the discussion in this chapter, is to truly empower people by raising issues that can help design better right-to-know laws.

Two other central insights of risk analysis, and risk communication research in particular, are that process matters and that procedural equity is a central dimension of equity. That is, people do not care to be talked down to or to merely be the recipients of one-way messages from government agencies. Rather, people are willing to accept creative risk management solutions provided they are involved in the decision process and there is adequate public participation in the choice of risk management solution before, during, and after a risk-related event (Leiss, 1996).

These insights of behavioral decision theory and risk analysis need to be considered in assessing the usefulness of information provision as a policy instrument. It is therefore worthwhile to examine the range of areas where information provision is being utilized as a policy instrument, and, interestingly, where it is being opposed, in order to see what relevance these insights have in such policy settings.

Action and Reaction in Information Provision

The first wave of laws utilizing information provision as a policy technique include product labeling requirements, occupational safety and health hazard warning requirements, and Proposition 65 – the Safe

Drinking Water and Toxic Enforcement Act, a California law passed by public referendum (Nordenstam & DiMento, 1990). Following this early application in toxics regulation, the right-to-know approach has been applied far afield in diverse policy areas.

For example, this approach is being utilized in the context of information about doctors' malpractice records. The State of Massachusetts has passed a law requiring such records to be made publicly available. In assessing such applications, one central question is whether malpractice claims have a systematic relationship with incompetence; the complex nature of medical decision making suggests that this may not necessarily be the case. Another key question is whether patients would avoid any doctor with a settlement in his or her record, interpreting this as evidence of incompetence. The resulting reaction will have effects not only in the context of patients' choices but also in terms of doctors' behavior, defensive medicine, and so on. In this case, significant opposition from the American Medical Association led the state to refine its information provision formats to include baseline information, such as their average rate of malpractice lawsuits, and other caveats (Pfeiffer, 1997).

I now focus in more detail on two recent information provision policies where the right-to-know ethic is being implemented and on another policy development where restrictions on information have become the central policy thrust.

SARA Title III

SARA Title III represents the most significant right-to-know policy in recent times. Formally called the Emergency Planning and Community Right-to-Know Act, it is Title III of the Superfund Amendments and Reauthorization Act of 1986. SARA Title III mandates that industries provide information to the communities in which their facilities are located to enable those communities to satisfy their right to know what chemicals are being emitted into their environment. This law's passage was spurred by the chemical accident in Bhopal, India, in 1984, which resulted in the deaths of people living near a Union Carbide plant who were exposed accidentally to toxic methyl isocyanate gas. SARA Title III creates an elaborate reporting mechanism called the Toxics Release Inventory. This imposes some costs on producers but is not resource intensive for the government, and is therefore in sync with the deregulatory fervor in policy circles.

Sunstein (1997) and Portney (2000) both consider this law a success based on its ability to get waste generators to reduce their emissions substantially. Grant and Downey (1995), based on an empirical study comparing the performance of SARA Title III in different states, conclude that it has reduced toxic pollution without displacing the problem to other states. Sunstein (1997) suggests that SARA Title III has induced change because producers are concerned about adverse public reactions to information about toxic emissions. Overall, this reduction in environmental pollution has entailed little regulatory cost to the government. Encouraged by SARA Title III's success, President Bill Clinton extended the number of industrial sectors that need to comply with these requirements. Similar laws are now in place in other parts of the world, such as the Seveso Directive in the European Union (Wiedemann & Henschel, 1998).

However, such laws may be working too well in the sense that they may be moving inefficient risk management responses away from regulators to corporations. This author was present at a conference where the president of a leading U.S. chemical company publicly committed his organization to a goal of zero emissions. Such corporate responses are reactions to public risk perceptions and are attempts to placate the zero risk bias or certainty effect. If so, the result is likely to be inefficient, because we will then have too much emission reduction, including the reduction of harmless emissions. Further, these corporations are setting themselves up for a public loss of trust due to the inevitability that they will be unable to meet their zero emissions goals.

Megan's Laws

In July 1994, Megan Kanka, a 7-year-old New Jersey girl, was raped and murdered by a paroled child molester who lived across the street. Outraged by this tragedy, her parents, Richard and Maureen Kanka, lobbied state and federal officials to enact tougher laws to prevent such tragedies in the future. They argued that Megan could have been saved if they had known of their neighbor's criminal background and taken care accordingly. They called for a law that would ensure that local law enforcement officials and parents would be informed when convicted child molesters and rapists moved into a community after their release (Bredlie, 1996). This right-to-know approach to addressing people's concerns about the risks posed to their children by released sex offenders quickly attracted attention all over the United States.

The publicity accorded to the Kankas' efforts and Megan's tragic death resulted in a wave of legislation whereby the right-to-know approach was implemented as the predominant policy response to managing the risks posed by released sex offenders. Although the term *Megan's law* applies specifically to the New Jersey state law, it has become synonymous with the broader policy approach.

New Jersey, which passed the first Megan's law, has a refined system for providing such information, which is tied to the judged seriousness of the risk posed by the released offender. That is, those people living in the immediate neighborhood of the released sex offender are provided detailed information and regular interaction with the police; those living farther away are merely informed that a released sex offender has taken up residence in their town. In spite of the care with which the actual Megan's law has been designed, the author of one of the few critical essays on Megan's law argues that it is an example of legislation passed in an election year that has not considered all the potential consequences and constitutional issues fully (Crimaldi, 1995). This criticism may be too strong in the case of New Jersey's law but is perhaps more appropriate in the context of similar programs in Louisiana and California. The law in Louisiana requires sex offenders to notify communities themselves by publishing notices in local newspapers that includes their names and addresses and their crimes. Further, local parole boards have the discretionary authority to require other forms of identification including bumper stickers that state "Sex Offender on Board" (Bredlie, 1996). This "Scarlet Letter" law is encountering legal challenges.

In California, the state attorney general, Dan Lungren, who was running (unsuccessfully) for election as governor, announced that the state would publish a CD-ROM containing information on upward of 60,000 convicted sex offenders. The CD-ROM would be available to the public at their local police departments. An article in the *New York Times* (Purdum, 1997) pointed out that the information contained in the database was not accurate, comprehensive, or up-to-date; for example, it included people who were convicted of same-sex consensual acts that have since been decriminalized. Thus, in California, some people whose names were found on the list ended up losing their jobs, even though their original crimes would no longer qualify them for the sex offender tag.

The same *New York Times* article refers to the public furor that often accompanies the discovery that a sex offender who has completed his term in prison is now living in the community. Although this public concern is legitimate in light of recidivism, it also hampers rehabilitation and provides governments with an excuse not to consider other forms of treatment for sex offenders. Further, although public hounding of sex offenders who have served their term clashes with values associated with the rule of law, larger dangers are vigilante justice and violations of constitutionally guaranteed rights. This is cause for concern because convicted sex offenders are less likely to have defenders other than key organizations such as the American Civil Liberties Union (ACLU). However, even the ACLU has chosen not to test the constitutionality of these laws except in the narrow context of double jeopardy – that released sex offenders were being unfairly punished again through the process of notification. Courts have generally ruled that notification does not constitute punishment and thus that Megan's laws do not constitute double jeopardy. In any case, commentators such as Schopf (1995) argue that Megan's laws can survive constitutional challenges on many different fronts. In considering the constitutionality of such laws, courts have ruled that the interests of the state and parents in protecting children outweigh any potential stigmatizing effects or threats of vigilantism (Bredlie, 1996).

Behavioral decision theory generates some insights into how people might respond to the information available under Megan's laws. People may react to such information and undertake different risk-management responses based on their estimates of how likely they are to encounter a released sex offender. Here the availability heuristic may come into play. If they base their estimates on media coverage, this may result in exaggerated risk perceptions. Further, the representativeness heuristic may also emerge. Representativeness may result in people's unwillingness or inability to differentiate between sex offenders based on their likelihood of recidivism, even if that were determined in some objective manner. In terms of the zero risk bias, this case raises an interesting challenge to the notion that it is a bias at all. Parents' desire to ensure that their children are exposed to absolutely no risk is quite understandable. Arguably, even one repeat offense by a released sex offender is one too many.

Such reactions may also be triggered by the NIMBY phenomenon. This may cause communities to reject the relocation of released offenders; some instances of this are already available (Nordheimer, 1995). The end result of such reactions could mean that released offenders lose their right to live in the location of their choice. It could also lead to more parole violations and the spreading of risks posed by released offenders if they are forced to move from place to place. Further, instances of vigilante justice suggest that people may be willing to go beyond the community's organizing efforts and undertake illegal acts, a troubling development in the range of ways that communities react to risks.

Again, in the Megan's law context, sex offenders may be stigmatized by the public knowledge of their background, and this may prevent them from reintegrating into the community. But there may be a more substantial stigma-related impact on communities as well. Once it becomes known that a community is host to released sex offenders, the whole community may be stigmatized as people "vote with their feet" and move out to avoid the risk. This potential impact has so far not been considered in the discussion surrounding Megan's laws.

More study will, it is hoped, reveal how a balance can be achieved in empowering citizens, preventing crimes, and protecting the civil rights of released offenders. The New Jersey law may offer a useful example in this regard. It contains the possibility of heeding the lesson from risk communication that process issues are central to the resolution of risk conflicts. If law enforcement agencies work together with communities to ensure that local residents are kept informed and even somehow involved in the monitoring of high-risk sex offenders, then the trust generated by such interaction could prevent vigilante attacks while also ensuring the protection of the community. Law enforcement agencies in the United States are moving toward active involvement with communities through community policing efforts; it is such efforts that could lead to more proactive, less legally violative risk management.

Although it appears that right-to-know legislation is finding its way into a variety of realms including the environment, health, and crime, we also note the emergence of reactions to right-to-know laws, motivated significantly by an understanding of their behavioral consequences. The prime example of laws aiming to constrain information sharing and discussion are veggie libel laws.

Veggie Libel Laws

In 1989, the National Resources Defense Council presented a scientifically debatable case against the apple growth retardant Alar on the widely watched *60 Minutes* television show. This story resulted in a significant public backlash against Alar-treated apples and a tremendous economic loss to apple growers (Wildavsky, 1995). This episode is one among many involving food-related risks. Every so often, the news media cover a study by a set of researchers purporting to find still more risks associated with commonly consumed products. Media coverage typically results in an economic loss to producers. Such developments have led politically powerful producer groups in various states to encourage the passage of a category of laws termed *food disparagement* or *veggie libel* laws. These laws provide for damages to food producers if they are harmed by falsely disparaging statements about the safety of their products (Pressley, 1998).

It is far from clear that such food disparagement laws will stand the test of judicial scrutiny on constitutional grounds because they potentially impinge on protected free speech – unless it can be proven that food-disparaging statements were made with malicious intent. Yet, at the current stage of development of these laws, such malicious intent is not required to be proven before damages can be assessed. This has the effect of suppressing free discussion of the risks associated with various products, which, given scientific uncertainty, is particularly open to debate. The most notable case in which these laws have been used was the lawsuit against Oprah Winfrey when she made offhand remarks about American beef in a television show discussing mad cow disease (Pressley, 1998).

Are such food disparagement laws a power play by producer groups and the food industry to suppress dissent and to allow them to continue to place potentially risky food products in the market (e.g., pesticide-contaminated food, genetically engineered products)? I suggest that the food industry's reaction results from its wariness about the behavioral effects of debates on the safety of food products drawn from its direct experience with the effects of risk perceptions and media coverage in the Alar case. This reaction therefore illustrates the need to understand the insights from behavioral research and risk analysis so as to avoid the adoption of information suppression policies such as food disparagement laws in other policy areas as a reaction to hastily drawn information provision laws. Overall, it is worthwhile to examine the politics of information provision to better understand whether these laws can be designed more carefully, taking into account the insights into actual behavior discussed in these policy areas.

The Politics of Information Provision

The growing popularity of information provision proposals may arise from their strategic superiority to opposing arguments. Because information is simply provided, such proposals are deceptively innocuous, and this makes them easier to implement politically. Information-related policy developments are also gaining momentum because political actors reason that by calling for such laws, they are demonstrating their commitment to public health and public empowerment goals. After all, such proponents seem to suggest, if risk-related information is available to producers, what is the harm in sharing it with those who may be affected by the risks? The implication is that risk producers who oppose such information provision have something to hide and that their actions are antidemocratic. Further, because information provision typically does not entail the establishment of a large regulatory apparatus, it is attractive to policymakers on cost considerations. Finally, given the hands-off nature of the information provision, any negative reactions on the part of the public are harder to pin directly to governmental actions.

The notion that right-to-know laws have inherently political features has already been emphasized by scholars such as Williams and Matheny (1995). They see right-to-know laws as empowering weapons in the hands of environmental activists and consumers against the powerful forces of industry. They believe that opposition to right-to-know laws arises from industry's efforts to suppress popular challenges to risk management decisions. Although I am in broad agreement with these points, my emphasis is on how right-to-know policies can be improved through the correction of potential implementation problems, so that the public can be empowered rather than misled. This is especially important given the growing propensity of policymakers to utilize information provision as a risk management tool in a variety of areas.

However, groups concerned about property rights are challenging Williams and Matheny's environmental activism. Property rights advocates are concerned that endangered species protection laws will affect their ability to develop their property if such resource use affects the habitat of an endangered species. These advocates consider the loss of their ability to develop their property as an unlawful taking on the part of governments and demand significant compensation in return. They have therefore developed a "property owners bill of rights" which includes the right to know when a governmental agency is about to declare a particular area a habitat for endangered species (Echeverria, 1997).

The potency of the right-to-know demands arises from the behavioral decision theoretic and risk analytic features discussed earlier. Once property owners are informed that their property is being targeted, it will enable them to organize a NIMBY-type opposition that can at least succeed in moving the habitat to be protected to a different back-yard or to even indulge in preemptive clearcutting of forests (Baron & Bazerman, this volume). From a behavioral perspective, the debate over the takings effects of endangered species legislation demonstrated sig-nificant efforts on the part of property rights advocates to exploit cog-nitive heuristics and biases through emotional anecdotes about small farmers being trampled upon by a governmental behemoth (Echeverria, 1997). Taken together, the right-to-know information and the nature of the debate could lead to the effective overturning of endangered species protection efforts, especially given the growing strength of property rights interests in Congress. This development illustrates how innova-tive tools such as information provision can be harnessed by either side of the debate.

Right-to-know laws have other features that enhance their political viability. Consider the nature of the legislative process in the United States. We may assume that lawmakers in a republican form of gov-ernment would consider various policy options thoroughly. For exam-ple, in the Megan's law case, we would expect that lawmakers would weigh the constitutional implications and the potential for vigilante attacks against popular pressure to enact right-to-know laws in the case of sex offenders. Indeed Suedfeld and Tetlock (1992, p. 51) point out that people generally assume that good political decision mak-ing is characterized by "extensive information, search, empathy for the positions of other participants, openness to disagreement, and the wish to find a mutually acceptable outcome." However, political de-cision making does not necessarily conform to this narrower concep-tion of rationality but focuses particularly on a broader strategic notion centered on elections and electability (Mayhew, 1974). The widespread and quick enactment of Megan's laws all over the country can instead be attributed to politicians catching on to a strategically advantageous policy option that would allow them to demonstrate their toughness on crime.

In general, both laypeople and policymakers may fundamentally behave as politicians, with a keen concern for reputation effects (Tetlock, 1998), and this can profoundly affect the debate over the poten-tial impacts of information provision. When risk-related incidents occur, the process of collective belief formation may be driven by *availability cascades* whereby a belief becomes accepted as the general consensus because people endorse the belief based on what they hear from others and by distorting their own views in order to ensure that they are socially acceptable (Kuran & Sunstein, 1999). Further, lawmakers may be loath to even appear to question popularly acceptable developments such as Megan's laws for fear of their views being used against them in negative advertisements in future elections (Gowda, 1999). Thus discussions about implementing information provision laws may often involve a debate characterized by one dominant viewpoint, and this may prevent judicious insights from being integrated with the policy solution.

Indeed, the quick passage of right-to-know laws soon after salient risk-related incidents can be regarded as the social amplification of risk in action (Kasperson 1992; Kasperson et al., 1988), where individual incidents have far-reaching consequences beyond their initial area of incidence. We argue that this may well have occurred because this is a policy solution that was easily enactable and electorally beneficial to the political players who propelled it forward. In terms of the enactability of right-to-know policies, consider how they fare in the context of Kingdon's (1984) model of agenda setting and the policy process. Kingdon points out that merely getting on the agenda does not guarantee success. Advocates of policy initiatives must take advantage of policy windows that have been opened by a salient, newsworthy event or problem. They must then argue that their policy solution is the most appropriate to deal with this problem. And the political climate should be receptive to such arguments, perhaps because politicians see electoral advantage in responding to the problem through the adoption of the proposed solution.

In the Megan's law case, we have a pressing problem (protecting children from the risks posed by released sex offenders) coupled with a policy solution (information provision) and a political climate favorable to such action (because right-to-know laws are politically difficult to oppose and financially easy to implement in an anticrime, anti-big-government era), which enabled the Kankas' public-spirited policy entrepreneurship to be amplified in the form of Megan's laws around the country. Information provision, because of its political viability, may thus enable quick legislative responses to risks that emerge on the public agenda, and thus the right-to-know policy technique may have an edge over alternative risk management policy techniques.[1]

Conclusion

One lesson from my exploration of various dimensions of information provision is that policy makers and scholars need to be alert to the implications of choosing a policy instrument such as the right to know. It is important that they pay attention to the findings of behavioral decision theory and risk analysis. These fields of knowledge are still works in progress. For example, much is yet to be learned about the role of noncognitive, affective factors in influencing decision making (Keren, 1996). Yet, as my discussion in this chapter has demonstrated, there are already sufficient insights available that need to be heeded by policy-makers as they utilize information provision as a policy instrument in different areas.

The goals of right-to-know laws are noble, and empowering people is an act of true democratic statesmanship. However, if this innovative policy instrument is misused as a populist measure through the provision of inaccurate information or in ignorance of behavioral responses, the consequences for public policy and particular disadvantaged groups may be far from positive. This may ultimately result in the rejection of innovative policy tools like information provision and make for a less open, less deliberative democracy, as is the case with veggie libel laws. The end result of empowering tools such as the right to know should not turn out to be grossly inefficient outcomes or even those that violate the fundamental tenets of the rule of law. If those unfortunate outcomes transpire, it will lead to a further erosion of trust in the political system, in contrast to the positive aspirations of the proponents of this policy approach. Integrating insights from behavioral decision theory and risk analysis will help prevent information provision from becoming a counterproductive policy instrument and yet another addition to the dreary catalogue of regulatory paradoxes where good intentions have often resulted in less than stellar policy outcomes (Sunstein, 1990).

Notes

1 This point can be illustrated by the Polly Klaas case, which provides an interesting and contemporaneous contrast to Megan's laws in addressing the risks posed to children by criminals. Polly Klaas, a pre-teen girl in the town of Petaluma, California, was found missing. A few days later her body was found and a vagrant, Richard Allen Davis, was ultimately convicted of her kidnapping and murder. Her father, Mark Klaas, responded to this incident by vowing to create conditions that would ensure the safety of children from criminals and other predators. His agenda involved generating collective action in communities, whereby towns formed committees to promote children's safety. His activities led to the establishment of the Polly Klaas Foundation (*http://www.pollyklaas.org*) and the Klaas Foundation for Children (*http://www.klaaskids.org*), which are lobbying entities and information providers in the area of children's safety.

Although the Polly Klaas tragedy was widely covered in the news media (problem identification) and occurred during an era favorable to tough action against criminals (politically propitious policy window), its overall impact may have been limited by the policy approach chosen by Mark Klaas – collective action. Collective action is particularly hard to bring about because of rational free-riding behavior (Olson, 1965), and arguably this will be the case even in the face of threats to children. Further, collective action takes away the responsibility of responding to the problem from the government and places it in the hands of citizens and community groups, thus lessening the potential for a large-scale policy response.

References

Baron, J. (1994). *Thinking and deciding* (2nd ed.). New York: Cambridge University Press.

Bredlie, K. R. (1996). Keeping children out of double jeopardy: An assessment of punishment and Megan's Law in *Doe* v. *Poritz*. *Minnesota Law Review, 81*, 501–545

Camerer, C. (1995). Individual decision making. In J. H. Kagel & A. E. Roth (Eds.), *Handbook of experimental economics* (pp. 587–673). Princeton, NJ: Princeton University Press.

Crimaldi, K. (1995). Megan's law: Election-year politics and constitutional rights. *Rutgers Law Journal. 27*, 169–204.

Echeverria, J. D. (1997). Politics of property rights. *Oklahoma Law Review, 50*, 351–376.

Fischhoff, B., Riley, D., Kovacs, D. C., & Small, M. (1998). What information belongs in a warning? *Psychology & Marketing, 15*, 663–686.

Gowda, M. V. R. (1999). Heuristics, biases, and the regulation of risk. *Policy Sciences, 32*, 59–78.

Grant, D. S., II, & Downey, L. (1995). Regulation through information: An empirical analysis of the effects of state-sponsored right-to-know programs on industrial toxic pollution. *Policy Studies Review, 14*, 337–352.

Hadden, S. G. (1989). *A citizen's right to know: Risk communication and public policy.* Boulder, CO: Westview.

Hadden, S. G. (1991). Public perception of hazardous waste. *Risk Analysis, 11*, 47–58.

Kahneman, D., Slovic, P., & Tversky, A. (Eds.). (1982). *Judgement under uncertainty: Heuristics and biases.* Cambridge: Cambridge University Press.

Kahneman, D., & Tversky, A. (1979). Prospect theory: An analysis of decision under risk. *Econometrica, 47*, 263–291.

Kasperson, R. E. (1992). The social amplification of risk: Progress in developing an integrative framework. In S. Krimsky & D. Golding (Eds.), *Social theories of risk* (pp. 153–178). Westport, CT: Praeger.

Kasperson, R. E., Renn, O., Slovic, P., Brown, H. S., Emel, J., Goble, R., Kasperson, J. X., & Ratick, S. (1988). The social amplification of risk: A conceptual framework. *Risk Analysis, 8*, 177–187.

Keren, G. (1996). Perspectives of behavioral decision making: Some critical notes. *Organizational Behavior and Human Decision Processes, 65*, 169–178.

Kingdon, J. W. (1984). *Agendas, alternatives, and public policies.* Boston: Little, Brown.

Knetsch, J. L. (1995). Assumptions, behavioral findings, and policy analysis. *Journal of Policy Analysis and Management, 14*, 68–78.

Kunreuther, H., & Slovic, P. (1996). Science, values, and risk. *Annals of the American Academy of Political and Social Science, 545*, 116–125.

Kuran, T., & Sunstein, C. R. (1999). Availability cascades and risk regulation. *Stanford Law Review, 51*, 683–768.

Leiss, W. (1992). Assessing and managing risks. *Policy Sciences 25*, 341–349.

Leiss, W. (1996). Three phases in the evolution of risk communication practice. *Annals of the American Academy of Political and Social Science, 545*, 85–94.

Magat, W. A., & Viscusi, W. K. (1992). *Informational approaches to regulation.* Cambridge, MA: MIT Press.

Mayhew, D. (1974). *Congress: The electoral connection.* New Haven, CT: Yale University Press.

Nordenstam, B. J., & DiMento, J. (1990). Right-to-know: Implications of risk communication research for regulatory policy. *University of California, Davis Law Review, 23*, 333–374.

Nordheimer, J. (1995, February 20). "Vigilante" attack in New Jersey is linked to sex-offenders law. *New York Times*, p. B1.

Olson, M. (1965). *The logic of collective action.* Cambridge, MA: Harvard University Press.

Pfeiffer, B. (1997). Six states join forces to offer doctor profiles that include malpractice claims on Internet. *State Health Watch, 4*, 1, 8.

Pidgeon, N., & Beattie, J. (1998). The psychology of risk and uncertainty. In P. Calow (Ed.), *Handbook of environmental risk assessment and management* (pp. 289–318). Oxford: Blackwell.

Plous, S. (1993). *The psychology of judgment and decision making.* New York: McGraw-Hill.

Portney, P. R. (2000). Environmental problems and policy: 2000–2050. *Journal of Economic Perspectives, 14*, 199–206.

Pressley, S. A. (1998, January 17). Testing a new brand of libel law. *Washington Post*, p. A1.

Purdum, T. S. (1997, July 1). Registry laws tar sex-crime convicts with broad brush. *New York Times*, pp. A1, A11.

Schopf, S. (1995). "Megan's law": Community notification and the Constitution. *Columbia Journal of Law and Social Problems, 29*, 117–146.

Slovic, P. (1987). Perception of risk. *Science, 236*, 280–285.

Slovic, P. (1992). Perception of risk: Reflections on the psychometric paradigm. In S. Krimsky & D. Golding (Eds.), *Social theories of risk* (pp. 117–152). Westport, CT: Praeger.

Slovic, P., Fischhoff, B., & Lichtenstein, S. (1979). Rating the risks. *Environment, 21*, 14–20, 36–39.

Suedfeld, P., & Tetlock, P. E. (1992). Psychological advice about political decision making: Heuristics, biases, and cognitive defects. In P. Suedfeld & P. E. Tetlock (Eds.), *Psychology and social policy* (pp. 51–70). New York: Hemisphere.

Sunstein, C. R. (1990). Paradoxes of the regulatory state. *University of Chicago Law Review, 57*, 407–441.

Sunstein, C. R. (1997). *Free markets and social justice.* New York: Oxford University Press.

Tetlock, P. E. (1998). An alternative metaphor in the study of choice: People as politicians. In W. M. Goldstein & R. M. Hogarth (Eds.), *Research on judgment and decision making: Currents, connections and controversies* (pp. 451–475). New York: Cambridge University Press.

Tversky, A., & Kahneman, D. (1974). Judgement under uncertainty: Heuristics and biases. *Science, 185,* 1124–1131.

Tversky, A., & Kahneman, D. (1982). Judgments of and by representativeness. In D. Kahneman, P. Slovic, & A. Tversky (Eds.), *Judgement under uncertainty: Heuristics and biases* (pp. 84–98). Cambridge: Cambridge University Press.

Tversky, A., & Kahneman, D. (1986). Rational choice and the framing of decisions. *Journal of Business, 59,* 251–278.

Weiss, J. A., & Tschirhart, M. (1994). Public information campaigns as policy instruments. *Journal of Policy Analysis and Management, 13,* 82–119.

Wiedemann, P. M., & Henschel, C. (1998). Implementing the Seveso Directive: Problems and progress. In P. C. R. Gray, R. M. Stern, & M. Biocca (Eds.), *Communicating about risks to the environment and health in Europe* (pp. 83–105). Dordrecht, the Netherlands: Kluwer.

Wildavsky, A. (1995). *But is it true?* Cambridge, MA: Harvard University Press.

Williams, B. A., & Matheny, A. R. (1995). *Democracy, dialogue, and environmental disputes: The contested languages of social regulation.* New Haven, CT: Yale University Press.

11 Behavioral Perceptions and Policies Toward the Environment

Anthony Patt and Richard J. Zeckhauser

There is a strong relationship between the ways people think about the behavior of nature – the probabilities, rewards, and penalties it metes out – and how we as a society confront environmental problems. Many characteristics of environmental problems stimulate the side of people's perceptions and responses that a band of psychologists and economists have recently worked together to describe. Environmental concerns frequently involve small and ill-defined probabilities, at times incorporating scenarios that are hard to envision. Many decisions of the potentially gravest import, such as destruction of the ozone layer or alteration of the global climate, are unique situations; they have no precedents and offer no repeat plays. Experts often disagree significantly about environmental problems and about the models to employ in thinking about them. The measuring rod of money, so helpful in dealing with many policy concerns, is absent or at best one step removed in measuring environmental outputs. Such outputs are not traded on markets, and people have difficulty making trade-offs between them and other valuable commodities. These conditions challenge wise choice. In this hostile soil for rationality, behavioral decision can flourish. In an unkindly moment, we may liken behavioral decision to an alien plant. To the rationalist, it is a weed in the garden where only rationality should bloom. To the realist, it is better to understand this plant's anatomy, learning how to live with it, even harvesting it at times, since eradication seems unlikely. Realists recognize that certain conditions make behavioral decision virtually inevitable. Environmental policy offers such conditions.

Economic theory, and decision theory as its complement, have developed around a few axioms of individual choice behavior. Generally, these axioms assume that individuals have consistent preferences, and that they make choices among competing bundles of goods to satisfy them. Utility theory assumes that we can define a utility function that describes these preferences, and that actors will follow the function in a consistent fashion such that choices made have higher utility than choices foregone. Decision theory posits further that individuals can extend the rational methods to make choices about uncertain outcomes, in effect maximizing the expected value of utility, given logically calibrated subjective probabilities of the possible outcomes. From these assumptions all manner of benefits flow. Most fundamental are consistency and transitivity in choice, implying the ability to extrapolate from an individual's choices in laboratory contexts.

Individuals do splendidly in choosing between apples and pears. Once uncertainty enters, unfortunately, the choice problem becomes more complex, and many people exhibit behavior that tends not to maximize the expectation of consistent utility functions. If these choices under uncertainty were random, decision theory could tie descriptions of behavior to physics, utilizing such concepts as Brownian motion, and could predict people's aggregate behavior in accordance with the law of large numbers. Instead, these behaviors tend to trace particular patterns in ways that we have begun to understand. Behavioral decision theory is the emerging discipline that describes how people draw inferences and act in choice situations more challenging than those involving preferences among certain alternatives. In this important class of cases, expected utility often fails as a predictive science, whereas behavioral decision theory frequently provides descriptive insights. A substantial amount of research has identified specific areas of economic life where these biases are apparent. For instance, many people suffer from the *money illusion*, thinking in terms of nominal rather than real units of money (Shafir, Diamond, & Tversky, 1997; Shiller, 1997). People simplify problems in predictable ways. Understanding these ways lends insight into how people will make decisions. By examining how they treat environmental problems – what simplifications they make – we can better understand where and why assumptions of perfect rationality may lead us astray in predicting behavior.

We might expect trained environmental experts to show the behavioral biases discussed here. But environmental problems often bring out sharp disagreements among experts, even among those who share a desire for a cleaner environment. An example is global climate change, one of the most important environmental issues of our age. Humankind faces the possibility of permanently altering its own habitat at a global level. But the climate change problem also engenders a tremendous diversity of opinion and often bitter debate. Many economic models of climate change, such as the Dynamic Integrated Climate Economy (DICE) model (Nordhaus, 1994b), treat the climate as a relatively linear system with no sharp corners. In effect, these models imply that past experience can guide future predictions to a large extent, and they counsel undertaking very gradual mitigation steps as we continue to learn. For validation they point to the majority of historical experience, which involves neither thresholds nor discontinuities, and in which technological innovation and market forces tended to solve the environmental problem in question. Treating the problem as one that can be guided by historical experience allows economists to model optimum levels of emissions abatement (Nordhaus, 1994b), optimum timing of emissions abatement given learning (Manne & Richels, 1991), and alternative strategies for achieving the same goals at a higher level of efficiency (Schelling, 1995).

By contrast, many ecologists – who are used to predator–prey and ecosystem models where there are booms and crashes in populations – tend to view climate change as part of a class of problems where salient thresholds may be passed unwittingly. Whereas economists have the single macro economy to study, which implies a restricted time series, ecologists tend to record extreme instances selected from dozens or millions of instances. Judged from a modeling perspective, the economists' sample is too small, the ecologists' too selective.

Ecologists' models suggest that unprecedented action is needed now. For validation they too draw on historical analogies; they point to the numerous instances when societies have passed thresholds, with results such as the desertification of their arable land or the exhaustion of a fishery (e.g., Ludwig, Hilborn, & Walters, 1993). Although exploitation has ruined local fish stocks or rendered agricultural areas infertile, current and future practices could influence human development worldwide. The two models, the economists' and the ecologists', rely on different mental models for thinking about climate change, and they strongly incline to opposite sets of advice (Patt, 1999b). Many environmentalists see technology as the source of global problems and disdain geoengineering solutions, even those that could potentially be simple and cost effective (National Research Council, 1992). Geoengineering, by contrast, sometimes entrances economists; they are used to seeing technological advances bolster the well-being of societies as a whole. Importantly, each side tends to think that it is behaving rationally and that disciplinary blinders hinder the other side.

This chapter examines the role of behavioral decision theory in illuminating issues of environmental policy, and the role of environmental issues in developing and testing the theory of behavioral decision. It does not present new data; rather, we highlight the places where environmental policy and behavioral decision theory overlap. In doing so, we look beyond health risks and contingent valuation – well-illuminated areas in the behavioral literature – to examine issues of environmental quality and change. The environment is special in the affinity between its problems and behavioral decision theory. Hence the analysis of environmental issues has potential for helping to develop general theory. Understanding how the individual addresses a problem in isolation can and should be useful for predicting how society as a whole will respond to complex threats, though the relationship is hardly one to one. Environmental problems range from local to global and from acute to chronic. They are prime real estate for mapping the relationships of individual decision making and societal responses.

In this chapter, we first review the best-known heuristics and biases identified by behavioral decision theory and outline their relevance to environmental policy. Second, we look at key features of environmental decision making, which enable behavioral decision theory to make such contributions. Third, we make two modest proposals to improve assessment and policymaking. The first is a framework for analyzing behavioral decisions in the multidimensional arena of environmental policy. The framework we propose – one of excessive and insensitive reactions – applies most of all to issues of poorly known probabilities, poorly defined preferences, and poorly understood policies. On these counts the environment is at the head of the class of issues facing policymakers. The second proposal is to develop a futures market for environmental problems and policies. Such a market would create incentives to generate and provide reliable information about the environment, and would promote research in the private sector geared not to advocacy, but to profits from accurate assessment.

Classic Heuristics and Biases

People subconsciously use shortcuts, or heuristics, to solve complicated problems (Kahneman & Tversky, 1974). These shortcuts produce answers to problems that are predictable but inconsistent with expected utility theory, and allow people to arrive quickly at answers that are usually "good enough" but quite poor in certain circumstances – circumstances that frequently characterize environmental decisions. For example, such decisions may involve low probabilities and long time spans, in which case decision makers will not have significant experience and feedback from earlier choices. Frequent feedback plays a role in decision making akin to competition in market products; each tends to drive out faulty decision making. As people become more familiar with a particular problem, they refine these shortcuts and gradually make choices that come closer to utility optimization. New problems will thus be solved using the tools that tended to work in the past. But when random variability is high, as it often is, many people have a hard time discriminating between good decisions and bad or seeing trends obscured by background noise. Changing seasons and interannual variability make it hard to perceive that human actions are likely changing the Earth's climate, for example. The investor Warren Buffett has noted that the best training for real-life decision making is the card game bridge, in which the successful player learns over time to discriminate between good strategies and good outcomes.

Decision-making heuristics combined with people's preferences can lead to predictable outcomes that are somewhat contradictory (e.g., Kahneman & Tversky, 1979; Tversky & Kahneman, 1988). If people are at a particular starting point, so that a change in wealth or some other commodity is perceived as a loss rather than a gain, they will take actions that simultaneously decrease the mean and increase the variance of the outcome they will face, in contrast to the action predicted by economic rationality. In short, framing a problem in a particular way can dramatically change an individual's decision in predictable ways. Empirical studies have also noted that real-world decision makers make consistent errors in judgment. One example is *bright line* behavior. DeGeorge, Patel, and Zeckhauser (1999) note that corporate managers manipulate reported earnings in order to meet specific targets such as positive net profits, the prior year's earnings, or earnings levels predicted by stock market analysts. Environmental policy provides its share of bright line anomalies, such as those associated with enshrining particular levels of environmental quality, setting standards at 1 part per some large number as opposed to 3 or 7 parts, or restoring quality to the level of some particular prior year, none of which may have a close connection with environmental protection outcomes.

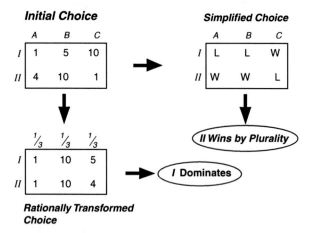

Figure 11.1. Simplified and rational transformation of two lotteries.

Bounded Rationality

Tversky and Kahneman (1988) identify a two-stage thought process when people confront tough decisions. First, people simplify the problem into an easier one; then they solve the easier problem. This is illustrated in Figure 11.1, which shows a choice between two lotteries, I and II, each giving payoffs in equally likely states of the world, A, B, and C. Here, a complicated choice between two different state-dependent lotteries is simplified to the perceived choice in the upper right. This is simpler, because it involves clear wins and losses; numbers are abandoned. Employing this simplification, many people will choose lottery I, because it gives them the better payoff two times out of three. An alternative but more complex way of viewing the problem would transform the choice by permutating the payoffs. This characterization of the problem – which employs the principle of stochastic dominance – shows that lottery I is the better choice. At every level of cumulative probability, lottery I gives a payoff at least as high as, and in one case higher than, that of lottery II. By simplifying the choice to a rule of thumb – wins and losses – people will choose the lottery that gives them the lower expected outcome and the greater degree of risk.

Two features of this type of problem are evident. First, when multiple rules of thumb can be applied to a problem, a number of competing problem frames suggest easy answers. Because deciding what rule of thumb to apply depends on the "norms, habits, and expectations" of the decision maker (Tversky & Kahneman, 1988, p. 172), we would expect differences of opinion to fall along lines correlated with other social and political factors. Put less nicely, interests influence biases. Not only will people disagree on what course of action the facts call for, they will disagree on what the facts are, based on their biased interpretations of ambiguous evidence. Following this logic, we would expect different academic disciplines to reach different answers to the same questions based on their different norms, habits, and expectations. Second, where the problem is one that is not repeated, so that feedback, which tends to push us beyond rule-of-thumb decision making, is limited, we would expect to see many people making the wrong decision.

A good example of this phenomenon can be seen with global warming. Although there is general scientific agreement that the problem is real and that cutbacks in greenhouse gas emissions would be wise, a great deal of uncertainty and some scientific controversy remain. Not surprisingly, there is much debate over what level of policy response is appropriate to address the problem; however, some also question the scientific findings that support the problem's existence in the first place. Industry groups, such as the Global Climate Coalition, argue that there is no sound evidence of the problem. As long as there remains a basis for reasonable doubt – and with issues of such complexity there almost always will – it is possible to give different interpretations to mixed evidence. For the problem of global warming this problem is especially serious because of the time delays involved. To be most effective, action to address the problem should probably occur before changes in climate are unambiguous to the lay observer.

Anchoring

Decision makers become anchored on their early estimates and fail to update those estimates as more reliable information becomes available (van der Sluijs, 1997). Walters (1986) developed the theory of *adaptive management*, in which environmental decision making approaches the optimum by incorporating feedback from past policy decisions. For example, if a fishery manager who wants to design the most effective salmon ladder to bypass a dam does not know what types of ladders salmon are likely to climb, she will have to monitor the salmon's reaction to preliminary designs, and change designs rapidly if the results do not match expectations. But Clark (in press) has observed that people are often unwilling to change a policy decision in midstream. At individual, social, and political levels of decision making, people dislike wavering, failing to change a decision even if doing so is the rational response to the best available knowledge. Behavioral decision theory suggests that if adaptive management is to occur, then people must take care to design institutions that will respond flexibly to new information. On their own, both individuals and groups show a profound resistance to incorporating new information and changing their decisions accordingly. In group settings, organizations rarely reward individuals for admitting that previous estimates were in error. Institutions should therefore incorporate incentive systems that correct for, rather than reinforce, the behavioral tendency to stick with original estimates and choices.

Availability

Environmental problems that are abstract or whose adverse consequences arise solely in the future are hard to contemplate because of the problem of availability or lack thereof. People tend to judge the frequency of a class of events by the ease with which they can bring to mind specific instances of that class (Thaler, 1991; Tversky & Kahneman, 1973). People worry about problems whose consequences are highly visible but underinvest when consequences are hard to bring to mind. In the context of endangered species protection, Metrick and Weitzman (1996) found that bodily characteristics (such as being a large mammal or bird) rather than scientific characteristics (such as the degree of endangerment or taxonomic uniqueness) better predicted governmental decisions to list a species as endangered and spend money for its preservation. It is not that bears or eagles are more endangered than smaller or more slimy species, or that preserving the larger animals benefits a given ecosystem more (arguably the reverse is true), but that people are more familiar with certain animals and care about them more for their symbolic value, in some sense attending to how much the wildlife reminds them of themselves.

As another example, climate change gained national policy attention during the summer of 1988, when abnormally hot temperatures plagued most of the country and much of Yellowstone National Park was lost to forest fires (Clark, in press). That same summer, Europe suffered through an abnormally cold season. The steamy summer in the United States did not necessarily indicate that the climate change was approaching, but it certainly helped people imagine what a climate-changed future could be like. Likewise, the loss of stratospheric ozone caused alarm, and the signing of an ambitious international treaty took place, only when scientists identified an ozone hole over Antarctica, an aspect of the problem that people could conceptualize, as opposed to a reduction in molecule concentrations, a more abstract but more accurate description. Relying on half-truth images can be misleading; some decision makers have expressed the view that were the ozone hole to be real, the atmosphere would "leak out." Since the air is still around us, they reasoned, ozone loss must be a myth.

Advocates can often take advantage of the availability problem (Patt, 1999a). In 1998, for example, an environmental advocacy group prepared a video demonstrating the potential effects of a sea level rise to Martha's Vineyard, an island off the New England coast. The video showed how a 1-meter rise in sea level – an eventual outcome foreseen as possible by global warming scientists – could inundate a small fraction of the island, but also how the effect would be magnified during a hurricane. The environmental organization that commissioned the video released it to the press the day before a major hurricane was predicted to strike Martha's Vineyard and the vacationing President Bill Clinton. The video was front-page news in the *Boston Globe*.

Many environmental problems are abstract, and are recognized as problems only because scientists tell us about them. People cannot directly sense ozone holes, increased climate variability, or the relationship between toxic waste and cancer rates. Thus they are readily subject to manipulating tales and images. For example, according to the Kemeny Commission (appointed by President Jimmy Carter to investigate the Three Mile Island nuclear accident), less than one statistical life was lost at Three Mile Island. Yet its highly visible status effectively ended the construction of new atomic generating facilities in the United States.

Further, the environmental commodities that advocates seek to protect are not traded on markets and have no price tag attached to indicate their value. In such situations, people do not do a good job at making trade-offs between competing needs and wants. Instead, they tend to frame issues in black and white terms, and use easily available arguments and salient but unrepresentative cases to support or justify their position. It is crucial that policymakers recognize the predictable biases in people's decision making. First, people will be overly sensitive to low-probability events, particularly scary ones they can bring to mind. Second, they will react insufficiently to changes in quantitative estimates of environmental harm, particularly if they are reported in hard-to-understand units, such as gallons of discharge or fractional concentrations. Third, people will have difficulty agreeing on consistent trade-offs between environmental quality and other competing societal objectives. Fourth, they will latch onto problems and push them onto the political agenda in response to events, not sound science. The challenge for policymakers is to design institutions that are capable of making sound and consistent environmental policy in this context. Such institutions should counter the claims of both alarmists and Pollyannas who attempt to manipulate the public's and policymaker's views of the environment.

Loss Aversion and Bias Toward the Status Quo

A central observation of behavioral decision theory is that people value losses more than equivalent gains. Prospect theory (Kahneman & Tversky, 1979) describes outcomes in terms of a departure from a starting reference point. It contrasts with traditional utility theory, which assumes that people view gains and losses along some absolute scale. Prospect theory incorporates two major findings. First, people respond to contingent gains with risk-averting behavior and to contingent losses with risk-taking behavior. Second, people have a strong aversion to losses, valuing them more, in an absolute sense, than gains of equivalent magnitude. Kahneman and Tversky suggested that instead of the standard concave utility function, people tend to operate in accordance with an S-shaped value function, as shown in Figure 11.2, with a sharp break in slope at 0. Since people value losses more than equivalent gains, they will generally reject any potential departure from their current

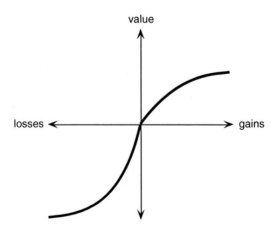

Figure 11.2. Value function.

position that involves gains and losses of roughly comparable magnitude on equally valued dimensions.

Samuelson and Zeckhauser (1988) found that people's decisions depend to a large extent on what they perceive as the current choice; they are biased toward the status quo. In the environmental context, status quo preference leads to inconsistent choices. It makes us forgo curtailing level H of harms, say by closing a plant, if J jobs must be sacrificed. Yet we might be unwilling to accept $H/3$ of environmental degradation nearby in order to create J jobs. Cost-benefit and cost-effectiveness analyses are supposed to curb such severe inconsistencies. However, many environmental advocates strongly oppose the use of such techniques for crafting policies, often as a strategy to capitalize on the status quo bias.

An important insight emerging from prospect theory and status quo bias is that the way a problem is framed can greatly affect the choices that are made. In some cases, it is possible for decision makers to adopt different reference points as the status quo, and the choice of reference point will largely determine the outcome of the decision. In other cases, decision makers anchor on an old reference point, even when conditions have changed enough to warrant a newly defined status quo. At other times, people have difficulty predicting how they will shift their reference points in the future if conditions change. In the environmental context, this class of problems has been most dramatically revealed in the contrast between people's willingness to pay for improved quality (WTP) versus their willingness to accept money in return for quality degradation (WTA). When consumers consider WTP, they consider what loss of wealth would be equal in value to a gain of environmental quality. For WTA, consumers answer the opposite question: What gain in wealth is required to counterbalance a given loss of environmental quality? As long as the change in environmental quality is the same (i.e., a gain from quality B to quality C or a loss from quality C to quality B), standard consumer theory predicts only a small discrepancy between WTP and WTA, arising out of the income effect. If we believe that people regard losses as worse than equivalent gains, however, we would expect estimates of WTA to be significantly larger than WTP. Survey data validate the latter prediction. Extensive empirical work has shown that WTA is two to five times higher in amount than WTP, a difference that cannot be explained by the income effects associated with utility theory (Gregory, Lichtenstein, & Slovic, 1993; Knetsch, 1990; Knetsch, this volume).

Overconfidence

People anchor on what they know and are insensitive to their level of ignorance. That is, they are overconfident. This has important consequences for the environment. Environmental policy problems require accurate predictions about the future of large, complex, poorly understood systems (Walters, 1986). Policymakers must ask, for example, what the likelihood is that sustained growth in carbon emissions will result in a 5-meter sea level rise, or some other disastrous outcome, in the next 200 years. Their answers to questions like this will probably be seriously in error. Over the years, we have asked students to estimate quantities such as the length of the Congo River, the oil production of Mexico, or the area of Thailand. To assess confidence, we have asked them to provide median estimates (best guesses), 25th and 75th percentiles, and 1st and 99th percentiles. The last two we have referred to as *surprise points*. Appropriately confident individuals ought to be surprised roughly 2% of the time. The thousands of people who have taken this test have been surprised more than one-third of the time, however. Whereas these questions were concerned with readily understood concepts, many environmental problems deal with outcomes that are difficult to imagine. Quite possibly, overconfidence will be more severe.

As expertise rises, does overconfidence diminish? Do experts, who presumably advise and make important policy decisions, better understand their ignorance? Experience with financial markets and energy resources is not reassuring. Gordon and Kammen (1996) find systematic overconfidence among professional financial analysts. In comparing forecasts to realized events, there is "a consistent underestimation of the probability of 'rare' events, or those lying far from the mean" (p. 190). Shlyakhter, Kammen, Broido, and Wilson (1994) find a similar pattern with projections of energy demand.

Frequently, uncertainties about the magnitude of interest are great because of cascading causes and effects, each with its own element of uncertainty. How likely is the temperature to rise by 3°C? If it does rise that much, how likely is it that a given glacier will disappear? If it does disappear, what will that do to river levels downstream, and how will that affect irrigation for agriculture? In the environmental context, looking specifically at flight in the stratosphere, Zeckhauser, Shearer, and Memishian (1975) provide a methodology for carrying such uncertainties through an analysis. More concretely, recent work by Morgan and Dowlatabadi (1996) and Morgan and Henrion (1990) modeling environmental problems such as climate change and acid rain has taken the approach of incorporating uncertainty at every stage of the modeling process, but these models are no more than attractive prototypes. Retail sensitivity analysis remains the norm. Rather than propagate uncertainty through their models, analysts continue to develop single-point estimates and then rework the estimates using alternative assumptions.

Many assessment agencies and decision makers attempt to correct for overconfidence by building margins of safety into administrative procedures, thus incorporating conservatism (Zeckhauser & Viscusi, 1990). But applying safety margins throughout a series of calculations can result in point estimates of health risks that are orders of magnitude higher than what is realistic. When these risks are compared to other risks, for which the number of calculations required is fewer or the safety margin less, society ends up doing more to protect people from the more complicated but often less dangerous risks. Alternatively, society shows an implicit preference to live with "old" risks that it understands and can estimate rather than replace them with "new" risks that may be of lesser magnitude but are less well understood (Huber & Litan, 1991).

Probability Weighting

Individuals make inconsistent choices when outcomes are uncertain. They simultaneously purchase insurance and lottery tickets. Such behavior appears counterproductive and contradicts the very core of the expected utility model. In risk analysis, the key question is why people respond to risks in ways that seem to violate rational interpretation of the magnitude of the expected loss. Behavioral decision theorists have theorized that people are predictable in their over- or underweighting of certain probabilities, and that this can affect their decision making. This predictability of behavior can be tested by environmental problems and can be important for setting effective environmental policy.

There is a large literature pointing out a correlation between people's subjective probability assessment of a risk and their feelings about the potential outcomes. In other words, people's perceived probabilities and the utilities associated with outcomes are not independent of each other. In normative decision theory, by contrast, the magnitude of the outcome should have no influence on the assessed probability. Kammen, Shlyakhter, and Wilson (1994) note that people tend to place higher probability assessments on catastrophic and insidious risks than on risks they feel they control. Authors such as Fischhoff (1996) have identified factors associated with outcomes that make people respond as if those outcomes were more likely. The fields of risk analysis, management, and communication have incorporated many of the lessons of behavioral decision theory, no doubt because, with low-probability risks, the norm for risks to the environment, decision theoretic predictions miss the mark so widely. We argue here that other environmental problems, not simply those involving health risks, warrant a similar analysis of decisions in behavioral terms.

Hyperbolic Discounting

Environmental decisions often have consequences that stretch for years, decades, or centuries. Traditional discounting methods provide a clear normative tool for considering benefits and costs that take place over extended periods of time. However, citizens' preferences and choices rarely reflect what discounting would prescribe. Behavioral decision theory has developed a framework, hyperbolic discounting, that much more closely approximates what people actually do.

Two findings are especially relevant. First, people demonstrate discount rates that are present-biased; that is, they tend to discount the near term by a large factor and events further in the future by a significantly smaller factor (Laibson, 1997). These disparities in discount rate are compounded by normal agency problems, such as if one generation or government regime controls the early decisions and others control the later decisions. Second, people resist applying any discounting methods to decisions that do not involve market transactions and the productive capacity of capital. Thus, they are ready to apply a discount factor to money in a bank account, and say that being paid $100 today is equivalent to being paid $110 a year from now. They are far less willing, for a variety of reasons, to say that a policy saving 100 lives today is as attractive as one that saves 110 lives a year from now. When policymakers do start to make such determinations, they lack the same intuition that they have with money. In addition, ethical concerns, albeit rarely formulated crisply, weigh against discounting. The result may be choices that are inconsistent and preferences that vary substantially over time. People may commit to protect the environment in the future, but once that future arrives they will defer until an even later date.

Importantly, people learn that they are inconsistent over time, which may strongly influence the choices they make. They search for devices to commit their own future behavior. With long-lived environmental problems, generations take the role of successive periods. Our generation might willingly bequeath an environmental legacy to the future if subsequent generations would behave accordingly, and those subsequent generations might be willing to agree. But given the absence of a commitment mechanism, they are not to be trusted; they will be selfish when their own time comes. The problem is that generation 1 values 3 relative to 2 more than generation 2 does.

Environmentalists and altruists toward the future confront this problem by seeking to constrain the behavior of future generations to conform to today's desires. A common adjustment is the use of precommitment devices, what Laibson (1997) calls *golden eggs*. For example, people set up investment accounts with substantial penalties for early withdrawal. They know that they will be tempted to withdraw money later on, as opportunities to spend money arise and their short-term discount rate makes leaving the money in savings accounts unattractive. The presence of an early withdrawal penalty makes it more likely that the money will stay put in the future. The policy equivalent may be to pass legislation; overturning the legislation is much more expensive politically than failing to enact it in the first place.

Fairness

Fairness gets a great deal of attention in environmental discussions. Is a policy fair to the people on the south side of town, who are closer to the dump, or to those on the south side of the equator, who have fewer economic resources to adapt to environmental change? Are we unfairly destroying the environmental legacy that was left to us, presumably with the intent that we pass it on to future generations? Is it fair that we destroy the breeding grounds of seals and the otters so that our economic activities can stretch even further? People place a high value on fairness, often overlaying this value on the others already discussed.

Fairness is an elusive concept and, like beauty, often lies in the eye of the beholder. Its opposite, unfairness, is more easily spotted. Despite difficulties of definition, fairness can be a trump card, even when it is fuzzily defined. An unfair policy may be defeated, even though no one can specify what a fair policy would be. Often the status quo reigns as fair, because at least no one is newly hurt by sticking with it.

Fairness is particularly relevant for environmental decision making involving the social costs of private action, as is typical of problems with externalities – such as pollution – and common pool resources, or public goods. People do not act in the purely self-interested mode that economic models predict. For example, demand-driven environmental decision making can be important. Some people pay more for tuna fish that is "dolphin safe" even if their contribution to the cause greatly exceeds any private benefit they derive from the slight increase in cetaceans that their contribution creates. Similarly, some people buy expensive solar power despite the fact that they could easily be free riders instead.

Recent research has focused on the relationships among fairness, self-serving bias, and framing. Are people paying for the dolphins they are saving, purchasing a warm glow cheaply, or voting for environmental protection in the only way they know how? Diekman, Samuels, Ross, and Bazerman (1997) conclude that "most of us want to see ourselves, and be seen by others, not only as fair but as generous, or at least less self-serving than other actors would be in similar circumstances" (p. 1061). They find that people are far more likely to support unequal allocations, in which they themselves receive a greater share of some common resource, when the allocations are dictated by another or are seen as the status quo. People are far less likely to propose a self-serving allocation themselves.

Key Features of Environmental Decision Making

It is in our blood to value the environment and environmental quality. But more than hemoglobin and plasma is required to think about how to make choices between different levels of environmental quality and hedonic pleasures. When people are asked to make these trade-offs, their cognitive processes let them down. They may become confused, they may make poor or inconsistent choices, or they may rebel. Many, for example, have criticized economic solutions to environmental problems as morally wrong, because they place an implicit price tag on the environment. Unless environmental quality is a trumping value, it is hard to see how implicit prices – which merely provide a way to value one output relative to another – could be avoided.

Economists assume that people at least have preferences that are consistent across choice sets. For example, the introduction of good C in a choice set will not affect a preference for good A over good B. A reasonable way of representing preferences among alternatives is in terms of willingness to pay (WTP). If I am willing to pay $5 for good A, $4 for good B, and $3 for good C, then I must prefer A to B to C. Goods that are traded on the market have prices associated with them, prices that to some extent reflect people's WTP. Decisions involving public welfare can take these prices for granted; importantly, they can also take into account WTP for nonmarket goods. By finding out people's WTP for nonmarket goods, such as different kinds of environmental quality, decision makers can evaluate the welfare implications of trade-offs between different allocations of market and nonmarket goods. Furthermore, they can predict the choices that people will make when faced with scarcity and uncertainty.

But a growing body of evidence from both psychology and neuroscience indicates that this method of decision making is not innate, and if it is present at all, it must be learned. Rather, people form emotional reactions (or attitudes) to things and ideas that vary sign and magnitude, and this mechanism often works quite well. For example, Damasio (1994) describes patients who through head injuries lost the ability to form emotional responses. Though these patients possess fully normal intellects and reasoning abilities, they have lost the ability to make good decisions and choices for their own well-being. Importantly, the emotional responses that form the basis for decision making can depend highly on context. I may choose a particular model of car over a particular model of pickup truck, but when a newer version of the car comes out, that could well affect my opinion of the now outdated car while leaving my emotional response to the pickup truck unchanged. With the introduction of the new car, my positive emotional response to the old car would be diminished, and I might now choose the pickup over it. The implication is that problems bring their own implicit choice sets.

In a study by Kahneman, Ritov, and Schkade (1999), researchers asked people to rate the importance of losses in environmental quality (due to cyanide fishing around coral reefs in Asia) and human health (increased rates of myeloma, a form of skin cancer, among the elderly). The coral reef issue was surmised to be an important and offensive issue within the environmental purview. The melanoma was perceived to be a relatively benign problem within a much more important area, human health. On a scale of 1 to 6, respondents rated both the importance of the problem and their expected satisfaction from making a contribution to the problem. As Table 11.1 shows, the answers depended on whether the issues were presented in isolation or after a question about the other issue. In isolation, myeloma received a relatively low rating, reflecting its low importance within the area of human health. However, when compared

Table 11.1. *Contextual Attitudes or Preference Reversals*

Importance Ratings (1–6)			Expected Satisfaction (1–6)		
	Coral Reefs	*Myeloma*		*Coral Reefs*	*Myeloma*
Judged alone	3.78	3.24	Judged alone	3.54	2.84
Judged second	3.62	4.36	Judged second	3.24	4.18

with the coral reef issue, myeloma gained in importance because it deals with human health.

If environmental issues are unusually important as a class, then asking about them in isolation will understate their importance, and vice versa. Trade-offs and priorities across classes of issues will be missed. If people do make choices that reflect consistent preferences, it may be because they learn to do so in some situations. We would expect these situations to be ones they face often, and where feedback is available for good or bad decisions. By contrast, when people have to make choices in unfamiliar territory, where they are neither experienced at making the choices nor receive feedback on their decisions, we would expect less consistency. Without consistency of preferences, both predicting future choices and determining the welfare implications of public policies become problematic.

Irreversible Phenomena

The nature of many environmental problems suggests that people's heuristic-driven choices will bias their decisions. For example, economists tend to treat problems as well behaved and continuous; many natural systems, by contrast, respond in ways that are extremely nonlinear and have thresholds where outcomes diverge qualitatively. Managing a renewable resource, such as a fishery, provides a good and well-documented example. Below certain rates of harvesting, the system changes slowly, but beyond some catch threshold the population decline is rapid and accelerating. As the threshold is approached, decision makers may continue to be guided by wisdom derived from prior experience. Yet if they do not perceive when they have crossed the critical threshold and respond immediately, irreversible damage, such as species extinction, may result (Ludwig et al., 1993). Plummeting fish stocks have afflicted the Grand Banks, the Columbia River, and numerous other locales.

The problem with irreversibility is not just that we can reach bad outcomes, but also that we are unlikely to understand our circumstances clearly as we progress toward them. If we are on the preferred side of the irreversibility threshold, we might never have been on the other side before. Many environmental decisions involve irreversible problems. If the decision is wrong, there will be no opportunity to correct the problem. When we characterize a problem as irreversible, we recognize that we cannot be guided by past experience, except on a meta-analysis basis, which looks across a wide class of problems. Irreversible problems demand extreme caution – though less extreme than the peddlers of irreversibility may claim. Such individuals portray irreversibility as a danger so bad that it cannot be risked. But this may well be a politically motivated framing ploy, and it is crucial to determine how bad the irreversible event may be.

People may also argue, however, that the irreversibility threshold is still a long way off. If a problem can be seen as potentially irreversible, decision makers will differ more widely in their predictions and prescriptions. Problems will be framed competitively as irreversible or as commonplace; these framings will matter for how decision makers actually act.

Ambiguous Status Quo

Previously, we explained the status quo's strong influence and how this can significantly affect outcomes. With real environmental problems, there is rarely an unambiguous definition of what comprises the status quo. Advocates in the environmental policy realm attempt to capitalize on this phenomenon, each presenting his or her own frame of what should be considered the status quo. Disciplinary analysts practice this game as well.

For example, in 1993, the State of Vermont faced a decision over an application by the Stowe Mountain Resort to install lights for night skiing on Mount Mansfield, the highest mountain in the region. Opponents claimed that the lights would ruin the region's rural character from one of moonlit pastures to one dominated by metal halide luminescence. Proponents claimed that the lights would bring economic development to the town. But Vermont was hesitant to grant the permit. Advocates for the resort convinced the state authorities to conduct a 1-year experiment, allowing the lights to be put up without a permanent permit. During that year, two things happened. First, the resort failed to generate its predicted revenues; economically, night skiing was a failure. Second, most people got used to the lights on Mount Mansfield. By the end of the ski season, most of the opposition to the lights had dissipated. The state decided that it would not require the lights to be taken down, but issued strict guidelines limiting such development salient elsewhere in Vermont. The advocates for the mountain had been clever; in 1 year, people's conception of the status quo shifted from an unilluminated mountain to one with lights. That fact proved critical in the decision to allow the lights to remain.

How the status quo is framed has important implications for policy. For instance, environmental economists traditionally classify development that is unregulated by new environmental laws as the status quo. When conducting cost-benefit or other forms of analysis, economists typically treat as costs the effects on the economy of regulating for environmental quality, and the benefits as the improved environmental amenities that result from the regulation. They are thinking of the status quo in terms of rates and directions of change. But it is also possible to define the status quo in terms of the present environmental state, without regard to how that state may or may not change if current practices continue. In some cases, these two definitions are compatible, as with the cleanup of a polluted site or the imposition of a tighter pollution standard. In other cases, however, the two potential definitions of the status quo yield quite different results.

With climate change, for instance, economists mostly prepare their baseline scenarios assuming no further constraints on carbon emissions, implying a given level of economic growth, along with significant environmental deterioration over time. The policy alternatives are predicted to slow both economic growth and the rate of environmental change. One could just as easily argue that both the current level of economic output and the current state of the environment are the status quo. Under this definition, the failure to regulate greenhouse gas emissions actually results in a greater departure from the status quo than would a policy significantly reducing greenhouse gas emissions. Since people tilt toward the stand-pat solution, how the status quo is defined matters a great deal. The economists' standard framing should dampen policy efforts to slow greenhouse warming. The alternative framing, suggested by many ecologists (e.g. Mintzer, 1987), will make people much fiercer about slowing emissions rates. The problem is politically salient because implicit property rights get assigned to the status quo. In the United States, for example, there is tremendous resistance to taxing pollution but not to granting tradable permits to pollute. Although the former is probably more efficient when information is incomplete, tradable permits give current polluters the right to continue doing so.

Low-Probability, High-Consequence Events

Many of the most significant environmental problems for the 21st century revolve around low-probability events that have monumental consequences. The problem with global warming, for example, is not that it is inevitable, but that it could have any of a range of unlikely consequences (e.g., significant shifts in the patterns of ocean currents), each of which would threaten most civilizations. As a global threat, it is not unlike nuclear war in the 1960s and 1970s, unlikely but extremely consequential. Other threats of this nature involve new viruses brought out by rapid population expansion in developing regions, such as AIDS (acquired immune deficiency syndrome), massive radioactive contamination, and the loss of human fertility from chronic exposure to endocrine disrupters. Unfortunately, we are very poor at assessing the likelihoods of such low-probability events, and history gives us little guidance on any particular one of them. Indeed, even a meta-analysis looking across events does not reveal whether society has been foolhardy or appropriately prudent. There simply is not enough experience to enable us to tell whether what we judge to be 1 in 1,000 global catastrophes are really 1 in 100 or 1 in 100,000.

Behavioral decision theory can help alleviate our difficulties in these areas. It has the most to say when subjective and objective probabilities associated with uncertain events are furthest apart, as they are with events of very low probability, and when the outcomes are especially frightful. Numerous environmental issues share the fundamental features of low probability and a high-magnitude outcome. For example, Kammen et al. (1994) discuss potential catastrophes resulting from nuclear power, climate change, air pollution, and other causes falling under the umbrella of the environment. In its report *Unfinished Business*, the U.S. Environmental Protection Agency (1987) highlights how many of its policies reduce environmental harm, devoting disproportionate attention to the risks that people care about. Hence environmental problems such as toxic waste dumps receive ample federal funding, whereas others such as indoor air pollution go largely unnoticed, even though the undernoticed risks pose a much greater statistical danger to society.

Most people are surprised to learn that there is little correlation between people's fears and typical objective measures of the dangers they face. For example, many people consider nuclear power to be the most substantial risk to public safety, whereas experts place it well down the list, after such risks as large construction, bicycles, and swimming (Slovic, 1987). Breyer (1993) identifies several causes of this result: public misperception of environmental risks; congressional attempts to mandate levels of safety; the difficulties that regulators face when trying to protect public safety in the face of uncertainty and ignorance; and at times ignorance about what the possibilities might be. In addition, people generally view risks differently based on where the risk comes from. Indoor air pollution is people's own responsibility, yet potential nuclear accidents occur because of factors beyond our control. People hate new risks that are imposed by other people, are willing to tolerate risks that they impose on themselves, and tend to ignore as background information risks generated by nature (e.g., Fischhoff, 1997).

The fact that many environmental risks are of low probability and thus subject to public misperception creates a substantial dilemma for policymakers: whether to leave the problem of these risks essentially to the market and people's private decision making, or to impose standards on risk regulation that are patently paternalistic (Zeckhauser & Viscusi, 1990, 1996). Although economists typically

argue that individuals' preferences are to be relied on and taken as given, economists are the first to question the underlying rationality of individuals' choices about risks and to suggest that informed expert opinion offers a superior guide to policy. . . . Yet the rational decision framework remains the appropriate normative reference point: policies should not institutionalize the errors people make but, rather, should promote the outcomes they would choose if they understood the risks accurately. (Zeckhauser & Viscusi 1996, p. 149)

In effect, though economists are very accepting of people's values, they are willing to override people's probability judgments when those judgments are demonstrably in error. They are even prone to question choices that deviate from what the economists believe people's values would dictate. As a result, many policy choices guided by expert opinion make people angry, and a rift can easily develop between expert assessment of environmental risks and grassroots opinion, complicating the ability of all concerned to address the problem (Wynne, 1996).

As Fischhoff (1985, 1995) describes, the creation of constructive policies requires a great deal of attention to communicating the risks effectively and making people feel involved in the process. Increasingly, communicators of risk have used devices to help people understand new risks, compare them to others with which they are already familiar, and finally take part in the decision-making process.

The fact that people are likely to respond irrationally to low-probability, high-consequence risks is well recognized by those who make a living out of communicating those risks, either in an advocacy or a coalition-building role. Patt (1999a) analyzed scientific assessments of one particular low-probability, high-consequence risk – the possibility that global warming would cause the West Antarctic Ice Sheet to collapse, resulting in a rapid 5-meter rise in sea level – and found a great deal of strategizing. Advocates on the two sides of the global warming debate either used the ice sheet's collapse to provide a reason to fear climate change or pointed to its implausibility as a recurring feature of the other side's arguments and fears. Importantly, consensus groups such as the Intergovernmental Panel on Climate Change (IPCC) tended not to discuss the particular risk. Two reasons can account for the omission. First, these groups would have been challenged to reach an internal consensus on how best to communicate the facts of the low-probability, high-consequence risk. Second, these groups realized that discussing the risk was likely to be counterproductive to building an external consensus about what actions to take to address the climate change issue. Since their job is to forge consensus rather than to stir up controversy, groups such as the IPCC steer clear of such risks altogether.

Contingent Valuation and Its Problems

Contingent valuation (CV) is a common method used to value environmental change. Researchers use it to measure things such as air quality (Irwin et al., 1990; Schultz, 1985), wildlife (Walsh, Bjonback, Aiken, & Rosenthal, 1990), or other resources for which market data do not exist. Basically, CV asks people how much they would pay for various environmental amenities. Often the questions address resources lost or at risk elsewhere, such as otters whose lives may be lost. Economists have always been suspicious of survey results; CV reinforces their suspicions. A large literature has shown that CV data are unreliable, partly due to a number of behavioral effects. First, the phenomenon of *embedding* shows up; people value a given resource and a significantly smaller subset of that resource essentially the same (Binger, Copple, & Hoffman, 1995;

Gregory et al., 1993; Irwin, Slovic, Lichtenstein, & McClelland, 1993). For example, respondents to a phone survey expressed essentially the same WTP to save fish in a particular lake in Ontario, in several lakes in the area, and in all of the lakes in the entire province (Kahneman, 1986). The embedding takes place not only for the resource, but also for the decision-making unit: Individuals express the same WTP for themselves and for their family as a whole, even though the latter ought to be several times higher (Binger et al., 1995).

Loss aversion also diminishes the reliability of CV. Individuals value losses more than they do equivalent gains (Kahneman & Tversky, 1979), and hence it matters a great deal whether the CV questionnaire is framed in terms of an existing environment resource to be preserved against loss (WTA) or a new environmental resource to be acquired (WTP). When framing effects become so important, the underlying methodology cannot be relied on to give consistent results. The challenge to design a CV methodology that provides credible results remains elusive (Binger et al., 1995), despite efforts of environmental regulators and policymakers to standardize the techniques (e.g., U.S. NOAA, 1993); behavioral theory suggests that this may be akin to the search for a unicorn.

In responding to the challenge of valuing environmental goods (which are unfamiliar commodities), people frequently exhibit preference reversals. In a series of surveys, Irwin et al. (1993) found that people react differently when asked to place relative values on environmental goods and when asked to rank them against other goods. In one survey, 92 subjects were asked whether they would prefer improved air quality or a new computer. When the question was framed as a direct choice between the two, the majority of them preferred better air quality. When instead they were asked to give monetary values to each of the choices, the majority gave a higher value to the new computer. Indeed, a third of the respondents showed a reversal of preferences: they placed a higher value on the computer but preferred the cleaner air. In a related study, Fischhoff et al. (1993) noted that subjects show the embedding phenomenon less frequently when asked to make direct choices rather than assign values. Often, the dollar figure they provide reflects merely a "feel good" statement for preserving the environment, giving them a "warm glow." In the context of a direct choice, individuals rely on different factors to decide whether they prefer environmental preservation to other goods (Fischhoff et al., 1993). Perhaps they are expressing their solidarity with the environmental movement when they are asked to make direct choices, an expression that is more difficult to quantify when assigning monetary values.

The environment is an issue area where people have rarely had to make trade-offs, where they have received little feedback on the consistency of their choices, and yet where there is a need to obtain WTP measures in order to evaluate important policy options. For example, global warming threatens to disrupt ecosystems and exacerbate natural hazards, such as hurricanes, in particular geographic regions. Most people would probably have a negative reaction to global warming and a positive response to averting it. Yet people also have a positive response to cars, light bulbs, and all of the energy-consuming gizmos that contribute to global warming; indeed, they consider these part of their endowment. People in industrialized nations may also have a positive response to allowing developing nations to acquire some of the same material luxuries, although probably not if doing so meant forgoing significant amounts of these luxuries themselves. People have also been choosing cars and electronic gizmos for decades, but have not typically seen these purchases as having a direct effect on climate, and certainly have received no immediate feedback from weather patterns when they drive their car an extra kilometer. So it is likely that people will have poorly informed and poorly defined preferences on the issue of global warming and measures to combat it. At the same time, the issue demands the attention of policymakers, who must take action.

Insufficiency of Private Markets

The status quo bias impedes private markets in their pursuit of economically efficient outcomes. Coase (1960) suggested, in his seminal article leading to the Coase theorem, that many externalities could be dealt with adequately through private negotiations or through markets operating among the affected parties. Assuming minimal transaction costs and well-defined property rights, markets would form between those harmed by externalities and those who create them. Hence, if the damage caused by pollution were smaller than the costs of avoiding it, those people suffering from pollution would pay the polluter to stop. An important element of the Coase theorem is that it does not matter to whom the initial property rights are assigned when income effects are small. Whether the polluter has an initial right to pollute, or the neighbor an initial right to clean air, does not determine the level of pollution they will negotiate. Numerous experiments have attempted to test the Coase theorem empirically (Hoffman & Spitzer, 1993; Knetsch, 1990). The results suggest that the way property rights are initially assigned determines the status quo, and this in turn influences the result of negotiations. If the polluter has property rights, we will end up producing far more pollution than if those who suffer the pollution begin with a right to a clean environment (Kahneman, Knetsch, & Thaler, 1991). Because unresolved externalities are a major environmental problem, government intervention may be necessary to supplement market-based decision making.

Bright Lines

People judge performance relative to bright lines. Usually one side of the bright line is good and the other is bad. How much the bright line is beaten is not so consequential. DeGeorge et al. (1999) find three bright lines (positive profit, last year's earnings, and the consensus of analysts' earnings estimates) for earnings in business firms, and find that businesses manipulate their earnings to get beyond them. These bright lines become important to managers, even if the means to achieve them, such as pushing sales by discounting when one is short of the target, are costly in the long run. Camerer, Babcock, Loewenstein, and Thaler (1997) examined the labor supply among New York City cabdrivers. They found that the drivers set daily earnings targets; on slow days they drive for many hours, whereas on busy days they leave work early. They could earn more money working fewer total hours by working the same number of hours each day, and could do better still by logging long hours on busy days and quitting early when the fares are slow. One way to explain the behavior of managers and cabbies is that people prefer to cross bright lines of some earnings target. They value having made their money goal in a given day or year and will strive to accomplish that goal.

With environmental problems as well, we often enshrine bright lines and struggle beyond them. For example, environmental negotiators in Europe have adopted the standard of *critical loads* for designing a regulatory framework for acid rain (United Nations, 1988). Recognizing that different ecosystems, and even different types of soil, can withstand different threshold levels of acidic deposition from air pollution, they have mapped the deposition levels across Europe that are the highest possible without any observable consequences. Using these maps and knowledge about how wind spreads pollution from factories to fields, they arrived at a very ambitious set of cost-effective emissions reductions, in some places as great as 90% from baseline amounts. Yet as Patt (1999c) discusses, these critical load models are highly arbitrary. The principal benefit of negotiating international policy around a critical load framework is that it provides an apparent bright line that helps to generate consensus.

There are two problems with bright lines. First, they take on too much importance. Moves that cross them are valued too much compared with equally important moves on either side of the bright line. Second, many bright lines in environmental policy are set inappropriately. They often revolve around some mathematical property, such as zero environmental impact or 1 part per million, when a little environmental impact or 3 parts per 10 million might be acceptable and far more achievable. To respond to concerns about equity, uniform bright lines are often set across situations where different standards would be desirable.

There is something particularly attractive about achieving the bright line of "no observable environmental impact." For the same policy problem, acid rain, U.S. policymakers have used equally bright lines of a different character. American air quality standards define an acceptable level of risk, and results are reported in terms of attainment or nonattainment, as opposed to quantitative risk levels. In another piece of regulation, the Clean Air Act Amendments of 1990, total sulfur emissions will be reduced by 10 million tons from baseline amounts. To achieve a cost-effective solution to this very different bright line, the amendments create a system of tradable emissions permits. Both the European and American regulations ensure that environmental targets are reached in a rational manner, but neither guarantees that the target itself is efficient or wise (Stavins & Whitehead, 1997).

Intergenerational Valuation and Commitment Devices

Environmental policy often involves issues that span generations. Schelling (1995) notes that this is a challenging problem. There is no reason, he suggests, that people should care less about the welfare of their great-great-grandchildren than they do about that of their great-grandchildren; they will never know either generation and have an attachment to them based only on genetic proximity. Thus, we should not expect people to continue to discount future events once those events are more than a few generations into the future. But people care very much about their own generation relative to the ones that follow. Should all generations that people will never know be discounted at some level more than those who are alive today should? If so, how does this compare to discounting the welfare of people who live overseas and whom we will never know? Schelling poses the question of whether it makes sense to invest our resources in avoiding climate change when we could potentially help far more people, over the long run, by investing in economic development programs to benefit today's poor and the poor to follow. Is there some sense from an intergenerational perspective in which environmental matters, such as preserving an ocean or the atmosphere from a measured amount of harm, count more than guaranteeing other aspects of material well-being through the provision of productive capital? We do not understand how people's altruism operates across time and space, and they do not seem to either. Absent this knowledge, it is difficult to implement preference-respecting decision making for global, long-term problems.

We argued earlier that long-term preferences might well be reflected with discounting models that consider problems of dynamic inconsistency and attempt to build in commitment devices (Laibson, 1997). Environmental policymaking shows these factors at work. For instance, leaders at the 1992 Earth Summit made a nonbinding commitment to reduce emissions to 1990 levels by the year 2000. The fact that this pledge proved unenforceable provided much of the impetus for the Kyoto Protocol (United Nations, 1997), which called on countries such as the United States to begin reducing greenhouse gas emissions toward a baseline starting in the year 2008. Given the excess weight, relative to straight discounting, that is placed on the present, policymakers are unwilling to take costly steps now to benefit the future, but they are willing to commit to such steps in the future. We can predict that in 2008 the United States and other nations will prefer not to reduce their greenhouse gas emissions to the extent called for by Kyoto, just as many holders of individual retirement accounts wish that they could withdraw their money early. But the agreements put in place now may be too much to overcome in the future and will be undertaken as planned. If we recognize that commitments to future action may be the only way to effect change, it is important to design mechanisms to create and enforce these commitments.

Destination-Driven Costs and Moving Equilibria

When choosing how to model the environment, economists have assumed that environmental cleanup can be represented by traditional supply-and-demand diagrams. Underlying such diagrams are the standard assumptions of continuity and diminishing returns to effort or scale. Even taking the economics approach, in many types of environmental problems this framework simply doesn't apply, as Philips and Zeckhauser (1998) argue. For example, for many types of environmental cleanup problems, the costs are driven not by the amount of cleanup undertaken, but by the level of cleanliness attained, regardless of the starting point. To make a toxic waste dump suitable for building a new school may require incinerating and replacing all of the soil that is contaminated. The cost depends little on the starting level of toxicity. A recognition that costs depend overwhelmingly on the destination and not the starting point, as the continuous case common in environmental economics assumes, leads to a different answer about what level of pollution is desirable, where the pollution should be, and what economic incentives the government should be using to achieve economic efficiency. It becomes desirable to concentrate pollution and to delay cleanup efforts, whereas in a standard economic model, pollution would be evenly spread and cleanup would be continuous.

The importance of increasing returns to scale and discontinuities in environmental problems is especially apparent when managers attempt to maintain a system in a steady state that is seen as most productive for humans. Often, the natural equilibrium is one that changes slowly for a period but then moves quite suddenly. For example, beaches shift in response to storms and accretion, small lakes fill with silt, and rivers alter course. Yet decision makers often perceive one of the various states of the resource as the only natural state and design human infrastructure around it. Oversimplifying the problem of what state or state of flux is natural puts human development at risk. Moreover, protecting that development means holding natural systems out of equilibrium. Shortsightedness creates environmental problems that conventional economics, with its emphasis on equilibrium, will both misperceive and misrepresent. Environmental realities move beyond the limited dimensions of our economic road maps, which have been honed through thinking about markets for apples and labor. Policy cannot be effective if environmental phenomena are crammed into the models and metaphors developed for worlds where property is owned, behavior is tidy, and extreme outcomes are not consequential.

Biased Risk Assessments

At best, expertise offers modest protection against behavioral propensities. For example, Nordhaus (1994a) surveyed a number of experts on climate change from several different disciplines. Economists tended to view climate change as far less of a problem than did the natural scientists – because the mental models of a discipline tend to fence in the imaginations of its practitioners. There was often a high correlation between the assessed seriousness of a particular problem, such as a rapid sea level rise from the melting of polar ice sheets, and the assessed probability of its occurrence. Ecologists, who worry about disruptions of natural systems, see these disruptions as quite probable. Economists, who are used to continuous behaviors, and who worry about the potential of mitigation strategies to produce economic inefficiency, think that acting to avoid climate change has risks at least as great as those of climate change itself. Because for climate change, as for many other environmental problems, there is no historical record on which to assess probabilities, there is little reason to believe that the experts are especially able to do a good job of forecasting the future. Moreover, experts are rewarded by the press or by advocacy groups by the attention they receive, and the spotlight shines when they predict the most extreme outcomes. This creates a substantial problem – selecting the proper estimates. There is no system in place to rate probability assessors, rewarding them after the fact should their estimates prove incisive.

Toward More Accurate Assessments and Superior Policies

A central theme of this chapter is that environmental problems bring behavioral decisions to the fore, challenging effective long-term decision making. We make two modest proposals: the first a diagnostic tool, the second a proposed therapy. First, we set forth a framework for thinking about the predictions of behavioral decision theory for environmental issues, which typically involve several heuristics and biases. The framework identifies a common thread: the human tendency to have either excessive or insensitive reactions to environmental problems. Second, we propose a mechanism that we believe could help increase the accuracy of assessments of environmental problems that drive policy. Basically, we propose the establishment of future markets, in effect betting markets, that would enable analysts to "put their money where their mouth is" when making predictions about environmental consequences. Such a mechanism would reduce the rewards for vociferous and extreme advocacy, and provide a venue where the best current estimates could be found.

Table 11.2. *Attributes of and Responses to Environmental Risks*

	Responses	
	---	---
Attributes	*Excessive Reactions*	*Insensitive Reactions*
Probabilities	Small probabilities; changes near 0 and 1	Changes elsewhere
Presence of money	Changes in money	Changes in other valued attributes
Direction of change	Losses; gains versus losses	Gains
Timing of problem	Now to $t + 1$	Periods after $t + 1$

A Behavioral Biases Framework: Excessive and Insensitive Reactions

Behavioral decision theory predicts how individuals' decisions deviate from a rational norm. With respect to environmental policy, these deviations take the form of excess or insensitive reactions: Sometimes policy responses are greater than the assessed risks justify; sometimes policy responses are too little, too late, or nonexistent. Because in many instances we can predict when each of these biases is likely to appear, this unidimensional characterization of biases informs us about our central policy concern: how policy should be shifted.

Table 11.2 organizes the typology. The dependent variable is the response to the problem and it is excessive or insensitive relative to the problem's magnitude. We address four attributes of risk: their probabilities, whether money (and hence other forms of consumption) is involved, the direction of change, and timing. To illustrate, an increase in a risk for the left-hand column – excessive reactions – will get more weight than one for the right-hand column. For example, a .01 reduction in risk when a risk starts at .01 will be valued more than when the initial risk is .4. Knowing the values of these four variables, one could predict the nature of the response to the environmental problem. Indeed, in theory, one could run a regression on a number of environmental problems and obtain beta values for each of the independent variables. Bright line thresholds are involved with each attribute. Thus, crossing the loss–gain threshold or approaching the 0 or 1 bright line for probabilities increases the importance of a fixed increment of something harmful or beneficial. Whether the risk is financial is important for two reasons: First, it changes a person's consumption in other areas of life; second, it is a means of accounting more familiar to most people than numbers of bacteria or adjusted life years. Other factors equal, we posit that people make better decisions when money is involved. For example, they are more sensitive to differences in money quantities than in quantities of air pollution.

Other heuristics or problems could be included in our table. For each, we would want to determine the circumstances in which society would over- and underact. For example, new risks get an excessive reaction because they come against a background of zero known risk in that category, and the benefits that come with those risks are not part of people's endowments. Politically, interest groups will not yet have formed to protect these benefits for a segment of society. There are, of course, other bright lines in the environmental field and perhaps other illuminated dimensions. The central point is that particular changes in outcomes will make the risk especially salient for decision making. For example, we strive for complete safety, we struggle hard to avoid losses in wealth, and we cater excessively to the present. Advocacy groups recognize these tendencies by citizens and policymakers. When confronting a real environmental problem, proenvironment groups attempt to frame the issue using the four independent variables to promote an excessive response. Their opposition, often industry groups, makes policymakers and citizens feel that an insensitive response is more appropriate.

Futures Market

One way to force more systematic analysis is to open up derivative markets for environmental problems. One of the great virtues of ordinary financial markets is that they elicit all available information, say about the value of a stock. If an individual knows that IBM is undervalued, she will purchase the company's stock until it is brought into line. The possible poaching on others' poor decisions ensures that prices reasonably represent value. A second great virtue of these markets, which reward foresightful decisions, is that extremely intelligent individuals research the value of securities. Some critics would claim that there is excess attention to securities valuation, because most of the return from research comes from extracting value from others, not from any social gain. This argument would hardly apply to research on the likely global warming consequences of our present emissions policies, where research leading to a convergence of beliefs would be of enormous value. If policymakers had a much firmer grasp of what would happen their policies would be much improved. In other words, the ratio of public benefit relative to private gain from a futures market is much greater for global warming than for the prices of computer stocks.

The third virtue of establishing a futures market is that it would dampen the ability of advocacy groups to misrepresent their true beliefs. For example, if an energy company confidently announced that global temperatures were unlikely to rise by more than 1°C over the next two decades but the futures market predicted a median increase of 3°C, the company would have a hard time explaining why the market had gotten the answer so wrong. Why hadn't experts and arbitrageurs listened to the company and driven down the estimates of the consequences? Why hadn't the company itself engaged in arbitrage to profit heavily from an incorrect assessment?

There would be a number of difficulties in developing a derivatives market relating to environmental consequences. We mention two. First, many of the consequences would be hard to measure. Second, the consequences may not become known for decades. In theory, the long time delays are not a problem. We might, in effect, have a security that would pay off in 50 years. Its current value will anticipate how each period would sell it to the next, in somewhat the same way that growth stocks, with no earnings expected for years, are able to value the far future. But whether investors would be willing to tie up their capital for such a long period is not clear. And arbitrageurs, whose participation would be welcome, have particularly high discount rates, given their ability to reap high returns from their capital at work. Recognizing these problems, we believe that an effective futures market might rely on indicators of environmental consequences, not the consequences themselves. The indicators might be available in a relatively short period of time. For example, we might use the degree of concentration of greenhouse gases in the environment as the surrogate for the longer-term problem of global warming.

An environmental futures market would bring a fourth benefit. It would provide immediate feedback on the expected environmental consequences of policy actions. This benefit is well understood now in the economics world. Financial markets discipline the behaviors of prime ministers and finance ministers, and punish those who boost the deficit. So too, a futures market for the environment would provide a continuous barometer of the consequences of policy, such as altering the Clean

Air Act or signing a global treaty on the environment. It would tell us which actions are consequential and which ones mere bandages.

Conclusion

Citizens confronting environmental issues have severe problems thinking systematically about the likelihood of and valuation of possible outcomes. And the disagreements between economists, the self-appointed guardians of material well-being, and ecologists, who view the environment as their domain of responsibility, are harsher still. When the experts disagree, it is harder for citizens to think clearly, much less advocate sensible decisions.

The most consequential environmental problems – climate change, loss of biodiversity, and sustainable development – involve uncertainty, requiring the calculation and use of probabilities, an area of profound misunderstanding for the public. Such problems are not mere exercises in computation; probabilistic phenomena do not lend themselves to determining in a dispute who was right and who was wrong. When the events involve relatively small probabilities of something consequential, as is frequently the case with the environment – living near this dump gives you 1 chance in 10,000 of developing cancer – learning is further diminished. And when something bad does happen, it often comes many years into the future, when it is too late to reverse course. Often, as with cancer, even if the outcome is known, it is hard to determine the contribution of environmental causes.

Legislators may be no better equipped than citizens to make decisions, but this matters little because citizens' perceptions, not reality as viewed by experts, are the primary basis for legislative actions pertaining to the environment. But some players do understand how citizens and legislators respond, whether behaviorally or rationally. Mostly these are the players in the environment – the activists, the lobbyists, and the expert witnesses. These actors seek to harness human proclivities to their own purposes, whether it be to get a high valuation of some environmental amenity or harm, or to frame the loss of jobs from some environmental measure as monumental.

Behavioral decision theory best models human intelligence in worlds with severe uncertainties, many attributes, long time frames, and a primordial measuring rod other than money. These are the conditions of the field of environmental decision making. Researchers in many fields – economics, political science, and sociology, to name three – would be wise to consider the lessons of behavioral decision theory as they examine people's motives for acting toward the environment. At the same time, researchers into behavioral decisions would be wise to look to the environment as a rich source of new data on people's decision-making abilities and predictable pathologies.

References

Binger, B., Copple, R., & Hoffman, E. (1995). Contingent valuation methodology in the natural resource damage regulatory process: Choice theory and the embedding phenomenon. *Natural Resources Journal, 35,* 443–459.

Breyer, S. (1993). *Breaking the vicious circle: Toward effective risk regulation.* Cambridge, MA: Harvard University Press.

Camerer, C., Babcock, L., Loewenstein, G., & Thaler, R. (1997). Labor supply of New York City cabdrivers: One day at a time. *The Quarterly Journal of Economics, 112,* 407–442.

Clark, W. (Ed.). (in press). *Social learning.* Cambridge, MA: MIT Press.

Coase, R. (1960). The problem of social cost. *Journal of Law and Economics, 3,* 1–31.

Damasio, A. (1994). *Descartes' error: Emotion, reason, and the human brain.* New York: G. P. Putnam.

DeGeorge, F., Patel, J., & Zeckhauser, R. (1999). Earnings management to exceed thresholds. *Journal of Business, 72,* 1–34.

Diekman, K., Samuels, S., Ross, L., & Bazerman, M. (1997). Self-interest and fairness in problems of resource allocation: Allocators versus recipients. *Journal of Personality and Social Psychology, 72,* 1061–1074.

Fischhoff, B. (1985). Risk perception and communication unplugged: Twenty years of progress. *Risk Analysis, 15,* 137–145.

Fischhoff, B. (1995). Managing risk perceptions. *Issues in Science and Technology, 2.* Washington, DC: National Academy of Sciences.

Fischhoff, B. (1996). Public values in risk research. *Annals of the American Academy of Political and Social Science, 545,* 75–84.

Fischhoff, B. (1997). Ranking risks. In M. Bazerman, D. Messick, A. Tenbrunsel, & K. Wade-Benzoni (Eds.), *Environment, ethics, and behavior* (pp. 342–372). San Francisco: New Lexington Press.

Fischhoff, B., Quadrel, M., Kamlet, M., Loewenstein, G., Dawes, R., Fishbeck, P., Klepper, S., Leland, J., & Stroh, P. (1993). Embedding effects: Stimulus representation and response mode. *Journal of Risk and Uncertainty, 6,* 211–234.

Gordon, D., & Kammen, D. (1996). Uncertainty and overconfidence in time series forecasts: Application to the Standard & Poor's 500 stock index. *Applied Financial Economics, 6,* 189–198.

Gregory, R., Lichtenstein, S., & Slovic, P. (1993). Valuing environmental resources: A constructive approach. *Journal of Risk and Uncertainty, 7,* 177–197.

Hoffman, E., & Spitzer, M. (1993). Willingness to pay vs. willingness to accept: Legal and economic implications. *Washington University Law Quarterly, 71,* 59–114.

Huber, P., & Litan, R. (Eds.). (1991). *The liability maze: The impact of liability law on safety and innovation.* Washington, DC: The Brookings Institution.

Irwin. J., Schenk, D., McClelland, G., Schultz, W., Stewart, T., & Thayer, M. (1990). Urban visibility: Some experiments on the contingent valuation method. In C. V. Mathei (Ed.), *Visibility and fine particles* (pp. 647–658). Pittsburgh: Air and Waste Management Association.

Irwin, J., Slovic, P., Lichtenstein, S., & McClelland, G. (1993). Preference reversals and the measurement of environmental values. *Journal of Risk and Uncertainty, 6*, 5–18.

Kahneman, D. (1986). Comments on the contingent valuation method. In R. D. Cummings, D. Brookshire, & W. Schulz (Eds.), *Valuing environmental goods: An assessment of the contingent valuation method* (pp. 185–194). Totowa, NJ: Rowman and Allenheld.

Kahneman, D., Retov, I., & Schkade, D. (1999). Economic preferences or attitude expression? An analysis of dollar responses to public issues. *Journal of Risk and Uncertainty, 19*, 203–236.

Kahneman, D., Knetsch, J., & Thaler, R. (1991). Experimental tests of the endowment effect and the coase theorem. In R. Thaler (Ed.), *Quasi-rational economics* (pp. 167–188). New York: Russell Sage Foundation.

Kahneman, D., & Tversky, A. (1974). Judgment under uncertainty: Heuristics and biases. *Science, 185*, 1124–1131.

Kahneman, D., & Tversky, A. (1979). Prospect theory: An analysis of decision under risk. *Econometrica, 47*, 263–291.

Kammen, D., Shlyakhter, A., & Wilson, R. (1994). What is the risk of the impossible? *Journal of the Franklin Institute, 331A*, 97–116.

Knetsch, J. (1990). Environmental policy implications of disparities between willingness-to-pay and compensation-demanded measures of values. *Journal of Environmental Economics and Management, 18*, 227–237.

Laibson, D. (1997). Golden eggs and hyperbolic discounting. *Quarterly Journal of Economics, 112*, 443–478.

Ludwig, D., Hilborn, R., & Walters, C. (1993). Uncertainty, resource exploitation, and conservation: Lessons from history. *Science, 260*, 17, 36.

Manne, A., & Richels, R. (1991). Buying greenhouse insurance. *Energy Policy, 19*, 543–552.

Metrick, A., & Weitzman, M. (1996). Patterns of behavior in endangered species preservation. *Land Economics, 72*, 1–16.

Mintzer, I. (1987). *A matter of degrees*. Washington, DC: World Resources Institute.

Morgan, G., & Dowlatabadi, H. (1996). Learning from integrated assessment of climate change. *Climatic Change, 34*, 337–368.

Morgan, G., & Henrion, M. (1990). *Uncertainty: A guide to dealing with uncertainty in quantitative risk and policy analysis*. New York: Cambridge University Press.

National Research Council (1992). *Policy implications of greenhouse warming: Mitigation, adaptation, and the science base*. Washington, DC: National Academy Press.

Nordhaus, W. (1994a). Expert opinion on climate change. *American Scientist, 80*, 45–51.

Nordhaus, W. (1994b). *Managing the global commons*. Cambridge, MA: MIT Press.

Patt, A. (1999a). Assessing extreme outcomes: The strategic treatment of low probability impacts in scientific assessment. *Risk, Decision, and Policy, 4*, 1–15.

Patt, A. (1999b). Economists and ecologists: Modeling global climate change to different conclusions. *International Journal of Sustainable Development*, 2, 245–62.

Patt, A. (1999c). Separating analysis from politics: Acid rain in Europe. *Policy Studies Review*, 16, 104–137.

Phillips, C., & Zeckhauser, R. (1998). Restoring natural resources with destination-driven costs. *Journal of Environmental Economics and Management*, 36, 225–242.

Samuelson, W., & Zeckhauser, R. (1988). Status quo bias in decision making. *Journal of Risk and Uncertainty*, 1, 7–59.

Schelling, T. (1995). Intergenerational discounting. *Energy Policy*, 23, 395–402.

Schultz, W. (1985). *Bessere Luft, was ist sie uns wert? Eine gesellschaftliche Bedarfsanalyse auf der Basis indivueller Zahlungsbereitschaften*. Berlin: Umweltbundesamt.

Shafir, E., Diamond, P., & Tversky, A. (1997). Money illusion. *The Quarterly Journal of Economics*, 112, 341–374.

Shiller, R. (1997). *Public resistance to indexation: A puzzle*. Paper No. 946. New Haven, CT: Cowles Foundation.

Shlyakhter, A., Kammen, D., Broido, C., & Wilson, R. (1994). Quantifying the credibility of energy projections from trends in past data. *Energy Policy* 22(2), 119–130.

Slovic, P. (1987). Perception of risk. *Science*, 236, 280–285.

Stavins, R., & Whitehead, B. (1997). *The next generation of market-based environmental policies*. Cambridge, MA: Kennedy School of Government Faculty Research Working Paper Series R96–17.

Thaler, R. (1991). The psychology of choice and the assumptions of economics. In R. Thaler (Ed.). *Quasi-rational economics* (pp. 137–166). New York: Russell Sage Foundation.

Tversky, A., & Kahneman, D. (1973). Availability: A heuristic for judging frequency and probability. *Cognitive Psychology* 5, 207–232.

Tversky, A., & Kahneman, D. (1988). Rational choice and the framing of decisions. In D. Bell, H. Raiffa, & A. Tversky (Eds.), *Decision making: Descriptive, normative, and prescriptive interactions* (pp. 167–192). Cambridge: Cambridge University Press.

United Nations (1988). *Cost-impact and economic impact analyses of different SO_x and NO_x abatement strategies*. Geneva: United Nations Economic Committee for Europe Executive Body for the Convention on Long-Range Transboundary Air Pollution, Group of Economic Experts on Air Pollution.

United Nations. (1997). *Kyoto protocol to the United Nations framework convention on climate change*. Kyoto: Conference of the Parties, Third Session.

U.S. Environmental Protection Agency. (1987). *Unfinished business*. Washington, DC: U.S. Government Printing Office.

U.S. NOAA Panel. (1993, January 15). Report of the NOAA panel on contingent valuation. *Federal Register*, 58, 4602–4614.

van der Sluijs, J. (1997). *Anchoring amid uncertainty: On the management of uncertainties in risk assessment of anthropogenic climate change*. Leiden: Ludy Feyen.

Walsh, R., Bjonback, R., Aiken, R., & Rosenthal, D. (1990). Estimating the public benefit of protecting forest quality. *Journal of Environmental Management*, 30, 175–189.

Walters, C. (1986). *Adaptive management of renewable resources*. New York: Cambridge University Press.

Wynne, B. (1996). Misunderstood misunderstandings: Social identities and the public uptake of science. In A. Irwin & B. Wynne (Eds.), *Misunderstanding science? The public reconstruction of science and technology* (pp. 19–40). Cambridge: Cambridge University Press.

Zeckhauser, R., Shearer, G., & Memishian, P. (1975). *Decision analysis for flight in the stratosphere*. Washington, DC: Department of Transportation, Climatic Impact Assessment Program.

Zeckhauser, R., & Viscusi, W. (1990). Risk within reason. *Science, 248*, 559–564.

Zeckhauser, R., & Viscusi, W. (1996). The risk management dilemma. *Annals of the American Academy of Political and Social Science, 545*, 144–155.

12 The Affect Heuristic: Implications for Understanding and Managing Risk-Induced Stigma

Howard Kunreuther and Paul Slovic

The word *stigma* was used by the ancient Greeks to refer to a mark placed on an individual to signify infamy or disgrace. One defining characteristic of a stigma is the risk that the marked person is perceived to pose to society. Within the social sciences, there is an extensive literature on the topic of stigma as it applies to people and social groups. By means of its association with risk, the concept of stigma has recently come to be generalized to technologies, places, and products that are perceived as unduly dangerous.

Stigma plays out socially in opposition to many industrial activities and products, particularly those involving the use of chemicals and radiation, and in the large and rapidly growing number of lawsuits claiming that one's property has been devalued by perceptions of risk.

The emergence of these new forms of stigma is a result of the modern world's concern about human health and ecological risks – a concern amplified by the vast power of communications media to spread the word about risks. But stigma goes beyond conceptions of hazard. Many conditions are known to be hazardous; stigma refers to something that is to be shunned or avoided not just because it is dangerous but also because it overturns or destroys a positive condition, signaling that what was or should be something good is now marked as blemished or tainted. As a result, stigmatization is a powerful component of public opposition to many technologies, products, and facilities. It represents an increasingly significant factor influencing the development and acceptance of scientific and technological innovations.

When stigmatization takes place, the social consequences and economic losses can be catastrophic (witness the impact of the bovine spongiform encephalopathy scare on the beef industry in Britain).

Risk-induced stigma thus exposes people and important social institutions to a new and extreme form of vulnerability.

This chapter examines the behavioral foundation of stigma and explores ways to manage it better. Particular emphasis is placed on the
role of imagery, affect, and emotion in creating and maintaining stigma.

Imagery, Affect, and Stigma

To create and evaluate strategies for dealing with the destructive effects
of stigma, we must understand something of its nature. Building on the
work of a large number of behavioral scientists, we propose a model in
which stigma is based on negative imagery that has become associated
with places, products, technologies, and, of course, people.

The eminent learning theorist Hobart Mowrer (1960a, 1960b), for
example, concluded that human behavior is guided and controlled in
a generally sensible and adaptive manner by conditioned emotional
responses to images that could be viewed as "prospective gains and
losses." More recently Damasio (1994) argues that human thought is
created largely from images, broadly construed to include perceptual
and symbolic representations. Through experience, these images become "marked" by positive and negative feelings (Mowrer and other
learning theorists would call this *conditioning*), and these feelings motivate action. When a negative marker is linked to an image, it sounds
an alarm and motivates avoidance. When we think of the prime targets for stigmatization in our society – members of minority groups, the
aged, homosexuals, drug addicts, and persons afflicted with physical
deformities and mental disabilities – we can appreciate the affect-laden
images that, rightly or wrongly, are associated with such individuals.

Empirical Evidence

Empirical support for the proposed relationship between images,
affect, decision making, and stigma has come from a program of research at Decision Research (Slovic et al., 1991). This work was initially
motivated by a practical question: What is the potential for a high-level
nuclear waste repository at Yucca Mountain to stigmatize the city of Las
Vegas and the State of Nevada, thus producing significant economic
impacts in those places? Building on previous research linking images
and behavior, the studies were designed to develop a measure of environmental imagery, assess the relationship between imagery and choice

behavior, and describe economic impacts that might occur as a result of altered images and choices.

Specifically, research was designed to test the following three propositions: (1) Images associated with environments have diverse positive and negative affective meanings that influence preferences (e.g., in this case, preferences for sites in which to vacation, retire, find a job, or start a new business); (2) a nuclear-waste repository evokes a wide variety of strongly negative images, consistent with extreme perceptions of risk and stigmatization; and (3) the repository at Yucca Mountain and the negative images it evokes will, over time, become increasingly salient in the images of Nevada and of Las Vegas. If these three propositions are true, it seems quite plausible that, as the imagery of Las Vegas and of Nevada becomes increasingly associated with the repository, the attractiveness of these places to tourists, job seekers, retirees, and business developers will decrease and their choices of Las Vegas and Nevada within sets of competing sites will decrease.

Our results showed that the concept of a nuclear-waste storage facility evoked extreme negative imagery (Proposition 2) indicative of stigmatization. Dominant associations to a repository were "dangerous," "death," "pollution," "bad," "undesirable," and "somewhere else." The nuclear-weapons test site, which has been around far longer than the Yucca Mountain nuclear-waste project, was found to have led to a modest amount of nuclear imagery becoming associated with the State of Nevada. This provided indirect evidence for Proposition 3, which asserts that nuclear-waste-related images will also become associated with Nevada and Las Vegas if the Yucca Mountain Project proceeds. Moreover, nuclear imagery, when present in a person's associations to Nevada, was found to be linked with much lower preference for Nevada as a vacation site, indicative of a stigmatization response. (This imagery is not shown in the set of images in Table 12.1.)

Table 12.1 illustrates the results obtained by asking one respondent to associate to each of four cities and, later, to rate each image affectively. An overall affective score is obtained for each stimulus city by summing the individual ratings. The cities in this example produce a clear affective ordering, with San Diego being perceived most favorably and Los Angeles most negatively. The research showed that image scores such as these were highly predictive of expressed preferences for living, working, and vacationing in different places (see Table 12.1). In one study we found that the image score predicted the location of actual vacations taken over the next 18 months.[1]

Table 12.1. *Images, Ratings, and Summation Scores for Respondent 132*

Stimulus	Image No.	Image	Rating	Stimulus	Image No.	Image	Rating
San Diego	1	Very nice	2	Denver	1	High	2
San Diego	2	Good beaches	2	Denver	2	Crowded	0
San Diego	3	Zoo	2	Denver	3	Cool	2
San Diego	4	Busy freeway	1	Denver	4	Pretty	1
San Diego	5	Easy to find way	1	Denver	5	Busy airport	−2
San Diego	6	Pretty town	2	Denver	6	Busy streets	−2
		SUM = 10				SUM = 1	
Las Vegas	1	Rowdy town	−2	Los Angeles	1	Smoggy	−2
Las Vegas	2	Busy town	−1	Los Angeles	2	Crowded	−2
Las Vegas	3	Casinos	−1	Los Angeles	3	Dirty	−2
Las Vegas	4	Bright lights	−1	Los Angeles	4	Foggy	−1
Las Vegas	5	Too much	−2	Los Angeles	5	Sunny	0
Las Vegas	6	Gambling out of the way	0	Los Angeles	6	Drug place	−2
		SUM = −7				SUM = −9	

Note: Based on these summation scores, this person's predicted preference for a vacation site would be San Diego.

Source: Reprinted from "Perceived Risk, Stigma, and Potential Economic Impacts of a High-Level Nuclear Waste Repository in Nevada" by P. Slovic, M. Layman, N. Kraus, J. Flynn, J. Chalmers, and G. Gesell, 1991, *Risk Analysis*, 11(4), p. 690. Copyright 1991 Society for Risk Analysis. Reprinted with permission.

In sum, the research pertaining to Yucca Mountain supported the three propositions that the study aimed to test: Images of cities and states, derived from a word-association technique, exhibited positive and negative affective meanings that were highly predictive of preferences for vacation sites, job and retirement locations, and business sites (Proposition 1).

The image of chemical technologies is so stigmatized that when you ask college students or members of the general public to tell you what first comes to mind when they hear the word *chemicals*, by far the most frequent response is "dangerous" or some similar response (e.g., "toxic," "hazardous," "poison," "deadly," "cancer"); beneficial uses of chemicals are rarely mentioned. National surveys have found that about 75% of the public agrees with the statement "I try hard to avoid contact with chemicals and chemical products in my everyday life" (Krewski, Slovic, Bartlett, Flynn, & Mertz, 1995).

The salience and availability of certain images may help explain why a product, place, or industry is likely to be stigmatized even when only one expert views a situation as being dangerous and points out what can happen from an adverse incident. There is considerable empirical evidence suggesting that individuals often focus on the consequences associated with specific events, particularly if they are characterized in a salient way. In these situations, little attention is given to the chances of its occurrence (Camerer & Kunreuther, 1989). Consider the following example of a failed attempt to site a liquefied natural gas (LNG) facility in California during the 1970s. Three locations were proposed for the facility. One was Oxnard, California, where there was considerable opposition by citizen groups. One of the opposition groups focused attention on a series of worst-case scenarios developed for them by a consulting firm showing the number of fatalities from accidents due to vapor cloud explosions without accompanying probabilities.

A series of maps of the community were drawn that depicted the impacts of these vapor cloud explosions should the wind be blowing in different directions. Any resident of Oxnard could find his or her house covered by a vapor cloud on at least one of the maps. This study was used by citizen groups to claim that an LNG facility would stigmatize Oxnard and decrease property values, even though scientific experts all reported extremely low probabilities of these events occurring.[2] The impact of the opposition was sufficiently strong that the California legislature passed a new Siting Act that redefined eligible siting areas so that Oxnard was officially excluded because it was viewed as too dangerous (Kunreuther & Linnerooth, 1982).

The Affect Heuristic

Recent research has further expanded our understanding of affect and demonstrated its strong influence on judgment and decision making. MacGregor, Slovic, Dreman, and Berry (in press) showed that the affective quality of images associated with an industry group (e.g., computer software companies, pharmaceuticals, railroads) was highly predictive of decisions to purchase stock in a new company within that industry. Benthin et al. (1995) found that images held by adolescents with regard to activities such as smoking and drinking were predictive of whether or not they engaged in those activities.

Finucane, Alhakami, Slovic, and Johnson (2000) linked the results just described to the operation of what they called the *affect heuristic*. Noting that representations of objects and events in people's minds (i.e., images) are tagged to varying degrees with affect, they argued that people consult or refer to an *affective pool* (containing all the positive and negative tags associated with the representations consciously or unconsciously) in the process of making judgments. Just as imaginability, memorability, and similarity serve as cues for probability judgments (e.g., the availability and representativeness heuristics), affect may serve as a cue for many important judgments. Using an overall, readily available affective impression can be far easier – more efficient – than weighing the pros and cons or retrieving from memory many relevant examples, especially when the required judgment or decision is complex or mental resources are limited. This characterization of a mental shortcut led them to label reliance on affect a heuristic. They went on to demonstrate how the affect heuristic produces the inverse relationship between perceived risk and perceived benefit that has been observed in many studies.

The Social Amplification of Risk and Stigma

Although negative images are created through direct experiences such as bad odors, ugly landscapes, accidents, illnesses, and so on, the greatest contributor to stigmatizing imagery, by far, is the news media, which play a major role in the social amplification of risk. Social amplification, as schematized in Figure 12.1, is triggered by the occurrence of

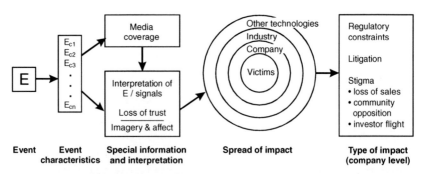

Figure 12.1. A preliminary model of social amplification of risk and stigma impacts. Development of the model will require knowledge of how the characteristics (E_c) associated with a hazard event interact to determine media coverage and the interpretation or message drawn from the event. The nature of the media coverage and the interpretation is presumed to determine the type and magnitude of ripple effects. Reprinted with permission from "Perception of Risk" by P. Slovic, *Science*, 236, 1987, p. 284. Copyright 1987 American Association for the Advancement of Science.

an adverse event, such as a major or minor accident, a discovery of pollution, an incident of sabotage, and so on.

Risk amplification reflects the fact that the adverse impacts of such an event sometimes extend far beyond the direct damage to victims and property, and may result in massive indirect impacts such as litigation against a company or loss of sales, increased regulation of an industry, and, of course, stigmatization. In some cases, all companies within an industry are affected, regardless of which company was responsible for the mishap. Thus, the event can be thought of as a stone dropped in a pond. The ripples spread outward, encompassing first the directly affected victims, then the responsible company or agency, and in the extreme, reaching other companies, agencies, or industries. In addition to the British beef incident mentioned earlier, other well-known examples of events resulting in extreme higher-order impacts include the chemical manufacturing accident at Bhopal, India, the disastrous launch of the space shuttle Challenger, the nuclear-reactor accidents at Three Mile Island and Chernobyl, the adverse effects of the drug thalidomide, the Exxon *Valdez* oil spill, and the adulteration of Tylenol capsules with cyanide. An important feature of social amplification is that the direct impacts need not be too large to trigger major indirect impacts. The seven deaths due to Tylenol tampering resulted in more than 125,000 stories in the print media alone, and inflicted losses of more than $1 billion on the Johnson & Johnson Company, due to the damaged image of the product (Mitchell, 1989).

It appears likely that multiple mechanisms contribute to the social amplification of risk. First, extensive media coverage of an event can contribute to heightened perceptions of risk, propagation of affect-laden, stigmatizing images, and amplified impacts (Burns, Slovic, Kasperson, Kasperson, Renn, & Emani, 1993). Second, a particular risk or risk event may enter into the agenda of social groups, or what Mazur (1981) terms the *partisans*, within the community or nation. The public relations attack on Alar by the Natural Resources Defense Council demonstrates the high media profile and important impacts that special interest groups can trigger (Moore, 1989).

A third amplification mechanism arises out of the interpretation of unfortunate events as clues or signals regarding the magnitude of the risk and the adequacy of the risk management process (Burns et al., 1993; Slovic, 1987). The informativeness or signal potential of a mishap, and thus its potential social impact, appears to be systematically related to the perceived characteristics of the hazard. An accident that takes many lives may produce relatively little social disturbance (beyond that caused to the victims' families and friends) if it occurs as part of a familiar and well-understood system (e.g., a train wreck). However, a small accident in an unfamiliar system (or one perceived as poorly understood), such as a nuclear-waste repository or a recombinant-DNA laboratory, may have immense social consequences if it is perceived as a harbinger of future and possibly catastrophic mishaps.

Carcinogens and Stigma: A Special Problem

Many substances, activities, and technologies have become stigmatized in our society because of their proven or suspected associations with cancer. Chemicals, radiation and radiation technologies (e.g., nuclear power, nuclear-waste storage), asbestos, and electromagnetic fields come quickly to mind in this regard. We shall briefly discuss why this is so and, in subsequent sections, point out its implications for managing stigma.

The pain and drawn-out suffering of cancer make it one of the most dreaded diseases in many societies. The very name *cancer* or the label *carcinogen* evokes dreaded images and stigmatizing avoidance responses. Avoidance responses to carcinogens are amplified when exposure is perceived as involuntary, when the risks are unfamiliar or viewed as poorly understood, when the victims are young and innocent, and when the benefits of the activity are small or distributed inequitably across society.

In addition, there are several major problems with risk assessment studies of carcinogens. First, it is now widely believed that animal studies overpredict cancer because the high doses used in such studies kill cells and overpower natural defense mechanisms in ways that would not happen in humans exposed to far lower doses of the chemical in question. Yet the public believes that chemicals that cause cancer in animals (at any dose) cause cancer in humans, even if scientists do not believe this (Kraus, Malmfors, & Slovic, 1992; Slovic, Satterfield, Mertz, & Flynn, 1996; Slovic, Malmfors, Mertz, Neil, & Purchase, 1997). Similar problems occur with epidemiological studies of risk that often seem better able to frighten the public than to reduce scientific uncertainty (MacGregor, Slovic, & Morgan, 1994).

Second, in order to be conservative and provide maximum protection for the public, cancer risk assessments are based on assumptions designed to minimize the chance that the risk will be underestimated. Data for animals exposed to chemicals at high doses are extrapolated to low doses using a linear, no-threshold model. No exposure is said to be without risk. A very small exposure to a carcinogen may be estimated as producing, say, 1 case of cancer per 100,000 people, but if 1 million people are exposed, this leads to an estimated 10 cases of cancer. In fact, such low risks could well be zero.

High signal potential and extensive media coverage typically accompany events or scenarios involving exposure to carcinogens. One of the most dramatic examples of media-amplified stigmatization of a product occurred in the spring of 1989, when millions of consumers stopped buying apples and apple products after CBS ran a news story on *60 Minutes* stating that the chemical Alar could cause cancer. The assertion that Alar was carcinogenic was based on animal studies that were considered suspect because the doses used had been so large as to have been acutely toxic. Moreover, there was no evidence from epidemiological studies showing Alar to be a human carcinogen. Nevertheless, the public reaction was extreme. The losses to apple growers would undoubtedly have been even greater had they not stopped using Alar soon after the CBS program was aired.

Within a year of the Alar scare, a minute amount of benzene (a known human carcinogen) was found in water bottled by Perrier. The contamination did not originate in the mineral water itself, but from dirty filters used in the process of adding carbon dioxide to the water to give it its fizz. Although the health risk was judged by the Food and Drug Administration (FDA) to be nil, every bottle of Perrier worldwide was withdrawn from the market in response to consumer pressure. Perrier estimated its short-term losses at $79 million (Reuters, 1990). During the year following the incident, Perrier lost half of its share of the U.S. imported mineral water market as a result of the stigmatization of its product.

These strong reactions to Alar and benzene are understandable in light of risk-perception studies that have found a high percentage of the public (70% or more) believing that any contact with a carcinogen (no matter how small or how brief) is likely to lead to cancer (Kraus et al., 1992). As a result of this belief, people want absolutely no contact with substances that are believed to be carcinogenic. Weinstein (1988), for example, found that 85% of the respondents in his survey of New Jersey residents agreed that "If even a tiny amount of a cancer-producing substance were found in my water, I wouldn't drink it." This *mental model of carcinogenesis* stands in stark contrast to the way that scientists think about the risks from chemicals. The fundamental principle of toxicology is the fact that *the dose makes the poison*.[3] Scientists believe that even very toxic substances, including carcinogens, may pose little risk if the dose is small enough.

Psychological and anthropological research provides insight into why people are so concerned about even minute exposures to carcinogenic substances. Frazer (1959) and Mauss (1972) described a belief, widespread in many cultures, that things that have been in contact with each other may influence each other through transfer of some of their properties via an *essence*. Thus, "once in contact, always in contact," even if that contact (exposure) is brief. Rozin, Millman, and Nemeroff (1986) show that this belief system, which they refer to as a *law of contagion*, is common in our present culture. The implication of this research is that even a minute amount of a toxic substance in one's food will be seen as imparting toxicity to the food; any amount of a carcinogenic substance will impart carcinogenicity, and so on.

The *essence of harm* that is contagious is typically referred to as *contamination*. Being contaminated has an all-or-none quality to it – like being alive or being pregnant. When a young child drops a sucker on the floor, the brief contact with "dirt" may be seen as contaminating the candy, causing the parent to throw it away rather than washing it off and returning it to the child's mouth. This all-or-none quality irrespective of the degree of exposure is evident in the observation by Erikson (1990) that "To be exposed to radiation or other toxins . . . is to be contaminated in some deep and lasting way, to feel dirtied, tainted, corrupted" (p. 122). The effect of contagion or contamination, in the public's view, is consistent with the workings of the affect heuristic described earlier. It is also very different from the scientist's model of how contact with a chemical induces carcinogenesis or other kinds of harm. In the scientific model, exposure (and the resulting risk) is viewed as a continuum, rather than as an all-or-none phenomenon.

The stigmatization and avoidance of such products as red apples treated with Alar and Perrier water containing benzene, and the decline in property values in neighborhoods exposed to contamination by carcinogenic pollutants, thus appear both understandable and to some extent predictable in light of research on perceived risk, affect, and social amplification of risk.

Strategies for Coping with Stigma

From the previous discussion, we can see why stigma is so powerful a phenomenon and so hard to manage. It arises from fundamental psychological processes of imagery, affect, and learned associations between the two, amplified by the media and by the use of risk assessment studies whose results are often uncertain or distrusted. It can lower demand for the affected goods, so that residents and businesses are economically harmed, sometimes severely.

In this section we discuss a number of potential strategies for reducing vulnerability to stigma. These include efforts to

- prevent the occurrence of stigmatizing events,
- reduce perceived risk, and
- reduce the number of stigmatizing messages and their social amplification.

Prevent Stigmatizing Events

One implication of signals, ripples, and stigma is that effort and expense beyond those indicated by the expected losses from direct impacts (the inner circle in Figure 12.1) might be warranted to reduce the frequency of occurrence of high-signal, stigmatizing events. For example, in the event of another "contained" core-damaging accident in a nuclear reactor such as the one that took place at Three Mile Island, the major costs of such an accident would not be those from immediate loss of life, latent cancers, and direct economic expenses (e.g., property damage, repairs, cleanup), important as these may be. Instead, the dominant costs might arise from secondary impacts such as public reaction, perhaps leading to shutdown of the industry, and the resulting higher-order consequences of shutdown (e.g., dependence on more costly and less reliable energy sources), which could total tens or hundreds of billions of dollars.

These sociopolitical and long-run economic impacts must be considered when determining how much should be spent on the facility to reduce the probability of a core-damaging accident. In other words, the design of nuclear safety criteria might be phrased in terms of the question "Given the cost of making a facility safer and the economic impacts of an accident, what probability of a core-damaging accident is tolerable?"

This notion calls for a more comprehensive modeling of the overall social costs (including stigma impacts) of nuclear accidents and the benefits of reducing the risk. If even small and contained (but frightening) accidents are likely to have immense costs, this would imply the need for strict criteria, even at great expense, to minimize the probability of such accidents. Similar logic might argue in favor of remote siting of hazardous facilities, dedicated trains for transporting hazardous materials, tamper-resistant packaging on products, expensive safety precautions in blood banks, and other measures to prevent stigma-producing events from taking place.

Of course, we need to better understand how to model and predict stigma impacts, but we already know a lot about the qualities of hazards and their victims that trigger media coverage, ominous signals, stigmatized images, and strong avoidance behavior, and this information should be incorporated into impact projections (for a related discussion of modeling and predicting potential future sources of toxic tort litigation see Foran, Goldstein, Moore, & Slovic, 1996).

Reduce Perceived Risk

Create and Maintain Trust. Reducing perceived risk should decrease stigma, but doing so is not easy. One key link to risk perception is through trust. If trust in experts, managers, and policymakers declines, perceived risk will increase and so will stigma. Unfortunately, trust in risk management is difficult to achieve and maintain (Slovic, 1993). Trust is fragile. It is typically created rather slowly, but it can be destroyed in an instant – by a single mishap or mistake. Once trust is lost, it may take a long time to rebuild it to its former state. In some instances, lost trust may never be regained.

The fact that trust is easier to destroy than to create reflects certain fundamental mechanisms of human psychology that Slovic (1993) called the *asymmetry principle*. When it comes to winning trust, the playing field is not level. It is tilted toward distrust because negative (trust-destroying) events are more visible or noticeable than positive (trust-building) events.

One way to generate trust is to encourage public participation as an integral part of the decision-making process. For example, in siting new facilities it is important to hear the concerns of the affected public and determine how to deal with them. As part of the monitoring and control procedures for making certain that the facility remains safe, a committee could be established to inspect the facility at regular intervals and report its findings back to the local community. The facility may have to be shut down temporarily to correct any defects. If such a process helps to establish trust and confidence between the developer and the affected parties, it could reduce perceived risk and stigmatization.

A set of guidelines for a fairer, wiser, and more workable siting process – the Facility Siting Credo – was developed during a National Facility Siting Workshop in 1990. A questionnaire based on the credo was completed by stakeholders in 29 waste facility siting cases, both successful and unsuccessful, across the United States and Canada. Using an independent determination of outcome (success), a preliminary rank of the importance of various credo principles was obtained. The data revealed that establishing trust between the developer and the host community was an important factor in facilitating the siting process. The siting process was most likely to be successful when the community perceived the facility design to be appropriate and to satisfy its needs. Public participation also was seen to be an important process variable, particularly when it led to the view that the facility did a good job of meeting community needs (Kunreuther, Fitzgerald, & Aarts, 1993).

Inform, Educate, and Desensitize the Public. It is natural to inform and educate people about risk in order to reduce stigma impacts by calming what technical experts may view as exaggerated fears. However, the affective nature of stigma limits the influence of quantitative risk information. Consider, for example, phobias, which are strong affective and aversive reactions to stimuli such as spiders, snakes, airplane travel, the outdoors, and so on. It is well known that risk communication (i.e., statistics showing that the risks are small or nonexistent) is virtually useless in treating phobias. We can expect the same to be true with stigma. What works with phobias is systematic desensitization or counterconditioning to reduce the negative affect. For example, a subject who developed an inability to take pills following the Tylenol poisonings in 1981 was "cured" by starting with relaxation training and then being exposed very gradually to stimuli increasing in similarity to medicine pills (first, simply imagining pill taking, then drinking wine, then taking a vitamin pill, etc.; see Pbert & Goetsch, 1988). Similar counterconditioning may be necessary to deal with the conditioned negative affect that drives stigmatization and avoidance behavior.

For example, in the difficult area of dealing with minute exposures to carcinogens, it may help people to learn of Bruce Ames's (1983) studies showing that many common fruits and vegetables contain natural carcinogens in far greater amounts than the small exposures they are concerned about (it is hoped that this will not stigmatize fruits and vegetables). It may also help if people understand that the body has defenses against the cell damage that might lead to cancer and if they understand the essence of current theories of carcinogenesis, so that they can appreciate that minute exposures may pose little or no risk.

Educating people about the benefits of such exposures (e.g., the great benefits of water chlorination, a procedure that may also expose people to very small amounts of carcinogens) may also reduce negative affect, as there is evidence to believe that the positive affect associated with benefits can partially offset the negative affect associated with risks (Alhakami & Slovic, 1994; Finucane, Alhakami, Slovic, & Johnson, 2000).

Educate Scientists: Risk Studies Breed Stigma. Risk assessment, as currently practiced and communicated, is part of the problem. The practice of quantitative risk assessment has steadily increased in prominence during the past several decades as government and industry officials have sought to develop more effective ways to meet public demands for a safer and healthier environment. Ironically, as society has expended great effort to make life safer and healthier, many persons have become more rather than less concerned about risk. This is particularly true for involuntary exposure to chemicals, which the public associates to a remarkable extent with danger, cancer, and death.

The linear, no-threshold model of cancer risk assessment has long been the subject of debate and criticism. Recently, Purchase and Auton (1995) described an alternative model in which the lowest dose at which the critical effect has been observed is identified and used to define the no observed adverse effect level (NOAEL) for that effect. Purchase and Auton show that one cannot distinguish empirically between the linear, no-threshold model and a model in which the NOAEL is divided by a safety factor. Thus, for example, the linear model used by the Environmental Protection Agency regulates any lifetime risk in excess of 1 chance in 1 million that can be shown to be equivalent to the NOAEL divided by a safety factor of about 250,000.

Use of a nonthreshold linear model to express risk in terms of relative frequencies leads to higher perceived risk than does the safety-factor format based on the same test results (Purchase & Slovic, 1999). More generally, Slovic, Monahan, and MacGregor (2000) found that any expression of risk in terms of relative frequencies (e.g., exposure to chemical X-rays produces an excess cancer risk of 1 in 1 million) raises the perceived risk by inducing affect-laden images of one or more people suffering. Expressing the same risk as a probability (.000001) does not produce such affect-laden images. Thus risk assessors and risk communicators are faced with a choice, given the same set of data, between asserting, say, that the probability that you will develop cancer from exposure to Chemical Y is about 1 chance in 100,000 and a statement that "Chemical Y has been observed to cause cancer in animals but only at doses more than 100,000 times greater than what you will ingest. At doses less than 100,000 times greater than what you will ingest, no cancer in animals has been found." The latter statement is not demonstrably less accurate than the former and may be less likely to contribute to the stigma-causing view that any exposure to this carcinogen is likely to cause cancer in the exposed person. Alternatively, the risk could be portrayed as a probability of .00001 or one-thousandth of 1%.

The point we are trying to argue here is that the rise of quantitative risk assessment, with its proliferation of high-dose animal studies and reliance on conservative extrapolation methods and probabilistic expressions of risk (e.g., 1 in X), may be a strong contributor to destructive stigmatization involving chemical products. This poses a dilemma for risk managers who cannot and should not abandon animal studies and risk assessment. However, they must recognize that stigma is a side effect of such efforts and consider ways to offset its damaging impacts without jeopardizing public health and safety.

Reduce Social Amplification

Another strategy would focus on possibly altering the number and type of stigma-producing messages reaching the public by educating the media and the regulatory community about the effects their messages may have.

Educate the Media

The media will not easily be persuaded to change their way of reporting on risk. They believe they are fulfilling an important duty to society in warning of potential threats, and this is true. Moreover, they are well protected by the First Amendment of the Constitution. Although apple growers in Washington State sued CBS for making numerous false statements about the risks of apples treated with Alar, the suit was dismissed by a federal judge who argued that "Even if CBS' statements were false, they were about an issue that mattered, cannot be proven as false and therefore must be protected." The judge further affirmed the right of a news-reporting service to rely on a scientific government report (which CBS did) and communicate the report's results.

However, we suspect that CBS, in reporting on Alar, did not intend to harm the apple growers. They wanted to motivate the EPA to take action against Alar and did not anticipate the massive stigmatizing response they created. Thus one strategy would be to educate the media about the nature and potency of stigma, and their responsibility to anticipate and weigh potential stigma losses against more direct risks when deciding what information to present about risk and how they should frame the data.

In response to the Alar incident, Florida, Washington, and other states have proposed (and in some cases passed) legislation allowing producers of agricultural commodities to recover damages for the disparagement of any agricultural commodity, where disparagement is defined as "dissemination to the public in any manner of any false information regarding the application of any agricultural chemical or process to agricultural commodities or products, or false information alleging a disease to agricultural commodities or products, that is not based on reliable scientific data, that the disseminator knows or should have known to be false, and that causes the consuming public to doubt the safety of any agricultural commodity" (quoted in Nelson, 1996).

Although antidisparagement legislation may discourage and punish some wanton attacks on products, it seems unlikely to penetrate the First Amendment defense of the news media.

Conclusion

The varieties of risk-induced stigma described in this chapter are noteworthy because they exemplify what has been called the *social amplification of risk* and illustrate a new form of societal vulnerability. Whereas in the past human health and safety were the primary vulnerable commodities, increasing technical and medical sophistication combined with hypervigilant monitoring systems to detect incipient problems certainly make our lives healthier and safer. If eating infected beef truly has the potential to trigger an epidemic of brain disease in humans, we will likely be able to limit the damage by publicizing the threat and measures to contain it.

The price of this vigilance is the impact that this information itself has upon social, political, industrial, and economic systems – witness the effect on the British beef industry and the reduction in beef consumption in other countries as well. Information has reduced our vulnerability to accidents and diseases at the cost of increasing our vulnerability to social and economic catastrophes of immense scale.

Although stigma has been studied by social psychologists, sociologists, and other social scientists as it applies to people, there is very little empirical research or stigmatization of places, products, industries, and technologies. It seems obvious that the better we understand the dynamics of these forms of stigmatization, the better we can forecast and manage in any given situation. Better communication with the public through the use of the media, and using policy tools, such as insurance to signal relative safety, may alleviate some unwarranted concerns by the public. More generally, an open dialogue with the public on the nature of the risks should help to reduce the stigma associated with specific products or facilities. The challenge before us is to learn how to manage stigma and reduce the vulnerability of important products, industries, and institutions to its effects.

Notes

1   The role of imagery in relocation decisions is illustrated by a Seattle friend's comment to one of the authors in a recent letter: "Ed's saying Montana may be the answer to middle-age[d] contentment. I think Montana has too many movie stars and militia, and too many creeps in cabins. I refuse to cross state lines in an Easterly direction."

2   The Federal Energy Regulatory Commission, the principal body at the federal level determining whether a proposed LNG project is in the public interest, indicated that the risk associated with one of the worst-case scenarios that caused 130,000 people in Oxnard to die was 1 in 710 septedecillion. A septedecillion has 55 zeros associated with it.

3   This maxim of toxicology dates back to the observation by Paracelsus in the 16th century that "All things are poison and nothing is without poison. It is the dose only that makes a thing not a poison" (as quoted in Ottoboni, 1984).

References

Alhakami, A. S., & Slovic, P. (1994). A psychological study of the inverse relationship between perceived risk and perceived benefit. *Risk Analysis, 14,* 1085–1096.

Ames, B. (1983). Dietary carcinogens and anticarcinogens. *Science, 221,* 1256–1264.

Benthin, A., Slovic, P., Moran, P., Severson, H., Mertz, C. K., & Gerrard, M. (1995). Adolescent health-threatening and health-enhancing behaviors: A study of word association and imagery. *Journal of Adolescent Health, 17,* 143–152.

Burns, W. J., Slovic, P., Kasperson, R. E., Kasperson, J. X., Renn, O., & Emani, S. (1993). Incorporating structural models into research on the social amplification of risk: Implications for theory construction and decision making. *Risk Analysis, 13*, 611–623.

Camerer, C., & Kunreuther, H. (1989). Decision processes for low probability events: Policy implications. *Journal of Policy Analysis and Management, 8,* 562–592.

Damasio, A. R. (1994). *Descartes' error: Emotion, reason, and the human brain.* New York: Avon.

Erikson, K. (1990). Toxic reckoning: Business faces a new kind of fear. *Harvard Business Review, 1,* 118–126.

Finucane, M. L., Alhakami, A., Slovic, P., & Johnson, S. M. (2000). The affect heuristic in judgments of risks and benefits. *Journal of Behavioral Decision Making, 13,* 1–17.

Foran, J. A., Goldstein, B. D., Moore, J. A., & Slovic, P. (1996). Predicting future sources of mass toxic tort litigation. *Risk: Health, Safety & Environment, 7,* 15–22.

Frazer, J. G. (1959). *The new golden bough: A study of magic and religion.* New York: Macmillan.

Kraus, N. N., Malmfors, T., & Slovic, P. (1992). Intuitive toxicology: Expert and lay judgments of chemical risks. *Risk Analysis, 12,* 215–232.

Krewski, D., Slovic, P., Bartlett, S., Flynn, J., & Mertz, C. K. (1995). Health risk perception in Canada II: Worldviews, attitudes and opinions. *Human and Ecological Risk Assessment, 1,* 231–248.

Kunreuther, H., Fitzgerald, K., & Aarts, T. D. (1993). Siting noxious facilities: A test of the facility siting credo. *Risk Analysis, 13,* 301–318.

Kunreuther, H., & Linnerooth, J. (1982). *Risk analysis and decision processes: The siting of LEG facilities in four countries.* Berlin: Springer Verlag.

MacGregor, D. G., Slovic, P., Dreman, D., & Berry, M. (in press). Imagery, affect, and financial judgment. *Journal of Psychology and Financial Markets.*

MacGregor, D. G., Slovic, P., & Morgan, M. G. (1994). Perception of risks from electromagnetic fields: A psychometric evaluation of a risk-communication approach. *Risk Analysis, 14,* 815–828.

Mauss, M. (1972). *A general theory of magic.* New York: W. W. Norton.

Mazur, A. (1981). *The dynamics of technical controversy.* Washington, DC: Communications Press.

Mitchell, M. L. (1989). The impact of external parties on brand-name capital: The 1982 Tylenol poisonings and subsequent cases. *Economic Inquiry, 27,* 601–618.

Moore, J. A. (1989). Speaking of data: The Alar controversy. *EPA Journal, 15,* 5–9.

Mowrer, O. H. (1960a). *Learning theory and behavior.* New York: Wiley.

Mowrer, O. H. (1960b). *Learning theory and the symbolic processes.* New York: Wiley.

Nelson, E. (1996, April/May). Lettuce libel: "Food disparagement" laws make groups eat their words. Washington Free Press. Available Internet: www.speakeasy.org/wfp/21/Enviro.html.

Ottoboni, M. A. (1984). *The dose makes the poison: A plain text guide to toxicology.* Berkeley, CA.: Vincente Books.

Pbert, L. A., & Goetsch, V. L. (1988). A multifaceted behavioral intervention for pill-taking avoidance associated with Tylenol poisoning. *Journal of Behavior Therapy and Experimental Psychiatry, 19,* 311–315.

Purchase, I. F. H., & Auton, T. (1995). Thresholds in chemical carcinogenesis. *Regulatory Toxicology and Pharmacology, 22,* 199–205.

Purchase, I. F. H., & Slovic, P. (1999). Quantitative risk assessment breeds fear. *Human and Ecological Risk Assessment, 5*, 445–453.

Reuter Library Report. (1990, May 10). *Perrier puts cost of Benzene scare at 79 million dollars*. Available through Nexis-Lexis.

Rozin, P., Millman, L., & Nemeroff, C. (1986). Operation of the laws of sympathetic magic in disgust and other domains. *Journal of Personality and Social Psychology, 50*, 703–712.

Slovic, P. (1987). Perception of risk. *Science, 236*, 280–285.

Slovic, P. (1993). Perceived risk, trust, and democracy. *Risk Analysis, 13*, 675–682.

Slovic, P., Flynn, J., Mertz, C. K., Mays, C., & Poumadere, M. (1996). *Nuclear power and the public: A comparative study of risk perception in France and the United States*. Report No. 96-6. Eugene, OR: Decision Research.

Slovic, P., Layman, M., Kraus, N., Flynn, J., Chalmers, J., & Gesell, G. (1991). Perceived risk, stigma, and potential economic impacts of a high-level nuclear waste repository in Nevada. *Risk Analysis, 11*, 683–696.

Slovic, P., Malmfors, T., Mertz, C. K., Neil, N., & Purchase, I. F. H. (1997). Evaluating chemical risks: Results of a survey of the British Toxicology Society. *Human & Experimental Toxicology, 16*, 289–304.

Slovic, P., Monahan, J., & MacGregor, D. M. (2000). Violence risk assessment and risk communication: The effects of using actual cases, providing instructions, and employing probability vs. frequency formats. *Law and Human Behavior, 24*, 271–296.

Slovic, P., Satterfield, T. A., Mertz, C. K., & Flynn, J. (1996). *Psychological and social impacts associated with contamination from the Woolfolk Chemical Works Plant in Fort Valley, Georgia* (Report No. 96-12). Eugene, OR: Decision Research.

Weinstein, N. D. (1988). *Attitudes of the public and the Department of Environmental Protection toward environmental hazards*. Final Report. Trenton: New Jersey Department of Environmental Protection.

13 Enlarging the Pie by Accepting Small Losses for Large Gains

Jonathan Baron and Max H. Bazerman

A forester named Ben Cone had been managing his land in a sustainable manner for 60 years when the Endangered Species Act (ESA) was passed. Suddenly, Ben faced a real threat. If the government found the red-cockaded woodpecker on his property, it would have the authority to constrain his forestry. Fearing the loss of his forest assets, Ben switched from sustainable management to clear-cutting: He cut down his entire forest. Clearly, this was not the goal of the ESA. The destruction of the forest benefited no one – not Ben Cone, not the environmental groups and politicians who fought for the new legislation, and least of all the red-cockaded woodpecker.

Ben Cone's decision to cut down his forest illustrates what happens when people assume that what is good for others is bad for them. Specifically, Ben viewed any gain for endangered species as an economic loss for him. Rather than seeing opportunities to enlarge the pie of assets, he regarded the pie as fixed in size. In failing to foresee the consequences of the new law, the government failed as well. Although the law allowed negotiations – which might have led to a win-win solution – neither side initiated them.

What can parties in a negotiation do to enlarge the pie of possible solutions? At what level can changes to the way we solve problems be made? We believe change occurs at two levels – how people think and how the government creates policy. These are related. Elected officials think like most citizens. Even if they didn't, they are responsible to their constituents. The most important constituents are members of organized groups that try to influence the government. These groups, however, represent other citizens who are less active.

The way that citizens and the government currently think about real-world problems is dangerously narrow in scope. Political actors at all levels would benefit by replacing the small pie mentality with a broader view. If we can improve how people inside and outside of government think, we will change how government acts, and what it does to influence the thinking and behavior of individuals and organizations. As citizens think differently and interest groups act differently, governments will create wiser legislation and more effective regulations, and they will implement these laws in more beneficial ways.

Although many of our own examples apply to the U.S. government, the United States is not unusual. In fact, recent studies suggest that the quality of government is a major determinant of national well-being. The poorest countries have the worst governments, and causation seems to run at least partly from government to poverty rather than the reverse. North Korea is a prime example, but some African countries are almost as bad, even ones that are democratic in their form of government. And governments can be good even when the people are extremely poor and uneducated, as seems to be the case in Mali right now. The quality of government amounts to the quality of decision making by those in the government and by those who influence them, which consists of voters and, especially, political activists (including contributors).

In the last 20 years, psychologists and other researchers have come to a better understanding of the errors that people commonly commit in making judgments and decisions, as the other chapters in this book attest. Much of this work has concerned the difficulties that people have making and understanding trade-offs. Our position is that citizens should become more familiar with the reasoning that decision scientists use when they think about government. It will not suffice if only those who work in government learn to incorporate principles of trade-offs when making decisions. Citizens, too, need to understand the logic of trade-offs. Anyone interested in making trade-offs must be willing to compare gains to losses.

In this chapter, we first categorize the types of missed opportunities that occur from our failure to find trades. Then we explore the psychological underpinning of these failures, followed by an exploration of the implications of these failures in three domains – negotiating about the environment, emissions trading, and subsidies.

Types of Missed Opportunities

Our core argument is that societal problems can be better solved by enlarging the pie through beneficial trades. A trade is an exchange resulting in both a gain and a loss, and a wise trade-off is one in which gains significantly exceed losses. People consistently overlook wise trade-offs. We see several categories of missed opportunities. We shall not discuss all of these in this chapter, but we include them as a map of the whole territory.

1. Each person faces a chance of a loss and a gain in the future. People often put themselves in the position of the loser or the gainer without seeing that they could be in either role. In thinking about lawsuits, people who take the role of the plaintiff but not the defendant fail to recognize the cost they pay for excessive lawsuits. In organ donation, people may see themselves or their families as potential donors whose wishes might be ignored, and then they fail to see themselves as potential recipients who might miss out on a lifesaving operation. In drug regulation, the same trade-off is between the side effects of drugs approved too early and the lost benefits of drugs approved too late.

2. In negotiation, the pie can be enlarged if each party is willing to give up what is relatively less important in return for what is more important. This requires being honest about what is relatively important even while playing close to the chest about how hard to bargain. An example is negotiation about Habitat Conservation Plans under the ESA, which was the relevant possibility for Ben Cone. Another example is the idea of emissions trading. Opponents of emissions trading want to limit the freedom to negotiate outcomes that are beneficial for everyone.

3. Competition is usually good, but often the costs of competition exceed the benefits. When this happens, potential gains can come from agreement or regulation to reduce competition. Collusion is not always a bad thing. When cities compete for sports teams and when states compete for factories, the winner is cursed by having promised too much, and the losers have wasted time and energy. The Ivy League universities used to agree on offers of financial aid to individual students. The courts said that this was illegal, but now the situation has degenerated into fighting over the best students. Some students play one offer against another, looking for the best deal. When one university makes a high offer in error, others match it, leaving too little money for students who need it more.

4. Special-interest groups try to get governments to help them, of-ten at the expense of others. Unions and firms alike try to win trade protection, subsidies, and tax reductions for their groups at the expense of other firms, workers, taxpayers, or consumers. An interesting example is the German coal miners, who have lobbied for a subsidy that amounts to twice their salary so that they do not lose their jobs. There is room here for negotiation: If the subsidy were given up, there would be plenty left over to help the miners in a way they might find acceptable, if not perfect.

5. The most difficult set of questions concern cases where net bene-fits result from sacrifices made by some people, who know who they are, for the benefit of others, and where there is no way to compensate those who make the sacrifices. One case con-cerns poverty. The distribution of income within and between nations is rising. Well-to-do people in advanced capitalist coun-tries live a life undreamed of by their predecessors. Meanwhile, the life expectancy in some African countries is falling, because of the acquired immune deficiency syndrome (AIDS) epidemic mostly, and people around the world are suffering from malnu-trition, epidemics of preventable disease, air pollution, and lack of the basic goods that others take for granted like education, housing, and medical care. Rich nations do try to help solve these problems in various ways, and sometimes the means are mutually beneficial in the long run. Even when they are not, we can ask whether the gains can be made by focusing on different methods.

6. We face similar trade-offs with people in the future. We are de-stroying species at a rate higher than any in the history of the Earth, including food fish. We are using resources, such as water from aquifers, at a rate that cannot be sustained. And we may be causing major problems by burning fossil fuels. Once again, we need to ask whether we are making the right sacrifices in return for the greatest protection of people in the future.

The solutions to these problems are all somewhat different, of course. But they all involve a willingness to accept losses in return for greater gains. Sometimes the losses and gains accrue to the same people when they make the decision. When the losses and gains affect different peo-ple, and when they know who they are, then government must bite the bullet and act, trying as hard as it can to ease the losses. When it does this, it must have the understanding of its constituents. So everyone must understand the basic principle of enlarging the pie.

Psychological Causes of These Effects

Scholars who study biased decision making have come up with a variety of explanations for why decisions do not always lead to optimal results. Sometimes people lack information, and the time required to get it and to deal with it would not be worthwhile. So people *satisfice* rather than maximize. In other cases, people distort information they are given because of basic psychological principles of judgment. These explanations do not help much in explaining the failure to integrate gains and losses.

What does help is the idea that people use heuristics. These are general rules or principles. The term, and the idea of heuristic methods, came from George Polya (1945), a mathematician. The term *heuristic* (an adjective) means "serving to discover." Heuristic methods were things to do when you didn't know what to do, like "Try to think of a related problem that you've solved before." They weren't guaranteed to work, but they were better than nothing.

Kahneman and Tversky (1972) used the term to refer to methods of inference that usually worked but sometimes led to error. This idea is closely related to the idea of satisficing. We would not need heuristics if we had sufficient computer power in our heads. But the new idea was that heuristics lead to systematic errors, not just random ones. For example, one of Kahneman and Tversky's heuristics was *representativeness*. The idea was that we judge the probability of some datum being in a category according to how similar the datum is to our stereotype of the category, that is, how representative it is of category members. Because the sequence heads–heads–heads–heads–tails is slightly more representative of a random sequence of coin tosses than the sequence heads–heads–heads–heads–heads, we tend to think that we will get tails after four heads in a row. This is the *gambler's fallacy*. It is fallacious because the coin has no memory.

Omission Bias

In our own case, people develop heuristics such as "do no harm." When we begin to learn morality, we are often chastised for some action that harms someone else. It is a good rule to avoid such actions. Cases in which we must cause harm as a means to a greater benefit are less common than those in which harm has little compensating advantage, except for satisfaction of an immediate sadistic urge or negligent carelessness.

In a study of hypothetical vaccination decisions, many subjects were unwilling to vaccinate children against a disease that could kill 10 out of 10,000 children when the vaccine itself would kill 5 out of 10,000 through side effects (Ritov & Baron, 1990). Some subjects would not tolerate any deaths from the "commission" of vaccinating. Opposition to real vaccines is based on the same principle: The Sabin polio vaccine can cause polio. The Salk vaccine can fail to prevent it. The total risk of polio is higher with the Salk vaccine, but some (e.g., Deber & Goel, 1990) argue against the Sabin vaccine because it causes polio through the action of vaccinating.

In another hypothetical scenario, John, the best tennis player at a club, wound up playing the final of the club's tournament against Ivan Lendl (then ranked first in the world). John knew that Ivan was allergic to cayenne pepper and that the salad dressing in the club restaurant contained it. When John went to dinner with Ivan the night before the final, he planned to recommend the house dressing to Ivan, hoping that Ivan would get a bit sick and lose the match. In one ending to the story, John recommended the dressing. In the other, Ivan ordered the dressing himself just before John was about to recommend it, and John, of course, said nothing. When asked whether John's behavior is worse in one ending or the other, about a third of the subjects said that it was worse when he acted (Spranca, Minsk, & Baron, 1991).

In sum, *omission bias* is the tendency to judge acts that are harmful (relative to the alternative option) as worse than omissions that are equally harmful (relative to the alternative) or even more harmful (as in the vaccination case) (Baron & Ritov, 1994). In any given case, some people display this bias and others do not. In this regard, at least, omission bias is like the other biases described in this book. In some cases, people can be persuaded to consider acts and omissions as equivalent, with an argument like the one just made (Baron, 1992).

Omission bias is related to issues of public controversy, such as whether active euthanasia should be allowed. Most countries (and most states of the United States) now allow passive euthanasia, the withholding of even standard medical treatment for those who are judged to be no worse off dead than alive, but active euthanasia is almost everywhere banned even for those who wish to die. Opponents of active euthanasia can, of course, find other arguments against it than the fact that it is active. But it is possible that these arguments would not be seen as so compelling if the distinction between acts and omissions were not made.

Omission bias could also justify a lack of concern with the problems of others (Singer, 1979). For example, much of the world's population lives in dire poverty today and into the foreseeable future. People – even people who take an interest in social issues – often think that they are not responsible for this poverty and need do nothing about it. It can be argued, however, that with a little effort we can think of all sorts of things we can do that will help the situation immensely at very low cost to ourselves, such as supporting beneficial policies. Failure to do these things can be seen as a harm, but many people do not see it that way. More generally, omission bias helps people believe that they are completely moral if they obey a list of prohibitions while otherwise pursuing their narrow self-interest.

Status Quo Bias

A closely related bias is that toward the status quo. We can think of omission as leading to the default option, that is, what you would get if you do nothing. Usually the default and the status quo are the same. They are different only when the default is new. The status quo bias can also be expressed by saying that losses, relative to the status quo, are weighed more than gains (Kahneman & Tversky, 1979). The same factor may help explain the omission bias if we think of doing nothing as the reference point against which actions are compared (Baron & Ritov, 1994).

The most direct effect of this idea is that people are often unwilling to give up what they already have, their *endowment*, for what they would otherwise prefer to it. The loss looms larger than the gain. People are therefore biased toward the status quo, or things the way they are. Consider the following example from Thaler (1980, pp. 43–44): Mr. R bought a case of good wine in the late 1950s for about $5 a bottle. A few years later, his wine merchant agreed to buy the wine back for $100 a bottle. He (Mr. R) refused, although he has never paid more than $35 for a bottle of wine.

In this example, Mr. R will not accept $100 for a bottle of wine, although he would not pay more than $35 for (presumably) the same bottle. In both cases, however, the choice is between wine and money. It might help to think of the true value of the wine as the amount of money that would have the same desirability as the wine *if Mr. R had to choose between a gift of money and a gift of wine* (having neither at the outset). Most likely, this value would be between $35 and $100, because the status quo bias induces an unwillingness to part with money when one has the money and with wine when one has the wine.

In an experiment using real goods and real money, members of a group of *sellers* were each given a coffee mug from their university bookstore and were asked to indicate on a form whether or not they would sell the mug at each of a series of prices ranging from $0 to $9.25 (Kahneman, Knetsch, & Thaler, 1990). A group of *buyers* indicated, on a similar form, whether they were willing to buy a mug at each price. At the end, a *market price* was picked at which there were enough sellers to meet the buyers' demands, and transactions were completed at that price for sellers willing to accept it and buyers willing to pay it, as in a real market. The median values assigned to the mug were $7.12 for sellers and $2.87 for buyers. Although we would expect that half of the buyers and half of the sellers would prefer the mug to the market price (since the mugs were assigned randomly), three-quarters of the sellers ended up keeping their mugs (and three-quarters of the buyers were unwilling to pay enough to get them). A group of *choosers* also indicated, for each price in the series, whether they preferred the mug or that amount in cash. The choosers preferred the mug if the cash amount was $3.12 on the average. This amount was still much lower than the average selling price ($7.12). Notice that the choosers differed from the sellers only in what they were told about ownership.

All of these situations involve a transaction, giving up one thing in exchange for something else. If we suppose that the thing given up (e.g., the bottle of wine) and the thing gotten in return (the $100) would have the *same* value if they were both received, we can see why Mr. R would not want to make the trade. The thing given up (the wine) would have a larger (absolute) value when it is perceived as a loss, because losses are valued more than gains. Therefore, Mr. R would require even more money in order to trade. On the other hand, when asked how much he would pay for the wine, the value of the money is increased, because the money is now seen as a loss. Therefore, he would not be willing to pay as much. The negative value of $35 would be greater than the value of the wine, because the $35 is now seen as a loss.

The status quo effect has several practical implications. One is that markets in which people buy and sell goods can be *sticky*. In the mugs experiments, far fewer than half of the mugs changed hands. The same effect may cause people to become attached to policies, or to their current position, or to the current position of others, so that they are generally unwilling to accept losses even for the sake of much larger gains.

The Mythical Fixed Pie

In negotiations, two or more dimensions are often at issue. For example, in the sale of a house, the parties often negotiate about both the price and the time when the transfer will occur. If the seller needs the money in a week to pay for a new house but the buyer is in no hurry, the speed of the sale can mean much more to the seller. Unless she gets the money right away, she will have to take out a loan at high interest in order to buy her new house.

Negotiations with two or more dimensions, where the parties have differing assessments about the importance of the issues, are called *integrative*. Most complex negotiations, including the societal negotiations that we focus on in this chapter, have integrative potential. The danger in integrative bargaining is to arrive at a result that is not Pareto-optimal. A result is Pareto-optimal when we cannot improve the outcome for one party without hurting the other party. If an outcome is not Pareto-optimal, then we can help one or both parties without hurting either one. That is what we mean by enlarging the pie.

The trouble is that people tend to view integrative negotiations as fixed pies (Neale & Bazerman, 1991). They think that what is good for the other side is bad for them, and vice versa. People therefore try to strengthen their bargaining position by pretending to care a lot about something they do not care about much. The buyer might pretend to be unable to move for months, once she hears that the seller is interested in moving quickly. The risk here is that the buyer will win, at the expense of something else that the seller would have been willing to give up more readily, like the sale price. If the buyer had been honest in saying that "the price is much more important to me than the time of sale," then each side would have been more willing to concede what it cared least about, especially if the seller, too, was candid about what was important. The same nonoptimal outcome can result if the parties negotiate about each dimension separately. The possibilities for trades that benefit both sides would simply not be recognized.

Floyd Spence, a South Carolina congressman, illustrates the fixed-pie assumption: "I have had a philosophy for some time in regard to SALT [the Strategic Arms Limitation Treaty] and it goes like this: The Russians will not accept a SALT treaty that is not in their best interest, and it seems to me that if it is their best interests, it can't be in our best interest." Spence's form of reasoning is surprisingly common.

Negotiators fail to find optimal outcomes because they fail to look for trade-offs that can enlarge the pool of resources to be distributed. They ignore the possibility of making trade-offs that will improve the overall quality of the agreement. The ESA's implementation did not cause Mr. Cone's actions. Rather, he misperceived the intentions of the Environmental Protection Agency (EPA).

Negotiators do not look for trade-offs that can enlarge the pool of resources to be distributed, so they miss these opportunities. The fixed-pie assumption leads to competitive behavior that ignores cooperative possibilities because it hides the opportunities in a complex negotiation situation. *Reactive devaluation*, the tendency of negotiators to interpret any proposal offered by the opponent as negative, sets in (Ross & Stillinger, 1991). When the other side is viewed as the enemy, this bias is exacerbated. This is the very antithesis of the cooperative processes necessary to make the wise trade-offs that can improve the overall quality of negotiated outcomes.

One of the authors (M.B.) conducts negotiation seminars with executives from corporate and environmental organizations. He asks why they fail to make mutually beneficial trade-offs in simulated negotiations. They commonly respond that they do not know trade-offs are possible. Negotiators may be willing to make trade-offs, but they assume that the parties' interests are perfectly opposed. The idea of creating trades across issues is simple, but it is not part of our intuitive repertoire of negotiation strategies.

Societal institutions encourage the fixed-pie assumption. Lawyers, often found at the core of legislative and regulatory disputes, have historically been trained in adversarial litigation. Only recently have leading legal scholars been arguing for reforms in legal education. A new text by Mnookin, Peppet, and Tulumello (2000) calls on lawyers to reconsider their traditional role as adversaries and become creative negotiators instead.

To avoid the fixed-pie bias, you must be specific about your trade-offs. If, for example, two roommates are negotiating about doing the housework, it helps to be able to say, "Two hours of cleaning are equivalent to one hour of cooking for me, since I hate cooking so much." If the other roommate feels the opposite, then the optimal solution is for one to do all the cooking and the other all the cleaning. This is far better than splitting everything equally.

Note that it is still possible to bargain hard while being honest about the *relative* importance of the dimensions to you. The point of honesty about relative importance is to make sure that you get to the Pareto frontier. The hard bargaining is about where on that frontier you wind up.

The danger here is real. Many laboratory studies show that college students left to their own devices will not arrive at Pareto-optimal solutions unless they are given specific advice about how to talk about their trade-offs or unless they have experience in the same situation (Bazerman, Magliozzi, & Neale, 1985; Pruitt & Lewis, 1975). Even in international negotiations (such as the Uruguay round of the General Agreement on Tariffs and Trade), experienced negotiators make the mistake of settling one issue at a time – first agriculture, then telecommunications, and so forth – when it is possible that these could be handled integratively. (An exception to the usual muddling was the Camp David negotiation mediated by President Jimmy Carter, as described by Raiffa, 1982.)

People seem to take a competitive, fixed-pie approach to division of resources between two groups. Interestingly, individuals are willing to sacrifice for the benefit of their own group, even when the gain to their group is exactly matched by a loss to the other group, so that the net loss is just their individual sacrifice. An experiment by Bornstein and Ben-Yossef (1994) shows this effect. Subjects came in groups of six and were assigned at random to a red group and a green group, with three in each group. Each subject started with 5 Israeli shekels (IS; about $2). If the subject contributed this endowment, each member of the subject's group would get 3 IS (including the subject). This amounts to a net loss of 2 IS for the subject but a total gain of 4 IS for the group. However, the contribution would also cause each member of the *other* group to *lose* 3 IS. Thus, taking both groups into account, the gains for one group matched the losses to the other, except that the contributor lost the 5 IS. The effect of this loss was simply to move goods from the other group to the subject's group. Still, the average rate of contribution was 55%, and this was substantially higher than the rate of contribution in control conditions in which the contribution did not affect the other group (27%). Of course, the control condition was a real social dilemma in which the net benefit of the contribution was truly positive. It seems that subjects were willing to sacrifice more for the sake of winning a competition than for the sake of increasing the amount their own group won.

Participants appear to see their own interest as tied more with their group than with the larger group consisting of all six players. This experiment might be a model for cases of real-world conflict, in which people sacrifice their own interest to help their group at the expense of some other group. Perhaps if people understood that such behavior was not really in their self-interest, they would not be so willing to do this, and we would see fewer of these kinds of conflicts.

In sum, these three biases – omission, status quo, and fixed pie – have in common the failure to look for ways to improve matters on the whole by sacrificing small losses for large gains. Part of the difficulty is that we don't like to compare apples and oranges. When we can express everything in dollars or hours, it is relatively easy. An investment is worthwhile if the payoff at the end is greater than the cost of the investment: We just subtract, because we can express everything in dollars. We are less willing to do this subtraction even when we must compare two different sources of risk of death (as in the fatal-disease example).

A related phenomenon is *belief overkill* (Baron, 1998). Many controversial issues are controversial because there are good arguments on both sides. A rational decision would involve balancing the arguments in a quantitative way, that takes into account their strengths or the magnitudes and probabilities of the possible results. But people find ways to avoid this balancing. Through wishful thinking, they convince themselves that all the good arguments are on one side. Robert Jervis (1976, pp. 128–142) provides many examples of this kind of overkill in judgments about foreign policy. In discussions of a ban on testing nuclear weapons, "People who favored a nuclear test-ban believed that testing created a serious medical danger, would not lead to major weapons improvements, and was a source of international tension. Those who opposed the treaty usually took the opposite position on all three issues. Yet neither logic nor experience indicates that there should be any such relationship. The health risks of testing are in no way connected with the military advantages" (p. 129). If people must think this way in order to make decisions, then they will find it difficult to make decisions when the options clearly involve both gains and losses. When this happens, they will tend to fall back on heuristics, such as "do no harm" or "stick with the status quo." Likewise, overcoming the fixed-pie bias involves comparing gains with losses. You must ask yourself how much of one thing to give up in return for some other amount of something else.

Negotiating About the Environment

When Benjamin Cone bought 7,200 acres in North Carolina's Pender County in the 1930s, the deforested land was considered so useless that his friends labeled it "Cone's Folly." By the time Ben Cone, Jr., inherited the land from his father in 1982, it had become a profitable forest full of songbirds, wild turkey, quail, and deer. For decades, the Cones managed their land for the benefit of wildlife by planting fodder, conducting controlled burns, and keeping their timber sales low.

In 1991, a wildlife biologist hired by Ben Cone, Jr., informed him that about 29 red-cockaded woodpeckers – members of an endangered species – were living on his property. Acting on the authority of the 1973 ESA, the U.S. Fish and Wildlife Service took control of about 15% of Cone's property (Baden, 1995).

After the Fish and Wildlife Service moved in, Cone no longer tried to conserve his property. Instead of limiting his clear-cutting to 50 acres every 5–10 years, he began clear-cutting up to 500 acres every year (Baden, 1995). Cone argued, "I cannot afford to let those woodpeckers take over the rest of the property" (Stroup, 1995). By harvesting the oldest trees on the land still under his control, Cone prevented the woodpeckers from expanding their habitat – and he ensured that the clear-cut land would once more become Cone's Folly in a new way.

The ESA, which was designed to protect and restore endangered or threatened species, forbids the killing, harassing, possessing, or removing of protected species from the wild. Cone's response was surely not what the writers of the ESA had in mind. Senators and members of the forestry industry have argued that the Cone story illustrates the failure of the ESA to consider the incentive effects of its provisions. However, the argument that the ESA is intractable in its dealings with landowners is simplistic. Only after the Cone story became a touchstone for ESA critics was it revealed that endangered species considerations affected only a small portion of Cone's property, for example.

Ben Cone, Jr., had many alternatives to his decision to begin clear-cutting huge stretches of forest. The ESA offered its own solution: a Habitat Conservation Plan (HCP). HCPs give private landowners permission to violate the specifics of the ESA by allowing *incidental take* of listed species in the course of lawful development activities, provided that the landowner takes certain steps to provide for conservation of that species. HCPs can lead to negotiated plans that serve both the interests of the endangered species and the economic interests of landowners.

The Fish and Wildlife Service approached Cone repeatedly with proposals for HCPs that would insulate him from future ESA responsibilities. He rejected the offers.

Cone seemed to assume that if the plan was desirable to environmentalists, it must be bad for his business. His fear of the devaluation of his assets led him toward a radical protective strategy. His belief in the win-lose nature of endangered species protection guided his unfortunate actions. Parties to other environmental disputes hold similar beliefs, with similar results.

Industry officials and environmentalists have chosen to view the situation as win-lose, a polarization that reinforces competitive rather than cooperative approaches. Politicians usually side with one group or the other. Both sides seem to believe that the environment can be saved only through economic sacrifices (Bazerman, Moore, & Gillespie, 1999). Economic and environmental interests try to claim as much as they can, often by demonizing the other side.

The ESA has been a successful piece of legislation (Hoffman, Bazerman, & Yaffe, 19997). Fifty-nine percent of the 128 species that were on the endangered species list when the ESA was passed in 1973 have since been recovered, have improved, or are in stable condition. But the ESA appears to pit the interests of economic development against those of environmental protection, and this has led the two sides to adopt a win-lose attitude toward negotiation. Protection of the human economy is paramount to ESA critics, so the idea of giving up jobs and crippling a regional economy to save a few animals is an absurd proposition. Many U.S. industry leaders view environmentalists as tree-huggers who are willing to sacrifice entire communities for a single owl or kangaroo rat. To proponents of the ESA, protection of the natural ecosystem is priceless (Baron & Spranca, 1997). Environmentalists tend to view loggers and fishers as villains eager to harvest every last tree and fish for their own personal profit.

In the typical ESA debate, both sides establish intractable positions and fight a distributive battle over concessions from the other side. For example, the Sierra Club membership voted to oppose all logging on all federal land, allowing no room for negotiations. By viewing their opponents from this fixed-pie perspective, these groups are ignoring mutually beneficial solutions that could arise through cooperative decision making. Almost all negotiations involve a distributive element, but these parties err by failing to look for integrative elements as well. Integrative elements can usually be found; the pool of resources is rarely fixed, and the parties can work together to increase its size. Win-win proponents claim that the U.S. economy can actually be improved by some methods that protect and restore the natural environment (Porter & van der Linde, 1995). For example, if a given piece of land is more valuable to environmental interests, it might be traded for a piece of land that a corporation values more highly. And much can be done about the details of the timing of harvests and the nature of specific habitat protection efforts.

Once these issues are identified, the two sides can weigh their values for the various attributes and find opportunities for integrative trade-offs. Of course, everything is not win-win, and there will still be some competition (Hoffman et al., 1999). The balance between economics and the environment is, at its core, a mixed-motive situation. Enlarging the pie through wise trade-offs does not eliminate the need to divide the pie; rather, actors can argue over a larger pool of resources.

Still, parties often miss easy gains because they are preoccupied with negotiating about distributive aspects. Ben Cone had the law on his side. With the endangered species not yet populating most of his land, he could have found a way to continue most of his customary behavior. Instead of clear-cutting, he could have negotiated with the government for an HCP that would strengthen his rights, increase the profitability of his forest, and contribute to the goal of taking the red-cockaded woodpecker off of the list of endangered species.

Flexibility and creativity are the key ingredients in efficient and satisfying economic and environmental agreements. Such solutions are not limited to such polarized issues as endangered species protection. Consider the large amount of money that oil companies must spend on environmental protection. The Unocal Corporation developed an innovative way to reduce its costs for complying with the hydrocarbon and nitrogen oxide standards in the Los Angeles basin. By collaborating rather than competing with the State of California and the general public, Unocal achieved the required emissions reductions at lower cost by means of a program initiated in 1990 for scrapping older, higher-polluting vehicles. The company removed nearly 13 million pounds of pollution per year from the air of the Los Angeles basin by buying pre-1971 cars for $600 apiece and scrapping them. The company computed the tailpipe emissions of each vehicle according to the number of miles the vehicle would have been driven. The resulting emissions reductions would have cost 10 times as much and taken 10 times as long had they been made at the company's Los Angeles refinery (Stegemeier, 1995). This outcome might initially appear to be win win, but it also possessed a distributive element: The final solution was negotiated, not fixed (Lax & Sebenius, 1986).

In another case, Amoco joined with the EPA to examine pollution reduction possibilities at its refinery in Yorktown, Virginia. Working together, they found that Amoco could meet the emission reductions required by the Clean Air Act Amendments of 1990 (CAAA) at one-quarter of its previous costs ($10 million versus $40 million) (Solomon, 1993). This result combined both the claiming of value (the EPA's insistence on CAAA compliance) and the creation of value (greater economic efficiency gained through flexible rule-making). The outcome allowed gains for both environmental and economic interests, even though the negotiation was still competitive as well.

The results described in the previous examples became visible because the parties took a mixed-motive perspective of the debate between economics and the environment. In each case, the pursuit of more efficient solutions led the parties away from a distinctly win-lose scenario. Although win-lose perceptions are present in many conflicts between economic and environmental interests, this perspective appears to predominate in the debate over endangered species. Yet, the implementation of the ESA shows that mixed-motive solutions can enhance both environmental and economic interests.

One way to make efficient agreements more likely is to provide landowners with a voice in negotiating their ESA compliance options. However, as long as the fixed-pie attitude persists, such solutions will be difficult to imagine. The HCPs discussed earlier are supposed to help overcome this attitude. Many creative private landowners have used these plans to work with other interested parties, from government agencies to citizens' groups, to identify optimal means of ESA compliance. As of 1997, there were 243 HCPs in 16 states covering 6.2 million acres of land. One of the best examples is the San Bruno Mountain HCP (*http://www.traenviro.com/specialties/sanbruno/sanbruno.html*). Consisting of 3,600 acres of unique habitat close to San Francisco, the San Bruno Mountain is the largest urban open space in the United States. It is home to 2 endangered and 1 threatened species of butterflies and 10 species of rare plants. Visatacion Associates, a major land-holding company, planned a development with 8,500 residential units and 2 million square feet of office space on the mountain. Environmentalists were outraged – especially when they learned that the government appeared powerless to stop the development. A 1982 HCP negotiation, however, led to a solution acceptable to both sides. The county bought 1,100 acres of the disputed land from Visatacion, Visatacion donated 546 acres to a county park and 256 acres to the state, and 368 acres were allocated for the planned development. This HCP did result in the loss of up to 14% of the habitat for the Mission Blue butterfly, but most of the habitat was preserved and a permanent funding source to manage the habitat was created.

HCPs do not eliminate conflict, but they increase the chances that the parties will bypass the traditional win-lose perspective. They are not used as often as they could be. The problems are many. The government agencies authorized to create HCPs often lack sufficient trained staff. Companies affected by the ESA often lack information about the HCP process. In addition, political changes continue to weaken and strengthen the ESA, and neither side can depend on the future enforcement of the law. As a result, environmentalists and landowners spend more time and effort lobbying to change the law than they spend to act wisely within it. Finally, scientists have not assessed the HCP process appropriately. Most current studies focus on the success or failure of species preservation efforts. Another question is whether the HCP process is creating improvement for the environment and the economy over what would have occurred without HCPs. Overall, the results seem to be positive, but they fall far short of what can be created. The biggest barrier to overcome is the fixed-pie approach to environmental negotiations.

We have focused on environmental negotiations, but problems like this are found throughout government, as we saw in Floyd Spence's quote and as we learn every day from discouraging news reports about gridlocked federal debates on education funding, health care, social freedoms, and so forth. In general, the political left and the political right often act as if they are fighting over a fixed pie – which they are if their only goal is to remain in office. However, politicians have other goals that attracted them to politics in the first place. They want to create wise policies within their own conception of wisdom. This goal is thwarted, however, once beating the other side becomes their primary focus. Unfortunately, the fixed-pie attitude is deeply engrained in politics, and it can be tough for wisdom to prevail.

Emissions Trading

The temperature of the Earth has, it seems, increased by about $1°C$ over the last 100 years. The increase fits with the theory that people are the cause. Many by-products of human activity contribute, but the main culprit – if that is the right word – is carbon. Most carbon in the air is carbon dioxide (CO_2). CO_2 prevents radiant heat from the Earth from escaping into outer space, yet it allows heat to enter in the form of light from the sun. So it helps to trap the heat, just as a greenhouse does. Hence the term *greenhouse effect* (an idea first proposed by S. Arrhenius in 1896).

We create CO_2 when we burn fuels like coal, oil, and natural gas – fuels from fossils of ancient plants, which grew at the time of the dinosaurs and before and became trapped in the Earth. These fuels are composed of carbon and hydrogen (except for coal, which has very little hydrogen). Both combine with oxygen and generate energy. The hydrogen becomes water (H_2O), and the carbon becomes CO_2.

One thing worth keeping in mind is that carbon itself is neither created nor destroyed in all of this. Most carbon is in rocks, and it pretty much stays there. The carbon we need to worry about is in four places. One, of course, is the air, in the form of CO_2. The other is in the ground in the form of fossil fuel. The third is the biosphere, the totality of living things. Almost every molecule in the bodies of living things contains carbon. Most living things are plants, including trees and plants that grow in the oceans. The fourth place is the oceans. Carbon dioxide dissolves in water.

If we want to reduce the carbon in the air, we can do it in two main ways. One is to leave it in the ground. The other is to grow more plants. Note, however, that once it is out of the ground, it is out forever. We can't put the oil back. Every barrel of oil we burn – to heat our homes, generate electricity, or run our car air conditioners while we sit in summer traffic jams – produces carbon that must go either into the air or into plants. And the more that goes into the air, the hotter the Earth will get. It is likely that, if present trends continue, we *will* use up a substantial fraction of the carbon in the ground. If we slow down the burning of fossil fuel, it must be for one of two purposes. Either we must admit that, eventually, the temperature of the Earth will be considerably higher than it would be otherwise, and we need to slow it down so that we can adapt. Or else we must plan to leave the carbon in the Earth for the foreseeable future and develop new sources of energy.

So one thing to bear in mind is the idea of the *carbon budget*. We can understand a lot about global warming by thinking about where the carbon is. For example, cutting forests would seem to be bad, because trees are full of carbon. But think about what happens to the carbon after the trees are cut. If the trees are made into houses and furniture, then the carbon stays locked up in these things. Most of this wood lasts longer than the wood from trees that die a natural death. And if the trees are replaced with more trees, so much the better. Think of your antique dining table or your wooden floors as a contribution to preventing global warming. If the trees are just burned, however, all the carbon goes into the air.

Under the auspices of the United Nations, several world bodies are addressing this problem. The last major step was taken in 1997 in Kyoto, Japan, where the nations of the world agreed to reduce the amount of carbon they produce. They plan to do this mostly by burning less fossil fuel than they would otherwise. Part of the treaty, and its subsequent elaboration in Buenos Aires in 1998, involves *joint implementation*.

The idea of joint implementation is to allow two countries to reach beneficial trades. Suppose that the United States promises to cut CO_2 emission by some amount to comply with the treaty. And suppose that, after the easy cuts are made, some of the cuts start to cost real money. They may, for example, involve replacing coal-burning power plants with wind power or nuclear power, both of which are more costly than coal in most areas. Meanwhile, the United States discovers that CO_2 can be reduced cheaply in some other country, but the other country cannot afford even the small cost involved. For example, that country may be using older equipment in its coal-burning plants. An investment to replace the equipment would vastly reduce the amount of coal required for a given amount of power and would ultimately save money too, but the country cannot afford the investment. So the United States lends the money at very low interest, or even provides the funds outright, for upgrading the plant. This is a beneficial trade because the United States reduces CO_2 money. The other country, meanwhile, gets a new, more efficient power plant. If the other country doesn't benefit, it doesn't have to agree. The idea is called joint implementation exactly because it involves the negotiated cooperation of two countries, with one of the outcomes being a reduction in CO_2 emissions.

In a recent test of this idea (Dunphy, 1999), residents in the Mexican cities of Monterrey and Guadalajara replaced ordinary light bulbs with energy-saving ones that are 75% more efficient and last 10 times longer. The objective was to require less electricity and thus reduce emissions of CO_2 from power plants. A Norwegian institute, Det Norske Veritas, acting as an impartial observer, confirmed that the new lights helped cut the equivalent of 171, 168 tons of CO_2 from 1995 to 1998. Of course, in the long run, the Mexicans will save money too, even though the costs of the installation were paid by the World Bank as part of an experiment.

A more extreme version of the idea is to make it part of the treaty for every nation. Then it amounts to tradable quotas. That is, each nation has a quota for CO_2 emission, but the quotas can be bought and sold in a free market. The United States could then buy some of the quota of a poor country. The poor country would thus have a smaller quota. It would meet this quota by using the money it got for selling part of its quota to the United States. For example, it could increase the efficiency of its power plants.

The same idea can be implemented within a nation, among firms that emit pollution of various sorts; then it is called a *tradable permit*. A permit allows a certain amount of pollution. The general term for all of these ideas is *emissions trading*. Emissions trading of all sorts enlarges the pie. Joint implementation is the easiest form of emissions trading because it requires only two nations. The issue at Kyoto was whether it would be allowed at all. The United States, its major proponent, prevailed for the time being.

Estimates suggest that emissions trading can save the rich countries as much as 30% of what they would otherwise pay for CO_2 reduction (Reuters/PlanetArc, 1999). The United States could save a lot more, up to 90% (Kaiser, 1998). Experience suggests the same. In the CAAA of 1990, the U.S. government set up a system of emissions trading for sulfur dioxide emissions, which were the major cause of acid rain. (Acid rain disturbs the ecology of lakes and has other negative effects.) Emissions of sulfur dioxide were cut, as required, and for far less than the cost originally predicted. Part of the credit for the lower cost must go to emissions trading (Kaiser, 1998).

Emissions trading is not free of problems, and it will surely pose special problems if it is extended to the whole world. One problem concerns the relation between it and retroactive credits. In order to encourage nations to begin cutbacks immediately instead of waiting for the treaty to be ratified, the treaty gives credit for cuts made since the time the treaty was initially signed. Since then, though, Russia has undergone a major economic collapse, and it would be fairly easy for the United States, say, to pay Russia for its reductions resulting from the collapse. Even this is not all bad: It is a mechanism for increased foreign aid to countries that need it. But it does undercut the purpose of the treaty. Still, this is a problem that is easily solved: Rather than scrap the whole idea of emissions trading, it could be limited to emissions reductions that did not result from economic collapse.

The biggest problem is perhaps to measure adherence to contracts. The whole scheme requires measurement of the effect of the actions agreed upon, as opposed to what would have been done without those actions. Still, this is a problem with any scheme that defines obligations in terms of reductions from a current level.

Opposition to emissions trading of any sort is fierce. One of the authors (J.B.) once had an acquaintance who worked for an environmental advocacy group. Let us call her N.F. They took the same train, and they chatted at the station while waiting for the train. They always talked about politics or environmental issues, and they often agreed. When they disagreed, the disagreements were always polite – until J.B. happened to mention his support for the idea of emissions trading. N.F. exploded into a moral rage. She said that emissions trading was just a way for rich companies to buy out of their obligations. She said every company should reduce its own pollution. She thought the whole thing was like paying someone to serve your jail sentence for you. J.B. made the mistake of arguing back. For the next few weeks, they stood at opposite ends of the station platform. Finally, they made up, but only after a few conversations in which they studiously avoided any political topics.

Emissions trading was a major point of controversy at the meeting held in Buenos Aires, Argentina, in November 1998 to flesh out the Kyoto treaty of 1997. The European countries wanted limits on the amount of trading that could be done. Even some developing countries, which stood to gain financially, were against unlimited trading. The opponents thought it would let the rich countries off the hook. They could get away with paying others to reduce pollution instead of reducing it themselves.

Michael Sandel, a professor of government at Harvard, argued that "turning pollution into a commodity to be bought and sold removes the moral stigma that is properly associated with it. If a company or a country is fined for spewing excessive pollutants into the air, the community conveys its judgment that the polluter has done something wrong. A fee, on the other hand, makes pollution just another cost of doing business, like wages, benefits and rent" (Sandel, 1997, p. 21A).

But is it really getting off the hook? And should there really be a stigma? Although the potential for global warming has been understood for a century, the potential seriousness of the problem has been recognized only in the last 20 years. Even now, it is not clear how serious the problem is. It may, for example, turn out to be a good antidote to what would turn out to be a small ice age. Or it may be solved more efficiently without cutting CO_2 emissions – for example, by growing more phytoplankton in the ocean (Kunzig & Zimmer, 1998). Possibly it is even cheaper to adapt to the effects of warming than to try to stop it. Jerry Mailman, director of the Geophysical Fluid Dynamics Laboratory at Princeton, has argued that even the most ambitious CO_2 reduction play may be nowhere near enough: "It might take another 30 Kyotos over the next century" (Malakoff, 1997, p. 2048).

Meanwhile, CO_2 has been seen as a completely innocent by-product of economic growth. It is a natural chemical, like water, found in abundance in nature and essential for the growth of plants. (Indeed, more of it will spur the growth of some plants.) It is not like soot or sewage. These *look* like pollution. It is more like water! Why should its emission be stigmatized? The problem, if it is a problem, is that we are simply producing too much of it. We may need to cut back.

Many of the critics of emissions trading made good points about particular projects. There are technical difficulties. Plans for emissions reduction may not work. Measurement may fail. But these are not problems with trading as such. They would happen with any proposal. The real objection seems to come from moral intuition. And the intuition, in turn, seems to result from an unwillingness to trade off small losses for larger gains. In particular, the loss is that the buying country reduces its CO_2 less. The gain is that the selling country reduces its CO_2 more. The gain outweighs the loss or the trade would not take place.

German Coal Miners

Some of the things that we can do to reduce global warming are things that we should do anyway. They are beneficial even if warming were not a problem at all. These are called *no-regrets* solutions. Let us look at one of them. Many countries subsidize the burning of fossil fuel. Developing countries such as Mexico, Nigeria, and Venezuela keep the price of gasoline artificially low by regulation or by selling it through state monopolies paid for from taxes. Highly developed countries such as Spain and Germany subsidize coal, again using taxes to keep the price artificially low.

This means that more fuel is burned. If fuel costs less, people will use more of it. If the price goes up, then some people will look for ways to use less. When the price of gasoline went up in the United States in the late 1970s, for example, use of gasoline declined. In the long run, it could have declined much more if people replaced their aging gas guzzlers with cars that burned less gasoline, but it did not get to that point in the United States. But it also means that people are paying taxes so as to make fuel cost less for other people. Some people are getting fuel at less than the cost of production, whereas others, who pay more taxes (or do without other benefits that government could provide), are doing without. When people pay less than the cost of production, money is being wasted. If we produced less coal, we could use the labor and capital to produce other things that people value at least as much, and we could produce more of them. So, subsidies lead to waste. Getting rid of subsidies is a no-brainer. It is all gain and no loss, even if there is no global warming. Or so it seems.

German coal mines are heavily subsidized. The price of German coal is more than three times the world market price. If the subsidy were to end, coal production would decline by 75% (Radetzki, 1995). Only 25% of production would be efficient enough to compete with other sources of energy (including imported coal). The number of coal workers would decline from 250,000 to 31,000. (Fewer workers would be needed for the more efficient production that would remain.) The average coal worker earned (in 1992) the equivalent of $36,000 per year, yet the size of the subsidy required came to $92,000 for every worker. The government would save quite a bit of money by paying each worker $36,000 to do nothing.

The main subsidy began in 1980, when German electricity suppliers agreed to burn expensive German coal instead of imported oil. The idea was to keep the coal mines going. Employment in the mines had declined since 1956, and a domestic source of energy was seen as more secure. The government was to compensate the electric suppliers for their extra cost, and the money for the compensation came from a tax on electricity. By 1986, Germany was under pressure from other members of (what would become) the European Union to cut these subsidies, in line with a more general move toward efficient economic policy, agreed to 10 years earlier. The government began to look for ways to cut the subsidy.

In 1994 the tax was found to be unconstitutional, and the subsidy was taken out of general funds (as well as contributions from the coal-producing states of Saarland and North-Rhine/Westphalia). The Kohl government proposed cuts in the subsidy.

In March 1997, coal miners went to Bonn to protest. Kohl's plan would cut mining jobs from 85,000 to 35,000 by 2005. The miners' union (IG Bergbau) wanted 45,000 jobs instead.

For three days, Chancellor Kohl negotiated with Hans Berger, the head of the miners' union, first about whether to meet and then about the size of the cuts. Meanwhile, up to 15,000 miners demonstrated in Bonn and about twice as many in the Saarland, in the heart of the mines. On one day, 3,500 of them blocked the main road through the capital's government center. Then they went to the nearby city of Cologne to camp out in a stadium while negotiations continued. A compromise was reached and the miners went home, accompanied by shouts of victory at their accomplishment. Specifically, as a result of the protest, the federal subsidy increased by 1.65 billion marks over the government's original offer of 56.6 billion marks (about $34 billion) until 2005, and an additional 1.75 billion was pledged by the state government of North Rhine/Wesphalia. By 2005, annual subsidies would be 5.5 billion marks. The miners did not get everything they wanted. Presumably, the number of jobs in 2005 – if anyone could predict – would be between 35,000 and 45,000.

One 40-year-old miner, Hans Zabcyk, said he was there because of "my job" (Kahl, 1977). He and his colleagues have known nothing else but mining, and, for many, they were preceded by several generations in the mine. Peter Kloss, another miner, asked, "Where will we work when everything is closed?" It was clearly jobs that were at issue.

Let us put aside the emotions of this protest and look at the numbers coldly. Half of the miners were demonstrating. The ones who went to Bonn lost 3 days of work. The others lost at least 1 day, maybe 2. So let us say that, on the average, each miner lost 1 day of work. If the protest were completely successful, about 11% of the 85,000 present jobs would be saved (10,000). But most protests are not completely successful, and this one was not. So let us say that 6% of the jobs were saved, and that was roughly the expectation. The savings would be spread out over an 8-year period, during which time some of the miners would retire or stop working for some other reason. Supposing that the average miner works for 20 years, we might expect the savings to be more like 10 years for 5% of the miners, so the benefit of the protest would be half a year per miner, perhaps even as much as 200 days of work. That is certainly worth 2 days of lost work to attend a demonstration.

But now let us look at the effect of one miner. Suppose that the government was sensitive to the size of the protest. If 10,000 miners were involved in the protest, then each additional protestor would contribute 1/10,000th of the total effect. Of course, the actual numbers were higher, so the actual fraction could be less, but we are trying to make a point. Each miner's participation thus contributed 1/10,000th of 200 days of extra work for all the miners. That comes to 2% of 1 day, or about 10 minutes.

Why the difference? From the perspective of the group, each miner's contribution was worth the effort. But from the selfish perspective of each miner, it was not. If the miner was concerned only about himself and not about the other miners, the 2 or 3 days spent participating in the protest were not worth it. Better to take off work early and go to a few soccer games than to camp out in a tent in a soccer stadium.

This is a classic example of what is called a *social dilemma*. Each miner is better off staying home (and even going to work, if possible), but all the miners benefit from every miner who participates in the protest. There is a conflict between self-interest and the interest of the group. It is analogous to many situations in which members of a group all face the same conflict. For example, each fisherman makes more money if he fishes as much as possible, but if all do that, the fish disappear and all are worse off.

This may be difficult to see. People are so used to thinking in terms of group interest that they lose the distinction between self-interest and group interest (Baron, 1997). We are not going to argue that self-interest is a good thing. Rather, we think that understanding the distinction is important in order to understand this entire situation.

In a way, this confusion is a good thing. It makes people willing to sacrifice their self-interest for others. The trouble is the group. The German coal miners saw themselves as the relevant group, not all the citizens of Germany and certainly not all of humanity. Yes, their actions represented a sacrifice of self-interest. But the beneficiaries were just the other miners. Everyone else was hurt, not helped. It would have been better on the whole if each miner had been selfish and stayed home. Then the government could have spent less money subsidizing the mines and left more money for other projects that would do more good, such as investing the development of the former East Germany, which would have created more jobs for less money than subsidizing the mines. (Note that nobody was arguing for an abrupt end to the subsidy. The argument was about how gradually it was reduced.)

Much scholarly writing about politics assumes that people behave in narrow, self-interested ways without noticing how strange it really is.

Many scholars see politics – from coal subsidies to taxes to Social Security – as a conflict between interest groups, each trying to influence a government to its own advantage. The groups collect money from their members for campaign contributions and publicity campaigns that could help these groups secure bigger shares of the pie for themselves. Economists call this *rent seeking*. The idea is that each group wants a larger share of the pie, and each group worries more about the size of its share than about the size of the whole pie. In the case of the miners, a larger share for them means a smaller pie for the rest of the country.

What is strange is that these scholars describe this process in terms of the pursuit of self-interest. But it is not self-interest. It is individual sacrifice on the part of a group, whether the sacrifice is in the form of making a contribution, writing a letter, or just taking the time to vote.

Yet, rent seeking is a *big* problem. Arguably, it is *the* biggest problem preventing the kinds of no-regrets solutions to global warming that have been suggested. All of these solutions involve a sacrifice of some group's interest for the common good, for they all involve change, and there is always some group that will be hurt by any change of this sort.

There are two levels of social dilemmas here. One level is that of the individual versus the small group. The self-interest of the individual miner conflicts with that of the group of miners. It is better for the individual to take a free ride on the participation of the other miners, but if they all did that, the group would not get the benefit.

But on the higher level, the group of miners is itself an actor in a society with other groups. Its interests conflict with those of the larger society. So we have a curious coincidence of the narrow self-interest of the individual miner – which is to stay home and do nothing – with the largest interest of the whole society.

This is not to say that people should be selfish. Rather, they should think about the largest group. The more people who do this, the easier it will be to solve the problems caused by rent seeking, including some of the problems of global warming. This should be easier to do when people understand that the interests of the largest society coincide with their narrow self-interest.

We also do not mean to say that these problems can be handled only by a change in the way people think. In particular, a short-term solution might involve a bargain between the government and the miners themselves, so that the miners are compensated out of the gains that come from cutting back on coal use. The compensation might take the form of retraining and subsidies for development of other industries. Even if such solutions are less efficient than other uses of the money, they might be necessary.

Conclusion: What to Do

We have argued that many of the problems of public policy result from an unwillingness to accept small losses in return for large gains. The losses and gains may be in the form of risks to the same people or to different people. The decision makers are often people who have little to gain or lose, so the issue is their moral intuition. Even when the decision makers are the apparent losers, as in the case of the German coal miners, the cost of political action to prevent losses is often greater than the expected losses themselves, so they, too, should be more willing to take a bird's-eye view.

What can be done about these problems, and who should do it? In general, we see implications for government officials, educators, journalists, and activists, that is, those citizens who are already politically involved in some way.

Government

Government officials are the prime movers, so the advice for them applies to everyone else. Here is what they should do: (1) look for gains that can be made through trade (and beware of the mythical fixed pie); (2) don't pass laws that discourage negotiation; (3) do pass laws that encourage negotiation; (4) compare options to their alternatives, rather than to the status quo or the ideal; (5) ask for quantities, because they matter; (6) recognize that trade-offs are real.

The point about passing laws requires comment. Many regulatory laws stipulate in detail what must be done, with the threat of penalties when it is not done. Often these stipulations are seen as intrusive by those who are affected. This is the essence of what people mean when they criticize bureaucracy. Sometimes these simplistic rules are necessary. It would be too complicated to negotiate one's income tax with a benevolent tax collector, for example. But, at other times, the laws are so intrusive that they become difficult to enforce. As in the case of Superfund, people fight, usually in court, rather than switch. It would serve everyone better if such laws allowed scope for negotiation. The next step, of course, is for government to encourage negotiation by providing helpful services.

Educators and Journalists

Another way to improve decisions is to educate leaders, and more generally the citizens who become the leaders and influence them. In the last 20 years, mutual gains negotiations have become central to management schools. Executive centers at management schools often include negotiations training, but this training must emphasize the broader context.

Government officials need training too, and too much evidence exists that they are not getting it. Governments at all levels, and nonprofit organizations, could place the same value on executive/professional education that we currently see in corporations. Some of this training could emphasize the issues addressed in this chapter.

Education in decision analysis in high schools can also make people aware of trade-offs (Baron & Brown, 1991). The study of formal methods, such as multiattribute utility theory (in a simple form), may help these students to avoid many of the errors that characterize informal decision making in others. It may also help them understand formal analyses carried out by others, even when these are only reported in the press. Feehrer and Adams, for example, wrote a curriculum for a unit in decision making as part of an eighth-grade program designed to increase intelligence (Adams, 1986). The curriculum deals with the analysis of decisions into possible choices and their probable consequences, consequences that differ in likelihood. Students are encouraged to trade off probability and utility informally; are taught to gather information that will improve probability estimates; and are urged to evaluate information for relevance and credibility. The curriculum also addresses trade-offs among attributes in the form of *preference tables*. All of the examples are based on detective stories.

Jared Curhan created an organization called the Program for Young Negotiators, based in Cambridge, Massachusetts, to teach children to solve their problems by negotiating rather than fighting. This education brings mutual-gains bargaining to the middle school level. Other such mutual-gain negotiation programs are being created earlier in the educational process. This is a great way to teach future voters to make wise decisions.

More generally, educators must help us learn to think quantitatively. This does not mean that we must have numbers. It does mean that we realize that a well-made decision requires comparisons of quantities. If we have a feeling for the quantities, we can make a good guess at what the decision would be even if we do not know the numbers themselves. This is what we do all the time in other domains. Tennis players, for example, realize that the intended placement of a shot is based on a trade-off of the probability of its going out and the probability of its winning the point if it does not go out. They do not know these probabilities as a function of where they aim, although some tennis statistician could, in principle, compile them. They do, however, think in this quantitative way even without the numbers.

When we think this way, we will be able to make everyday decisions in a sensible way, and we will also know when some public decision, such as whether to build more nuclear power plants, requires a more detailed quantitative analysis by experts. We will also understand that it does not matter whether risks arise through commission or omission, or whether the cause of a risk is human or natural. And we will understand why we should not pay more to reduce risk to zero if we can use the money better in other ways by reducing some other risk imperfectly.

Quantitative thinking of this sort is not widespread. People do not even notice its absence. Many people, for example, say that decisions such as whether to recommend estrogen replacement are "difficult" because there are costs as well as benefits. Many of these people do not seem to consider the possibility of looking at some overall measure, such as death rates or life expectancy. Or one can even get a more precise measure by weighing each condition (various cancers, heart disease, strokes, hip fractures) by some measure of its seriousness and their duration.

Journalists are, in fact, educators. Perhaps they do more to educate people about relevant issues and ways of thinking than schools do. They must see themselves this way, and they must help people understand both the idea of trade-offs and the idea of quantitative thinking.

Activists and Potential Activists

Political activists must understand all the things we have just described, and they must use their energy to get government officials, educators, and journalists to help. Moreover, activists would do well to understand that the tangible benefit that they get from their own activism will rarely be worth the effort. They must thus see themselves as what they are, altruists who work primarily for others. If they derive a sense of satisfaction from such altruism, so much the better for them, but it does not change the fact that most of the tangible effects of their actions are on others. If they see themselves this way, then they will be less inclined to participate in what they see as battles over a larger slice of a fixed pie. They will, instead, look for ways to expand the pie even if it requires a real sacrifice. They are already sacrificing their time and energy.

References

Adams, M. J. (Coordinator). (1986). *Odyssey: A curriculum for thinking*. Watertown, MA: Mastery Education Corporation.

Baden, J. (1995, October 25). The adverse consequences of the ESA. *The Seattle Times*, p. B5.

Baron, J. (1992). The effect of normative beliefs on anticipated emotions. *Journal of Personality and Social Psychology, 63*, 320–330.

Baron, J. (1997). The illusion of morality as self-interest: A reason to cooperate in social dilemmas. *Psychological Science, 8*, 330–335.

Baron, J. (1998). *Judgment misguided: Intuition and error in public decision making*. New York: Oxford University Press.

Baron, J., & Brown, R. V. (Eds.). (1991). *Teaching decision making to adolescents*. Hillsdale, NJ: Erlbaum.

Baron, J., & Ritov, I. (1994). Reference points and omission bias. *Organizational Behavior and Human Decision Processes, 59*, 475–498.

Baron, J., & Spranca, M. (1997). Protected values. *Organizational Behavior and Human Decision Processes, 70*, 1–16.

Bazerman, M. H., Magliozzi, T., & Neale, M. A. (1985). The acquisition of an integrative response in a competitive market. *Organizational Behavior and Human Performance, 34*, 294–313.

Bazerman, M. H., Moore, M. A., & Gillespie, J. J. (1999). The human mind as a barrier to wiser environmental agreements. *American Behavioral Scientist, 42*, 1277–1300.

Bornstein, G., & Ben-Yossef, M. (1994). Cooperation in intergroup and single-group social dilemmas. *Journal of Experimental Social Psychology, 30*, 52–67.

Deber, R. B., & Goel, V. (1990). Using explicit decision rules to manage issues of justice, risk, and ethics in decision analysis. *Medical Decision Making, 10*, 181–194.

Dunphy, H. (1999, July 8). Market for pollution credits viable. Associated Press dispatch.

Hoffman, A. J., Bazerman, M. H., & Yaffe, S. L. (1997). The Endangered Species Act and the U.S. economy. *Sloan Management Review, 39*, 59–73.

Hoffman, A. J., Gillespie, J., Moore, D., Wade-Benzoni, K. A., Thompson, L. L., & Bazerman, M. H. (1999). A mixed-motive perspective on the economics versus environment debate. *American Behavioral Scientist, 42*, 1254–1276.

Jervis, R. (1976). *Perception and misperception in international politics*. Princeton, NJ: Princeton University Press.

Kahl, J. (1977, March 13). Ein Kumpel ist Kein Kumpan. *Suddeutche Zeitung*, p. 3.

Kahneman, D., Knetsch, J. L., & Thaler, R. H. (1990). Experimental tests of the endowment effect and the Coase theorem. *Journal of Political Economy, 98*, 1325–1348.

Kahneman, D., & Tversky, A. (1972). Subjective probability: A judgment of representativeness. *Cognitive Psychology, 3*, 430–454.

Kahneman, D., & Tversky, A. (1979). Prospect theory: An analysis of decision under risk. *Econometrica, 47,* 263–291.

Kaiser, J. (1998). Pollution permits for greenhouse gases? *Science, 282,* 1025.

Kunzig, R., & Zimmer, C. (1998). Carbon cuts and techno-fixes: 10 things to do about the greenhouse effect some of which aren't crazy. *Discover, 19,* 60.

Lax, D., & Sebenius, J. (1986). *The manager as negotiator.* New York: Free Press.

Malakoff, D. (1997). Thirty Kyotos needed to control warming. *Science, 278,* 2048.

Mnookin, R., Peppet, S., & Tulumello, A. (2000). *Beyond winning: How lawyers help clients create value in negotiation.* Cambridge, MA: Harvard University Press.

Neale, M. A., and Bazerman, M. H. (1991). *Cognition and rationality in negotiation.* New York: Free Press.

Polya, G. (1945). *How to solve it: A new aspect of mathematical method.* Princeton, NJ: Princeton University Press.

Porter, M., & van der Linde, C. (1995). Green and competitive: Ending the stalemate. *Harvard Business Review, 73,* 120–134.

Pruitt, D. G., & Lewis, S. A. (1975). Development of integrative solutions in bilateral negotiation. *Journal of Personality and Social Psychology, 31,* 621–633.

Radetzki, M. (1995). Elimination of West European coal subsidies. *Energy Policy, 23,* 509–518.

Raiffa, H. (1982). *The art and science of negotiation.* Cambridge, MA: Harvard University Press.

Reuters/PlanetArc. (1999, June 15). Emissions trading could save money. Reuters press release.

Ritov, I., & Baron, J. (1990). Reluctance to vaccinate: Omission bias and ambiguity. *Journal of Behavioral Decision Making, 3,* 263–277.

Ross, L., & Stillinger, C. (1991). Barriers to conflict resolution. *Negotiation Journal, 7,* 389–404.

Sandel, M. (1997, December 16). Emissions trading defeats purpose of global pact. *Minneapolis Star Tribune,* p. 21A.

Solomon, C. (1993, March 29). Clearing the air: What really pollutes? *Wall Street Journal,* p. A1.

Singer, P. (1979). *Practical ethics.* Cambridge: Cambridge University Press.

Spranca, M., Minsk, E., & Baron, J. (1991). Omission and commission in judgment and choice. *Journal of Experimental Social Psychology, 27,* 76–105.

Stegemeier, R. (1995). *Straight talk: The future of energy in the global economy.* Los Angeles: Unocal.

Stroup, R. L. (1995). Endangered Species Act: Making innocent species the enemy. Political Economy Research Center Policy Series, Issue PS–3. *http://www.perc.org/ps3.htm.*

Thaler, R. (1980). Toward a positive theory of consumer choice. *Journal of Economic Behavior and Organization, 1,* 39–60.

Part V

Commentary and Cautionary Note

14 The Virtues of Cognitive Humility: For Us as Well as Them

Philip E. Tetlock

Experimental research on judgment and choice was once an esoteric specialty of a small cadre of cognitive psychologists. To judge just by citation counts, this research program has become psychology's leading intellectual export to the social sciences, as well as to a host of applied fields. The influence of experimental work on judgment and choice has spread (critics might say *metastasized*) into such diverse domains as behavioral finance, marketing, medical diagnosis, international relations, public opinion, organizational behavior, and the law (Arkes, 1991; Goldstein & Hogarth, 1986; Mellers, Schwarz, & Cooke, 1998; Payne, Bettman, & Johnson, 1992). Scholars with little else in common share a familiarity with foundational concepts and behavioral decision theory such as heuristics and biases, framing and choice, and the psychopsychics of gain and loss functions.

This chapter is, in one sense, testimony to how profoundly successful the heuristics-and-biases research program has been in extending cognitivist concepts into a vast array of disciples. By advancing one ingenious demonstration after another, investigators faithful to the core tenets of the program have converted many sophisticated skeptics to the view that our human limitations as information processors, especially our reliance on simplifying heuristics, produce systematic deviations from rationality across diverse spheres of professional endeavor. The research program thus advances a core scientific value of psychology: the parsimonious reduction of superficial diversity to unifying principles.

Inevitably, though, some skeptics have resisted conversion. In my experience, the most outspoken skeptics cluster into four categories, each a variant of the school of thought that stresses the power of perfect competition to extinguish systematic irrationality quickly and completely:

true-believer neorealists in world politics, neoclassical economists, orthodox game theorists, and evolutionary theorists (who are sometimes unflatteringly called *ultra-Darwinians*). For each camp, the notion of systematic deviations from rationality is just plain silly. Systematically irrational players were plucked long ago from the competitive game. What looks parsimonious from a particular psychological point of view looks like a gratuitous complication of existing models from these more macro, competitive-logic perspectives.

In this chapter, however, I wish to mount a more modest and less strident challenge to the heuristics-and-biases research program. I do not deny that people do often make mistakes, sometimes systematic ones, in a wide range of ecologically significant inferential tasks (that is to say, the errors and biases are not limited to laboratory tests concocted with the express purpose of tricking subjects). But I do warn of the dangers of jumping the inferential gun – of assuming a tad too glibly that people have exactly the goals that our theoretical models specify and that, therefore, when human judgment strays from our normative guidelines, they must be making mistakes. To reinvoke the game metaphor, people may often be playing a different game altogether from the one that we supposed – a game that fits into broader functional/dysfunctional patterns of social activity and that leads them to attach unexpected meanings to both experimental manipulations and dependent measures.

Let's designate this challenger as *functionalist pluralism*. Functionalist pluralists remind us that the normative benchmarks that judgment and decision-making (JDM) researchers typically use for identifying errors and biases implicitly or explicitly assume that people are either trying to be intuitive scientists (with the goal of achieving cognitive mastery of the causal structure of their environment and whatever predicted leverage that may confer) or are trying to become intuitive economists (with the goal of maximizing subjective expected utility). The standards for rationality flow naturally from these underlying functionalist metaphors. Good intuitive scientists should assess covariation between hypothesized causes and effects accurately and update their hypotheses in a roughly Bayesian fashion. Good intuitive economists should make choices in rigorous conformity to the logical precepts of utility-maximization.

Functionalist pluralists then go on to argue for broadening the motivational matrix of assumptions, for taking seriously the possibility that people are trying to achieve a miscellaneous host of objectives. These *deviant functionalist metaphors* – as I have called them elsewhere

(Tetlock, 1992; Tetlock, Kristel, Elson, Green, & Lerner, 2000) – include the intuitive politician (trying to maintain valued relationships and social identities vis-à-vis key constituencies in his or her life), the intuitive theologian (trying to protect sacred values from secular encroachments), and intuitive prosecutors (trying to deter wrongdoing and to exact retribution that restores the moral status quo ante). The deviant metaphors highlight social functions of judgment and choice that would otherwise have been overlooked had theorizing been confined to epistemic or narrowly utilitarian premises. Middle-range theories of people as intuitive politicians, theologians, and prosecutors call to our attention the importance of the social context within which decision makers work (who is accountable to whom, for what, under what ground rules?) as well as the social content of the information decision makers process (Do trade-offs implicate sacred values? Do statistical generalizations trespass into the domain of forbidden base rates?). In the process, these middle-range theories reveal new moderators of old effects: empirical boundary conditions under which well-replicated errors are either attenuated or amplified (Tetlock & Lerner, 1999). These theories also reveal new ways of normatively evaluating old effects: normative boundary conditions under which judgmental tendencies regarded as errors or biases within the mainstream intuitive scientist/economist frameworks often look quite adaptive or appropriate within one of the deviant social-functionalist frameworks. I will consider four examples of such normative boundary conditions of special relevance to public policy.

Aspiring Intuitive Economists Meet Angry Intuitive Theologians

Trade-off reasoning is widely viewed as a minimal prerequisite for economic rationality. Utility-maximization presupposes that people routinely factor reality constraints into their deliberations and explicitly weigh conflicting values. Indeed, economic survival in competitive markets requires that people make at least implicit trade-offs between objectives such as work versus leisure, saving versus consumption, and consumption of alternative products. If, however, we think of people not as intuitive economists but rather as intuitive moralists/theologians, we should expect sharp resistance to efforts to translate all values into a common utility metric. Fiske and Tetlock (1997) document that, in most cultures, people are chronic *compartmentalizers* who deem some trade-offs legitimate (goods and services routinely subject to market-pricing rules) but vehemently reject others – in particular, those that treat *sacred values* like honor, love, justice and life as fungible.

This sharp resistance is rooted, in part, in the familiar incommensurability problem that mainstream models of bounded rationality can readily handle. People are still trying to be good intuitive economists, but they have limited mental resources and they (rationally enough) seek out quick-and-dirty shortcuts. There are no surprises here. Decision theorists have long known that people find interdimensional comparisons cognitively difficult and often resort to noncompensatory choice heuristics such as elimination-by-aspects to avoid them (Payne et al., 1992). The moralist/theologian framework, however, finds this explanation incomplete. Apple–orange comparisons are difficult, but people do make them when they go to the supermarket. Moreover, people do not find it shameful to make trade-offs between money and consumption goods. The moralist/theologian framework traces opposition to reducing all values to a single utility metric to a deeper form of incommensurability: *constitutive incommensurability*, a pivotal concept in modern moral philosophy (Raz, 1986) as well as in classic sociological theory (Durkheim, 1925/1976). As Tetlock, Peterson, and Lerner (1996) argue, the guiding idea is that our commitments to other people require us to deny that we can compare certain things – in particular, things of finite value to things that our moral community insists on formally treating as possessing transcendental or infinite significance. To transgress this boundary, to attach a monetary value to one's friendships, children, or loyalty to one's country, is to disqualify oneself from the accompanying social roles. Constitutive incommensurability can thus be said to exist whenever comparing values subverts one of the values (the putatively infinitely significant value) in the trade-off calculus. Taboo trade-offs are, in this sense, morally corrosive: The longer one contemplates indecent proposals, the more irreparably one compromises one's moral identity. To compare is to destroy.

This framework helps us to understand an otherwise baffling phenomenon. Why do corporate or government agencies often suffer punishing legal or political consequences when they try to do the right (microeconomic) thing and perform cost-benefit analyses that monetize human lives, justice, or other sacred values? Rather than being applauded for their candor and rigor (for puncturing the moral pretentiousness of communities that claim to place infinite values on things that, revealed preference indicates, they regularly trade off), these decision makers are figuratively pilloried and pelted with moral outrage.

As Tetlock (2000a) has shown in experimental vignettes, decision makers who violate trade-off taboos are denounced as callous, inhuman, technocrats, or ruthless profit-maximizers, becoming objects of contempt and ridicule and the target of exorbitant punitive-damage award seekers. It is surprisingly easy, however, to escape scorn: Instead of revealing the gruesome details of their cost-benefit deliberations, decision makers can simply mask the thought process by invoking either a vague utilitarian rationale (on balance, after weighing the pros and cons, we opted to do ×) or a vague deontic rationale (morally this seems like the right thing to do). It is small wonder that, as Calabresi and Bobbitt (1978) documented, decision makers do their best to obfuscate trade-offs that implicitly affix dollar values to life, justice, or honor.

Honesty is, to be sure, a virtue and hypocrisy a vice. But it may well be a mistake to dismiss understandings central to our collective self-concept – nurtured over centuries – as mere illusions that serve no social functions worth preserving (Bell, 1976). Sociological commentators warn that a world in which we candidly monetize all competing values will turn out to be a cold, mean place where no one knows when to stop calculating, where – to paraphrase Oscar Wilde's definition of an economist – people know the price of everything but the value of nothing. The question then becomes: How much truth – about our own mental processes – can we tolerate? Whatever the answer, it is safe to say that efforts to debias choice by flushing trade-offs into the open will often be controversial, sometimes intensely so.

Curious Intuitive Scientists Meet Punitive Intuitive Prosecutors

When we work from the assumption that people are intuitive scientists trying to achieve cognitive mastery of causal relationships and predictive leverage, it is reasonable to judge social perceivers against the normative benchmarks of scientific inference (Fiske & Taylor, 1991). Do people accurately assess patterns of covariation? Do people integrate information in ways that win them the seal of Bayesian approval? Insofar as people are too quick to jump to conclusions about the character of an actor from fragmentary evidence or insofar as people are reluctant to change their minds in response to probative evidence, we feel justified in concluding that people are indeed flawed intuitive scientists. One often invoked example of our limitations as intuitive scientists is the *fundamental attribution error* (Jones, 1979). People do not seem to give as much weight as they should to situational constraints on behavior and make excessively confident dispositional attributions to actors. This error – which can work to the decided advantage of the disadvantaged in society at large – is often traced to overreliance on simple heuristics such as availability or representativeness or on cultural schemata that exaggerate individual agency at the expense of the interpersonal/institutional context. Another much-discussed bias is the *severity effect*. People are often far more punitive to perpetrators of negligent acts when the consequences are severe than when the consequences are mild. This experimental effect holds up when we hold constant both the nature of the act and the context within which it occurred. Here, some have suggested, is evidence of how the certainty-of-hindsight effect can bias attributions of responsibility. As soon as observers learn of an outcome, they quickly forget how difficult that outcome was to foresee ex ante. Because the outcome now seems so retrospectively obvious, the actor should have known what could/would happen before the fact and should therefore be culpable.

No doubt, the overattribution and severity effects do sometimes represent irrational social inference. It is curious to note, however, that there is systematic ideological variation among managers in private and public sector organizations about the classification of these effects as errors or biases. Using repeated-measures designs that make transparent which cues are being manipulated, Tetlock (2000b) documents that more conservative managers view the fundamental attribution error as neither fundamental nor erroneous. In their view, setting a low threshold for drawing dispositional conclusions about others, especially for the disappointing conduct and performance of others, is a shrewd prosecutorial strategy of pressuring others to behave themselves rather than an illustration of our shortcomings as intuitive scientists. In a similar vein, more conservative managers are not at all embarrassed – again, in repeated-measures designs – to attach greater blame as outcome severity rises. Their reasoning often is: When you break norms you take chances, and sometimes you are lucky and sometimes you are not. Liberal managers, by contrast, are influenced by severity manipulations only in the between-subjects component of the design when it is not obvious that outcome severity may be shaping their judgments. Here we have an interesting example of what may be a cognitive bias within one ideological subculture (a cue that people regard as embarrassing to use and use only when they are not aware of using it) but that represents a prudent policy posture within another ideological subculture. These diverging ideological reactions suggest, at minimum, that efforts to debias attributions of responsibility are likely to prove politically contentious.

Pragmatic Economists Meet Punitive Prosecutors

Economic models of legal reasoning depict people who approach the problem of maintaining social control in a relentlessly pragmatic way. In the judicial arena, *Homo economicus* is continually seeking out the most cost-effective societal strategies for deterring wrongdoing. In real life, however, people are systematically both more punitive and less punitive than this framework would predict. Moreover, people are disinclined to accept characterizations of their deviations from ideal-type economic logic as errors or biases. Consider, first, contexts in which people seem to be unnecessarily punitive, going beyond the requirements of both specific and general deterrence. Several investigators (including myself) have found that people are willing to punish both individuals and corporations long after all plausible utilitarian rationales for punishment have been removed. For example, Baron and Ritov (1993) have shown that the desire to punish a company for misdeeds persisted even when the penalty had to be secret, the company had insurance to pay the penalty, and – in any case – the company was about to go out of business. They also demonstrated that, in setting punishments for companies dumping hazardous wastes, people preferred to require companies to clean up their own waste, even if the waste did not threaten anyone and even if it were possible to spend the same amount of money to clean up the waste of a now-defunct company – waste that posed a far greater health hazard. From a microeconomic point of view, these choices are perversely Pareto-suboptimal. But these choices are easily reconciled normatively with a portrait of the intuitive prosecutor as guided by the "primitive" Durkheimian intuition that those who harm others (including nature) should be responsible for bringing us back to the status quo ante. Justice is supposed to restore social equilibrium, and this retributive function of punishment – the desire to bring low those who have treated others with contempt – is still widely viewed as a legitimate, indeed as an essential, defining feature of justice.

People can also be systematically less punitive than economic models suggest that they should be. One implication of the doctrine of optimal deterrence is that punitive damages should make up for the shortfall in compensatory damages produced by the failure of many potential plaintiffs either to be aware of their injuries or to be successful in securing compensation. This leads to a counterintuitive prediction that is also counter to reality: *Homo economicus* in the legal arena should multiply compensatory awards by the inverse of the probability that any given person from the population of injured persons would receive compensation. The fewer perpetrators who are caught, the more harshly those who are caught should be punished. Kahneman, Schkade, and Sunstein (1998) document that people are understandably reluctant to do this (a line of reasoning that, taken to its extreme in the domain of criminal law, would lead us to save money on police enforcement of traffic rules by laying off large percentages of the highway patrol but beheading the unlucky few reckless or drunk drivers who are apprehended). I suppose that, from a purely economic standpoint, this refusal should count as a judgmental defect, but it is more plausible to posit a theoretical model of people as intuitive prosecutors whose shared conceptions of equity and procedural justice are deeply offended by punishing a few so severely *because* so many are escaping the enforcement net. Again, efforts to debias judgment to bring people's intuitions into conformity with those of the normative model are likely to be sharply contested.

Intuitive Scientists/Economists Meet Adroit Intuitive Politicians

One advantage of working from the functionalist postulate that people are trying to understand and predict events in order to maximize expected utility is the resulting clarity of the normative criteria for gauging errors and biases. By these standards, a wide array of policy-relevant judgmental tendencies look decidedly dysfunctional. Let's look at some alleged biases and errors not yet considered. In the case of ambiguity aversion (a preference for outcomes with precisely known probabilities), one appears to be leaving money on the proverbial table. In the case of efforts to recoup sunk costs from money-hemorrhaging projects, one appears to be throwing good money after bad. In the case of the dilution effect, one appears to be sacrificing predictive accuracy and wasting cognitive effort by trying to incorporate irrelevant or nondiagnostic cues into one's impressions of a target person or institution. In the case of the attraction effect in three-option choice sets, one appears to be violating one of the basic axioms of rational choice by giving considerable weight to logically irrelevant alternatives.

But what happens when we shift functionalist frameworks and posit now that people are intuitive politicians whose guiding goal is claiming desired social identities in the eyes of key constituencies? Turning to ambiguity aversion, decision makers may be right inferring that they will incur greater blame for choosing options that have consequences with ambiguous probabilities of occurrence than for choosing options that have consequences with well-defined probabilities of occurrence (holding expected values constant). They just need to imagine the recriminations that will ensue if they choose an ambiguous gamble with a probability of winning between 10% and 90% and that gamble turns out to have had only a 10% chance of yielding a positive payoff (Curley, Yates, & Abrams, 1986). In the case of sunk costs, leaders may sometimes be well advised to stay the course insofar as the groups to whom they are accountable hold an implicit theory of leadership that identifies staying the course, not with intellectual rigidity or economic illiteracy, but rather with principled determination to uphold certain values or to implement a certain vision (Staw & Ross, 1980). In the case of the dilution effect, people may often try too hard to integrate irrelevant cues into their subjective-prediction formulas, because they are working from the conversational premise that the experimenter would not give them the information unless it had some connection to the task (Schwarz, 1994; Tetlock, Lerner, & Boettger, 1996). People value getting along smoothly with their prospective conversation partners (in this case, the experimenter) and make good faith efforts to find relevance in irrelevant data that the experimenter has supplied. In the case of the attraction effect, decision makers may be right when they infer that they have a more persuasive justification for choosing option A over B when A and not B dominates the logically irrelevant alternative C. Although introducing C does not in any way alter the offsetting strengths of options A and B, asserting that "A dominates C but B does not" should persuade at least cognitively superficial audiences that one chose wisely (Simonson, 1989). Again, efforts to debias judgment and choice will be resisted – resisted now because they threaten to strip away political defenses that are useful in protecting or enhancing decision makers' social identities vis-à-vis key constituencies.

Taken to its extreme, functionalist pluralism quickly becomes a dangerous doctrine. Shifting functionalist premises makes it suspiciously easy to concoct post hoc rationalizations for virtually anything people do, no matter how incoherent or foolhardy. Skeptics are right to ask where the limits of functionalist forgiveness lie. When people appear to be defective intuitive statisticians, the tolerant functionalist proposes that they are attentive conversationalists on the lookout for predictive cues in even the most vacuous utterances. When people appear to be flawed intuitive psychologists who jump the inferential gun in drawing conclusions about character, the functionalist cautions that people are shrewd intuitive prosecutors who know how to pressure other people to behave. When people appear to be clueless intuitive economists who refuse to treat certain values – say, loyalty to family or other collectivities – as fungible, the functionalist suggests that people are devout intuitive theologians struggling to protect sacred values from secular encroachments. Within this Panglossian worldview, no one can ever make a mistake.

How far down this permissive path should we stray? Those who treat parsimony as a trump scientific value will urge us to turn back right away. And a few postmodernists might counsel going all the way: The more metaphorical lenses we possess for viewing reality, the wiser we are. This chapter adopts a middle-ground stance. It endorses a moderately conservative epistemological stopping rule: Consider seriously only those functionalist reinterpretations of putative biases that lead to testable hypotheses and to corroborative evidence that we would not have discovered had theorizing been confined to traditional frameworks. This is indeed the direction that my own research on judgment and choice has taken. The thrust has been to advance beyond abstract metaphorical posturing and to delineate middle-range theories that advance knowledge by highlighting empirical boundary conditions on the error-and-bias portrait of human nature (When do features of the social-institutional context amplify or attenuate particular cognitive shortcomings?) as well as normative boundary conditions (When does it cease to be reasonable to label particular judgmental tendencies as cognitive shortcomings, as opposed to adaptive solutions to functionalist challenges not previously given their due weight?) (cf. Tetlock, 1992; Tetlock et al., 2000).

Here, however, it is instructive to dwell on the dangers of functionalist misclassifications in applying JDM insights to the realm of public policy. This chapter may therefore aggravate many readers. There is understandably a pent-up missionary zeal to push forward with clearing out the irrationality – at the levels of both the mass public and elite decision makers – that has for so long been ignored by policy analysts trained in mainstream economics. Still, replacing one deformation professionelle with another can carry costs, and my job is to highlight them.

Policy missionaries of JDM – who are impatient with the ambiguity that inevitably comes with functionalist pluralism – might be persuaded to be a bit more patient if they consider analogies between their movement and the vast array of other reform movements of the 20th century – from urban planning to collectivizing agriculture to eliminating corruption to enhancing public health – that have been animated by rationality and efficiency goals, some of which have succeeded splendidly and some of which have failed spectacularly. In a thoughtful book, James Scott (1999) has clustered these ideologically diverse efforts under the rubric of *high modernism*, which he defines as a strong (even musclebound) belief in scientific and technological progress that arose in the late Industrial Revolution (say, 1820) and has persisted in various forms right up to the present. Le Corbusier, the planner of cities, personifies high modernism (although, following Scott, we could just as well have selected Robert McNamara, the shah of Iran, Vladimir Lenin, or Walter Rathenau). Here is Scott's characterization of Le Corbusier's approach to urban planning:

> Le Corbusier had little patience for the physical environments that centuries of urban living had created. He heaped scorn on the tangle, darkness, and disorder, the crowded and pestilential conditions of Paris and other European cities at the turn of the century. His new urban order was to be a lyrical marriage between Cartesian pure forms and the implacable requirements of the machine. In characteristically bombastic terms, he declared: "We claim in the name of the steamship, the airplane, and the automobile, the right to health, logic, daring, harmony, perfection." Unlike the existing city of Paris, which to him resembled a porcupine and a vision of Dante's Inferno, his city would be an "organized, serene, forceful, airy, ordered entity." (Scott, 1999, pp. 106–107)

It is perhaps obvious now what is wrong with this stance. Any effort to plan a city or a language or a decision process will soon run afoul of an intricate web of existing social arrangements and understandings. Cities, languages, and decision procedures are the unintended products of many minds. Reformers who insist on replacing this complex web of meanings and activities with new, often formal, procedures run the risk of disrupting the web in unforeseeable ways (cf. Jervis, 1997). This point is often made by proponents of laissez-faire such as Friedrich Hayek, who tirelessly stressed that a command economy, however deftly designed, could never replace the myriad rapid-fire mutual adjustments of free markets and the price system. Moreover, high modernism does not just ruffle the ideological feathers of libertarians (although virtually all state-mandated forms of high modernism do). Cognitive egalitarians in anthropology have long been wary of the imperialistic pretensions of Western epistemic practices and ideals. In a Geertzian spirit, they often stress the importance of avoiding a condescending attitude toward local knowledge that is deeply embedded in local experience. One cannot understand a Balinese cockfight without understanding the webs of significance attached to the events by the participants. And one cannot understand opposition to labeling certain judgmental tendencies as errors and bias unless one understands the rationales and ways of life within which those judgmental tendencies are embedded.

Just as it is possible to stretch functionalist pluralism to its Panglossian reductio ad absurdum, so too it is possible to push critiques of high modernism too far – to the point where one becomes an apologist for the most oppressive and bizarre societal arrangements. Any balanced critique of high modernism – or of applications of JDM to public policy – needs to be both nuanced and sharply qualified. High modernism has contributed enormously to human welfare via public-health programs, transportation, communication, and universal public education. And high modernism has inflicted enormous suffering in totalitarian states whose leaders embraced all-encompassing social theories that permitted them to treat the people as though they were "a blank piece of paper" on which the new regime could inscribe the new revealed truths (Mao Zedong quoted in Scott, 1999, p. 341). Between these endpoints, there is plenty of room for reasonable observers to disagree over whether the pursuit of some abstract epistemic ideal such as rationality should trump existing practices and local knowledge.

So where does this leave us? Applied to public policy, JDM investigators can make a good case for compulsory vaccinations (over the irrational objections of those who blow tiny probabilities of risk out of all proportion and weight sins of commission far more heavily than sins of omission), for requiring cost-benefit analyses that affix explicit values to human life or other ostensibly sacred values (over the objections of moral or religious figures), for explicitly trading off Type I (convict the innocent) and Type II (acquit the guilty) errors in the criminal justice system (over the objections of those such as Tribe, 1971), and even for using forbidden base rates in setting insurance rates or in law-enforcement decisions of whom to search at airports or on the highways (over the objections of representatives of minority groups). More generally, in a thought-provoking overview of the implications of limited rationality for public policy, Sunstein (1997) has shown how JDM research that reveals biases and inconsistencies in human preferences can be deployed to justify a vast range of paternalistic policies. Why treat misguided beliefs and muddled preferences of individual citizens as sacrosanct guides to public policy? Advocates of functionalist pluralism worry, though, that in the pursuit of microeconomic or scientific rationality in public policy, other values are trampled underfoot and disturbing precedents are set for even more high-handed interventions. The line between telling people *how* to think and telling people *what* to think can be a blurry one. Functionalist pluralists are inclined to agree with value pluralists like Isaiah Berlin (1969) that "from the crooked timber of humanity, no straight thing can be built" and to worry that when we insist on trying to straighten things out, we run the risk of cracking the entire gnarly and knotted structure.

References

Arkes, H. R. (1991). Costs and benefits of judgment errors: Implications for debiasing. *Psychological Bulletin, 110,* 486–498.

Baron, J., & Ritov, I. (1993). Intuitions about penalties and compensation in the context of tort law. *Journal of Risk and Uncertainty, 7,* 17–31.

Bell, D. (1976). *The cultural contradictions of capitalism.* New York: Basic Books.

Berlin, I. (1969). Two concepts of liberty. In Isaiah Berlin, *Four essays on liberty* (pp. 118–172). Oxford: Oxford University Press.

Calabresi, G., & Bobbitt, P. (1978). *Tragic choices.* New York: W. W. Norton.

Curley, S. P., Yates, J. F., & Abrams, R. A. (1986). Psychological sources of ambiguity avoidance. *Organizational Behavior and Human Decision Processes, 38,* 230–256.

Durkheim, E. (1925/1976). *The elementary forms of the religious life* (2nd ed.). London: Allen & Unwin.

Fiske, S. T., & Taylor, S. (1991). *Social cognition* (2nd ed.). New York: McGraw-Hill.

Fiske, A., & Tetlock, P. E. (1997). Taboo trade-offs: Reactions to transactions that transgress spheres of justice. *Political Psychology, 18,* 255–297.

Goldstein, W., & Hogarth, R. (1986). *Research on judgment and decision making.* Cambridge: Cambridge University Press.

Jervis, R. (1997). *System effects: Complexity in social and political life.* Princeton, NJ: Princeton University Press.

Jones, E. E. (1979). The rocky road from acts to dispositions. *American Psychologist, 34,* 107–117.

Kahneman, D., Schkade, D., & Sunstein, C.R. (1998). Shared outrage and erratic awards: The psychology of punitive damages. *Journal of Risk and Uncertainty, 16,* 1–42.

Mellers, B. A., Schwartz, A., & Cooke, A. D. J. (1998). Judgment and decision making. *Annual Review of Psychology, 49,* 447–477.

Payne, J. W., Bettman, J. R., & Johnson, E. J. (1992). Behavioral decision research: A constructive processing perspective. *Annual Review of Psychology, 43,* 87–131.

Raz, J. (1986) *The morality of freedom.* New York: Oxford University Press.

Schwarz, N. (1994). Judgment in a social context: Biases, shortcomings, and the logic of conversation. In M. P. Zanna (Ed.), *Advances in experimental social psychology* (pp. 123–162). San Diego, CA: Academic Press.

Scott, J. (1999). *Seeing like a state.* New Haven, CT: Yale University Press.

Simonson, I. (1989). Choice based on reasons: The case of attraction and compromise effects. *Journal of Consumer Research, 16*, 158–174.

Staw, B. M., & Ross, J. (1980). Commitment in an experimenting society: A study of the attribution of leadership from administrative scenarios. *Journal of Applied Psychology, 65*, 249–260.

Sunstein, C. R. (1997). *Free markets and social justice.* New York: Oxford University Press.

Tetlock, P. E. (1992). The impact of accountability on judgment and choice: Toward a social contingency model. *Advances in Experimental Social Psychology, 25*, 331–376.

Tetlock, P. E. (1998). Losing our religion: On the collapse of precise normative standards in complex accountability systems. In R. Kramer & M. Neale (Eds.), *Power and influence in organizations: Emerging themes in theory and research* (pp. 121–144). Thousand Oaks, CA: Sage.

Tetlock, P. E. (2000a). Coping with trade-offs: Psychological constraints and political implications. In S. Lupia, M. McCubbins, & S. Popkin (Eds.), *Political reasoning and choice* (pp. 239–263). Berkeley: University of California Press.

Tetlock, P. E. (2000b). Cognitive biases and organizational correctives: Do both disease and cure depend on the political beholder? *Administrative Science Quarterly, 45*, 293–327.

Tetlock, P. E., Kristel, O., Elson, B., Green, M., & Lerner, J. (2000). Attitudes and social cognition – the psychology of the unthinkable: Taboo trade-offs, forbidden base rates, and heretical counterfactuals. *Journal of Personality and Social Psychology, 78*, 853–870.

Tetlock, P. E. & Lerner, J. (1999). The social contingency model: Identifying empirical and normative boundary conditions on the error-and-bias portrait of human nature. In S. Chaiken & Y. Trope (Eds.), *Dual-process theories in social psychology* (pp. 571–585). New York: Guilford Press.

Tetlock, P. E., Lerner, J., & Boettger, R. (1996). The dilution effect: Judgmental bias, conversational convention, or a bit of both? *European Journal of Social Psychology, 26*, 915–935.

Tetlock, P. E., Peterson, R., & Lerner, J. (1996). Revisiting the value pluralism model: Incorporating social content and context postulates. In C. Seligman, J. Olson, & M. Zanna (Eds.), *Ontario symposium on social and personality psychology: Values* (pp. 25–52). Hillsdale, NJ: Erlbaum.

Tribe, L. (1971). Trial by mathematics: Precision and ritual in the legal process. *Harvard Law Review, 84*, 1329–1393.

Index